The Harbrace Reader for Canadians

The Harbrace Reader for Canadians

Joanne Buckley
McMaster University

THOMSON
NELSON

Australia Canada Mexico Singapore Spain United Kingdom United States

Canadian Cataloguing in Publication Data

Main entry under title:

The Harbrace reader for Canadians

ISBN 0-7747-3681-X

1. College readers. 2. English language – Rhetoric.

I. Buckley, Joanne, 1953–

PE1417.H372 2000 808'.0427 C00-930177-1

Acquisitions Editors: Heather McWhinney/Anne Williams
Developmental Editor: Camille Isaacs
Production Editors: Shana Hayes/Emily Ferguson
Production Coordinator: Cheryl Tiongson

Copy Editor: Claudia Kutchukian

Cover and Interior Design: The Brookview Group

Typesetting and Assembly: Carolyn Hutchings Sebestyen

Printing and Binding: Transcontinental Printing Inc.

Cover art: *Dreaming Heads 5* by Irina Florov. Colour pencil:
8 1/2" by 11", 1999. Copyright © Irina Florov. All rights reserved.

Thomson Nelson
1120 Birchmount Road
Toronto, Ontario M1K 4G5
1-800-668-0671
www.nelson.com

This book was printed in Canada.
4 5 6 7 10 09 08 07

ISBN-13: 978-0-7747-3681-7
ISBN-10: 0-7747-3681-X

TO THE INSTRUCTOR

The Harbrace Reader for Canadians, in its first edition, is a composition anthology meant to provide instructors and teachers at the college and university level with a broad selection of readings for use in a writing class. One of the premises of most writing classes is that students learn best when they are actively invited to emulate the techniques and processes that they see. Another premise, of course, is that we all write best when we are given the opportunity to use what we know already, combined with some judicious reflection and research. The essays that have been gathered in this collection are, for that reason, topical and in some respects controversial, in an effort to provide classes with food for thought and for discussion and debate.

To assure that a variety of readers will be stimulated by the book, every effort has been made to include materials with a broad sweep: there are articles on sports, on business, on psychology, on literature, on nature, on science, and on many aspects of contemporary culture. Many of the pieces that have been chosen are hot off the presses, though a number of popular and well-known essays have also been included for their historical significance as well as for their grace and pertinence. The content of the volume is not entirely Canadian, but a high proportion of the works chosen do have Canadian origins. To give students an opportunity to read beyond Canadian and American examples, however, a number of authors of different nationalities are also part of the package.

The essays in this volume are divided according to rhetorical mode, though no single essay purports to be wholly an example of that mode. The essays are grouped into these categories:

Description and Narration
Illustration
Definition
Process
Comparison and Contrast
Division and Classification
Cause and Effect
Persuasion and Argument
Variations on a Theme: Exploring Multiculturalism

Each of these groupings contains essays that, in some of their aspects, exemplify the modes under discussion. In each case, a brief introduction to that mode is provided, followed by a short paragraph that illustrates how the rhetorical technique functions. After that, each mode is illustrated with a short annotated essay that shows how the mode might be approached by student writers. These brief examples may well be taken as the most succinct models of how a rhetorical mode functions. Students should be invited to read and comment on these simpler essays, particularly as they illustrate how the mode might operate in the hands of someone writing within an academic environment, rather than for a newspaper or a magazine, as is sometimes the case with the selected materials.

The selections follow, each with a concise profile of the author. After each selection, there is a vocabulary list for ease of reading. As well, there are questions that may be adapted for classroom discussion or for written assignments, which deal with the audience and purpose of the piece, with broader content concerns, and with the issues of style and structure. Use these questions to guide discussion in class of the elements of each rhetorical mode and of how they may each be adapted for use by student writers. The questions vary to illustrate the complexity and the notable features of particular essays. They are guides to careful reading, too, and students are encouraged to read the questions as part of their preparation of the essays for class. The questions are intended to provoke discussion and to improve appreciation of the style and substance of the pieces that have been selected.

ACKNOWLEDGEMENTS

Special thanks are due to several people who contributed essays and ideas to this collection, among them Heather McWhinney, who always kept in touch and came up with great workable ideas; Camille Isaacs, who always was there with wise suggestions and good advice; and Geoffrey Rockwell and Andrew Mactavish, who supported the endeavour and made worthwhile suggestions for selections. I would like to thank the reviewers, whose comments helped shape this manuscript: Glenn Deer, University of British Columbia; Patricia Rigg, Acadia University; Alex Kizuk, University of Lethbridge; Anita Hurwitz, University of Windsor; and Douglas Babington, Queen's University. Special thanks are also due to Donna Millar, Sachi Morris, and Tina Furlanetto, who helped me and comforted me as the project proceeded. Other friends and contributors to the volume include Rhonda Hustler, Marie Davis, Sandy Shaw, and David Gates. David, as always, was a wealth of information and of constructive assistance, distraction, and kindness. My mother, Mary Buckley, was the patient, strong, and helpful person she always is.

A Note from the Publisher

Thank you for selecting *The Harbrace Reader for Canadians*, edited by Joanne Buckley. The editor and publisher have devoted considerable time and care to the development of this book. We appreciate your recognition of this effort and accomplishment.

RHETORICAL TABLE OF CONTENTS

THEMATIC TABLE OF CONTENTS

CLASSIC ESSAYS

ESSAYS ABOUT WRITING

ESSAYS ABOUT TECHNOLOGY

ESSAYS ABOUT SEX, LOVE, AND GENDER

ESSAYS ABOUT CULTURE

ESSAYS ABOUT CANADIAN IDENTITY

ESSAYS ABOUT RACIAL IDENTITY

ESSAYS ON A HUMOROUS OR LIGHT THEME

ESSAYS ON A PERSONAL THEME

ESSAYS ABOUT LANGUAGE

INTRODUCTION TO READING THIS VOLUME AND WRITING IN RESPONSE

A book like this one assumes that writers learn not only by writing, but also by reading. The assumption is not far-fetched, given that no writer could reasonably be expected to write an essay without having read one, preferably many, before beginning. Although the essay remains the favoured written format in college and university, it is not the form we are most inclined to read. Except for editorials in newspapers and newsmagazines, the essay sometimes gets overlooked as an important form, particularly by a public whose preferred reading in fiction is fantasy and in nonfiction is the cookbook. Since a large segment of the population gets its news from broadcast media and not from print, the essay, like a sonnet or a villanelle, is at a disadvantage. That said, few students are able to articulate written opinions without recourse to the form, and the essay is in its own way as rigorous and demanding as the sonnet or the villanelle, even if its expression allows for considerable variation, as this volume alone can testify.

The essay is composed of a number of essential component parts. Although some variations are possible in expert hands, numerous expected conventions are part of this form, and a reader can safely bring a number of expectations to its reading. An essay, for example, will typically have a thesis statement or a claim that it is the function of the essay to demonstrate by presenting evidence to the reader in the form of examples, statistics, and reasoned arguments. An essay, apart from this structure, might also be defined as an attempt to arrive at the truth about something by presenting, as fair-mindedly as possible, the facts of the case. The subject matter, of course, may vary widely, but the manner of presentation tends to follow this expected pattern.

To enhance its credibility, the essay also typically may be broken down into three integral parts: the introduction, in which the reader is brought up to speed on the issue at hand; the body, in which most of the key arguments are laid out; and the conclusion, which sums up and reflects on the findings and sometimes makes recommendations about what questions the next researcher would be wise to take up. But knowing what the essay is composed of does not ensure that a writer can produce one to his or her satisfaction. That is a different matter, one that demands regular practice and long experience of the form. One of the best ways to get such experience is through reading a broad array of others' work in the essay form and using it as the foundation of one's own work.

This textbook, then, aims at encouraging the reading, critical understanding, and emulation of a variety of essay forms to enable students who are obliged to write them as part of their academic education to do so from a broad base of knowledge. Let's take some time to consider each of these requirements in turn. Reading may seem the simplest, but what we mean in the context of a course is a more complicated and thoughtful kind of reading —more than the cursory skimming of a text with the hope of getting its gist.

Readers approaching these essays will be asked to read carefully in order to discuss and assess the claims that are made and the techniques by which the authors make them. Such reading is assuredly very active and demands that the reader take a position with regard to what is being said. A good deal of preparation is necessary for a reader to comment knowledgeably on the contents of a sophisticated thought piece written by an expert.

In the ideal world, no reader called upon to enter into or engage with an essay would be content with reading it just once. While short, the essays in this collection were selected because they represent a broad spectrum of opinion and a wide range of styles. You can make their acquaintance by reading them once, but you cannot claim to have any intimate knowledge of them after just one brief encounter. Nor is it just a thorough reading that is demanded—the hope of this book is that your reading will make you think about how an author put the essay in question together, and why he or she did so. So, far from reading an essay in this anthology to grasp its content, you will be reading to grasp its technique. Now, admittedly, that is like watching Fred Astaire dancing and then hoping to dance like that yourself. You may well be able to develop your own style or imitate his, but you won't do it without a lot of practice.

That's where the critical engagement part comes in. What does it mean? How can you, as a reader, be sure that you have engaged the reading and that you are in a good position to assess its claims? This kind of reading calls for a dialogue between the writer and the reader—a conversation, if you will, that you deliberately and carefully engage in as you read. Such an imagined conversation would enable you, if need be, to discuss the work with the writer if he or she were to make a cameo appearance in your classroom. This is not as outlandish as it may at first sound. In these days of e-mail, there are more and more opportunities for readers to engage with authors. The medium by which the conversation must be carried on is, of course, written down, and that, some think, is the hard part.

SOME ADVICE ON READING ESSAYS EFFECTIVELY

To guarantee that you grant each essay the kind of reading it deserves, aim to read each one at least three times, or at the very least twice. That way, you can plan to read once just to orient yourself, and once to begin to engage in the kind of dialogue that will get you involved in the author's train of thought. The first time through, ask the kinds of questions that you need answers to: questions that help you determine where you are, sometimes the kinds of questions that people are embarrassed to ask. For instance, start by making a list of words or phrases that you do not understand, with the aim of looking them up in the dictionary as soon as you get the chance. More than that, take an active approach toward learning. Since you are expected to have a sound working knowledge of the arguments you are presented with in this volume, make the effort to incorporate the terminology of the essays into your own thinking. Your ability to use the terms the experts use with some degree of facility is a mark that you are qualified to speak on the subjects in question yourself. The tools of the trade are often part of a subject matter's vocabulary. Don't overlook the value of assimilating this vocabulary, both in your speech and in your written responses.

Given the list of structural components that we have suggested you need to watch out for, it is also a good idea to make a note of the location of the thesis statement, as well as the topics that branch out from it. That way, you will be in a good position to draw up an outline of the author's argument, one more crucial step toward understanding it and feeling competent to comment on it. This kind of preliminary reading, or preview of coming attractions, will stand you in good stead when you begin to concentrate more deeply on the details of the writing itself. The first thing you need is a sense of the essay's direction. Ask of it: Where are we going? This is a crucial step before you try to determine how the author took you there.

Used book sales aside, don't be afraid to write in your textbook. If the book is borrowed or the thought of defacing a book offends you, invest in some sticky notes that will allow you to leave a discreet trail through your reading, jotting down ideas and counterarguments as they occur to you. The first time through, you don't need to follow any rigid kind of structure; you need only ask your own authentic questions of the piece in front of you. To facilitate this activity, make sure to give yourself enough time to reflect after reading: deliberately pause, put the book down, and think about the reading after you have finished.

The next reading is different. At this point, it does become appropriate for you to read with a particular slant. If you are planning to do three complete readings, in this second pass you should attempt to absorb the meaning of the essay without too much in the way of critical disagreement. In other words, try to take in, as open-mindedly as possible, what the author is saying. While your final assessment need not be so accepting, it is important at this stage to make your best effort to understand the point of view of the author. Imagine, during this reading, that you are obliged to take the author's side in any debate that might ensue after the reading. What arguments can you muster that would prepare you to defend the position that he or she has chosen? Add examples and elaborate on points, drawing on your own experience and expertise. This reading might be called the "reading of assent." After you do it, take the time to read the questions that follow the essay; they are meant to make you pause over specific points in the writing and to open up questions that might profitably be asked of it.

As you might anticipate, the third reading is then the "reading of dissent." Now, instead of trying to be the ideal reader of the essay as you have just been doing, you try to take apart, or unpack, some of the author's assumptions and evidence to show that his or her position is in some way not as good as it could be. Even at this point, it is of the utmost importance to remain reasonable in your proceedings: you do not want to launch a fierce attack against something when perhaps only minor objections may be reasonably raised. The objections you raise need to be credible; they cannot be half-baked or wildly overstated. Use materials and ideas you have gleaned from the questions to inform some of the thinking you do about the essay at this point. Reinforce this thinking by rereading the questions at the end to determine what answers you are now prepared to give them, based on your readings of the essay.

In this stage of critical assessment, you are free to take either of two tacks: (1) you can argue from your own position, provided you don't give way to emotion to the detriment of reason; and (2) you can argue just that the stated position is unsatisfactory from a number of points of view, perhaps none of them recognizably your own. Either way, you need to preserve your dignity and that of the author. Imagine how this conversation would be conducted if he or she were physically present in the room and free to respond to your critique. Only if you set yourself up for this kind of dialogue can you appreciate the genuine search for truth that is involved in a critical assessment of this nature.

Reading in layers, in this way, will enable you to "try on" the position that the author supports and to see whether it fits your notion of how the subject ought to be handled. It will also enrich your understanding of how and why the author chose to put an argument together the way it is. This focus on the methods of argumentation is vital to a working understanding of essay writing and the kind of complicated persuasive writing that it asks of you.

Bear in mind as you read that many of the selections in this volume are here because they serve two functions. First, they might be models of good writing whose techniques and strategies are available to you as an apprentice writer. Second, they are essays whose themes or manner of exposition is provocative in some marked ways and hence can promote discussion and reflection on a number of issues that might well adapt themselves to subject matter for your own writing. Think about this bigger picture as you evaluate what you have read. Ask yourself why the material is included or whether it ought, in fact, to be included. These larger questions put you in a stronger position to assess the validity and importance of what you have read.

To Summarize

1. Read each essay at least twice.
2. Ideally, read for orientation, for assent, and for dissent—at least three separate readings.
3. Locate the thesis statement and the essay's preview.
4. Be prepared to write a brief outline of the author's arguments.
5. Keep track of vocabulary and terminology that is new or unfamiliar to you.
6. Don't get mesmerized by the fact that something is in print; read critically.

7. Keep an open mind: ask questions that engage the piece, but allow yourself to reflect on its claims fairly.
8. Take note of the questions provided before reading the piece a second time.
9. Keep notes on what techniques are used to make the author's point.
10. Read with an eye to emulation. How can you use what you have learned?

SOME ADVICE ON WRITING IN REACTION

If reading in layers is a new and unfamiliar skill, writing in layers may be even more so. Yet writing in layers is one of the best ways to proceed if you are asked to write an essay or a response to an essay, such as a reaction paper. Part of the difficulty of this kind of assignment is that it asks you to talk fluently with the experts and sometimes leaves you unsure of your ground. Assuming that responding to something is easier than initiating a highly serious subject matter on your own, the reaction or response paper is the place to start. It is simpler to write than a formal essay; it lets you in on the conversation, so to speak; and it helps you formulate your attitudes toward a given subject much more readily than a paper that you must construct from scratch. A reaction or response paper takes on the challenge handed to you by an essay that you have read, though the resulting piece of writing may take the assignment in unexpected directions.

What you are asked to write in response is, like what you read, expository prose. Before you get to the part where you produce your first piece of official expository prose, though, you need to allow your writing to develop through a few essential stages. You need to ask how to get from the notes to the argument to the reasoned essay.

Your first writing toward the reaction paper is not meant to be completely coherent: it is only a tentative first step. You begin with stray thoughts, notes toward the final coherent product that will be your response paper. Don't try to impose too much order on your thoughts at this early phase; just let your ideas flow, even if they initially seem contradictory.

After you have decided what your main position toward the essay will be and what you think is in need of further, deeper discussion, you are ready to establish a firmer structure for your response paper. You begin this part of the essay writing as you would any other: you need to ascertain for yourself what you want to claim about the essay you have just read. Remember, though, that your function as a reader is not to write an appreciation of the piece, but instead to move toward an analysis of its ideas.

Let us draw an analogy here. Imagine that your friend is contemplating buying a new suit. He or she asks you your opinion of it. Assuming that you do not feel it is the perfect example of a suit, prepare to make constructive suggestions about it for your friend's benefit. That is, get ready to analyze the suit's appropriateness rather than just to praise or revile it. Instead of saying, "You look fat in such a light colour," a comment that dismisses the suit but makes no constructive suggestion, a question such as "Is a darker colour that would suit you better available?" This second kind of comment is more analytic in nature than the first. Although both involve your opinions, the second is aimed at making appropriate changes to the existing idea by exploring what can feasibly be modified. Similarly, your role as a reader is not just to praise or blame but to do so with an eye to producing a better result, either your perspective in contrast to the first essay or a modified version of it, altered by your constructive thinking. Or failing that, a reader can go further and suggest that the ideas be scrapped entirely. This would be tantamount to telling your friend that you don't understand why he or she needs a new suit at all and would involve a more radical dismantling of the claim that he or she does. In short, you aim at analyzing rather than appreciating, at taking apart rather than accepting or rejecting the whole of an idea, except on rare occasions when the idea seems completely unworkable, unacceptable, or reprehensible.

Your first effort should be directed toward arriving at a thesis statement in response to the work in front of you. Such a statement must be general, but it can be reined in by providing the reader with a sense of what direction your argument is going in. In other words, it is a good idea to write a thesis statement to conform to the following formula: "X is good/bad because it has these results: ..." Remember, however, that it is not the essay that you are rating good or bad; it is the position that essay takes with regard to the subject under discussion. You won't wind up writing: "X's essay was good because...." That would be an appreciation. Instead, you will write: "X's view of Y is flawed because it doesn't take one important thing into account...." It is your engagement with the argument that is the focal point here—not an acceptance or rejection of the essay itself. So allow yourself plenty of room to get into the argument, allowing your real reactions, formulated through multiple readings, to show through.

To demonstrate real engagement with another's work, you need to show that you have carefully considered what is being argued. That does not mean you are obliged to accept the author's structure as the backbone of your own essay. On the contrary, it is probably a good idea for you to come up with a structure of your own, at the same time acknowledging points made in the essay that you are reacting to. Use the author's work to make your points, either quoting or paraphrasing where appropriate. Make sure that the connection between your work and the catalyst essay is clear; the two pieces should be clearly linked in your reader's mind. Nevertheless, the catalyst essay should not hamper you: it should simply serve as a launching point for your ideas on the same subject.

Remember throughout that you are responsible for what you say. As a result, you must think through your ideas clearly and make sure that they are fully explained and can be easily understood by the reader. One of the best ways to make sure that real communication is taking place is to read your first draft to a fellow classmate. Then be prepared to take his or her suggestions for improving your writing, whether the suggestions involve fine details such as spelling or proofreading or whether they involve larger structural issues, such as the order that materials are presented in or weaknesses in your reasoning. The development of your ideas demands that you supply readers with sufficient evidence to convince them that your point is a valid one. Bear in mind that evidence comes in a number of different forms. Work on improving your abilities in gathering and presenting evidence, whether in the form of examples (the most common form), in the more sophisticated form of statistics, in the use of authoritative evidence (quotations or paraphrases of learned sources), or in terms of complex reasoning. All of us have some degree of proficiency with presenting these forms of evidence. Part of your task as a reader and a responder to the articles in this textbook is to improve your capacity to present such evidence, and to assess other writers' skills in presenting it. Finding evidence to support your arguments is only one part of the task, and one that is increasingly easy with new electronic access to materials that are at a distance. Besides finding evidence, you need to know how to use it, and there is no better place to look than at the precedent established by published writers with similar aims, who appeal to a wide variety of audiences. Developing your ideas necessitates giving readers good and compelling reasons for believing as you do. Make sure that you do not lose sight of the need for strong evidence when you write in any of the expository modes, either as a responder or on your own.

Revise your work carefully, starting with its larger aspects and moving to the smaller ones. In other words, begin by asking what ideas should be added or deleted, moved or changed in the larger structure of what you have written. After you are satisfied that the body of the piece is adequate and your thesis statement is strong, move on to the paragraph level and assess the line your argument takes and the topic sentences that accompany each paragraph as guides to the reader. After completing this examination, make sure that your essay is coherent and consistent. Can the reader move easily from the first argument to the second and so on? Check transitions between paragraphs, repetition of key words, and consistency of argument throughout. Another reader at this point may be valuable, especially if he is or she is willing simply to write in the margins, "I don't get this point" whenever your writing gets hazy. And, of course, little things mean a lot. Make sure that the reader doesn't feel that he or she has become merely your proofreader, confronted with typos, spelling mistakes, and grammatical errors. These details matter a lot to the overall impression that your work makes on the audience it finds. See to it that no distractions of this sort interfere with a reader's understanding and enjoyment of the material you present.

To Summarize

1. Decide where you stand in relation to what is being argued.
2. Develop your own "platform" that will allow you to discuss pertinent points that need to be addressed.
3. Make sure your own claim is clear.
4. Keep a clear head and a rational, not overly emotional, perspective.
5. Ask questions that relate to the written piece you're reacting to.
6. Use material from the piece to support your own claims.
7. Remain constructive in your suggestions.
8. Develop ideas fully.
9. Revise carefully.

EXPOSITORY PROSE AND ITS PATTERNS

Expository prose seeks to explain things to the reader, and it may undertake to do this in any number of ways. Through expository prose, writers share their understanding of a given subject. In other words, the main function of this kind of writing is to teach rather than to tell a story. As a student, you have likely been exposed to numerous teaching methods, all aimed at giving you a better explanation of events, a better understanding of someone else's ideas.

This volume aims to isolate several techniques for explaining things in writing by giving you examples of their use in the hands of respected writers. While not all of the writers collected in this volume are writing academic expository prose, many of the techniques they use to explain something can be readily adapted to your purposes as a writer in school. None of the essays collected here is a pure example of a particular kind of exposition, but all of them employ a variety of techniques that help to make their points better understood by the reader.

This volume aims at something more as well. Since the object of good expository prose is to explain ideas and to provoke them, the range of materials aims to give you, as a member of a writing class, something to argue about with your class, some issues to discuss and debate, and some launching points for your thinking. What you write in response and what you come to discuss in class may broach on a variety of topics that may be just slightly beyond the range of the kind of material you typically study in your academic courses. No one would argue that writing that seeks an audience cannot afford not to be interesting; the selections here may have a variety of audiences in mind, but all have the fixed goal of interesting and enlightening their audiences.

The patterns of exposition that will be explored here include description and narration, illustration, definition, process, comparison and contrast, division and classification, cause and effect, and persuasion and argument. In the last section on exploring multiculturalism, a number of essays are gathered that deal with questions of identity and culture. These essays consider the conflicts and challenges of identity in a variety of ways. Each of these patterns can be employed as a means of teaching something, or explaining it clearly. They are all tactics that can be used to make a point by good writers with a command of their tools. When you can use these techniques to explain something to your satisfaction, you have mastered some of the significant methods of argumentation demanded by an expert writer. You may notice in reading that seldom does an entire essay conform to the strictures of comparison and contrast, for example, but that instead selected parts of the larger work provide marked examples of how comparison and contrast work. Only rarely does a complete essay follow just one rhetorical pattern of exposition. But while the categories may seem, to some extent, arbitrary, the methods used by various authors to present them can be invaluable to those of us who are learning to perfect our own communication skills. Undoubtedly, you use all these techniques to some extent already in your day-to-day conversations with friends, in your correspondence, and in practical applications of ordinary life. This textbook and the course it is connected to will work together to make you more conscious of the ways in which you use the techniques to achieve particular stylistic effects in your writing. Judicious use of these effects, in turn, will combine to convince your readers that you know what you are talking about and that what you have to say is worth attending to. Remember as you read that the essays are valued not only for what they say, but for the skilled ways in which they say it. Read with an eye to imitating them.

When you are asked to write in a particular expository mode, try to incorporate materials that really interest you and that form part of your thinking, your conversation, and your work on a daily basis. Then the writing task will become less onerous, and you will kill two birds with one stone: you will learn more, and you will reinforce your learning by articulating your thoughts and opinions about the subject matter in question. Then too, the writing will seem less like an assignment and will become more a part of what you want to say. Concentrate on making a good case, and the reader will be impressed by your command of the modes and by the rhetorical flourish with which you support your arguments. Remember that how you argue is at least as important as what you argue, and write your essays with a conscious awareness of the tactics of argument you have learned in the course of reading this book.

Consult the book as a reference guide to the modes of expository writing. Think about what arguments you found most persuasive and why. This method will help you identify ways to proceed when you are faced with the task of writing an essay with a deliberate communicative purpose.

And now for the disclaimer: Although many of the tactics of argument are admirable, the pieces that are gathered in this collection do not always perfectly represent the way you ought to write as a student. Each of these essays was written with a specific audience in mind. Some of them are journalistic pieces, which make more use of slang and other conventions of informal language. In other words, the writers of these selections often get away with more in their treatment of language than you can in a college or university setting. Bear in mind that correct grammar and formal academic usage are usually called for in the papers you write for a course. Although you may not be granted the kind of professional licence that some of these writers are, the general requirements of writing remain the same. Your first duty is to be interesting (and convincing) to your audience. Absorb the techniques used in these short pieces, and your writing will be the better for it.

Description and Narration

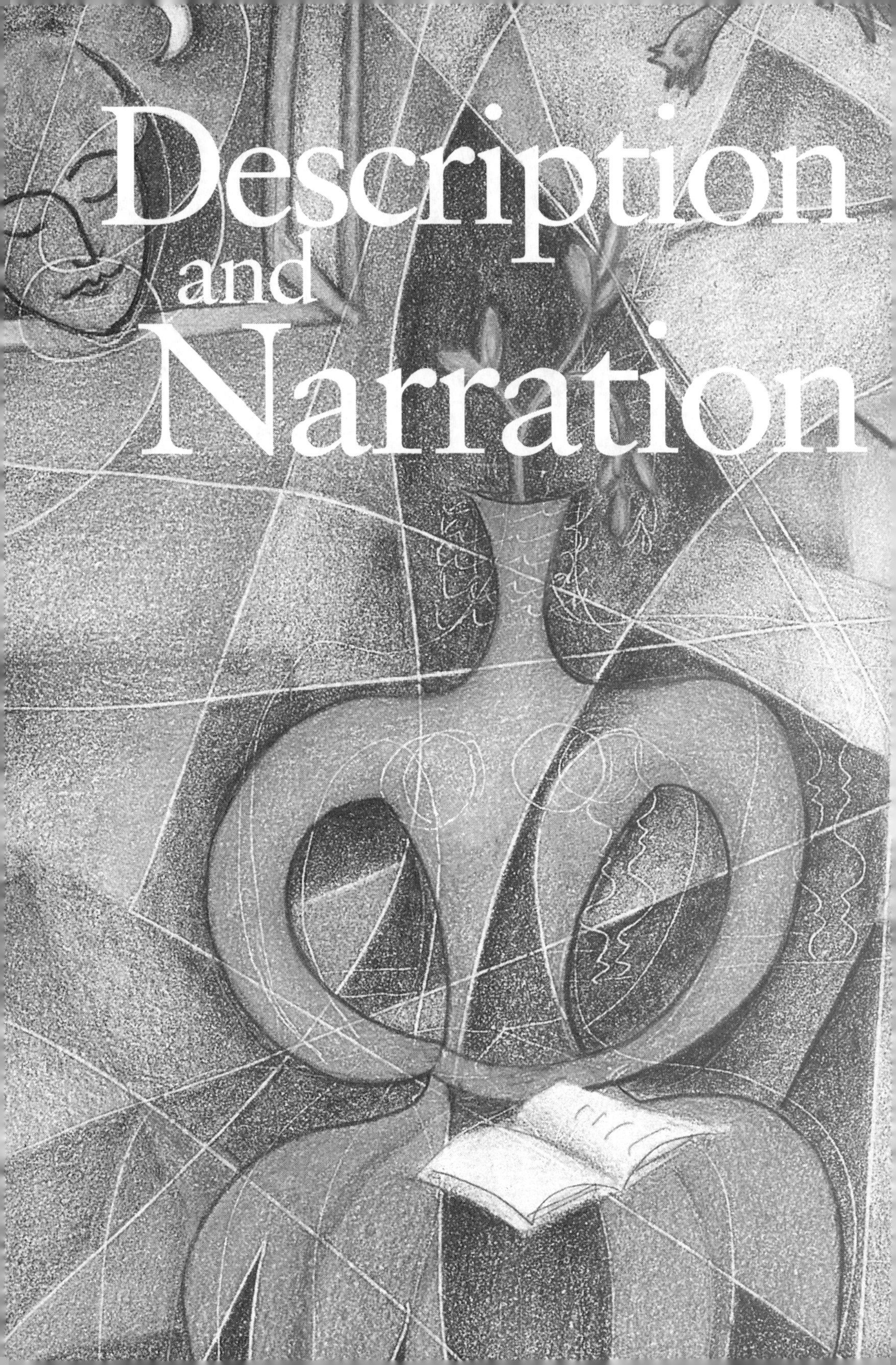

DESCRIPTION AND NARRATION

Show and Tell: Some Tricks of the Trade

Perhaps no other modes depend more on detail than description and narration. In order either to describe something clearly enough to evoke it for your reader or to tell the story of an incident —real or imagined—you need to supply plenty of detail. That said, description and narrative in essays are not there for their own sakes. They are there to provide support for a point that you, the writer, are intent on making. Still, for these patterns of expository writing to perform effectively, you need to learn how to tell stories with the kind of confidence that fiction writers often have. It's not a simple task, because telling a story well is an art. Let's look at the narrative mode first.

When you narrate an event, you tell a story according to a structured sequence of events. The focus of the narrative is consequently the action being described, or, more precisely, your account of what happened. For this reason, transition words that describe when something took place—like "now," "later," "soon"—become prominent in this kind of writing, as do verb tenses, which are at their most vibrant when active rather than passive. Pay close attention to these words as you write. They help readers orient themselves in the story you are telling.

To the extent that verbs are active, they allow the action to unfold before the readers' eyes. Immediacy is an important feature of successful narratives, as is suspense. When you tell a story, you need to ensure that it builds toward some kind of dénouement, some kind of satisfactory ending. As joke-telling makes clear, good storytelling is often hard to come by. There must, after all, be a point to the story—a punch line, so to speak.

When telling a story, you need to keep a few things in mind. First, detail is of the utmost importance. Any detail that you decide to include should supply something relevant to the story and something important for readers to know. The details are props that support the framework of the story, and the bare bones of the plot would be nothing without them. Your record of an event is dead on the page without specific detail.

Next, make sure that you understand what the story is doing in your essay. Why is it there? What does it show? If you can't articulate its function, chances are the reader will be at a similar loss. The story or description should clearly be a parable of meaning for readers.

Last, make sure that the story engages your readers. To achieve this goal, you have to call upon a fair amount of definite, concrete, sensory detail that will sufficiently call up the story in readers' minds. Narrative and description must draw readers in, invite them to turn pages, or the point you are making will be forever obscured. Narratives must adhere to readers' expectations of stories. Most of what you write will be done in the first person, with occasional forays into the third-person narrative. You need to provide a plot, some carefully drawn characters, a setting that establishes important background. Even more vital, you need to make sure that your story builds to a satisfactory ending. The structure of the story is your chief concern.

The joke that follows takes up more than one paragraph because of dialogue between a pair of speakers, but otherwise it shows the importance of timing and structure in the development of a narrative. This narrative/joke might be used as part of a larger essay to illustrate the importance of stating the obvious.

Narratives often start "in the middle of things" without preamble.

Sherlock Holmes and Dr. Watson went on a camping trip. After a good meal and a bottle of wine, they lay down for the night and went to sleep. Some hours later, Holmes awoke and nudged his faithful friend.

Dialogue is included to foster the sense of immediacy.

"Watson, look up at the sky and tell me what you see."

Watson replied, "I see millions and millions of stars."

"What does that tell you?" queried Holmes.

Watson pondered for a minute. "Astronomically, it tells me that there are millions of galaxies and potentially billions of planets. Astrologically, I observe that Saturn is in Leo. Chronologically, I deduce that the time is approximately a quarter past three. Theologically, I can see that God is all-powerful and that we are small and insignificant. Meteorologically, I suspect that we will have a beautiful day tomorrow. What does it tell you?"

> Holmes was silent for a minute, then spoke, "Watson, you idiot. Someone has stolen our tent."

Description is not very different from narrative, though its emphasis is less on plot and more on the pictures you are able to paint with words. Don't forget, however, that any description hinges on the point of view taken by the observer, so the context of any description must take your own position in relation to the object described into account. Perhaps the best analogy to illustrate steadiness of point of view when composing descriptive passages comes from the camera. Descriptions, if they are to be clear to readers and not blurred or vague, must seem to come from a steady source. Put simply, readers need to know where you are coming from. Without a clear point of view, descriptions lose their relation to you as the writer and to the audience. Keep your point of view in check by making your position and your purpose clear as you go along. Descriptions must have a clear purpose to be effective. Consider carefully what mood or attitude you wish to create for your readers' benefit. Often the scope of a descriptive essay is small; rather than describing events, it confines itself to characteristics of people, things, or moments in time.

To write a satisfactory description of something, you might invest some time in composing an inventory of details about it. Try to circle the object, person, or place in your mind, taking in its importance, its relation to you, its placement, its associations, its sensory characteristics, your feelings about it, and the feelings you wish to create in the readers. To test your ability to capture your subject, read your written piece over, adding details to arrive at a complete mental image for the readers' benefit. A strong descriptive essay can conjure up the sight, smell, taste, sound, and feel of a given object and, consequently, can reproduce in readers the emotions that you yourself feel upon contemplating it.

Balance is the key to a powerful description. You want to include details relevant to the impression you wish to make on the reader, but not so many that readers start to nod off. The most difficult part of creating a strong description is learning what to put in and what to cut out. A good rule of thumb is not to rely too heavily on adjectives. Adjectives laid on too thickly can be dull and inactive, rather than stimulating or impressive. Use careful judgement, and test your pieces on your readers' pulses by trying your phrases out on listeners, in an effort to elicit their responses.

Most of the time, the purpose of a descriptive piece is this kind of sensory sharing; sometimes, however, an object, person, or place may need to be described in a more forthright, simple way to make it a source of clear information for readers. This kind of description may occur in a technical document as a kind of "word diagram" for readers, who may need it to supplement instructions, or, perhaps, to decide the legal consequences of a traffic accident. Whatever kind of description you are asked to write, whether coolly objective or thick with subjective impressions, be scrupulous in your choice of details. The picture you create in the readers' minds depends on it.

This descriptive paragraph moves from the general (in the first line) to the specific.

The office was a shambles. True, custodians did attempt to put it to rights every ten days, but given that she virtually lived in her office, this low level of care did not suffice. Beneath the clutter, you could see that there had once been an attempt at decoration, but the borrowed modernist painting on the wall and the bland, colourless drapes were about as far as it went. There were books on the shelves, as you might expect. But there were also books on two out of three chairs, books on the floor, and a plastic bag full of books on the radiator. These books weren't stacked neatly either, just piled higgledy-piggledy, in one spot on top of the computer in a dangerous-looking leaning tower. There was paper, too —some stacked on the desk, some flung on one chair, some crumpled on the floor beside the garbage pails. And there was garbage, pop cans, waxed paper, torn envelopes, and coffee containers, heaped in and beside the garbage bins. While it was clear that someone worked in this office, it wasn't clear how she managed in the midst of such debris.

Death Comes Uninvited

It was a warm night in June, and most of the clientele in the posh restaurant were experiencing the lull that usually comes after dinner. The taped music droned in the background like buzzing bees, and most customers gave in to post-prandial calm. The only other noise was the clink of silverware against plate, the ring of crystal, and the murmur of voices. Then over these gentle sounds there was the sound of a cough, first relatively calm and polite and then more persistent and urgent.

One well-heeled diner turned her head to see what was the matter, and saw a sudden flurry of panic and pandemonium as guests at the man's table realized that he was in distress. He clutched his throat frantically, choking. The waiter stood by helplessly, the other guests woke from their peacefulness, and one of the women in the room shrieked.

An older man at a nearby table leaped up and ran toward the ailing gentleman, flung him quickly out of his chair onto the floor, and proceeded to pound his chest in a resolute attempt to administer the Heimlich manoeuvre. The gasping man seemed not to respond, but, in fact, to crumple in the face of this solicitude. He uttered just one more gasp, this one more audible and more frightening in its suddenness, and then he lay on the floor, inert.

This is an example of a narrative essay.

Undeterred, the older man crouched over him and began mouth-to-mouth resuscitation. He continued for what seemed hours, now watched over by all the customers, whose conversations were halted in mid-word and who looked on eagerly, hoping desperately for signs of life from the man's body as it lay, indecorously, on the carpeted floor. The resuscitation continued unabated, at a steady pace, but the man's face beneath was now an expressionless mask, slackened and pale, not tortured and reddened as it had been. The older man reached helplessly for the victim's wrist. His face revealed his frenzied despair — all the hope seemed at once to drain out of it. He placed the man's hand back on the floor beside him and told someone to dial 911. Mercifully, someone had already thought to make the call.

The hushed dinner crowd now felt ridiculously out of place as they awaited the outcome. Most yearned to leave but felt constrained to see out the whole event and its aftermath. Besides, it was too late to leave the scene unscathed by what they had witnessed. Death is an uninvited guest who nevertheless shows up even among the young, the wealthy, the happy, and the elegant. Death, evidently, comes like a thief in the night.

An autopsy report later revealed that the unfortunate dinner guest, who had inadvertently choked on a piece of steak, died from complications: a punctured lung suffered when his rib broke as the other guest administered the Heimlich manoeuvre and from a coma induced by an allergic reaction. It seems the older man had been eating peanuts, and the mouth-to-mouth resuscitation he gave was, in fact, the kiss of death.

David Suzuki

David Suzuki (b. 1936) is a geneticist, writer, and journalist. His CBC TV show, *The Nature of Things,* has been broadcast for many years. He has published many books, including *Metamorphosis: Stages in a Life* (1987), as well as ten books for children. Suzuki holds a PhD in Zoology from the University of Chicago, and is currently working in the Sustainable Development Research Institute (SDRI) at the University of British Columbia.

LESSONS TAUGHT BY NATURE

"Look at that insect," the grandmother said, pointing at the beetle lying motionless on the sidewalk. "Oh, its battery must be dead!" responded the boy.

This story was related to me in Japan in 1994. Apocryphal or not, it was meant to illustrate how disconnected from nature modern people have become. To the boy, even an insect is merely an object manufactured by humans.

I thought of that anecdote while lying on a dock on the shores of Smoke Lake in Algonquin Park. The reason we have become so reckless with the ecological birthright of our children must be the illusion that we are in total command of our surroundings. Here in Algonquin, we have an opportunity to see that nature is complex beyond our understanding.

The brilliant panoply of stars overhead at night is a startling contrast to the limited display visible in any large city on a "clear" night. Gazing at the spectacular starscape above me, I wondered whether urban children responded to their first sight of an Algonquin night sky with awe or fear. I suspected a bit of both.

5 Our perceptions and values are formed by our experiences and surroundings. For example, Prairie people have told me of their great love of the big sky and the distant horizon, which makes them feel claustrophobic in Vancouver, hemmed in by mountains that seem to push them into the ocean. For most people today, the human-created environment of cities shapes priorities and the way we see the world. Here in Algonquin, we have to recognize that there is a different rhythm, driven by the seasons, the climate, the forest, and the animals, over which humans have no control at all.

"Tonight is 'wolf night' in Algonquin," someone said, to explain the people who had gathered to howl into the forest. The haunting reply of a wolf confirmed an inter-species communication and sent squeals of delight through the crowd. This is quite a change in attitude from that reflected in fairy-tales where vicious wolves try to make a meal of Little Red Riding Hood or the three little pigs.

This summer I have been able to spend time relaxing on Quadra Island and rafting down the Babine River in British Columbia, travelling in the Arctic around Baffin Island and Greenland, and now holidaying in Algonquin, the jewel of Ontario's park system. Taken together, these places give an overwhelming sense of the awesome beauty of this part of the planet. But these islands of wilderness are decreasing in number and size under the relentless pressure of human beings. Too many of us want too much to be sustained indefinitely by the productive capacity of even the most distant ecosystems. Communities of organisms with whom we are discovering a spiritual kinship—grizzlies, walruses, wolves—are threatened by our need for "development" and "resources."

The degradation of natural systems has become inevitable because of an economic system that is fatally flawed by its species chauvinism. Economists appraise everything in the world on the basis of perceived utility for human beings alone—if we can use it, it has a value; if we can't, it's worthless. That might work if implicit in such a system was an understanding that our survival and quality of life depend on what we extract from the Earth—air, water, soil, biodiversity. Unfortunately, that isn't how it works. Economists have traditionally defined those things—the very things that keep us alive—as externalities to the system they've invented! And therein is the basis of our destructiveness.

And nowhere in such a system is there any acknowledgement of the importance and reality of spiritual values. The immense expanse we call Canada includes some of the most dazzling and biologically rich places on this planet. The chortle of a loon, which has inspired generations of Canadian artists and writers, brings me back to a reality too easily forgotten in cities. Loons and moose remind me how important it is to me to be able to share this Earth with other species. They inform us that we must temper our impulse to exploit and profit because there are forces and phenomena that lie beyond our scientific understanding.

10 Away from Ontario's wilderness gem at Algonquin, we travelled to northern British Columbia. Rafting the Babine River along a 160-kilometre arc above Smithers, we are transported back in time. For three days, the only hint of the existence of other people is the whisper of a far-off jet. Away from the familiar urban setting, we live by a different rhythm and rules and see through different eyes. There is much to think about and time to do it.

"Daddy, is it safe to drink the water?" my daughter asks, reminding me how much our world has changed since camping in my childhood, when we drank from rivers and lakes without a worry. Her whoop of delight when I answer yes reassures me that the simple joy of being in a pristine environment persists.

Hundreds of eagles precede us in a steady relay. Drifting by rock strata pointing straight up, we can only speculate at the forces that caused these geological upheavals. And everywhere we wonder at trees that have somehow found a roothold on rock cliffs or whole forests growing out of thin topsoil coating solid stone.

From where we start just below Babine Lake to our finish at the Kispiox River, the water drops almost 500 metres, creating both spectacular scenery and a navigational challenge. On the way, we meet the early arrivals of the sockeye-salmon run. They leap past one of the hundreds of obstacles on the way to spawning channels almost a thousand kilometres from the sea. And all along the route, fewer and fewer evade the deadly string of predators depending on them.

We sight twelve grizzly bears, perhaps 10 percent of the population in this watershed, and watch three of them fishing in a narrow canyon. Wild and free, large animals like grizzlies need a lot of room to move. As powerful as they are, they are extremely wary of humans and almost always vanish with a shout. But as the relentless pressure of human activity encroaches on their homes, bears can't just move away or squeeze in tighter. I wonder how much room we will leave for these magnificent animals, for whom this is ancestral land.

15 At each camp site, the children are respectful but unafraid. They know the bears will give us a wide berth if we are careful and make enough noise to let them know we're here. River guides tell stories of urban dwellers for whom this kind of wilderness is terrifying because it is beyond human understanding and predictability. Yet it is exhilarating and somehow reassuring to discover forces of nature still intact and beyond our comprehension and domination.

For four days, the forest around is intact, untouched by road or logging, but at the junction with the Skeena River we sight the first patches of clearcuts. A massive fire in 1978 on Cutoff Mountain gave forest companies an excuse to "salvage" the burned trees by clearcutting. Those companies often argue that fires and outbreaks of insects and disease are the natural analogues of clearcuts, but after such logging there's nothing left to salvage. The unlogged parts of the Cutoff burn have much more vegetation and regrowth. Standing or fallen dead trees continue to hold the thin soil and nourish a host of organisms, including small trees.

Along the Skeena, fresh clearings far exceeding the legal limit of fifty hectares appear on both sides of the river. Forest companies boast that for every tree cut, two or three more are planted, as if a few seedlings crudely stuck in the ground are an equal exchange for trees hundreds of years old. A mature tree bears hundreds of cones, each producing hundreds of seeds. Of tens of thousands of seeds, perhaps a few hundred will actually sprout and begin to grow, while only a few dozen may reach small treehood. Of them, a handful may reach full maturity. Every merchantable tree, then, is a survivor of tens of thousands of mini experiments, not two or three seedlings.

The forests, fish, and bears here, as in most parts of the planet, are threatened by the relentless demands of human numbers, consumption, and economics. Those calling for the preservation of areas like the Babine River basin are called "greedy" because only a few hundred people may actually experience it annually. But when such an area is developed, an exquisitely balanced and complex ecosystem thousands of years in the making vanishes in a geological blink of an eye.

Human beings have needs that are more than just physical and social; we are spiritual animals. I believe we have a built-in need to experience wilderness and nature, a craving that can be fulfilled partially by knowing that there are such cathedrals to nourish the soul. In trashing wilderness areas that only time and nature create, we diminish ourselves with the loss of an integral component of our spiritual make-up.

20 When we began the trip at the head of the Babine River, we put our rafts in at a weir built by the federal government. Sockeye salmon completing their long journey from the sea up the Skeena River and then the Babine are stopped by that weir so scientists can determine the number and make-up of the run and regulate the number of fish in the spawning beds.

Driven by the powerful urges of their genes, the fish gather restlessly behind the barrier until they find a series of slots through which they swim only to be trapped in metal cages. At regular intervals, summer students open a horizontal slit so the fish can slither by and be counted and classed as mature or "jacks" (immature males).

Impounded in the metal cage, the fish frantically leap into the air, repeatedly smashing themselves against the metal sides. It was a horrifying reminder of a giant dam on the Parana River in

South America. Many of the fish in the Parana migrate up and down the river, foraging for food or spawning beds. So a fish "elevator" was installed to carry the fish from one side of the dam to the other. Fish attempting to escape the elevator made the same sickening clank of flesh on metal as the desperate animals on the Babine. The elevator is a cruel and ridiculous technological solution to fulfill the natural instincts of fish. And here in Canada, in the name of science, experts were treating fish in a similarly unnecessary and destructive way.

Tourist rafting on the Babine has increased the human traffic considerably. This summer (1994), two or three hundred people will probably make the trip. Since there are very few sites along the rugged banks that can comfortably accommodate tents and rafts, there is increasing pressure on them. There is also concern that, though wild, animals could become habituated to humans by rooting through any refuse or even digging up latrines.

Our rafting guides went to impressive lengths to minimize our impact. There wasn't a sign of human detritus like packaging, bottle tops, or cans on the entire trip. Every bit of food that was brought in was consumed, carried back out unused, or burned and the ashes spread on the river. Only small branches of dead driftwood were collected and used for firewood so they could be burned completely and the ashes dispersed. Most surprising was the collection of all human feces so it could be transported away from the river. Of course we did have an impact on the ecosystem, but every effort was made to minimize it.

25 It was a privilege to enter territory where the wild creatures —eagles, salmon, and bears—so clearly belonged. Without even being aware of it, we showed our respect by our own behaviour. When we encountered grizzly bears fishing, we waited and watched quietly until they had finished and left before we continued on our way.

At the Skeena River, we encountered our first evidence of clearcut logging on both sides of the river. Along the riverbanks, a fringe of trees was left all the way up to the tops of the banks. But the sky was visible through the highest trees and the narrow strip of trees became an insult, an inadequate illusion of a real forest. There was a striking contrast between the river banks along the Babine and those on the Skeena. Slides where rock and dirt had come away and dropped towards the river carrying trees with them were not at all noticeable on the Babine—in fact, I didn't see any. But once we hit the logged area, slide after slide was obvious along the banks, many of them recent.

It may be true that the bottoms of natural slides are places where some of the largest trees in a wild forest can be found. When thin soil piles up at a slide's bottom, it can be an exceptionally fertile area for future trees. But along a river, the soil slides right off the hills and into the water, while the gashes remaining are inhospitable challenges for any future trees. So even where trees are left for cosmetic purposes, clearcut logging nearby has visible effects.

In the wild, the interconnectedness of living systems becomes obvious. The salmon and steelhead runs up the Skeena and Babine are famous and important for sport, commercial, and Native food fisheries. But they are also intimately connected to biophysical and meteorological rhythms that are disrupted by large-scale clearcutting. And the populations of bear, eagles, and micro-organisms are intertwined with the fate of salmon. An experience of the wild uplifts the human spirit and also makes us rethink some of our assumptions and beliefs.

VOCABULARY

apocryphal: of doubtful authenticity 2
panoply: ceremonial attire 4
chortle: laugh, chuckle 9
strata: layers 12
encroaches: trespasses 14
analogues: similar things 16
weir: a dam 20
impounded: trapped 22
latrines: bathrooms 23
detritus: waste, garbage 24

AUDIENCE AND PURPOSE

1. What is the purpose of Suzuki's description of his visit to the wilderness?
2. Why does he begin with a child's confused remark about a natural creature?
3. Describe how Suzuki intersperses natural description with arguments about the importance of maintaining the ecosystem.

CONTENT

1. What unclear thinking accounts for the human destruction of ecosystems, according to Suzuki?

2. What, does Suzuki argue, is the spiritual value of the wilderness?
3. Why does replanting after clear-cutting not replenish the trees?
4. How are salmon being destroyed in the name of science in Canada?

STYLE AND STRUCTURE

1. Find examples of Suzuki's vocabulary that show the spiritual value of nature.
2. Why does Suzuki use children's comments and other references to them to punctuate his thoughts about nature?
3. Why is a personal account of the wilderness a more effective way to explain dangers to the wilderness than simple facts and figures?

Robertson Davies

Robertson Davies (1913–95) was a Canadian essayist and novelist and a professor at the University of Toronto. His best-known novels include *Fifth Business* (1970), *The Manticore* (1972), and *World of Wonders* (1975), collectively known as the Deptford Trilogy. Davies was the first Canadian to become an Honorary Member of the American Academy and Institute of Arts and Letters, and he was a Companion of the Order of Canada.

STRATFORD FORTY YEARS AGO

Stratford fifty years ago is easily described; what does the infallible Karl Baedeker have to say in his *Handbook for Travellers in Canada*? ... "a divisional point and important railway centre ... an agricultural and industrial city ... prettily situated on the Avon ... its schools include a Collegiate Institute and a Provincial Normal School." But in 1953 Stratford underwent a transformation which nobody had foreseen, not even Tom Patterson, who brought it about.

Stratford forty years ago suddenly became a theatre town, and saw the beginnings of what is now generally admitted to be the foremost centre of classical theatre in North America. Nobody forty years ago thought that would happen or had a clear idea of what it might mean. I well recall my own early visits to Stratford, for I was one of the few non-Stratfordians to be a member of its earliest Board of Governors. Why I was so honoured I cannot truly say, except that I was a friend of Tyrone Guthrie's, who knew that I liked long chances and would do anything to give the theatre in Canada a lift. My personal expectations for the infant Festival were high, because I had great faith in Guthrie, whose organizing ability and theatrical wizardry I knew well, but as I sat at those early Board meetings, I knew that I was an outsider and carried little of the real responsibility for what was happening; the Stratford citizens who sat there with me were undertaking a venture which could cost them dear in reputation and good hard cash. They hadn't much notion of what a theatre festival might be, but they knew that their town was no longer an important railway centre and something must be done if it were not to lose significance. They were prepared to take a very long chance—for chances don't come longer anywhere than in the theatre. So they listened with caution to Tom Patterson, and very soon they were listening in astonishment to Tyrone Guthrie.

His impact on Stratford was immediate and extraordinary; the town had never seen anything like him before. He was not like anybody's idea of a great theatrical director. With his height, air of command, and informal dress he was often described as looking like a policeman off duty. And indeed there was something of the policeman about him — his gimlet eye, which awoke a sense of guilt in the sluggard; his remarkable physical strength, which showed itself in immense endurance and an ability to absorb malt liquor without visible consequence; his sometimes rough and peremptory dismissal of arguments he did not choose to consider. This was his Scottish side. But he had an Irish side, which showed itself in a light-hearted approach to difficulties that looked insurmountable, a brilliant wit, and very often in a sort of inspired silliness, which confused people who had, a moment before, heard him uttering what sounded like the thunderings of Jove. Not an easy man for the sober citizens of an Ontario community to understand.

He was, however, irresistible, or almost so, for there were Stratfordians who resisted him and did so until they had reluctantly to admit the success of what he had done for the town. But everybody associated with the Festival venture was hypnotized by him. To be with him was to breathe a finer air, to be swept into a world where life was strenuous but entrancing.

5 So, the Festival came into being with Tony as its inspiring spirit. And how lucky that was for Stratford, because he was, in all things that related to the theatre, a man of unimpeachable probity, and he recommended nothing, insisted on nothing, that he was not prepared to support with every ounce of his remarkable energy.

Suddenly, there was the Festival, and that story has been told many times and need not be repeated here. Tony's enthusiasm spread through the town and the town responded in ways that were both characteristic and admirable. Actors had to be housed; people found houses and overcame the fears of those who thought actors must be fly-by-nights and fallen women. Visitors had to be housed, and people were found who threw open their homes, charging minimal prices for excellent beds, and breakfasts of astounding variety and quantity. Churches undertook to provide hot meals for the playgoers who could not squeeze into the town's few hotels and cafés. The Festival was a town festival and everybody with an ounce of daring wanted to get in on the action. It was thus that the town made the Festival its own, and not an exotic visitor.

As a dweller in Eastern Ontario I watched this development with astonishment, for, though Eastern Ontario has virtues of its own, enthusiasm and bounteous hospitality are not among them. Was it a matter of heritage? The people of Western Ontario tend to be descendants of English settlers, from the gentler parts of the Old Land, and from Germany. The Scots and Irish of Eastern Ontario are a different breed.

Not everything went smoothly, of course. The press was not pleased that Guthrie would not admit its representatives to rehearsals. What could he be hiding? He was, of course, protecting artistic creation on a high level, which is something the press has never been quick to understand. But when the uttermost is being demanded of Canadian actors who have never been so stretched before, it is not fair to invite reporters to watch them. Nor, if reporters had been present, could Guthrie have spoken in the combination of extravagant rhetoric and quarter-deck profanity which was his rehearsal mode.

The actors were a puzzle to some Stratfordians. "What do you do in the daytime?" was a question often heard, from people who had never known what hard work make-believe can be.

There was turbulence. The local newspaper did not, at first, favour the Festival, and it had its following. *Maclean's* magazine, a national publication, carried an article which was somewhat jocose and patronizing about Stratford's presumption in attempting a Festival of the first rank, as big-city papers tend to be when writing about smaller places. The writer went so far as to say that Alec Guinness who was, with Irene Worth, at the head of the acting company, was cold and standoffish and kept the local people at a distance. This was trivial and untrue, but for some reason Guinness was deeply offended and wanted to sue the magazine for libel. He was not to be deflected from this determination, and because I knew something about the press, I was deputed by the Board to reason with him. It was not easy, but when I pointed out that such a suit would be a long time coming before the court, and would simply give further circulation to an inept article, he withdrew, without being wholly appeased.

The public could not peep at rehearsals, but it could, and did, take the keenest interest in the digging of the hole, and the pouring of the cement, for the amphitheatre. Most of all, it loved the huge tent. The master of the tent was Skip Manley, a circus man, gaudy in dress and richly be-ringed; he worked with his crew for sixty hours without a break to raise the poles, the guy-wires, and the canvas. It was such a tent as sultans dream of, for inside the heavy canvas shell it was hung with cloth of royal blue, establishing an atmosphere of opulence and distinction which Canadians do not associate with tents. Manley slept in the tent, and managed it through winds and storms like the captain of a great galleon, for there was unceasing and unrelenting need to ease it here, tighten it there, and adjust the stress on the four huge cedar poles that bore the greatest strain.

All this was to be seen, and Stratford saw it. What could not be seen, but which hung like a storm cloud over the Board, was the terrible financial responsibility for demands were daily—hourly—and there was never enough money. But great acts of faith were called forth, courage was demanded and shown, the people who had decided to back the venture bent—sometimes distressingly—but they did not break. This was municipal heroism, a virtue we seldom hear celebrated.

At last came July 13—not a date of happy omen—and the opening performance. A few minutes before *Richard III* began, my wife and I were standing with Tony and Judy Guthrie between the canvas and the blue inner tent, far down on the right side of the amphitheatre. It was the only time we had seen them a prey to nerves. They were deeply apprehensive, for they knew how much hung on what happened in the next three hours. They were not fearful for themselves, but for the troops of friends they had made in Stratford. Could this absurd adventure succeed?

If it had not done so, you would not be reading this recollection now.

VOCABULARY

gimlet: perceiving 3
peremptory: admitting no denial, imperious 3
quarter-deck: part of a ship's upper deck, near the stern 8
jocose: playful, joking 10
guy-wires: ropes or chains to secure a tent 11
opulence: wealth 11

AUDIENCE AND PURPOSE

1. Why does Davies begin his narrative with a description of Stratford from the Baedeker *Handbook for Travellers in Canada*?
2. How does Davies characterize the people he finds in small-town Ontario without offending some of his readership?
3. In what ways might this piece of writing be characterized as a celebration?

CONTENT

1. Note how Davies uses detail to describe Tyrone Guthrie in one short paragraph. What telling details does he include?
2. Davies says that the town made the Festival its own. How did this occur?
3. Why does Davies stress the "circus" atmosphere and the dark side of the Festival's beginning?

STYLE AND STRUCTURE

1. Davies' title conjures up a world gone by, and much of this language harkens back to the way it used to be. Why does he talk so much about the Stratford of the past instead of the one we know now?
2. Davies takes the perspective of the Stratfordian in this essay. How is this approach effective in demonstrating the success of the Stratford festival today?
3. Why does Davies conclude with just one brief question?

Dylan Thomas

Dylan Thomas (1914–53) was a Welsh poet whose works include *Portrait of the Artist as a Young Dog* (1940), and *Under Milkwood* (1952), a radio play for voices. A few of his best-known works include "A Child's Christmas in Wales," which is the poetic version of this piece; "Do Not Go Gentle into That Good Night" (1952); and "Fern Hill" (1946).

MEMORIES OF CHRISTMAS

One Christmas was so much like another, in those years, around the sea-town corner now, and out of all sound except the distant speaking of the voices I sometimes hear a moment before sleep, that I can never remember whether it snowed for six days and six nights when I was twelve or whether it snowed for twelve days and twelve nights when I was six; or whether the ice broke and the skating grocer vanished like a snowman through a white trap-door on that same Christmas Day that the mince-pies finished Uncle Arnold and we tobogganed down the seaward hill, all the afternoon, on the best tea-tray, and Mrs Griffiths complained, and we threw a snowball at her niece, and my hands burned so, with the heat and the cold, when I held them in front of the fire, that I cried for twenty minutes and then had some jelly.

All the Christmases roll down the hill towards the Welsh-speaking sea, like a snowball growing whiter and bigger and rounder, like a cold and headlong moon bundling down the sky that was our street; and they stop at the rim of the ice-edged, fish-freezing waves, and I plunge my hands in the snow and bring out whatever I can find; holly or robins or pudding, squabbles and carols and oranges and tin whistles, and the fire in the front room, and bang go the crackers, and holy, holy, holy, ring the bells, and the glass bells shaking on the tree, and Mother Goose, and Struwelpeter—oh! the baby-burning flames and the clacking scissorman!—Billy Bunter and Black Beauty. Little Women and boys who have three helpings, Alice and Mrs Potter's badgers, penknives, teddy-bears—named after a Mr Theodore Bear, their inventor, or father, who died recently in the United States—mouth-organs, tin-soldiers, and blancmange, and Auntie Bessie playing "Pop Goes the Weasel" and "Nuts in May" and "Oranges and Lemons" on the untuned piano in the parlour all through the thimble-hiding musical-chairing blind-man's-buffing party at the end of the never-to-be-forgotten day at the end of the unremembered year.

In goes my hand into that wool-white bell-tongued ball of holidays resting at the margin of the carol-singing sea, and out come Mrs Prothero and the firemen.

It was on the afternoon of the day of Christmas Eve, and I was in Mrs Prothero's garden, waiting for cats, with her son Jim. It was snowing. It was always snowing at Christmas; December, in my memory, is white as Lapland, though there were no reindeers. But there were cats. Patient, cold, and callous, our hands wrapped in socks, we waited to snowball the cats. Sleek and long as jaguars and terrible-whiskered, spitting and snarling they would slink and sidle over the white back-garden walls, and the lynx-eyed hunters, Jim and I, fur-capped and moccasined trappers from Hudson's Bay off Eversley Road, would hurl our deadly snowballs at the green of their eyes. The wise cats never appeared. We were so still, Eskimo-footed arctic marksmen in the muffling silence of the eternal snows — eternal, ever since Wednesday — that we never heard Mrs Prothero's first cry from her igloo at the bottom of the garden. Or, if we heard it at all, it was, to us, like the far-off challenge of our enemy and prey, the neighbour's Polar Cat. But soon the voice grew louder. "Fire!" cried Mrs Prothero, and she beat the dinner-gong. And we ran down the garden, with the snowballs in our arms, towards the house, and smoke, indeed, was pouring out of the dining-room, and the gong was bombilating, and Mrs Prothero was announcing ruin like a town-crier in Pompeii. This was better than all the cats in Wales standing on the wall in a row. We bounded into the house, laden with snowballs, and stopped at the open door of the smoke-filled room. Something was burning all right; perhaps it was Mr Prothero, who always slept there after midday dinner with a newspaper over his face; but he was standing in the middle of the room, saying "A fine Christmas!" and smacking at the smoke with a slipper.

"Call the fire-brigade," cried Mrs Prothero as she beat the gong.

"They won't be there," said Mr Prothero, "it's Christmas."

There was no fire to be seen, only clouds of smoke and Mr Prothero standing in the middle of them, waving his slipper as though he were conducting.

"Do something," he said.

And we threw all our snowballs into the smoke — I think we missed Mr Prothero — and ran out of the house to the telephone-box. "Let's call the police as well," Jim said.

"And the ambulance."

"And Ernie Jenkins, he likes fires."

But we only called the fire-brigade, and soon the fire-engine came and three tall men in helmets brought a hose into the house and Mr Prothero got out just in time before they turned it on. Nobody could have had a noisier Christmas Eve. And when the firemen turned off the hose and were standing in the wet and smoky room, Jim's aunt, Miss Prothero, came downstairs and peered in at them. Jim and I waited, very quietly, to hear what she would say to them. She said the right thing, always. She looked at the three tall firemen in their shining helmets, standing among the smoke and cinders and dissolving snowballs, and she said: "Would you like something to read?"

Now out of that bright white snowball of Christmas gone comes the stocking, the stocking of stockings, that hung at the foot of the bed with the arm of a golliwog dangling over the top and small bells ringing in the toes. There was a company, gallant and scarlet but never nice to taste though I always tried when very young, of belted and busbied and musketed lead soldiers so soon to lose their heads and legs in the wars on the kitchen table after the tea-things, the mince-pies, and the cakes that I helped to make by stoning the raisins and eating them, had been cleared away; and a bag of moist and many-coloured jelly-babies and a folded flag and a false nose and a tram-conductor's cap and a machine that punched tickets and rang a bell; never a catapult; once, by a mistake that no one could explain, a little hatchet; and a rubber buffalo, or it may have been a horse, with a yellow head and haphazard legs; and a celluloid duck that made, when you pressed it, a most unducklike noise, a mewing moo that an ambitious cat might make who wishes to be a cow; and a painting-book in which I could make the grass, the trees, the sea, and the animals any colour I pleased; and still the dazzling sky-blue sheep are grazing in the red field under a flight of rainbow-beaked and pea-green birds.

Christmas morning was always over before you could say Jack Frost. And look! suddenly the pudding was burning! Bang the gong and call the fire-brigade and the book-loving firemen! Someone found the silver threepenny-bit with a currant on it; and the someone was always Uncle Arnold. The motto in my cracker read:

Let's all have fun this Christmas Day,
Let's play and sing and shout hooray!

and the grown-ups turned their eyes towards the ceiling, and Auntie Bessie, who had already been frightened, twice, by a clockwork mouse, whimpered at the sideboard and had some elderberry wine. And someone put a glass bowl full of nuts on the littered table, and my uncle said, as he said once every year: "I've got a shoe-nut here. Fetch me a shoe-horn to open it, boy."

And dinner was ended.

And I remember that on the afternoon of Christmas Day, when the others sat around the fire and told each other that this was nothing, no, nothing, to the great snowbound and turkey-proud yule-log-crackling holly-berry-bedizined and kissing-under-the-mistletoe Christmas when *they* were children, I would go out, school-capped and gloved and mufflered, with my bright new boots squeaking, into the white world on to the seaward hill, to call on Jim and Dan and Jack and to walk with them through the silent snowscape of our town.

We went padding through the streets, leaving huge deep footprints in the snow, on the hidden pavements.

"I bet people'll think there's been hippoes."

"What would you do if you saw a hippo coming down Terrace Road?"

"I'd go like this, bang! I'd throw him over the railings and roll him down the hill and then I'd tickle him under the ear and he'd wag his tail ..."

"What would you do if you saw *two* hippoes ... ?"

Iron-flanked and bellowing he-hippoes clanked and blundered and battered through the scudding snow towards us by Mr Daniel's house.

"Let's post Mr Daniel a snowball through his letterbox."

"Let's write things in the snow."

"Let's write 'Mr Daniel looks like a spaniel' all over his lawn."

"Look," Jack said, "I'm eating snow-pie."

"What's it taste like?"

"Like snow-pie," Jack said.

Or we walked on the white shore.

"Can the fishes see it's snowing?"

"They think it's the sky falling down."

The silent one-clouded heavens drifted on to the sea.

"All the old dogs have gone."

Dogs of a hundred mingled makes yapped in the summer at the sea-rim and yelped at the trespassing mountains of the waves.

"I bet St Bernards would like it now."

And we were snowblind travellers lost on the north hills, and the great dewlapped dogs, with brandy-flasks round their necks, ambled and shambled up to us, baying "Excelsior."

We returned home through the desolate poor sea-facing streets where only a few children fumbled with bare red fingers in the thick wheel-rutted snow and cat-called after us, their voices fading away, as we trudged uphill, into the cries of the dock-birds and the hooters of ships out in the white and whirling bay.

Bring out the tall tales now that we told by the fire as we roasted chestnuts and the gaslight bubbled low. Ghosts with their heads under their arms trailed their chains and said "whooo" like owls in the long nights when I dared not look over my shoulder; wild beasts lurked in the cubby-hole under the stairs where the gas-meter ticked. "Once upon a time," Jim said, "there were three boys, just like us, who got lost in the dark in the snow, near Bethesda Chapel, and this is what happened to them...." It was the most dreadful happening I had ever heard.

And I remember that we went singing carols once, a night or two before Christmas Eve, when there wasn't the shaving of a moon to light the secret, white-flying streets. At the end of a long road was a drive that led to a large house, and we stumbled up the darkness of the drive that night, each one of us afraid, each one holding a stone in his hand in case, and all of us too brave to say a word. The wind made through the drive-trees noises as of old and unpleasant and maybe web-footed men wheezing in caves. We reached the black bulk of the house.

"What shall we give them?" Dan whispered.

"'Hark the Herald'? 'Christmas comes but Once a Year'?"

"No," Jack said: "We'll sing 'Good King Wenceslas.' I'll count three."

One, two, three, and we began to sing, our voices high and seemingly distant in the snow-felted darkness round the house that was occupied by nobody we knew. We stood close together, near the dark door.

Good King Wenceslas looked out
On the Feast of Stephen.

And then a small, dry voice, like the voice of someone who has not spoken for a long time, suddenly joined our singing: a small, dry voice from the other side of the door: a small, dry voice through the keyhole. And when we stopped running we were outside *our* house; the front room was lovely and bright; the gramophone was playing; we saw the red and white balloons hanging from the gas-bracket; uncles and aunts sat by the fire; I thought I smelt our supper being fried in the kitchen. Everything was good again, and Christmas shone through all the familiar town.

"Perhaps it was a ghost," Jim said.

"Perhaps it was trolls," Dan said, who was always reading.

"Let's go in and see if there's any jelly left," Jack said. And we did that.

VOCABULARY

Struwelpeter: a classic children's book by Heinrich Hoffman, known for its tales of wicked children who are cruelly punished 2
blancmange: pudding 2
golliwog: a grotesque black doll used in illustrations by Florence K. Upton for a series of children's books 13
busbied: wearing a busby—a military full-dress hat 13
bedizened: decorated in a cheap, showy way 16
dewlapped: having loose folds of skin hanging at the throat 36

AUDIENCE AND PURPOSE

1. How does Thomas create the sense of an age difference between the narrator and the child he once was?
2. Why do anecdotes end so abruptly in Thomas's telling of them?
3. What is important to children, according to Thomas? What in the essay makes you think so?

CONTENT

1. What characters appear in the narrative aside from the narrator? What do you find out about them?
2. What makes the story of Mr. and Mrs. Prothero so memorable?
3. What is the effect of the accumulated detail relating to the Christmas presents?
4. Why does Thomas record so much of the children's dialogue? How would you describe it?

STYLE AND STRUCTURE

1. How does Thomas give you memories from many different Christmases without making the structure disjointed?
2. How does Thomas create humour? Give examples.
3. How do the long sentences of the narrative contribute to the sense of a child's way of telling a story? Analyze a few of them closely with this question in mind.
4. Why does Thomas end with the story of the voice behind the door?

E.B. White

E.B. White (1899–1985) was the preeminent American essayist of his time. He was on the staff of *The New Yorker*, and also wrote several children's classics: *Charlotte's Web* (1952), *Stuart Little* (1945), and *The Trumpet of the Swan* (1970). His 1972 revision of William Strunk, Jr.'s *The Elements of Style* set the standard for conciseness and clarity in prose writing.

ONCE MORE TO THE LAKE

One summer, along about 1904, my father rented a camp on a lake in Maine and took us all there for the month of August. We all got ringworm from some kittens and had to rub Pond's Extract on our arms and legs night and morning, and my father rolled over in a canoe with all his clothes on; but outside of that the vacation was a success and from then on none of us ever thought there was any place in the world like that lake in Maine. We returned summer after summer—always on August 1 for one month. I have since become a salt-water man, but sometimes in summer there are days when the restlessness of the tides and the fearful cold of the sea water and the incessant wind that blows across the afternoon and into the evening make me wish for the placidity of a lake in the woods. A few weeks ago this feeling got so strong I bought myself a couple of bass hooks and a spinner and returned to the lake where we used to go, for a week's fishing and to revisit old haunts.

I took along my son, who had never had any fresh water up his nose and who had seen lily pads only from train windows. On the journey over to the lake I began to wonder what it would be like. I wondered how time would have marred this unique, this holy spot—the coves and streams, the hills that the sun set behind, the camps and the paths behind the camps. I was sure that the tarred road would have found it out, and I wondered in what other ways it would be desolated. It is strange how much you can remember about places like that once you allow your mind to return into the grooves that lead back. You remember one thing, and that suddenly reminds you of another thing. I guess I remembered clearest of all the early mornings, when the lake was cool and motionless, remembered how the bedroom smelled of the lumber it was made of and of the wet woods whose scent entered through the screen. The partitions in the camp were thin and did not extend clear to the top of the rooms, and as I was always the first up I would dress softly so as not to wake the others, and sneak out into the sweet outdoors and start out in the canoe, keeping close along the shore in the long shadows of the pines. I remembered being very careful never to rub my paddle against the gunwale for fear of disturbing the stillness of the cathedral.

The lake had never been what you would call a wild lake. There were cottages sprinkled around the shores, and it was in farming country although the shores of the lake were quite heavily wooded. Some of the cottages were owned by nearby farmers, and you would live at the shore and eat your meals at the farmhouse. That's what our family did. But although it wasn't wild, it was a fairly large and undisturbed lake and there were places in it that, to a child at least, seemed infinitely remote and primeval.

I was right about the tar: it led to within half a mile of the shore. But when I got back there, with my boy, and we settled into a camp near a farmhouse and into the kind of summertime I had known, I could tell that it was going to be pretty much the same as it had been before—I knew it, lying in bed the first morning, smelling the bedroom and hearing the boy sneak quietly out and go off along the shore in a boat. I began to sustain the illusion that he was I, and therefore, by simple transposition, that I was my father. This sensation persisted, kept cropping up all the time we were there. It was not an entirely new feeling, but in this setting it grew much stronger. I seemed to be living a dual existence. I would be in the middle of some simple act, I would be picking up a bait box or laying down a table fork, or I would be saying something, and suddenly it would be not I but my father who was saying the words or making the gesture. It gave me a creepy sensation.

5 We went fishing the first morning. I felt the same damp moss covering the worms in the bait can, and saw the dragonfly alight on the tip of my rod as it hovered a few inches from the surface of the water. It was the arrival of this fly that convinced me beyond any doubt that everything was as it always had been, that the years were a mirage and that there had been no years. The small waves were the same, chucking the rowboat under the chin as we fished at anchor, and the boat was the same boat, the same color green and the ribs broken in the same places, and under the floor-boards the same fresh-water leavings and débris—the dead helgramite, the wisps of moss, the rusty discarded fishhook, the dried blood from yesterday's catch. We stared silently at the tips of our rods, at the dragonflies that came and went. I lowered the tip of mine into the water, tentatively, pensively dislodging the fly, which darted two feet away, poised, darted two feet back, and

came to rest again a little farther up the rod. There had been no years between the ducking of this dragonfly and the other one—the one that was part of memory. I looked at the boy, who was silently watching his fly, and it was my hands that held his rod, my eyes watching. I felt dizzy and didn't know which rod I was at the end of.

We caught two bass, hauling them in briskly as though they were mackerel, pulling them over the side of the boat in a businesslike manner without any landing net, and stunning them with a blow on the back of the head. When we got back for a swim before lunch, the lake was exactly where we had left it, the same number of inches from the dock, and there was only the merest suggestion of a breeze. This seemed an utterly enchanted sea, this lake you could leave to its own devices for a few hours and come back to, and find that it had not stirred, this constant and trustworthy body of water. In the shallows, the dark, water-soaked sticks and twigs, smooth and old, were undulating in clusters on the bottom against the clean ribbed sand, and the track of the mussel was plain. A school of minnows swam by, each minnow with its small individual shadow, doubling the attendance, so clear and sharp in the sunlight. Some of the other campers were in swimming, along the shore, one of them with a cake of soap, and the water felt thin and clear and unsubstantial. Over the years there had been this person with the cake of soap, this cultist, and here he was. There had been no years.

Up to the farmhouse to dinner through the teeming, dusty field, the road under our sneakers was only a two-track road. The middle track was missing, the one with the marks of the hooves and the splotches of dried, flaky manure. There had always been three tracks to choose from in choosing which track to walk in; now the choice was narrowed down to two. For a moment I missed terribly the middle alternative. But the way led past the tennis court, and something about the way it lay there in the sun reassured me; the tape had loosened along the backline, the alleys were green with plantains and other weeds, and the net (installed in June and removed in September) sagged in the dry noon, and the whole place steamed with midday heat and hunger and emptiness. There was a choice of pie for dessert, and one was blueberry and one was apple, and the waitresses were the same country girls, there having been no passage of time, only the illusion of it as in a dropped curtain—the waitresses were still fifteen; their hair had been washed, that was the only difference—they had been to the movies and seen the pretty girls with the clean hair.

Summertime, oh, summertime, pattern of life indelible, the fade-proof lake, the woods unshatterable, the pasture with the sweetfern and the juniper forever and ever, summer without end; this was the background, and the life along the shore was the design, the cottages with their innocent and tranquil design, their tiny docks with the flagpole and the American flag floating against the white clouds in the blue sky, the little paths over the roots of the trees leading from camp to camp and the paths leading back to the outhouses and the can of lime for sprinkling, and at the souvenir counters at the store the miniature birch-bark canoes and the postcards that showed things looking a little better than they looked. This was the American family at play, escaping the city heat, wondering whether the newcomers in the camp at the head of the cove were "common" or "nice," wondering whether it was true that the people who drove up for Sunday dinner at the farmhouse were turned away because there wasn't enough chicken.

It seemed to me, as I kept remembering all this, that those times and those summers had been infinitely precious and worth saving. There had been jollity and peace and goodness. The arriving (at the beginning of August) had been so big a business in itself, at the railway station the farm wagon drawn up, the first smell of the pine-laden air, the first glimpse of the smiling farmer, and the great importance of the trunks and your father's enormous authority in such matters, and the feel of the wagon under you for the long ten-mile haul, and at the top of the last long hill catching the first view of the lake after eleven months of not seeing this cherished body of water. The shouts and cries of the other campers when they saw you, and the trunks to be unpacked, to give up their rich burden. (Arriving was less exciting nowadays, when you sneaked up in your car and parked it under a tree near the camp and took out the bags and in five minutes it was all over, no fuss, no loud wonderful fuss about trunks.)

10 Peace and goodness and jollity. The only thing that was wrong now, really, was the sound of the place, an unfamiliar nervous sound of the outboard motors. This was the note that jarred, the one thing that would sometimes break the illusion and set the years moving. In those other summertimes all motors were inboard; and when they were at a little distance, the noise they made was a sedative, an ingredient of summer sleep. They were one-cylinder and two-cylinder engines, and some were make-and-break and some were jump-spark, but they all made a sleepy sound across the lake. The one-lungers throbbed and fluttered, and the twin-cylinder ones purred and purred, and that was a

quiet sound, too. But now the campers all had outboards. In the daytime, in the hot mornings, these motors made a petulant, irritable sound; at night, in the still evening when the afterglow lit the water, they whined about one's ears like mosquitoes. My boy loved our rented outboard, and his great desire was to achieve single-handed mastery over it, and authority, and he soon learned the trick of choking it a little (but not too much), and the adjustment of the needle valve. Watching him I would remember the things you could do with the old one-cylinder engine with the heavy flywheel, how you could have it eating out of your hand if you got really close to it spiritually. Motorboats in those days didn't have clutches, and you would make a landing by shutting off the motor at the proper time and coasting in with a dead rudder. But there was a way of reversing them, if you learned the trick, by cutting the switch and putting it on again exactly on the final dying revolution of the flywheel, so that it would kick back against compression and begin reversing. Approaching a dock in a strong following breeze, it was difficult to slow up sufficiently by the ordinary coasting method, and if a boy felt he had complete mastery over his motor, he was tempted to keep it running beyond its time and then reverse it a few feet from the dock. It took a cool nerve, because if you threw the switch a twentieth of a second too soon you would catch the flywheel when it still had speed enough to go up past center, and the boat would leap ahead, charging bull-fashion at the dock.

We had a good week at the camp. The bass were biting well and the sun shone endlessly, day after day. We would be tired at night and lie down in the accumulated heat of the little bedrooms after the long hot day and the breeze would stir almost imperceptibly outside and the smell of the swamp drift in through the rusty screens. Sleep would come easily and in the morning the red squirrel would be on the roof, tapping out his gay routine. I kept remembering everything, lying in bed in the mornings—the small steamboat that had a long rounded stern like the lip of a Ubangi, and how quietly she ran on the moonlight sails, when the older boys played their mandolins and the girls sang and we ate doughnuts dipped in sugar, and how sweet the music was on the water in the shining night, and what it had felt like to think about girls then. After breakfast we would go up to the store and the things were in the same place—the minnows in a bottle, the plugs and spinners disarranged and pawed over by the youngsters from the boys' camp, the Fig Newtons and the Beeman's gum. Outside, the road was tarred and cars stood in front of the store. Inside, all was just as it had always been, except there was more Coca-Cola and not so much Moxie and root beer and birch beer and sarsaparilla. We would walk out with the bottle of pop apiece and sometimes the pop would backfire up our noses and hurt. We explored the streams, quietly, where the turtles slid off the sunny logs and dug their way into the soft bottom; and we lay on the town wharf and fed worms to the tame bass. Everywhere we went I had trouble making out which was I, the one walking at my side, the one walking in my pants.

One afternoon while we were there at that lake a thunderstorm came up. It was like the revival of an old melodrama that I had seen long ago with childish awe. The second-act climax of the drama of the electrical disturbance over a lake in America had not changed in any important respect. This was the big scene, still the big scene. The whole thing was so familiar, the first feeling of oppression and heat and a general air around camp of not wanting to go very far away. In mid-afternoon (it was all the same) a curious darkening of the sky, and a lull in everything that had made life tick; and then the way the boats suddenly swung the other way at their moorings with the coming of a breeze out of the new quarter, and the premonitory rumble. Then the kettle drum, then the snare, then the bass drum and cymbals, then crackling light against the dark, and the gods grinning and licking their chops in the hills. Afterward the calm, the rain steadily rustling in the calm lake, the return of light and hope and spirits, and the campers running out in joy and relief to go swimming in the rain, their bright cries perpetuating the deathless joke about how they were getting simply drenched, and the children screaming with delight at the new sensation of bathing in the rain, and the joke about getting drenched linking the generations in a strong indestructible chain. And the comedian who waded in carrying an umbrella.

When the others went swimming, my son said he was going in, too. He pulled his dripping trunks from the line where they had hung all through the shower and wrung them out. Languidly, and with no thought of going in, I watched him, his hard little body, skinny and bare, saw him wince slightly as he pulled up around his vitals the small, soggy, icy garment. As he buckled the swollen belt, suddenly my groin felt the chill of death.

VOCABULARY

gunwale: side of the boat 2
primeval: ancient, primitive 3

undulating: flowing, waving 6
indelible: permanent 8
petulant: peevish 10
Ubangi: a woman from the district of Kyabé village in Africa with pierced and distended lips 11
sarsaparilla: a sweetened, carbonated beverage 11
melodrama: sensational story 12
premonitory: warning 12
languidly: slowly 13

AUDIENCE AND PURPOSE

1. What is the effect of the juxtaposition of the two dates at the start of the essay?
2. How does White draw on his readers' memories of their youth?
3. How does the conclusion make the reader aware of change?

CONTENT

1. What is the significance of the narrator's feeling that he is his father, and his son is him?
2. What are the differences between then and now that the narrator catalogues?
3. What is the significance of the storm at the end of the essay?

STYLE AND STRUCTURE

1. Why does the narrator include in the opening such precise details of his first visit?
2. What is the effect of the repetition of the sentence, "There had been no years"?
3. The conclusion depends on a visceral image. Why is this technique effective?

Howard Rheingold

Howard Rheingold (b. 1947) is the author of *The Virtual Community: Homesteading on the Electronic Frontier* (1993). Rheingold is one of the creators and former founding Executive Editor of *HotWired*, the on-line World Wide Web multimedia publication of Wired Ventures. He is also founder of Electric Minds (named by *Time* magazine one of the ten best Web sites of 1996), Editor-in-Chief of *The Millennium Whole Earth Catalog* (1994), and Editor Emeritus of *Whole Earth Review* (1990–94).

LOOK WHO'S TALKING

Technology is my native tongue. I'm online six hours a day. I have a cell phone, voicemail, fax, laptop, and palmtop. I'm connected—and lately, I've been wondering where all this equipment is leading me. I've found myself asking a question that's both disquieting and intriguing: What kind of person am I becoming as a result of all this stuff?

Of course, I'm not the only one asking. And a while ago it occurred to me that, in addition to measuring my reactions against those of others in comparable circumstances, I might learn something entirely new by looking at a civilization of which I am not a member. The Amish communities of Pennsylvania, despite the retro image of horse-drawn buggies and straw hats, have long been engaged in a productive debate about the consequences of technology. So I turned to them for a glimpse of the future.

Amish settlements have become a cliché for refusing technology. Tens of thousands of people wear identical, plain, homemade clothing, cultivate their rich fields with horse-drawn machinery, and live in houses lacking that basic modern spirit called electricity. But the Amish do use such 20th-century consumer technologies as disposable diapers, in-line skates, and gas barbecue grills. Some might call this combination paradoxical, even contradictory. But it could also be called sophisticated, because the Amish have an elaborate system by which they evaluate the tools they use; their tentative, at times reluctant use of technology is more complex than a simple rejection or a wholehearted embrace. What if modern Americans could possibly agree upon criteria for acceptance, as the Amish have? Might we find better ways to wield technological power, other than simply unleashing it and seeing what happens? What can we learn from a culture that habitually negotiates the rules for new tools?

Last summer, armed with these questions and in the company of an acquaintance with Amish contacts, I traveled around the countryside of Lancaster County, Pennsylvania. Everywhere, there were freshly planted fields, farmhouses with handsome, immaculate barns and outbuildings. At one farm we passed, a woman was sitting a hundred yards from her house on the edge of a kitchen garden. She wore the traditional garb of the conservative Old Order—a long, unadorned dress sheathed by an apron, her hair covered by a prayer bonnet. She was sitting in the middle of the garden, alone, the very image of technology-free simplicity. But she was holding her hand up to her ear. She appeared to be intent on something, strangely engaged.

"Whenever you see an Amish woman sitting in the field like that," my guide said, "she's probably talking on a cell phone."

"It's a controversy in the making," he continued. A rather large one, it turns out—yet part of the continuum of determining whether a particular technology belongs in Amish life. They've adopted horses, kerosene lamps, and propane refrigerators; should they add cell phones?

Collective negotiations over the use of telephones have ignited intense controversies in the Amish community since the beginning of the 20th century. In fact, a dispute over the role of the phone was the principal issue behind the 1920s division of the Amish church, wherein one-fifth of the membership broke away to form their own church.

Eventually, certain Amish communities accepted the telephone for its aid in summoning doctors and veterinarians, and in calling suppliers. But even these Amish did not allow the telephone into the home. Rather, they required that phones be used communally. Typically, a neighborhood of two or three extended families shares a telephone housed in a wooden shanty, located either at the intersection of several fields or at the end of a common lane. These structures look like small bus shelters or privies; indeed, some phones are in outhouses. Sometimes the telephone shanties have answering machines in them. (After all, who wants to wait in the privy on the off chance someone will call?)

The first Amish person I contacted, I reached by answering machine. He was a woodworker who, unlike some of his brethren, occasionally talked to outsiders. I left a message on his phone, which I later learned was located in a shanty in his neighbor's pasture. The next day the man, whom I'll call Amos, returned my call. We agreed to meet at his farmstead a few days later.

10 I couldn't help thinking it was awfully complicated to have a phone you used only for calling back—from a booth in a meadow. Why not make life easier and just put one in the house?

"What would that lead to?" another Amish man asked me. "We don't want to be the kind of people who will interrupt a conversation at home to answer a telephone. It's not just how you use the technology that concerns us. We're also concerned about what kind of person you become when you use it."

The Amish are famously shy. Their commitment to "plain" living is most obvious in their unadorned clothing—Old Order Amish even eschew buttons, requiring humble hooks instead. Any sign of individuality is cause for concern. Until fairly recently, Amish teachers would reprimand the student who raised his or her hand as being too individualistic. Calling attention to oneself, or being "prideful," is one of the cardinal Amish worries. Having your name or photo in the papers, even talking to the press, is almost a sin.

Like most modern Americans, I assume individuality is not only a fundamental value, but a goal in life, an art form. The garish technicolor shirts and hand-painted shoes I usually wear sometimes startle business audiences who show up for my speaking engagements. My reasoning: If I think for myself, why not dress for myself? Dye technology has given us all these colors, so let's use 'em! Still, I didn't want to make my idiosyncrasies the focus of my visit to Amish country. So I bought a plain blue work shirt, dark blue gabardine pants, and brown shoes. I hadn't traveled so drably in many years.

Amos runs a factory of sorts in the vicinity of three memorably named Pennsylvania towns: Bird-in-Hand, Paradise, and Intercourse. The sun was setting as I drove slowly down his unpaved driveway. I found myself inside a tableau that must have looked almost exactly the same 200 years ago. Several men and young boys in identical black trousers, suspenders, and straw hats were operating horse-drawn equipment in the fields beyond. One of Amos's grandsons pointed me to a plain wooden building beside the barn.

15 The aroma of cows gave way to the pungent smell of diesel fuel and woodchips as I entered the workshop. The whine of a wood-milling machine made it futile to talk. This was not the serene place the words "Amish woodshop" conjure up. My host finished cutting a 12-foot-long plank before we greeted each other. He then lit a kerosene lamp in the small office next to his workshop and invited me in. The office had no modern technology in it, but railroad posters were tacked on the walls, and wooden locomotive models sat on the shelves.

Amos had sawdust and hydraulic fluid in his beard. His blue-gray eyes fastened on me as he bounced back his own questions in reply to my queries. He had received the same eighth-grade education that all Amish youth are given, but it was obvious that Amos did some outside reading. When I asked him to describe his sense of community, he started out, "Hmm, how do you pronounce s-c-e-n-a-r-i-o?"

Amos runs a successful business crafting wooden furniture, which he sells throughout Pennsylvania and beyond—primarily to the "English" (the Amish term for non-Amish). It's a trade more and more Amish are getting into. Inside Amos's home there are no telephones, radios, televisions, vacuum cleaners, dishwashers, or other electrical appliances. In his shop, routers, mills, and sanders are powered by specially adapted hydraulic mechanisms connected to a diesel engine located near a large open door, exhausting outside the building.

This was a good case study in Amish reasoning: Far from knee-jerk technophobes, these are very adaptive techno-selectives who devise remarkable technologies that fit within their self-imposed limits. The price of good farmland and the number of Amish families are both increasing so rapidly that in recent decades they have adopted nonagricultural enterprises for livelihood—woodworking, construction, light factory work. This, in turn, has forced the Amish to adopt technologies that can enhance their productivity. And the interface with the English brings its own set of demands: When the State of Pennsylvania refused to certify Amish-produced milk unless it was stirred mechanically and refrigerated according to state health codes, the Amish installed stirring machines and refrigeration—operated by batteries or propane gas.

Amos, like many other Amish craftsmen, uses electricity in his workshop for certain tools. But the electricity does not come from public utility lines. Amos runs a diesel generator to charge a bank of 12-volt batteries. The batteries' DC charge is then sent through a converter to create homegrown 110-volt "Amish electricity." To generate more, he has to haul the diesel fuel in from town on his horse-drawn buggy.

20 To the obvious question why allow Amish electricity but not public electricity, Amos answered slowly and deliberately, "The Bible teaches us not to conform to the world, to keep a separation. Connecting to the electric lines would make too many things too easy. Pretty soon, people would start plugging in radios and televisions, and that's like a hot line to the modern world. We use batteries and generators because you can use the

batteries for only a short time and because you have to fuel and maintain the generator yourself. It's a way of controlling our use of electricity. We try to restrict things that would lead to us losing that sense of being separate, to put the brakes on how fast we change."

Despite the reputation today's Amish have as old-fashioned diehards, their departure from Europe several centuries ago was driven by their success as innovators. They started out as radical religious libertarians—at a time when the price of religious radicalism was martyrdom. Catholics and Protestants were killing each other in a major religious war, but both sides took a serious dislike to these defiant theological purists, known at the time as Anabaptists, for their emphasis on adult baptism. (Today, every Amish household has a copy of *Martyrs' Mirror*, a text of more than 1,000 pages that details the excruciating and humiliating public executions suffered by Anabaptist martyrs in Switzerland, Germany, and Holland.) The Anabaptists developed a soil technology based on crop rotation, planting clover in their pastures, and sweetening their earth with lime and gypsum; they dramatically increased the yield of their land, and some of them became wealthy.

Ironically, those same Anabaptists helped set the stage for the fast-paced changes of modern life that today's Amish reject. It was the widespread adoption of Anabaptist practices that eventually produced enough food to free other agricultural laborers, creating the workforce that would be needed for the industrial revolution.

Toward the end of the 17th century, one of the Anabaptist leaders, Jakob Ammann, decided that his Swiss brethren had not been radical enough. Ammann and his followers, who came to be known as "Amish," broke with traditional Anabaptists, moved to the New World, and started farming in Lancaster County in 1710.

In today's Pennsylvania Amish country, a group of 20 to 30 families who live near one another constitute a "district." Each district has a bishop, and the bishops get together twice a year to discuss church matters. This includes raising the recurring questions about which technologies should be permitted in the community, and which banned or regulated.

While the say of the bishops is binding, the Amish come to their decisions quite consensually. New things are not outright forbidden, nor is there a rush to judgment. Rather, technologies filter in when one of the more daring members of the community starts to use, or even purchases, something new. Then others try it. Then reports circulate about the results. What happens with daily use? Does it bring people together? Or have the opposite effect?

Despite the almost organic ebb and flow of this evaluation process, the common goal is constant submission to the judgment of one's peers. On my visit, I was constantly struck by what seemed an alien conception of community. As a kid I was encouraged to "do my thing" while being nice to others; I've lived in five states and dozens of neighborhoods. Amish communities are not just tightly knit and immobile, they're authoritarian.

Yet there is some room for disagreement; consider how the bishops judged the automobile in the 1960s. Typically, the Amish have large extended families; most have dozens of cousins within walking or buggy distance. Every other Sunday, instead of attending church, the Amish are encouraged to visit relatives and the sick. Over time, it was felt that the automobile was enlarging people's traveling radius too far beyond their extended family, to diversions and recreations not related to the community, decreasing the social cohesion and personal connection the Amish so cherish. Some bishops accepted the use of the automobile under certain conditions, while others rejected it outright. The Amish are now split into traditional "Old Order" Amish who still stick to horse and buggy, "New Order" Amish who approve use of telephones and powered farm equipment but shun public electricity, and "Beachy Amish," named for the '20s liberal leader Moses Beachy, who permit both public electricity and automobiles.

While all orders now allow diesel engines in the barn to blow silage, their use is still resisted in the fields—the bishops don't want increased efficiency to interfere with the practice of fathers and sons, mothers and daughters, working together with horse-drawn machinery and handheld implements. Notably, some Old Order Amish allow some diesel-powered equipment in the fields—if it's hauled by animals. "Does it bring us together, or draw us apart?" is the primary question the bishops ask in considering whether to permit or put away a technology.

The bishops' rulings can take decades. In daily life, the Amish take their directions in dress, thought, behavior, and custom from a body of unwritten but detailed rules known as the "Ordnung." Individuals and communities maintain a separation from the world (by not connecting their houses to telephones or electricity), a closeness to one another (through regular meetings), and an attitude of humility so specific they have a name for it ("Gelassenheit"). Decisions about technology hinge on these collective criteria. If a telephone in the home interferes with face-to-face visiting, or an electrical hookup fosters unthinking dependence on the outside world, or a new pickup truck in the driveway elevates one person above his neighbors, then people start to talk about it. The talk reaches the bishops' ears.

30 In the middle of Amish country, it occurs to me that Internet culture itself grew out of a kind of virtual Ordnung—the norms of cooperation, information-sharing, and netiquette taught to newbies by the first generations of users. The celebrated "anarchy" of the early days was possible only because of the near-universal adherence to largely unwritten rules. But the Internet population has grown fast—so fast that the sudden influx of tens of millions of newbies has overwhelmed the capacity of the old-timers to pass on the Ordnung. In the process, the Internet loses its unique hallmarks, coming to resemble and reflect the rest of contemporary culture.

"The Amish employ an intuitive sense about what will build solidarity and what will pull them apart," says Donald Kraybill, author of *The Riddle of Amish Culture*. "You find state-of-the-art barbecues on some Amish porches. Here is a tool they see as increasing family coherence: Barbecues bring people together." Asked what kinds of questions the bishops will likely raise about cell phones, Kraybill replies, "Are cell phones being used 'to make a living' or just for gossip and frivolous chatter? Will permitting cell phones lead to having phones in homes, and where will that lead ... to fax machines and the Internet?"

"We don't want to stop progress, we just want to slow it down," several Amish told me. Conversations about technology often turn on where to "hold the line" against the too-rapid advance of innovation. Riding in automobiles to work, but not owning them, putting telephone shanties in fields, requiring battery power instead of electrical lines are all ways of holding the line.

And clearly a lot could be learned about the Amish hold-the-line philosophy by looking at those who either crossed the line or pushed it further out. So I sought out several of the more boldly experimental members of the greater Plain community (Amish and Mennonites and other religious groups sharing a kindred commitment to plain living). In ranging from farmers who ran small enterprises in barnside sheds to well-equipped machine workshops and multimillion-dollar crafts factories, I soon was directed to Moses Smucker, who runs a harness shop in Churchtown, Pennsylvania.

Moses is an early adopter. He didn't mind if I used his real name, a liberty that has made him the subject of a few other journalists' stories. When I arrived at his manufacturing headquarters, I took a look at some of the harnesses on display—one of them had a price tag of $12,000. If you've ever seen the Budweiser Clydesdales Christmas commercials, you've seen harness bells from Moses Smucker's Churchtown workshop.

35 In the back of the store, more than a dozen young Amish men were working at modern machinery powered by hydraulics and diesel-generated electricity. Upstairs, I saw a woman in traditional plain clothing seated in front of a PC.

Moses Smucker might look like Abe Lincoln, in his black suit and mustache-free beard, but he bore the same time-is-money air of any factory manager taking a few minutes out of a busy day to talk to the press. Where Amos was rough hewn and wry, Moses seemed shrewd and slick. His office was certainly in a different century from Amos's. An electronic rolodex and an electric calculator sat atop an old roll-top desk. I noticed a clock in the shape of a horse and buggy. The whip ticked back and forth.

"When I started this business in 1970," Moses said, "it wasn't accepted to have a telephone in the building, even in a business. But the telephone began to be accepted through popular disobedience. More businesses put them in and the bishops didn't stop them."

Will the bishops also eventually allow phones in the home? I asked.

"When the telephone first came out here, people put them in their homes," explained Moses. "But they were party lines. One time a woman overheard two other women gossiping about her. She objected. That wasn't what we wanted for our families or our community, so the bishops met and home telephones were banned."

40 I had heard the same story from several other Amish—in fact, this story seemed to be a key part of community mythology. A writer named Diane Zimmerman Umble, who grew up in Lancaster County and had family roots in the Plain orders, traced the story to its origin, a 1986 memoir written by an Old Order Amishman born in 1897. As a graduate student, Zimmerman Umble started investigating Amish community telephones for a course on contemporary social theory, and ended up writing a book on the subject, *Holding the Line: The Telephone in Old Order Mennonite and Amish Life*. Among her findings was the power of anecdote in the Amish decisionmaking process.

Anecdote, of course, is a key currency on the Internet, so I asked Moses if he'd heard stories about it. Although he used a computer in his business, he didn't believe the Internet as currently constituted would ever be permitted. Based on anecdotal evidence, he said, "It's too unregulated, there's too much trash, and there's a worry people will use it for purposes unrelated to work."

I asked another Amish workshop owner whom I'll call Caleb what he thought about technology. He pulled some papers out of a file cabinet, handed them to me, and said, "I share some of this fellow's opinions," pointing to a magazine interview with virtual reality pioneer Jaron Lanier. Asked for an opinion he shared with the dreadlocked-and-dashikied Jaron, he replied, "I agree with his statement that you can't design foolproof machines, because fools are so clever."

Caleb also discussed the Amish resistance to becoming "modern." They're not worried about becoming people without religion or people who use lots of technology, he explained; rather, the Amish fear assimilating the far more dangerous ideas that "progress" and new technologies are usually beneficial, that individuality is a precious value, that the goal of life is to "get ahead." This mind-set, not specific technologies, is what the Amish most object to.

"The thing I noticed about the telephone is the way it invades who you are," Caleb said. "We're all losing who we are because of the telephone and other machines—not just the Amish."

45 In *Holding the Line*, Zimmerman Umble writes: "Some Old Order people feel that relaxation of telephone rules reflects a movement toward an 'uncontrollable drift' which must be halted. Others see these steps as pragmatic choices necessary to hold the community together economically. The paradox in the Old Order story is that the telephone does both: It holds people together by making communication among community members possible, and it separates them from the world and from each other. The telephone is both evil and good."

Donald Kraybill, who is also provost of Messiah College, on the outskirts of Amish country, believes taboos about telephones are "a symbolic way of keeping the technology at a distance and making it your servant, rather than the other way around."

Can they make the cell phone a servant? My questions on this score were answered mostly with anecdote. I heard of one Amish man who was going to be late to a chiropractor appointment, so he pulled out his cell phone and called the receptionist from the bus he was on. Zimmerman Umble heard of a Plain order businessman who called his stockbroker from his company car phone, pushing three taboos at once past their boundaries.

Zimmerman Umble pointed out that part of what makes cell phones so handy—the lack of a wire—also poses a special challenge for the Amish. "In the early part of the community discussion, electrical and telephone lines carried substantial symbolic freight," she said. The wires meant that anyone in the community could easily see who was using electricity and phones. "But now, in the absence of the line, behavior can't be monitored in the same way. It is harder to maintain separation between home and business when you have a cell phone in your pocket. In that sense it tests the community consensus about what is allowable."

It's a pretty safe prediction that when the bishops get around to their formal ruling, cell phones will not be deemed appropriate for personal use. In the 1910s, when the telephone was only beginning to change the world at large, the Old Order Amish recognized that the caller at the other end of the line was an interloper, someone who presumed to take precedence over the family's normal, sacred, communications. Keeping the telephone in an unheated shanty in a field, or even an outhouse, was keeping the phone in its proper place.

Though the Amish determination to allow phones at work but ban them at home might seem hard to accept, I appreciate the deliberation put into their decision. In fact, similar reflection might highlight conflicts between our own practices and values. How often do we interrupt a conversation with someone who is physically present in order to answer the telephone? Is the family meal enhanced by a beeper? Who exactly is benefiting from call waiting? Is automated voicemail a dark hint about the way our institutions value human time and life? Can pagers and cell phones that vibrate instead of ring solve the problem? Does the enjoyment of virtual communities by growing numbers of people enhance or erode citizen participation in the civic life of geographic communities?

"What does the Old Order story have to say to members of postmodern society?" asks Diane Zimmerman Umble. "The struggle of Old Order groups to mold technology in the service of community provides a provocative model of resistance for those who have come to recognize that technology brings both benefits and costs.... Their example invites reflection on a modern dilemma: how to balance the rights of the individual with the needs of the community. For them, community comes first."

Indeed, what does one's use of a tool say to other people, particularly loved ones, about where they stand in our priorities? In my own house, we decided to get a rollover to voicemail instead of call waiting—experiences on the receiving end of call waiting convinced us that both parties on the other end of the line get pissed off when you interrupt the conversation. No matter how absorbing the flame war of the moment might be, I make a point of suspending online communication when someone in my presence attempts to talk with me. And I've come to believe that face-to-face conversation should outrank disembodied conversation via cell phone or email.

I never expected the Amish to provide precise philosophical yardsticks that could guide the use of technological power. What drew me in was their long conversation with their tools. We technology-enmeshed "English" don't have much of this sort of discussion. And yet we'll need many such conversations, because a modern heterogeneous society is going to have different values, different trade-offs, and different discourses. It's time we start talking about the most important influence on our lives today.

I came away from my journey with a question to contribute to these conversations: If we decided that community came first, how would we use our tools differently?

VOCABULARY

eschew: avoid 12
garish: loud, bright 13
dreadlocked: wearing long, thin braids 42
dashikied: wearing a loose-fitting, bright-coloured tunic 42
interloper: someone who meddles in others' affairs 49
heterogeneous: mixed, various 53

AUDIENCE AND PURPOSE

1. Why does Rheingold tell the story of his visit to the Amish rather than just summarizing his findings about them?
2. What does Rheingold learn from the Amish about how technology should be used in a society?
3. How does Rheingold avoid being judgmental in the essay?
4. Why does Rheingold choose the title that he does?

CONTENT

1. Why does Rheingold disguise the names of his interlocutors?
2. Why does Rheingold provide information about the founding of the Amish?
3. How does Rheingold view the bishops' rulings that decide things for the Amish? What does he learn from them?

STYLE AND STRUCTURE

1. Why does Rheingold write this essay in the first person?
2. Why does Rheingold name those he interviewed, though in most cases the names are fictitious?
3. How does Rheingold encourage readers to take the message of the essay home to their own situation?

Illustration

ILLUSTRATION: USING EXAMPLES TO MAKE YOUR POINT

Why a Picture Really Is Worth a Thousand Words

Examples are the most straightforward and obvious way to support your arguments. They are straightforward because they *show* readers something in the most concrete way rather than just telling them in the abstract. When things start to get unclear, good speakers and writers know instinctively to resort to examples that will make a visual, visceral impression on their readers. The whole point, after all, is to communicate the feeling of an experience in one's writing. If you don't have access to a picture, you can still create a visual image for readers that will make your point clear.

If I tell you, a hungry tourist, that you would be better off ordering an American breakfast than a continental breakfast, you probably would need more information to make that decision wisely. Instead, let me offer some illustrating details. Let me start with the fact that an American breakfast typically includes eggs, bacon, toast, jam, and a number of other dishes. A continental breakfast, on the other hand, typically includes only some kind of bread, some toppings for it, and coffee. Including these detailed examples, my point would be much clearer and your decision would be much easier to make.

If you use examples as a means of clarifying and supporting the arguments you make in your writing, you need to choose them carefully. Examples must be typical if they are to be convincing. You can't successfully argue that Australian directors are superior to Hollywood directors simply by listing the examples of Peter Weir, director of *Witness*, and Baz Luhrman, director of the newest film version of *Romeo and Juliet*. Two examples are probably not enough to make such a grand claim, since the two directors in question are almost certainly not representative examples. But you could use these examples for building the case that Australian directors have a unique and creative vision that is refreshing compared with many Hollywood directors. Another way to strengthen your point may be to add several more examples. One long, extended example may, nevertheless, do the trick. This technique is the one employed in many textbooks that use case studies as a way of making a subject area clearer to readers. Even here, though, the addition of shorter, well-developed examples is often a good idea. However, remember that you shouldn't be writing a "laundry list." If you find yourself tempted to add "etc.," you probably aren't developing your ideas fully enough. Never forget that the onus is on you as the writer to supply details substantial enough for readers to follow your thinking and share your insights.

Examples do not have to be taken from real life to be convincing—often a good example is hypothetical. You might begin to elaborate it with the word "Suppose ..." in an effort to make readers imagine a case. Good teaching often involves this kind of strategy. Think of the use of parables in the Bible, for instance, or of the moral power of fables. The story of the fox and the grapes goes a long way toward showing what we mean by "sour grapes," the psychology by which we rein in our unsatisfied desires.

Examples must be as lively as possible. Your object in selecting them is to make the reader see what you see, feel what you feel. Say, for example, that you want to argue that city and town councils need to pay more attention to neighbourhood concerns about threats to the environment. One good way to support this point is to draw, as vividly as you can, from your own experience. The following paragraph is such a concrete example:

This is the topic sentence. ⟶

It is crucial that development plans for a neighbourhood take into account residents' concerns about the impact on the quality of life in the area. At the last town council meeting, several angry citizens in my neighbourhood protested a proposed development that would have a pronounced negative effect on the natural environment. They argued that developers' plans would jeopardize the deer, birds, and other wildlife now living in the open, wooded space behind their houses. Residents wanted to protect several endangered species of oak that had been planted in the hilly area behind their homes. They also hoped to prevent excessive development from affecting flora and fauna in the larger, connected escarpment area of which their neighbourhood formed a small part. To keep the ecosystem intact, they maintained, it is essential to respect the requirements of plants and animals living in the region. They also contended that drainage problems caused by the new development would create flooding problems for nearby residents. Another argument was that the proposal to clear-cut the forested areas behind current homes would lower property values and reduce privacy. If councils are to make decisions with the potential to affect neighbourhood environments, they must take into account residents' concerns about the beauty, value, privacy, and health requirements of their surroundings.

This repeats the point of the topic sentence.

The Importance of Technology in Modern Education

Introduction

Currently, there is considerable controversy about the changes being brought about by technology in the classroom. Those who fear technology often argue that its alleged "progress" is actually detrimental to education, charging that students become progressively reliant on technical innovations and incapable of using their own intelligence in the quest for knowledge. Another argument raised is that the cost of computer equipment makes education inaccessible. It can be argued, however, that technology is an important part of modern education, offering significant benefits to students: first, it collapses space and thus makes distance education a reality; second, it allows for more equal opportunity for participation through electronic discussion lists and for self-paced education among students through the use of drill software; and finally, it allows for quicker

The thesis statement acts as a route map.

access to more information than was ever dreamed possible through the research tools of the Internet.

The first example is developed.

The use of computer-assisted teaching in classrooms means that students who do not live near colleges and universities can still actively take courses without the need to give up their shift work, leave their children with baby sitters, or find parking spaces. Increasingly, students are finding it possible to study at home, receiving materials and engaging in classroom interactions with other students, all through the medium of their computers. This one feature alone means that a student in Yellowknife can participate in a class in Edmonton or Toronto without any impediments to learning. The lack of need for physical classroom space and scheduled times frees both student and teacher from problems that used to exclude some people from involvement in higher education.

The second example is developed.

Secondly, the computer-assisted classroom can level some inequalities among students. For example, students in a regular classroom must usually compete for class time and for the instructor's attention when they are called upon to participate. The advancement of electronic discussion lists, however, ensures that students are able to ask and answer questions, state opinions, and engage in active debate with other students without imposing on actual class time. Such electronic discussion lists also provide students with more opportunity to write, and provide instructors and students alike with a written record of the discussions that took place in the course. This feature allows students to engage more collaboratively and less competitively with one another and with the teacher. Because there are fewer demands in actual time, technology also enables students to work more often at their own pace, particularly with the lessons that involve painstaking and time-consuming drill exercises, which may be more necessary to some students than to others. This freedom to work through material on one's own promotes independent thinking and problem solving, and it allows everyone to work at a comfortable pace.

The third example is developed.

The last and most significant benefit of technology in the classroom comes from using the Internet itself. The Internet, while still a "wild and woolly" medium, and still part of the frontier of technology, is nonetheless a remarkable step forward for education. It allows students to engage in speedy research that goes far beyond the constraints of the school or regional public library. It is quick in its response and democratic in its subject matter, so that, as a research tool, it is a factor in helping students learn to make their own judgements about the reliability of evidence and the differences between fact and opinion. Far from making students more dependent, the Internet obliges those who use it — both teacher and student — to form their own opinions in the light of a broad and mixed base of evidence, no longer driven by sanctioned authorities and limited classroom discussion. The Internet, unregulated by governments and unlimited by national boundaries, offers quick access to virtually anything that might be pertinent in the classroom.

Conclusion

The examples of distance education, electronic discussion lists, drill software, and the Internet as a research tool all show the value of technological advancement in education, both as an improvement to student access and as a promoter of independent thinking in the classroom.

Alleen Pace Nilsen

Alleen Pace Nilsen (b. 1936) is a specialist in children's literature who teaches at Arizona State University. She first wrote this essay for a volume entitled *Sexism and Language* (1977) but has updated the piece for the 1990s. Nilsen's most recent publication is the *Encyclopedia of Twentieth Century American Humor* (2000), which she co-authored with Don L.F. Nilsen.

SEXISM IN ENGLISH: A 1990S UPDATE

Twenty years ago I embarked on a study of the sexism inherent in American English. I had just returned to Ann Arbor, Michigan, after living for two years (1967–69) in Kabul, Afghanistan, where I had begun to look critically at the role society assigned to women. The Afghan version of *chaderi* prescribed for Moslem women was particularly confining. Afghan jokes and folklore were blatantly sexist, such as this proverb: "If you see an old man, sit down and take a lesson; if you see an old woman, throw a stone."

But it wasn't only the native culture that made me question women's roles, it was also the American community.

Most of the American women were like myself—wives and mothers whose husbands were either career diplomats, employees of USAID, or college professors who had been recruited to work on various contract teams. We were suddenly bereft of our traditional roles: some of us became alcoholics, others got very good at bridge, while still others searched desperately for ways to contribute either to our families or to the Afghans. The local economy provided few jobs for women and certainly none for foreigners; we were isolated from former friends and the social goals we had grown up with.

When I returned in the fall of 1969 to the University of Michigan in Ann Arbor, I was surprised to find that many other women were also questioning the expectations they had grown up with. In the spring of 1970, a women's conference was announced. I hired a babysitter and attended, but I returned home more troubled than ever. The militancy of these women frightened me. Since I wasn't ready for a revolution, I decided I would have my own feminist movement. I would study the English language and see what it could tell me about sexism. I started reading a desk dictionary and making notecards on every entry that seemed to tell something about male and female. I soon had a dog-eared dictionary, along with a collection of note cards filling two shoe boxes.

5 Ironically, I started reading the dictionary because I wanted to avoid getting involved in social issues, but what happened was that my notecards brought me right back to looking at society. Language and society are as intertwined as a chicken and an egg. The language a culture uses is telltale evidence of the values and beliefs of that culture. And because there is a lag in how fast a language changes — new words can easily be introduced, but it takes a long time for old words and usages to disappear — a careful look at English will reveal the attitudes that our ancestors held and that we as a culture are therefore predisposed to hold. My notecards revealed three main points. Friends have offered the opinion that I didn't need to read the dictionary to learn such obvious facts. Nevertheless, it was interesting to have linguistic evidence of sociological observations.

WOMEN ARE SEXY; MEN ARE SUCCESSFUL

First, in American culture a woman is valued for the attractiveness and sexiness of her body, while a man is valued for his physical strength and accomplishments. A woman is sexy. A man is successful.

A persuasive piece of evidence supporting this view are the eponyms — words that have come from someone's name — found in English. I had a two-and-a-half inch stack of cards taken from men's names but less than a half-inch stack from women's names, and most of those came from Greek mythology. In the words that came into American English since we separated from Britain, there are many eponyms based on the names of famous American men: *Bartlett pear, boysenberry, diesel engine, Franklin stove, Ferris wheel, Gatling gun, mason jar, sideburns, sousaphone, Schick test,* and *Winchester rifle*. The only common eponyms taken from American women's names are *Alice blue* (after Alice Roosevelt Longworth), *bloomers* (after Amelia Jenks Bloomer), and *Mae West jacket* (after the buxom actress). Two out of the three feminine eponyms relate closely to a woman's physical anatomy, while the masculine eponyms (except for *sideburns* after General Burnsides) have nothing to do with the namesake's body but, instead, honor the man for an accomplishment of some kind.

Although in Greek mythology women played a bigger role than they did in the biblical stories of the Judeo-Christian cultures and so the names of goddesses are accepted parts of the language in such place names as Pomona from the goddess of fruit and Athens from Athena and in such common words as *cereal* from Ceres, *psychology* from Psyche, and *arachnoid* from Arachne, the same tendency to think of women in relation to sexuality is seen in the eponym *aphrodisiac* from Aphrodite, the Greek name for the goddess of love and beauty, and *venereal disease* from Venus, the Roman name for Aphrodite.

Another interesting word from Greek mythology is *Amazon*. According to Greek folk etymology, the *a* means "without" as in *atypical* or *amoral*, while *mazon* comes from *mazos* meaning "breast" as still seen in *mastectomy*. In the Greek legend, Amazon women cut off their right breasts so that they could better shoot their bows. Apparently, the storytellers had a feeling that for women to play the active, "masculine" role the Amazons adopted for themselves, they had to trade in part of their femininity.

10 This preoccupation with women's breasts is not limited to ancient stories. As a volunteer for the University of Wisconsin's *Dictionary of American Regional English (DARE)*, I read a western trapper's diary from the 1930s. I was to make notes of any unusual usages or language patterns. My most interesting finding was that the trapper referred to a range of mountains as *The Teats*, a metaphor based on the similarity between the shapes of the mountains and women's breasts. Because today we use the French wording, *The Grand Tetons*, the metaphor isn't as obvious, but I wrote to mapmakers and found the following listings: *Nippletop* and *Little Nipple Top* near Mount Marcy in the Adirondacks; *Nipple Mountain* in Archuleta County, Colorado; *Nipple Peak* in Coke County, Texas; *Nipple Butte* in Pennington, South Dakota, *Squaw Peak* in Placer County, California (and many other locations); *Maiden's Peak* and *Squaw Tit* (they're the same mountain) in the Cascade Range in Oregon; *Mary's Nipple* near Salt Lake City, Utah; and *Jane Russell Peaks* near Stark, New Hampshire.

Except for the movie star Jane Russell, the women being referred to are anonymous—it's only a sexual part of their body that is mentioned. When topographical features are named after men, it's probably not going to be to draw attention to a sexual part of their bodies but instead to honor individuals for an accomplishment. For example, no one thinks of a part of the male body when hearing a reference to Pike's Peak, Colorado, or Jackson Hole, Wyoming.

Going back to what I learned from my dictionary cards, I was surprised to realize how many pairs of words we have in which the feminine word has acquired sexual connotations while the masculine word retains a serious businesslike aura. For example, a *callboy* is the person who calls actors when it is time for them to go on stage, but a *call girl* is a prostitute. Compare *sir* and *madam*. *Sir* is a term of respect, while *madam* has acquired the specialized meaning of a brothel manager. Something similar has happened to *master* and *mistress*. Would you rather have a painting by an *old master* or an *old mistress*?

It's because the word *woman* had sexual connotations, as in "She's his woman," that people began avoiding its use, hence such terminology as *ladies' room, lady of the house,* and *girls' school* or *school for young ladies*. Feminists, who ask that people use the term *woman* rather than *girl* or *lady*, are rejecting the idea that *woman* is primarily a sexual term. They have been at least partially successful in that today *woman* is commonly used to communicate gender without intending implications about sexuality.

I found two hundred pairs of words with masculine and feminine forms, e.g., *heir–heiress, hero–heroine, steward–stewardess, usher–usherette*. In nearly all such pairs, the masculine word is considered the base, with some kind of a feminine suffix being added. The masculine form is the one from which compounds are made, e.g., from *king–queen* comes *kingdom* but not *queendom*, from *sportsman–sportslady* comes *sportsmanship* but not *sportsladyship*. There is one—and only one—semantic area in which the masculine word is not the base or more powerful word. This is in the area dealing with sex and marriage. When someone refers to a *virgin*, a listener will probably think of a female, unless the speaker specifies *male* or uses a masculine pronoun. The same is true for *prostitute*.

15 In relation to marriage, there is much linguistic evidence showing that weddings are more important to women than to men. A woman cherishes the wedding and is considered a bride for a whole year, but a man is referred to as a groom only on the day of the wedding. The word *bride* appears in *bridal attendant, bridal gown, bridesmaid, bridal shower,* and even *bridegroom*. *Groom* comes from the Middle English *grom,* meaning "man," and in the sense is seldom used outside of the wedding. With most pairs of male/female words, people habitually put the masculine word first, *Mr. and Mrs., his and hers, boys and girls, men and women, kings and queens, brothers and sisters, guys and dolls,* and *host and hostess,* but it is the *bride and groom* who are talked about, not the *groom and bride*.

The importance of marriage to a woman is also shown by the fact that when a marriage ends in death, the woman gets the title of *widow*. A man gets the derived title of *widower*. This term is not used in other phrases or contexts, but *widow* is seen in *widowhood*, *widow's peak*, and *widow's walk*. A *widow* in a card game is an extra hand of cards, while in typesetting it is an extra line of type.

How changing cultural ideas bring changes to language is clearly visible in this semantic area. The feminist movement has caused the differences between the sexes to be downplayed, and since I did my dictionary study two decades ago, the word *singles* has largely replaced such sex specific and value-laden terms as *bachelor, old maid, spinster, divorcée, widow*, and *widower.* And in 1970 I wrote that when a man is called a *professional* he is thought to be a doctor or a lawyer, but when people hear a woman referred to as a *professional* they are likely to think of a prostitute. That's not as true today because so many women have become doctors and lawyers that it's no longer incongruous to think of women in these professional roles.

Another change that has taken place is in wedding announcements. They used to be sent out from the bride's parents and did not even give the name of the groom's parents. Today, most couples choose to list either all or none of the parents' names. Also it is now much more likely that both the bride and groom's picture will be in the newspaper, while a decade ago only the bride's picture was published on the "Women's" or the "Society" page. Even the traditional wording of the wedding ceremony is being changed. Many officials now pronounce the couple "husband and wife" instead of the old "man and wife," and they ask the bride if she promises "to love, honor, and cherish," instead of "to love, honor, and obey."

WOMEN ARE PASSIVE; MEN ARE ACTIVE

The wording of the wedding ceremony also relates to the second point that my cards showed, which is that women are expected to play a passive or weak role while men play an active or strong role. In the traditional ceremony, the official asks, "Who gives the bride away?" and the father answers, "I do." Some fathers answer, "Her mother and I do," but that doesn't solve the problem inherent in the question. The idea that a bride is something to be handed over from one man to another bothers people because it goes back to the days when a man's servants, his children, and his wife were all considered to be his property. They were known by his name because they belonged to him, and he was responsible for their actions and their debts.

20 The grammar used in talking or writing about weddings as well as other sexual relationships shows the expectation of men playing the active role. Men *wed* women while women *become* brides of men. A man *possesses* a woman; he *deflowers* her; he *performs*; he *scores*; he *takes away* her virginity. Although a woman can *seduce* a man, she cannot offer him her virginity. When talking about virginity, the only way to make the woman the actor in the sentence is to say that "She lost her virginity," but people lose things by accident rather than by purposeful actions, and so she's only the grammatical, not the real-life, actor.

The reason that women tried to bring the term *Ms.* into the language to replace *Miss* and *Mrs.* relates to this point. Married women resent being identified only under their husbands' names. For example, when Susan Glascoe did something noteworthy, she would be identified in the newspaper only as Mrs. John Glascoe. The dictionary cards showed what appeared to be an attitude on the part of the editors that it was almost indecent to let a respectable woman's name march unaccompanied across the pages of a dictionary. Women were listed with male names whether or not the male contributed to the woman's reason for being in the dictionary or in his own right was as famous as the woman. For example, Charlotte Brontë was identified as Mrs. Arthur B. Nicholls, Amelia Earhart as Mrs. George Palmer Putnam, Helen Hayes as Mrs. Charles MacArthur, Jenny Lind as Mme. Otto Goldschmit, Cornelia Otis Skinner as the daughter of Otis, Harriet Beecher Stowe as the sister of Henry Ward Beecher, and Edith Sitwell as the sister of Osbert and Sacheverell. A very small number of women got into the dictionary without the benefit of a masculine escort. They were rebels and crusaders: temperance leaders Frances Elizabeth Caroline Willard and Carry Nation, women's rights leaders Carrie Chapman Catt and Elizabeth Cady Stanton, birth control educator Margaret Sanger, religious leader Mary Baker Eddy, and slaves Harriet Tubman and Phillis Wheatley.

Etiquette books used to teach that if a woman had *Mrs.* in front of her name, then the husband's name should follow because *Mrs.* is an abbreviated form of *Mistress* and a woman couldn't be a mistress of herself. As with many arguments about "correct" language usage, this isn't very logical because *Miss* is also an abbreviation of *Mistress*. Feminists hoped to simplify matters by introducing *Ms.* as an alternative to both *Mrs.* and *Miss*, but what happened is that *Ms.* largely replaced *Miss*, to become a catch-all business title for women. Many married women still prefer the title *Mrs.*, and some resent being addressed with the term *Ms.* As one frustrated newspaper reporter complained, "Before I can write about a woman, I have to know not only her marital status but also her political philosophy." The result of such complications may contribute to the demise of titles, which are already being ignored by many computer programmers who find it more efficient to simply use names, for example in a business letter: "Dear Joan Garcia," instead of "Dear Mrs. Joan Garcia," "Dear Ms. Garcia," or "Dear Mrs. Louis Garcia."

The titles given to royalty provide an example of how males can be disadvantaged by the assumption that they are always to play the more powerful role. In British royalty, when a man holds a title, his wife is automatically given the feminine equivalent. But the reverse is not true. For example, a *count* is a high political officer with a *countess* being his wife. The same is true for a *duke* and a *duchess* and a *king* and a *queen.* But when a female holds the royal title, the man she marries does not automatically acquire the matching title. For example, Queen Elizabeth's husband has the title of *prince* rather than *king*, but if Prince Charles had become king while he was still married to Lady or Princess Diana, she would have been known as the queen. The reasoning appears to be that since masculine words are stronger, they are reserved for true heirs and withheld from males coming into the royal family by marriage. If Prince Philip were called *King Philip*, it would be much easier for British subjects to forget where the true power lies.

The names that people give their children show the hopes and dreams they have for them, and when we look at the differences between male and female names in a culture, we can see the cumulative expectations of that culture. In our culture girls often have names taken from small, aesthetically pleasing items, e.g., *Ruby*, *Jewel*, and *Pearl*. *Esther* and *Stella* mean "star," *Ada* means "ornament," and *Vanessa* means "butterfly." Boys are more likely to be given names with meanings of power and strength, e.g., *Neil* means "champion," *Martin* is from Mars, the God of War, *Raymond* means "wise protection," *Harold* means "chief of the army," *Ira* means "vigilant," *Rex* means "king," and *Richard* means "strong king."

25 We see similar differences in food metaphors. Food is a passive substance just sitting there waiting to be eaten. Many people have recognized this and so no longer feel comfortable describing women as "delectable morsels." However, when I was a teenager, it was considered a compliment to refer to a girl (we didn't call anyone a *woman* until she was middle-aged) as a *cute tomato*, a *peach*, a *dish*, a *cookie*, *honey*, *sugar*, or *sweetie-pie*. When being affectionate, women will occasionally call a man

honey or *sweetie*, but in general, food metaphors are used much less often with men than with women. If a man is called a *fruit*, his masculinity is being questioned. But it's perfectly acceptable to use a food metaphor if the food is heavier and more substantive than that used for women. For example pin-up pictures of women have long been known as *cheesecake*, but when Burt Reynolds posed for a nude centerfold the picture was immediately dubbed *beefcake*, cf. *a hunk of meat*. That such sexual references to men have come into the language is another reflection of how society is beginning to lessen the differences between their attitudes toward men and women.

Something similar to the *fruit* metaphor happens with references to plants. We insult a man by calling him a *pansy*, but it wasn't considered particularly insulting to talk about a girl being a *wallflower*, *a clinging vine*, or a *shrinking violet*, or to give girls such names as *Ivy*, *Rose*, *Lily*, *Iris*, *Daisy*, *Camellia*, *Heather*, and *Flora*. A plant metaphor can be used with a man if the plant is big and strong, for example, Andrew Jackson's nickname of *Old Hickory*. Also, the phrases *blooming idiots* and *budding geniuses* can be used with either sex, but notice how they are based on the most active thing a plant can do which is to bloom or bud.

Animal metaphors also illustrate the different expectations for males and females. Men are referred to as *studs*, *bucks*, and *wolves* while women are referred to with such metaphors as *kitten*, *bunny*, *beaver*, *bird*, *chick*, and *lamb*. In the 1950s we said that boys went *tomcatting*, but today it's just *catting around* and both boys and girls do it. When the term *foxy*, meaning that someone was sexy, first became popular it was used only for girls, but now someone of either sex can be described as a *fox*. Some animal metaphors that are used predominantly with men have negative connotations based on the size and/or strength of the animals, e.g., *beast*, *bull-headed*, *jackass*, *rat*, *loanshark*, and *vulture*. Negative metaphors used with women are based on smaller animals, e.g., *social butterfly*, *mousy*, *catty*, and *vixen*. The feminine terms connote action, but not the same kind of large scale action as with the masculine terms.

WOMEN ARE CONNECTED WITH NEGATIVE CONNOTATIONS; MEN WITH POSITIVE CONNOTATIONS

The final point that my notecards illustrated was how many positive connotations are associated with the concept of masculine, while there are rather trivial or negative connotations connected with the corresponding feminine concept. An example from the animal metaphors makes a good illustration. The word *shrew* taken from the name of a small but especially vicious animal was defined in my dictionary as "an ill-tempered scolding woman," but the word *shrewd* taken from the same root was defined as "marked by clever, discerning awareness" and was illustrated with the phrase "a shrewd businessman."

Early in life, children are conditioned to the superiority of the masculine role. As child psychologists point out, little girls have much more freedom to experiment with sex roles than do little boys. If a little girl acts like a *tomboy*, most parents have mixed feelings, being at least partially proud. But if their little boy acts like a *sissy* (derived from *sister*), they call a psychologist. It's perfectly acceptable for a little girl to sleep in the crib that was purchased for her brother, to wear his hand-me-down jeans and shirts, and to ride the bicycle that he has outgrown. But few parents would put a boy baby in a white and gold crib decorated with frills and lace, and virtually no parents would have their little boy wear his sister's hand-me-down dresses, nor would they have their son ride a girl's pink bicycle with a flower-bedecked basket. The proper names given to girls and boys show this same attitude. Girls can have "boy" names—*Chris*, *Craig*, *Jo*, *Kelly*, *Shawn*, *Teri*, *Toni*, and *Sam*—but it doesn't work the other way around. A couple of generations ago, *Beverly*, *Francis*, *Hazel*, *Marion*, and *Shirley* were common boys' names. As parents gave these names to more and more girls, they fell into disuse for males, and some older men who have these names prefer to go by their initials or by such abbreviated forms as *Haze* or *Shirl*.

30 When a little girl is told to *be a lady*, she is being told to sit with her knees together and to be quiet and dainty. But when a little boy is told to *be a man* he is being told to be noble, strong, and virtuous—to have all the qualities that the speaker looks on as desirable. The concept of manliness has such positive connotations that it used to be a compliment to call someone a *he-man*, to say that he was doubly a man. Today many people are more ambivalent about this term and respond to it much as they do to the word *macho*. But calling someone a *manly man* or a *virile man* is nearly always meant as a compliment. *Virile* comes from the Indo-European *vir* meaning "man," which is also the basis of *virtuous*. Contrast the positive connotations of both *virile* and *virtuous* with the negative connotations of *hysterical*. The Greeks took this latter word from their name for *uterus* (as still seen in *hysterectomy*). They thought that women were the only ones

who experienced uncontrolled emotional outbursts, and so the condition must have something to do with a part of the body that only women have.

Differences in the connotations between positive male and negative female connotations can be seen in several pairs of words that differ denotatively only in the matter of sex. *Bachelor* as compared to *spinster* or *old maid* has such positive connotations that women try to adopt them by using the term *bachelor-girl* or *bachelorette*. *Old maid* is so negative that it's the basis for metaphors: pretentious and fussy old men are called *old maids*, as are the leftover kernels of unpopped popcorn, and the last card in a popular children's game.

Patron and *matron* (Middle English for *father* and *mother*) have such different levels of prestige that women try to borrow the more positive masculine connotations with the word *patroness*, literally "female father." Such a peculiar term came about because of the high prestige attached to *patron* in such phrases as *a patron of the arts* or *a patron saint*. *Matron* is more apt to be used in talking about a woman in charge of a jail or a public restroom.

When men are doing jobs that women often do, we apparently try to pay the men extra by giving them fancy titles, for example, a male cook is more likely to be called a *chef* while a male seamstress will get the title of *tailor*. The armed forces have a special problem in that they recruit under such slogans as "The Marine Corps builds men!" and "Join the Army! Become a Man." Once the recruits are enlisted, they find themselves doing much of the work that has been traditionally thought of as "women's work." The solution to getting the work done and not insulting anyone's masculinity was to change the titles as shown below:

waitress	orderly
nurse	medic or corpsman
secretary	clerk-typist
assistant	adjutant
dishwasher or kitchen helper	KP (kitchen police)

Compare *brave* and *squaw*. Early settlers in America truly admired Indian men and hence named them with a word that carried connotations of youth, vigor, courage. But they used the Algonquin's name for "woman" and over the years it developed almost opposite connotations to those of *brave*. *Wizard* and *witch* contrast almost as much. The masculine *wizard* implies skill and wisdom combined with magic, while the feminine *witch* implies evil intentions combined with magic. Part of the unattractiveness of both *witch* and *squaw* is that they have been used so often to refer to old women, something with which our culture is particularly uncomfortable, just as the Afghans were. Imagine my surprise when I ran across the phrases *grandfatherly advice* and *old wives' tales* and realized that the underlying implication is the same as the Afghan proverb about the old men being worth listening to while old women talk only foolishness.

35 Other terms that show how negatively we view old women as compared to young women are *old nag* as compared to *filly*, *old crow* or *old bat* as compared to *bird*, and of being *catty* as compared to being *kittenish*. There is no matching set of metaphors for men. The chicken metaphor tells the whole story of a woman's life. In her youth she is a *chick*. Then she marries and begins *feathering her nest*. Soon she begins feeling *cooped up*, so she goes to *hen parties* where she *cackles* with her friends. Then she has her *brood*, begins to *henpeck* her husband, and finally turns into an *old biddy*.

I embarked on my study of the dictionary not with the intention of prescribing language change but simply to see what the language would tell me about sexism. Nevertheless I have been both surprised and pleased as I've watched the changes that have occurred over the past two decades. I'm one of those linguists who believes that new language customs will cause a new generation of speakers to grow up with different expectations. This is why I'm happy about people's efforts to use inclusive language, to say *he or she* or *they* when speaking about individuals whose names they do not know. I'm glad that leading publishers have developed guidelines to help writers use language that is fair to both sexes, and I'm glad that most newspapers and magazines list women by their own names instead of only by their husbands' names and that educated and thoughtful people no longer begin their business letters with "Dear Sir" or "Gentlemen," but instead use a memo form or begin with such salutations as "Dear Colleagues," "Dear Reader," or "Dear Committee Members." I'm also glad that such words as *poetess*, *authoress*, *conductress*, and *aviatrix* now sound quaint and old-fashioned and that *chairman* is giving way to *chair* or *head*, *mailman* to *letter carrier*, *clergyman* to *clergy*, and *stewardess* to *flight attendant*. I was also pleased when the National Oceanic and Atmospheric Administration bowed to feminist complaints and in the late 1970s began to alternate men's and women's names for hurricanes. However, I wasn't so pleased to discover that the change did not immediately erase sexist thoughts from everyone's mind, as shown by a headline about Hurricane David in a 1979 New York tabloid, "David Rapes Virgin Islands." More recently a similar metaphor appeared in a headline in the *Arizona Republic* about Hurricane Charlie, "Charlie Quits Carolinas, Flirts with Virginia."

What these incidents show is that sexism is not something existing independently in American English or in the particular dictionary that I happened to read. Rather, it exists in people's minds. Language is like an X ray in providing visible evidence of invisible thoughts. The best thing about people being interested in and discussing sexist language is that as they make conscious decisions about what pronouns they will use, what jokes they will tell or laugh at, how they will write their names, or how they will begin their letters, they are forced to think about the underlying issue of sexism. This is good because as a problem that begins in people's assumptions and expectations, it's a problem that will be solved only when a great many people have given it a great deal of thought.

VOCABULARY

chaderi: a large piece of cloth used as a long cloak and veil 1
connotations: associated meanings of words 12
temperance: moderation in or total abstinence from drinking liquors 21

AUDIENCE AND PURPOSE

1. What is Nilsen's thesis?
2. What is the tone of this essay?
3. Why does Nilsen believe that changes to language will affect culture?

CONTENT

1. What evidence does Nilsen collect to show that men are valued for their minds and women for their bodies?
2. How does Nilsen show the sexual connotations of feminine words? Give examples.
3. What evidence does Nilsen find of passivity in words that describe women's roles?
4. What evidence does Nilsen have of the negativity or triviality of the feminine?

STYLE AND STRUCTURE

1. Why does Nilsen tell you the simple techniques that she used to do her research?
2. How does Nilsen use humour? Give examples.
3. How is Nilsen's conclusion an effective example?

Margaret Atwood

Margaret Atwood (b. 1939) is a Canadian writer best known for her novels, including *The Edible Woman* (1969), *The Handmaid's Tale* (1985), and *Alias Grace* (1996), and her poetry, the most recent volume of which is called *Morning in the Burned House* (1995).

GOD IS IN THE DETAILS: THE SHAKERS KNEW WHEN TO STOP

Utopia is a paradoxical concept. As a motivating idea — "improvement is desirable" — we can't do without it. But every time we try to implement it on a grand scale, we accomplish its disastrous opposite. Perhaps that is why the word itself means "no place."

The first proto-utopias of our millennium were religious communities — monks and nuns renouncing this world to get into the next one. The Puritans shifted the locus: they wanted to realize God's spiritual kingdom here on earth. As the 19th century embraced "progress," and living conditions improved — though not for everyone — utopian plans of a more material kind flourished. The new sciences of archeology and anthropology encouraged speculative thinking: why were women doomed to wear corsets? They didn't in ancient Greece, so why not the bloomer suit or the pre-Raphaelite gown? Literary utopias like William Morris's "News From Nowhere" show a parallel interest in easily shed undergarments.

Among the other areas of human life utopians itched to redesign were: material goods, and how they should be made (handicrafts were encouraged); money, and whether it should be scrapped; the class system, and whether to eliminate it or just recostume it; sex, and how to do away with it or else spread it around (monogamy was rarely endorsed); children, and who should have them (not people with squints), and who ought to bring them up (not their mothers); the environment, and how to clean it up (do away with factories), and health — everyone in utopia always has a lot of health, not to mention beauty. If yesterday's utopia sounds like today's life-style magazine, who's to wonder? Both are the products of desire.

But utopia usually contains the seeds of its obverse, the dreaded dystopia. All utopias face a problem: what do you do with those who don't agree with you? Utopias are Procrustean beds; few actual human beings fit their grand schemes. Bits must be stretched or else chopped off. The French Revolution was a utopian idea, and the guillotine was originally intended as a pain-saving device.

How many heads have to roll to achieve "the perfect society"? Often a lot. Lovely robes turn to nasty uniforms; sex is either coerced or denied; the orderliness of the ant, so admired by some utopians, becomes robotic; the working class turns cannabalistic, as in H.G. Wells's "Time Machine," or thanks to brain-altering chemicals, the Brave New World ends, not with a bang but a simper. We should remember too that laissez-faire capitalism was once considered a utopian idea: the system that would save us all through unregulated market forces, if only we would stay the course.

So what's the best utopia of the last thousand years? I'd vote for the Shakers. These were a breakaway group of Quakers who went to America in 1774 under the leadership of "Mother" Ann Lee. They believed that the divine principle was both male and female, the former having been manifested in Christ, the latter in (surprise) Ann Lee herself, who had begun the establishment of (you guessed it) God's kingdom on earth. God, it appeared, favored cloth weaving, furniture making, a cappella singing, worshipful dancing in concentric circles with men on the outside and minimalist clothing—unadorned black and white were his/her preferred fashion colors. The Shakers lived in "family groups" of 30 to 90; they practiced celibacy, replenishing their numbers through conversions and the adoption of foundlings. At their zenith, in 1874, they numbered 58 communities; by 1905, however, there were only 1,000 of them left.

As utopians go, the Shakers were a kindly, melodious and harmless bunch. They never took up with Big Brother—Big Mother was about as far as they went. They were pacifists; they didn't kill anyone; they didn't try to impose their ideas by force. They made a lasting contribution to furniture design and music, which is more than some can say, and best of all, they were self-limiting.

However, a recent archeological dig has revealed that the latter-day Shakers had backslid to a degree and were making use of such worldly products as alcohol, corsets and hair ointment. Utopia is a grab at Paradise, so why should it surprise us that there's always a worm in its apple?

VOCABULARY

utopia: ideal place, literally "no place" 1
locus: place 2
obverse: flip side 4
dystopia: example of perfect society gone wrong 4
Procrustean: like Procrustes, a creature from Greek myth who was said to seize travellers, tie them to a bedstead, and then either stretch them or cut off their legs to make them fit; someone or something that insists on conformity 4
a cappella: voices without instrumental accompaniment 6

AUDIENCE AND PURPOSE

1. Atwood discusses utopias and how unrealizable they are. How does she give the reader a sense of her own mixed attitude toward them?
2. What is Atwood's attitude toward the Shakers?
3. Why does Atwood remind us of so many utopias that were either quaint or disastrous?

CONTENT

1. What do utopias usually attempt to change, according to Atwood?
2. What is the inherent problem of the utopia, according to her?
3. What was the best feature of the Shakers, according to Atwood?

STYLE AND STRUCTURE

1. Atwood moves from the general to the particular. Discuss how she does this and why it works.
2. Why does Atwood so often use parentheses?
3. Why does the conclusion take us back to the fall of Adam and Eve?

A.S. Byatt

A.S. Byatt (b. 1936) is a British author best known in North America for writing *Possession: A Romance* (1990), a novel that became a bestseller. She is also the author of a novella called "Morpho Eugenia" (1992), which was made into the successful film *Angels and Insects* directed by Phillip Haas in 1996. Byatt's most recent novel is entitled *The Biographer's Tale* (2000).

NARRATE OR DIE: WHY SCHEHERAZADE KEEPS ON TALKING

The best story ever told? Perhaps the story of the two brothers, both kings, who found that their wives were unfaithful, took bloody vengeance, and set out into the world to travel until they found someone less fortunate than they were. They encountered a demon who kept a woman in a glass chest with four locks; she came out while he slept and showed them 98 rings she had collected from chance lovers and insisted on having sex with the princes to make it a round 100. The princes decided that the demon was more unfortunate than they were and returned to their kingdoms. There the elder brother, Shahrayar, still angry over his wife's betrayal, instituted a reign of terror, marrying a virgin each day and handing her to his vizier for execution at dawn. The vizier's daughter Shahrazad, a woman both wise and learned, beseeched her father to give her to the king. On the wedding night, the bride asked that her younger sister, Dinarzad, might sleep under the bed, so that when the king had "finished with Shahrazad," the younger girl, as the sisters had agreed, might ask Shahrazad to tell a story to while away the time until dawn. When dawn came, the story was not finished, and the curious king stayed execution for a night. Shahrazad continued to tell tales, which gave rise to other tales, all of which were unfinished at dawn. The king's narrative curiosity kept Shahrazad alive, day after day. She narrated a stay of execution, a space in which she bore three chidren. And in the end, the king removed the sentence of death, and they lived happily ever after.

This story has everything a tale should have. Sex, death, treachery, vengeance, magic, humor, warmth, wit, surprise and a happy ending. Though it appears to be a story against women, it actually marks the creation of one of the strongest and cleverest heroines in world literature. Shahrazad, who has been better known in the West as Scheherazade, triumphs because she is endlessly inventive and keeps her head. The stories in "The Thousand and One Nights" (interchangeably known as "The Arabian Nights") are stories about storytelling without ever ceasing to be stories about love and life and death and money and food and other human necessities. Narration is as much a part of human nature as breath and the circulation of the blood. Modernist literature tried to do away with storytelling, which it thought vulgar, replacing it with flashbacks, epiphanies, streams of consciousness. But storytelling is intrinsic to biological time, which we cannot escape. Life, Pascal said, is like living in a prison from which every day fellow prisoners are taken away to be executed. We are all, like Scheherazade, under sentence of death, and we all think of our lives as narratives, with beginnings, middles and ends.

Storytelling in general, and "The Thousand and One Nights" in particular, consoles us for endings with endless new beginnings. I have just finished my own telling of the frame story with the European fairy-tale ending, "they lived happily ever after," which is a consolatory false eternity, for no one does, except in the endless repetitions of storytelling. Stories keep part of us alive after the end of our story, and there is something very moving about Scheherazade entering on the happiness ever after, not at her wedding, but after 1,001 tales and three children.

Great stories, and great story collections, are shape shifters. "The Thousand and One Nights," with its roots in Persia and India, has probably been circulating in one form or another since the ninth century. It first appeared in Europe in the French translation of Antoine Galland between 1704 and 1717. He used a 14th-century Syrian text but adapted and rewrote and added for French taste—it is possible that both Aladdin and Ali Baba as we read them originate with the Frenchman. Subsequent translators took liberties, or used their imaginations. Richard Burton invented a curious Victorian-medieval style. Joseph Charles Mardrus, in 1899, according to Robert Irwin, whose "Companion to the Arabian Nights" is gripping and indispensable, "reshaped the 'Nights' in such a manner that the stories appear to have been written by Oscar Wilde or Stéphane Mallarmé.

5 Eastern and Western literature contain other related collections of interlinked tales—"Katha Sarit Sagara" ("The Ocean of Story"), Ovid's "Metamorphoses," Chaucer's "Canterbury Tales" and Boccaccio's "Decameron," whose frame story has its characters defying the Black Death by retreating to the country and telling tales. Out of such works came 19th-century Gothic fantasy and the intricate, paranoid nightmare plottings of such story webs as "The Crying of Lot 49" and Lawrence Norfolk's

"Lemprière's Dictionary." Collections of tales talk to one another and borrow from one another; motifs glide from culture to culture, century to century. If the origin of stories is the human ability to remember the past, speculate about beginnings and imagine the ending, it doesn't follow that the search for any "pure" or undisputed origin for any story will lead to definiteness.

Scheherazade's tales have lived on, like germ cells, in many literatures. Dickens, who became the master of serial narration and endless beginnings, comforted his lonely and miserable childhood with "The Arabian Nights," living in their world and learning their craft. In British Romantic poetry, "The Arabian Nights" stood for the wonderful against the mundane, the imaginative against the prosaically and reductively rational. Coleridge said his mind had been "habituated to the vast" by his early reading of "Romances, & Relations of Giants & Magicians, & Genii." He used the tale of the angry and vengeful Djinn whose invisible child had been killed by a thrown date stone as an example of pure chance or fate. Wordsworth, in the fifth book of his "Prelude," describes his childhood treasure as "a little yellow, canvas-covered book, / A slender abstract of the Arabian tales," and the "promise scarcely earthly" of his discovery that there were four large volumes of the work.

Various Western writers have been tempted to write the 1,002d tale. Edgar Allan Poe's Scheherazade makes the mistake of telling her aging husband about modern marvels like steamships, radio and the telegraph. He finds these true tales so incredible that he concludes that she has lost her touch and has her strangled after all. Poe is a combative and irreverent Yankee at the Persian court. Joseph Roth's Scheherazade resides in the decadent days of the Austrian Empire; while John Barth, in his "Dunyazadiad," appears in person as a balding, bespectacled genie who tells the nervous Scheherazade the tales she will tell because he has read them in the future and she is his heroine — thus creating another false eternity, a circular time loop, in which storytellers hand on stories of storytellers.

Then there are the modern Oriental fabulists, Naguib Mahfouz and Salman Rushdie, both threatened with death for storytelling. Mahfouz's "Arabian Nights and Days" is a collection of magical tales with a political edge and a spiritual depth. His stories rework "The Thousand and One Nights": his Shahriyar slowly learns about justice and mercy, the Angel of Death is a bric-a-brac merchant and genies play tricks with fate. Salman Rushdie's narratives are intertwined with the storytelling of the "Nights."

"Haroun and the Sea of Stories" pits a resourceful child, Haroun, against the evil Kattam-Shud, who wants to drain the ocean of the streams of story, which are alive, and replace it with silence and darkness. Rushdie's tale, like Scheherazade's, equates storytelling with life, but his characters and wit owe as much to Western fantasies — "Alice in Wonderland" and "The Wizard of Oz" — as they do to "The Thousand and One Nights." Another cross-fertilization, another conversation.

Rushdie's sea of stories is "the biggest library in the universe." Jorge Luis Borges, to whom libraries, labyrinths and books were all images of infinity, wrote in "The Garden of Forking Paths" of "that night which is at the middle of the 'Thousand and One Nights' when Scheherazade (through a magical oversight of the copyist) begins to repeat her stories over again...." This circular tale fascinated Italo Calvino. It also inspired him, for his "If on a Winter's Night a Traveler" is the endless tale of a lost reader who starts a book only to find that the rest is missing; when he replaces the book, he finds that it has a new beginning. This novel contains a novelist — as Borges's tale contains Scheherazade within Scheherazade — who wants to write a book that will contain only the pure pleasure of anticipation of the beginning, "a book that is only an incipit," a book with no ending, perhaps like "The Arabian Nights."

10 Marcel Proust saw himself as Scheherazade, in relation to both sex and death. At the end of the almost endless novel, "Remembrance of Things Past," he writes a triumphant meditation on the presence of death, which has in fact driven him to create his great and comprehensive book, the book of his life. At one point he even personifies this presence of death as "le sultan Sheriar," who might or might not put a dawn end to his nocturnal writing. Malcolm Bowie, in "Proust Among the Stars," comments that "the big book of death-defying stories" with which Proust's novel compares itself is not Boccaccio's "Decameron," in which death appears as a "horrifying initial trigger to tale-telling," but the "Nights," where stories are life. "Narrate or die," for Proust's narrator as for Scheherazade, is the imperative. "By mere sentences placed end on end, one's sentence is commuted for a while, and the end is postponed."

The Judeo-Christian culture is founded on a linear narrative in time. It moves forward from creation through history, to redemption in the Christian case, and looks forward to the promised end, when time and death will cease to be. The great novels of Western culture, from "Don Quixote" to "War and Peace," from "Moby Dick" to "Dr. Faustus," were constructed in the shadow of this story. People are excited by millennial events as images of beginnings and endings. There is a difference between these great, portentous histories and small tales that are handed down like gifts for delight and contemplation.

Storytellers like Calvino and Scheherazade can offer readers and listeners an infinity of incipits, an illusion of inexhaustibility. Calvino's imaginary novelist sits and stares at a cartoon of Snoopy, sitting at a typewriter, with the caption "It was a dark and stormy night," the beginning of a circular shaggy-dog story. Both cartoons and soap operas are versions of Scheherazade's tale telling, worlds in which death and endings are put off indefinitely—and age too, in the case of Charlie Brown.

High modernism escaped time with epiphanic visions of timeless moments, imagined infinities that have always seemed to me strained, for they fail to offer any counter to fear and death. But the small artifices of elegant, well-made tales and the vulgar satisfaction of narrative curiosity do stand against death. The romantic novelist Georgette Heyer kept few fan letters, but I saw two: one from a man who had laughed at one of her comic fops on the trolley going to a life-threatening operation, and one from a Polish woman who had kept her fellow prisoners alive during the war by reciting, night after night, a Heyer novel she knew by heart.

During the bombardment of Sarajevo in 1994, a group of theater workers in Amsterdam commissioned tales, from different European writers, to be read aloud, simultaneously, in theaters in Sarajevo itself and all over Europe, every Friday until the fighting ended. This project pitted storytelling against destruction, imaginative life against real death. It may not have saved lives, but it was a form of living energy. It looked back to "The Thousand and One Nights" and forward to the millennium. It was called Scheherazade 2001.

VOCABULARY

vizier: a high executive Turkish officer 1
beseeched: pleaded 1
epiphanies: moments of discovery or understanding 2
intrinsic: part of something's essential nature 2
Black Death: the bubonic plague 5
prosaically: dully, unimaginatively 6
fabulists: writers of fables 8
bric-a-brac: small ornaments 8

incipit: opening words 9
nocturnal: nightly 10
portentous: ominous 11

AUDIENCE AND PURPOSE

1. Why does Byatt think that Scheherazade's story is the best story ever told?
2. Why does Byatt use both Eastern and Western, as well as ancient and modern, examples to make her point?
3. How are we like Scheherazade, in Byatt's view, and why do we need storytelling?
4. What, according to Byatt, is the reason that storytelling is consoling for readers and listeners?

CONTENT

1. Byatt draws on a range of stories from intellectual works to soap operas and comic strips. Why does she include such a range?
2. Why does Byatt consider modernist writers often unsuccessful in storytelling?

STYLE AND STRUCTURE

1. Why does Byatt begin her essay by retelling the story of Scheherazade?
2. Why is the title of her essay effective?
3. Show how some of Byatt's examples of writers used or use storytelling to stave off death.
4. Why does Byatt use a recent political event to form her conclusion?

Wayne Grady

Wayne Grady (b. 1948) is an award-winning journalist who worked for *Saturday Night* (1980–84) and *Harrowsmith* (1984–89). He is currently the science editor for *Equinox*. His first book was an anthology of Canadian short stories. He has also written on Canadian literature, history, geography, and science. His most recent work is *Chasing the Chinook: On the Trail of Canadian Words and Culture* (1998).

THE METRIC SYSTEM (SORT OF)

Canada was declared a metric nation in 1971, and after 2.8 decades, it's safe to say that we're as metric as we're going to get. At first the two systems, metric and imperial, battled it out—the metricists seized the road signs and thermostats, while the stubborn imperialists refused to buy anything that wasn't measured out according to some body part. You may recall extremists in Ottawa driving all the way to Carleton Place, a distance of sixty-three kilometres, to fill up at a service station that still sold gasoline in gallons. But that's all over now. Resistance and insistence proved equally futile.

Purists on both sides have lamented the resulting mishmash, failing to see that what we have now is a system that's uniquely Canadian. By combining the more sensible features of the metric system, or SI (for Système Internationale d'Unités) with some long-cherished aspects of the imperial system, we've come up with a seamless hybrid that makes perfect sense to us all. Let's call it simperial. Like franglais and "Progressive Conservative," simperial is the ideal Canadian compromise.

For example, the other day I asked directions to an auction sale: "Drive ten kilometres down this road," I was told, "and you'll see a barn about two hundred feet in from the highway." That's simperial. Only in Canada can a river be half a mile wide and thirty metres deep. At building supply yards, you can buy 100 square metres of shingles and a box of three-quarter inch roofing nails to hold them down. When I ask my daughter, who is fourteen and has been raised metric, how tall she is, she says "Five four." What's the temperature outside? "Plus three." Simperial.

In our quiet, peacekeeping way, we took the best features from each extreme and consigned the rest to oblivion. Simperial simply makes more sense than either of its two feeder systems. Nobody's feet should be size forty-two anything. But at the same time, zero degrees, not thirty-two, is obviously the temperature at which water should freeze; if anyone knows that, it's us.

After the auction, I stopped at that gas station in Carleton Place. The pump registers gasoline by the litre now, of course, and when I went in to pay, the guy in the booth pointed his chin at my car.

"How is she on gas?" he asked.

"I get 100 kilometres on six litres," I said, quoting the manual; I had no idea what it meant.

He nodded appreciatively. "That's pretty good mileage."

AUDIENCE AND PURPOSE

1. What is Grady's thesis statement?
2. How does the introductory paragraph function to give Grady's audience essential background?
3. Why does Grady make such precise reference to 2.8 decades in the introduction?

CONTENT

1. Why does Grady believe that "simperial" is uniquely Canadian?
2. How does Grady try to illustrate the common sense that underlies the Canadian use of the metric system?
3. How old do you think the author is? Why? Is he right that Canada will never become more metric than it is now? Why or why not?

STYLE AND STRUCTURE

1. Why does Grady use so much dialogue in his examples?
2. Why does the word "simperial" work so well to describe the hybrid system? What is the word itself a hybrid of?
3. Grady uses "homey" examples — building supply yards, auctions, gas stations. What is the effect of such familiar examples?
4. What does Grady's story in the conclusion show about his and his listener's understanding of the metric system?

Jeffrey Moussaieff Masson and Susan McCarthy

Jeffrey Moussaieff Masson (b. 1941) and Susan McCarthy are the authors of *When Elephants Weep: The Emotional Lives of Animals* (1995). Masson was briefly the project director of the Sigmund Freud Archives and found documents there on child abuse that created a major controversy in psychoanalysis. He is also the author of *The Assault on Truth* (1984), *Against Therapy: Emotional Theory and the Myth of Psychological Healing* (1988), and *Final Analysis: The Making and Unmaking of a Psychoanalyst* (1990). His work on the emotions of animals has been a spectacular success, selling nearly half a million copies in America alone. McCarthy has degrees in biology and journalism.

SHAME, BLUSHING, AND HIDDEN SECRETS

Darwin argued that only humans blush. In the years since, the self-aware social emotions like shame, shyness, guilt, embarrassment, and self-consciousness—all feelings revolving around how the self is perceived by others—have usually been considered exclusively human. Yet there is evidence that many animals feel them, too, and shame may prove to be a surprisingly basic emotion.

Asked whether wild chimpanzees ever appear ashamed or embarrassed, Jane Goodall laughed. "They do, actually. In the wild you don't see that very often. The best story I know of clear embarrassment was young Freud when he was about six years old. He was showing off—really, you could only describe it as showing off—in front of Uncle Figan, who was the alpha male. Figan was trying to groom Fifi, the new baby was there, and Freud was just prancing around and shaking branches and making a real big nuisance of himself. He went up into a tall plantain tree: they have a rather weak trunk like a banana. He was swaying it to and fro, to and fro, and suddenly it snapped!—and he *crashed* onto the ground. He just happened to land very close to me. I was able to see his face, and the first thing he did when he emerged from the grass was to take a quick little glance at Figan and then he crept quietly away and began feeding. That was quite clearly a big comedown for him."

Shame is one of the most vividly remembered feelings. Recalling happiness or fear or anger, people do not usually experience the emotion again at the time of recalling it. But remembering an incident of embarrassment or shame can often bring a flood of shame sweeping back. Those who blush may blush again at a memory. In human psychology and psychotherapy, shame received little attention for years but has recently begun to be considered important. It has been called "the master emotion," which societies use to enforce norms. Guilt refers to a particular event, but shame, which is more global, is said to refer to the individual's entire being. Thus a person might feel guilt about going off their diet, and shame at being fat. Guilt can also result from a private event, while shame tends to require that others know or observe or are imagined to judge.

Some argue—not especially vigorously, as they have met little opposition—that only humans have self-conscious emotions. It is said that animals are intellectually incapable of self-consciousness—although this is generally meant to show the low level of animal intelligence rather than a lack of emotion.

5 But while it may seem logical to conclude that such emotions cannot exist without an intellectual comprehension of how one is viewed by other creatures, this need not be the case. There is no reason to suppose that an animal couldn't feel shame without understanding why. As Darwin noted, mental confusion is a prominent symptom of shame. "I can't think clearly in the moment of embarrassment, and I don't know anybody else who can," psychiatrist Donald Nathanson has written. Emotion can exist with or without understanding the reasons for it. One animal might be ashamed or embarrassed without being entirely conscious of the reason; another might be ashamed or embarrassed and understand the reason perfectly.

Self-consciousness denotes both emotional and intellectual states. Emotionally, it can be an uncomfortable feeling of being observed (or observing oneself)—a form of embarrassment. Intellectually, it is the reflective knowledge of one's own mind, existence, and acts—a philosophical minefield.

Mirror studies with primates have been a focus of the debate over whether animals have or can have self-awareness. A chimpanzee allowed to become familiar with mirrors appears to learn that the image is its own. If such apes are anesthetized, dabbed on the face with a dot of paint, and given a mirror upon awakening, when they see the paint in their reflection they will touch their face with their fingers, examine their fingers, and then try to remove the paint. Orangutans also learn that the image in the mirror is of themselves; so far, monkeys have not done so. To some observers, this is evidence of self-consciousness. Others have sought to prove that it is nothing of the sort. John S.

Kennedy follows some critics in arguing that it is more parsimonious to assume that the chimpanzee merely "forms a point-to-point association between the movements of the mirror image and his own movements." This tortuous explanation assigns mental powers to the chimpanzee that are at least as complex as saying that it knows it is seeing itself in the mirror. Its appeal is simply that it denies the possibility of self-consciousness in a nonhuman being.

The chimpanzees Sherman and Austin, part of an ape language experiment in Atlanta, are monitored by video cameras that they have learned to use in a variety of ways. After several months of exposure to their own images on the video monitors, each ape appeared to suddenly realize that the image was of himself. They then used the monitor to observe themselves make faces, eat, or swirl water around in their mouths. Both have learned to distinguish between a live image and a taped image of themselves, by testing to see if their actions are duplicated on the screen. Sherman was using a hand mirror to guide his application of Crayola makeup one day, tired of the mirror and gestured to have the video camera aimed at his face instead. He used the image to apply the makeup and to locate and remove any that had stained his teeth. Austin made valiant attempts one day to use the monitor to look down his throat while simultaneously shining a flashlight into it.

The practice of saving face is another chimpanzee behavior that implies consciousness of self. At the zoo in Arnhem, the chimpanzee Yeroen was slightly injured in a fight with another chimp, Nikkie. To the astonishment of researchers, Yeroen spent the next week limping dramatically—but only in Nikkie's view. A chimpanzee wishing to make peace with another sometimes will not approach directly, but will pretend to discover a nonexistent object and use the resulting gathering of many chimps to make contact with the former adversary, a strategy Frans de Waal thinks is used to save face.

10 In a diverse range of species, evidence that animals know when they are being observed suggests self-awareness. When a male baboon yawns, his impressive canine teeth are ostentatiously displayed. Observing wild baboons, biologist Craig Packer found that males with worn or broken teeth yawn less than males with teeth in good condition—unless there are no other males around, in which case they yawn just as often. Chimpanzees have been known to avoid glancing at a food source they know about but other chimps do not. On several occasions, lions in the Serengeti who had caught prey in high grass broke with the

usual lion habit of beginning to eat at once. Instead the lion sat down and glanced around for as much as five minutes, as if it had caught nothing. When other nearby lions departed, the lion began to eat. A mountain goat who sees a predator will often walk away calmly and slowly and then, the moment it is out of the predator's line of sight, take off, running at full speed. These animals act as if they were conscious of others perceiving their behavior and want to affect that perception. This level of self-consciousness might not permit a goat to look into a mirror and think, "That's me," but might show self-consciousness nonetheless. Self-awareness need not be all or nothing.

SHYNESS, MODESTY, AND EMBARRASSMENT

Embarrassment and shyness, also considered self-aware emotions, seem to be about being seen—in a bad light, or when one does not wish to be seen. Koko, the signing gorilla, has shown a rather touching form of embarrassment. Among her toys are a number of puppets and dolls. She was once seen signing "kiss" to her alligator puppet. On another occasion Koko signed "kiss" to her blue gorilla doll and "bad bad" to her pink gorilla doll. Then she signed "chase tickle," slammed the dolls together, made them wrestle, and signed "good gorilla good good." On each occasion, and other similar occasions, the moment she saw that she was being watched, she stopped playing.

Animals do not wear clothing to conceal parts of their bodies that humans in many cultures consider vital for adults to conceal. They do not hide many actions that correspond to actions people often prefer to hide. This does not necessarily mean that there is nothing they choose to hide or keep private. The courtship of one captive bird may be an example.

Alex, the verbally accomplished African grey parrot, may be imprinted on human beings. According to Irene Pepperberg, he attempts to court certain of her male students. When courting, Alex may regurgitate food and do a little ritualized dance. "If he is courting one of my students and I walk in, he immediately stops," says Pepperberg. Perhaps Alex is embarrassed. If, on the other hand, he merely wants a little privacy, why does he want it? Perhaps he is trying to avoid competition. Is he shy? Shyness is an emotion that seems to shade into fear, the fear of being seen, and it may be that shame is also related to fear.

The essence of shame is the unpleasant feeling that one appears badly—weak, stupid, dirty, helpless, or inadequate—and the dread of appearing this way. At first sight, shame need have no connection with fear. At one oceanarium (where the animals were never punished) a bottle-nosed porpoise, Wela, was trained to jump out of the water and take a fish from a person's hand. One day when this stunt was being photographed, trainer Karen Pryor was distracted and forgot to drop the fish as she usually did. As a result, when Wela grabbed the fish, she inadvertently bit Pryor's hand. Wela, appearing "hideously embarrassed," went to the bottom of the tank, put her snout in a corner, and would not come out until Pryor got in with her, petted her, and coaxed her into calmness.

Wela's behavior is comparable to that of a dog who barks and threatens someone coming into the house—and suddenly realizes that the someone is its owner. From a barking, bristling, menacing creature, the dog suddenly deflates to a wriggling, whining, tail-wagging pup. It has been argued that the comic reversal of behavior in such a dog does not mean he or she is embarrassed, only seeking to appease a dominant animal—its owner—by showing submission. Whether this is accurate or not, it does not seem to describe Wela's behavior, which looks more like embarrassment, a form of shame. The chimpanzee Washoe was seen to make a similar mistake, threatening an old friend (who had grown four or five inches since they had last met) before she recognized who it was and reacted with what would be called embarrassment if Washoe were human. One might say that such behavior is merely ritual submission, but then the same description could apply to an embarrassed human apology.

Dog trainers at Guide Dogs for the Blind say that old dogs who have lost bladder or sphincter control seem to be embarrassed or ashamed. One otherwise healthy sixteen-year-old dog in this condition refused to go indoors as she had always done.

One text on animal behavior evades acknowledging animal emotion by insisting, "It is certainly acceptable to say our misbehaving dog is acting as if embarrassed. It would be entirely without foundation to say it was embarrassed, even though we admit to the probable existence of emotions in animals."

BLUSHING

The blush is a primary evidence of shame in people. Charles Darwin, who investigated blushing at great length, seems to have been surrounded by people who blushed at the least provocation. He noted that it was usually accompanied by other signs of shame such as averting the eyes, the face, or the whole body. He had difficulty explaining the value of this phenomenon, and gave a rather Lamarckian explanation for it. Humans, he said, care about their personal appearance and the opinion of others. When people feel attention, especially critical attention, being directed at them, this "excite[s] into activity that part of the sensorium which receives the sensory nerves of the face; and this will react through the vaso-motor system on the facial capillaries. By frequent reiteration through numberless generations, the process will have become so habitual ... that even a suspicion of ... depreciation suffices to relax the capillaries, without any conscious thought about our faces."

After questioning British missionaries stationed around the world on this subject, Darwin concluded that people of all races blush, and that it is not learned, since people who have been born blind also blush. (His data contradicted those defenders of slavery who alleged that Negroes did not blush because they were incapable of shame and hence not fully human.) He called blushing "the most peculiar and the most human of all expressions. Monkeys redden from passion, but it would require an overwhelming amount of evidence to make us believe that any animal could blush."

It would have interested Darwin to know that animals other than monkeys also exhibit reddening skin. The ears of a Tasmanian devil (a small, carnivorous marsupial) in the Frankfurt Zoo turned red "during a state of excitement." Some birds blush, as can be seen on featherless areas of skin. Like the turkey, the spangled honeyeater and the smoky honeyeater have unfeathered wattles that blush "when the bird is excited." Macaws that have bare skin on their cheeks can be seen to blush. They do so when excited or enraged, and, according to parrot behaviorist Mattie Sue Athan, they have also been seen to do so if they fall accidentally while clambering down from a perch. This certainly looks like embarrassment. On the other hand the macaw might just be angry that it has fallen. Perhaps it will turn out to be true that humans are the only animals to blush self-consciously. Humans are unusually devoid of fur, feathers, and other coverings, after all, and so provide a large canvas for this effect.

On the other hand, it may be that the function of blushing is not, or not wholly, a visual one. The phenomenon of blushing need not be visible. Many people feel tingling skin — and shame — without visibly reddening. If people flushed, paled, and turned green with the frequency found in fiction, society would be a much more colorful place. Perhaps many species of animals blush unnoticed. No one has checked to see if, under the fur, a raccoon tingles with mortification or flushes with pride. Whether macaws also blush on the parts of their bodies covered by feathers or whether other parrots flush beneath their feathers is unknown. But even if they do not, it does not necessarily follow that if animals do not blush, they do not feel shame.

THE ADVANTAGES OF SHAME

If shame proves to be widespread in the animal kingdom, the evolutionary approach would predict that it should confer some advantage. Just what might be adaptive about global self-accusation is not immediately apparent.

The self-conscious emotions seem to appear early in the lives of humans. In one series of experiments, researchers gave small children toys cunningly designed to fall apart and then videotaped their play. When a toy broke, some children cried; some looked for another toy; some appeared ashamed or guilty. Some children looked away, their bodies "collapsed" in what is considered a typical shame response. A child who appeared tense and averted its gaze, but then tried to fix the toy, was thought to be showing a guilt response. Helen Block Lewis, an early theorist in the field of shame and guilt, viewed human shame and guilt as regulators of social interactions that combat narcissism and punish transgressions of group mores. Blushing signals to other group members that the blusher recognizes such transgression and, therefore, recognizes the group rules.

Psychiatrist Donald Nathanson does not consider shame a social emotion. He cites an experiment in which three- to four-month-old infants could control a display of flashing colored lights by turning their heads. The babies apparently loved doing this and squealed with pleasure when the lights went on. When the experimenters changed the apparatus so that the babies' efforts were unsuccessful, the infants' heads and necks slumped, their breathing quickened, blood flow to their skin increased, and they turned their faces away. Nathanson and other theorists interpret this as a primitive shame response that was independent of whether or not other people were present, and hence argue that shame is not necessarily a social emotion. (It is not clear how disappointment and frustration can be excluded as possible explanations.) In Nathanson's analysis, shame is "a biological system by which the organism controls its affective output so that it will not remain interested or content when it may not be safe to do so, or so that it will not remain in affective resonance with an organism that fails to match patterns stored in memory." He believes that it evolved comparatively recently.

As for the advantages of global self-accusation, Nathanson argues: "If you were going to design a system capable of learning from experience and educating itself, you might as well build in the capacity to magnify failure. Shame augments our memory of failure and protects us from whatever danger might occur, when, in a moment of need, we might try something well beyond our capacity."

Another possibility is that shame might keep animals from attracting the attention of predators. Humans feel ashamed not only of their actual or perceived faults, but often of their differences from others, even when those differences are neutral or even positive. To be stared at can be unnerving, even when the stare is an admiring one. Often people are uncomfortable when praised. To be singled out in any way can be acutely embarrassing—and may also feel perilous.

Predators single out prey. Some predators select prey on the basis of physical condition, thus culling out sick and injured animals, as well as young animals. They may study herds of prey animals, chase some of them, and make an all-out effort to catch only a few. An examination of the bone marrow of wildebeest killed by lions revealed that a large percentage were in poor condition. Hyenas hunting make random passes at herds, or zigzag through, then stop and watch them run, switching their attention from animal to animal, apparently looking for potential weakness. One experimenter who was shooting wildebeest with anesthetic darts in order to measure and tag them found that, if he was not careful, these animals would at once be killed by hyenas when he released them. Although they looked normal to humans, and seemed to be able to run as fast as ever, the hyenas noted some difference. He had to herd the hyenas away with his vehicle until the wildebeest had more time to recover.

Predators also notice other differences. A researcher once marked some wildebeest by painting their horns white. Within a few months, almost all of these animals had been killed by hyenas. Hans Kruuk has noted instances in which hyenas pursued animals who were presumably in good physical condition but were acting oddly and were then singled out by hyenas. At night, when dazzled by the headlights of a car, wildebeest ran in an odd way—and were instantly pursued by hyenas. Away from the headlights, the wildebeest quickly got their bearings and escaped.

Kruuk also saw a herd of several hundred wildebeest in which only one was rolling and showing territorial behavior.

These actions, unremarkable in another context, instantly attracted a hyena's pursuit. The wildebeest escaped easily. That the wildebeest escaped in these instances supports the idea that the hyenas were detecting difference rather than weakness.

Schooling or flocking behavior can baffle some predators in a very simple way: by preventing them from focusing on individual prey. When a few members of a school of small silver fish were dyed blue, not only were they more frequently attacked by predators, but so were the normal silver fish next to them. Faced by a cloud of identical fish, the predator could not pick out an individual, but it was able to pick out the blue one or the one next to the blue one.

Prey animals often seem aware of the assessment of predators. In Zaire, Paul Leyhausen saw two uneasy-looking male kobs (large antelope) near a river. Presently he saw two lions lurking near the kobs, moving from behind one bush to another. The kob closest to the lions appeared to grow calmer and began grazing, but the other began to run back and forth in alarm. It soon became clear from their movements, Leyhausen says, that the lions were stalking the farther kob—and that both kobs knew this well before the human observer figured out that the lions were not going for the closest prey.

Prey animals also seem able to tell when predators are hunting and when they are bent on other business entirely, and adjust their flight distance accordingly. A wish to conceal weakness and difference—behavior resulting from fear or dislike of being scrutinized—could lead animals to take actions to avoid predation. They could pretend not to be weak, minimize their difference, or hide from the view of predators.

Predators are not the only creatures who might take advantage of an animal's display of vulnerability or weakness. Animals of the same species are all too likely to be alert to signs of such weakness and to exploit them. When lions in the Serengeti were shot with anesthetic darts, some of the other lions took the opportunity to attack them (and were driven off by the researchers). Thus, shame might motivate animals to hide weakness from members of their herd or pack. If a caribou appears visibly weak or lame, it will be the first in the herd to be attacked by wolves, but the wolf who appears weak or sick may lose status in the pack. This can have consequences in terms of having offspring.

To survive, then, an animal must not only be fit, it must look fit. The sense of shame, painful to experience, may provide an emotional reason to hide infirmity.

35 Sickness and injury are often concealed. To the despair of animal breeders and veterinarians, many captive animals will diligently conceal all signs of sickness until they are too far gone to be saved. Birds are particularly adept at this, sometimes hiding all symptoms and enduring secretly until the moment when they literally topple from their perches.

Scottish red deer leave the herd when they become sick or are injured. At one time it was suggested that they did this for the good of the herd, but it seems probable that a lone deer is less likely to be spotted by a predator than a herd of deer—and if a herd of deer is spotted, then the sick or injured one is most likely to be the first animal attacked. If the deer recovers, it returns to the herd. If predators zero in on difference, not merely weakness, animals might feel vulnerable or ashamed of things that attract the gaze of others.

It might seem odd that shame could lead to blushing. At first glance it seems counterproductive for an animal to blush visibly or physically show embarrassment: it does not look good, and isn't the objective to look good or at least not to stand out? The tingle of the blush could conceivably signal the blusher to hide (or give them something to hide), which serves the purpose of concealing the original weakness that the blusher was embarrassed about. Most animals do not blush visibly, if at all, so it may be that humans (some of us) do have a small claim to distinction in being the most visible blushers, even if we do not prove unique in feeling shame.

Pet owners often say that their cat or dog hates to be laughed at. Elephant keepers have reported that elephants who are laughed at have responded by filling their trunks with water and spraying those who are mocking them. It seems curious that animals that do not laugh might recognize and resent laughter. But perhaps laughter should be considered the equivalent expression of something they do feel themselves, and they are better translators than we are.

GUILT

Guilt—feeling remorse for a particular act—can be trickier to pin down than shame. An action that carries overtones of guilt usually does so because our culture has informed us that it is wrong. Guilt is easily confounded with fear of discovery and subsequent disapproval or punishment. The chimpanzee Nim Chimpsky ... was taught the sign for "sorry" and used it when he had "misbehaved," just as Alex the parrot has said "I'm sorry" after biting his trainer. The examples of Nim's misdeeds that are cited — breaking a toy or jumping around too much — do not seem to be things that a chimpanzee would naturally regard as bad. Like human children, he knew it was misbehavior only because he had been taught so. Sometimes Nim signed "sorry" before his teachers noticed what he had done. Whether Nim felt something other than the desire to avert possible wrath is unclear. On the other hand, this is often unclear in humans, as well.

40 Washoe's adopted son Loulis was teasing Roger Fouts one day, "just being a pill," and poked him harder than usual, cutting Fouts with his nail. "I made a big deal of it, crying and so on. Later, whenever I showed him that, to make him feel guilty, if you will, to use it to exploit that, he would squeeze his eyes tight and turn away. He would refuse to look at me whenever I tried to show him or talk about this old, old scratch that he had given me." There are a variety of possible interpretations for this extraordinarily familiar behavior, but guilt is very strongly suggested.

Dogs are the most familiar guilty animal for most people. Desmond Morris has argued persuasively that dogs do feel remorse for their actions at times. When a dog that has committed some misdeed greets a human in an unusually submissive manner before the person has any reason to guess what has happened, Morris says, it cannot be getting cues from human behavior. "It has an understanding that it has done something 'wrong.'"

Human shame has only recently been deemed a respectable field of study. Donald Nathanson recounts how, early in his career, he organized a symposium on shame. When it was over a friend took him aside, complimented him on the success of the symposium, and urged him not to do any more work on shame, lest he get a reputation for it. "It was in that moment that I learned that the very idea of shame is embarrassing to most people," Nathanson says. These are emotions to be hidden. Perhaps animals have been successful in hiding them from our gaze.

If social animals feel guilt and shame, other animals might learn to take advantage of this. When a young chimpanzee makes a fool of itself, as Freud did in the incident recounted by Jane Goodall, it would seem possible for other chimpanzees to ridicule the young animal, to draw the attention of their companions to the situation, and to exaggerate their reactions. There does not seem to be any evidence that they do in fact mock each other this way, and if so, in this they differ from human animals.

VOCABULARY

parisimonious: sparing, miserly 7
ostentatiously: deliberately seeking attention, grandly 10
provocation: stimulation 18
Lamarckian: relating to the theory of organic evolution that claims that changes to animals and plants are transmitted to their offspring 18
sensorium: parts of the mind that receive and interpret sensory signals 18
carnivorous: meat-eating 20
wattles: hanging flesh around the head or neck of a bird 20
mortification: embarrassment, humiliation 21
transgression: misbehaviour 23
mores: customs or moral attitudes 23
culling: collecting, gathering 27
wrath: anger 39
symposium: a meeting for the interchange of ideas 42

AUDIENCE AND PURPOSE

1. Why do Masson and McCarthy begin with Darwin, whose view of the subject differs so completely from theirs?
2. At what point do they return to Darwin in the essay? Why?
3. Look at the authors' attempts to define shame, embarrassment, and guilt. How do the definitions work to convince the reader of their aptness?

CONTENT

1. Can you determine why Darwin and nineteenth-century scientists preferred to believe that animals were incapable of feelings such as shame, embarrassment, and guilt?
2. Why do the authors use proper names when referring to the animals in their examples?
3. Masson and McCarthy use accumulated anecdotal examples to reinforce their view that animals experience emotions similar to ours. This tactic shows just how forceful examples can be. Analyze one or two examples to show how they are convincing and memorable for readers.

STYLE AND STRUCTURE

1. Why have the authors chosen to use headings to structure their essay?

2. Why do the authors not draw more explicit conclusions at the end of each section?
3. How do the authors give a sense of finality to their essay?
4. This essay is scientific, but its approach is not statistical or objective. How do the observations the authors include contribute to making the essay readable?

Definition

DEFINITION: CHARACTERIZING PRECISELY TO MAKE YOUR POINT

How Can I Know What I Mean Till I See What I Say?

Communication depends on shared meaning, the faith that what the writer meant to convey has been understood by the reader. One of the safeguards of clear communication is thus the inclusion of careful definition. As a result, almost any essay, using any rhetorical pattern, will demand that you define your terms at the outset. It's the one way to be sure that you have made clear what the boundaries of your discussion are intended to be.

Definition is seldom used in isolation. It is a means to an end, and that end is, ultimately, readers' understanding. More important, it is often the first step toward clarifying something in your readers' minds. When asked to define something in a formal way, most writers turn to the dictionary. In the dictionary, you find assembled words and meanings that a community of speakers has agreed on. If, for instance, you look up the word "comedy," you find something like the following in the dictionary: "A work (perhaps a novel, play, or film) that is amusing and usually has a happy ending." Such a dictionary definition is known as a formal definition. The job of a formal definition is to identify the class of things to which a particular term belongs and then to add other characteristics that distinguish it. Consequently, definitions of the formal kind should always take this form: "X may be classified as Y with distinguishing characteristic Z." You want to avoid writing imprecise definitions that don't follow this form, such as "A tornado is when whirling winds and funnel-shaped clouds create violent weather." It would be more appropriate to fall back on the suggested form: "A tornado is a violent storm with whirling winds and funnel-shaped clouds."

What is more important to you as a writer, however, is what you mean by a term that you are using. Many crucial questions that are suitable subjects for discussion in essays are founded on the need for a clear understanding of the meaning of terminology that is being used. Remember that you are building a case when you write an essay. It is as important for you to know what you mean by the term "self-defense," for example, as it would be for your lawyer in a trial. Your credibility as a writer hangs on your ability to convince the reader that your definition of a term is fair and appropriate.

When you set out to define something, you may use a number of other strategies to supplement the notion of formal definition with which we began. Often, writers use extended definition to provide reflections or meditations on a particular word or phrase with an eye to clarifying its meaning. In fact, that is often the technique of the sermon, which may take as its subject a single word like "charity" and from there go on to create a meditation on the meaning of the word and how it is enacted in one's daily life.

Other strategies may involve discussing the derivation of a word or phrase, often with the purpose of explaining how its meaning gradually changed to the current one. Such an etymological approach reminds us that definition is first and foremost a matter of words, how we choose them, and how our understanding of their meaning can change subtly or dramatically over time. A glance at a dictionary reveals that a ubiquitous word like "nice" has a complex history: despite its namby-pamby personality these days, it meant in Middle English something or someone "stupid" and in Old French something or someone "silly" or "naive." Discussions of the historical nuances in the meaning of a word can enlighten the reader about how human nature has changed too. Take the history of the word "inflammable," for example. It meant and means "easy to inflame or set on fire," but because the word is liable to be misunderstood (on spray cans and the like), the word "flammable" has also been coined to mean exactly the same thing, but perhaps with less ambiguity than its prefixed partner.

Another common approach to the problem of defining a term is to explain what it is not. This strategy of exclusion is a useful one because it allows the writer to set a term apart for special consideration. As Shakespeare writes, "Love is not love that alters when it alteration finds." Such an attempt at definition shows that one of the distinguishing features of love, as Shakespeare sees it, is its constancy, even in the face of change. This exclusionary or negative tactic goes some way toward establishing what sets love apart from other emotions.

The following paragraph shows some of these tactics in operation:

The topic sentence is followed by a definition in support of it. →

In these days of conspicuous consumption, there seems to be no such thing as enough. Even by definition, this seems true. Take, for example, the word "luxury," now common as dirt in advertisements, and coupled with everything from cars to condominiums. Changes in attitude toward material possessions are part of the interwoven meaning of this word, evidently. "Luxury" began life as a pejorative term that was ascribed to self-indulgent, excessive, indeed sinful, behaviour. Sometime in the 17th century, however, the word "luxury" underwent a sea-change. Then it began to acquire its current modern meaning, and things luxurious were assumed to be comfortable, costly, and — above all — desirable. Some people might argue that the word "luxury" may yet return to something closer to its humble roots, now that it seems to describe almost any new accommodation or vehicle that contains what have become standard requirements. What, to most of us, is luxury anyway? Do two bathrooms or the presence of carpet make for luxury, as contemporary realtors and car dealers are wont to suggest? Luxury, now, apparently has come to mean something close to "standard," at least in citified civilization. Whatever the case, there is no longer even the hint of sin or excess about the luxurious. Luxury now seems to describe what every civilized city dweller has a right to expect of his or her material possessions.

The Meaning of Integrity

Introduction →

When someone celebrates another for his or her "integrity," what is usually meant is that the person in question shows signs of admirable moral uprightness and exceptionally unshakable honesty. Built into the word is the notion that that is the

Thesis statement →

way it should be. Integrity is somehow what ought to be expected of a decent human being, who is, one supposes, capable of being safely integrated into the fabric of human society of which he or she forms a part.

The first point is developed through etymology.

At its core, integrity means "wholeness," and knowing that connection is a vital part of understanding what it means to have integrity. You could say that people who possess integrity leave no one in doubt about them, that they are wholeheartedly involved in something with nothing on reserve or nothing unaccounted for. As the Latin root suggests, they are "in touch," that is, rooted in their connections with others and hence wholly to be trusted. People with integrity leave no one in doubt, or divided, about them. It is no accident that the word "doubt," in turn, comes from roots that imply division or hesitation, being undecided, about something. Like the Latin origins of the word, the concept of "doubt" continues to carry the notion of division or "twoness" about it, in many languages, as in German, for example, which translates the word "doubt" as "das Zweifel" or literally "twoness." If you have integrity, then, no one has cause to doubt you or feel hesitant about you. You are sound as a dollar, and given the state of Canadian currency lately, probably sounder.

The second point is a reflection on the meaning using an example.

It might be said that a person acts with integrity when he or she never has any doubts about the actions to be taken. Think for a moment of the popular notion of the good angel and the bad angel, a device made familiar by Renaissance writers such as Christopher Marlowe. In one famous work, Marlowe portrayed his central character, Dr. Faustus, as a man beset by temptations embodied by these two creatures, one who spoke for his conscience, and the other who incited him to all sorts of doomed pleasures in exchange for his mortal soul. If one is able to resist such divisions and such bad angels, then one can be said to be at peace with oneself, or even more explicitly, at one with oneself. This last notion of at + one + ment is the source of the word "atonement," which describes the reconciliation of the divine and the human. Human beings, having fallen from the grace of God, need to overcome their division from God in order to reattain the statement of unity described in atonement. One of the moral requirements of regaining such a state of grace would seem to be moral integrity.

Conclusion

If you have integrity, then, you are wholly honest. Think about how this concept of wholeness underlies so many of our notions of what is morally good. Good people are wholehearted, go the whole nine yards, are ready to devote their whole lives to something. That kind of unflinching completeness is a mark of what we would like to expect of one another. People with integrity are not going to cross their fingers behind their backs when they make a promise; they are not going to say one thing to you, and quite another thing to somebody else; they are not, by definition, "two-faced." Integrity, it seems, means knowing and following the one true path.

Joyce Carol Oates

Joyce Carol Oates (b. 1938) is a writer whose most recent work is *The Collector of Hearts: New Tales of the Grotesque* (1998). She has taught at the University of Windsor and now teaches creative writing at Princeton. She began with psychological realism in novels such as *You Must Remember This* (1987), and *Because It Is Bitter, and Because It Is My Heart* (1990), and in the 1980s produced a series of Gothic novels (such as *Bellefleur* [1980]). An eclectic writer, Oates has even produced a series of pseudonymous suspense novels published under the name Rosamond Smith.

WHEN TRISTRAM MET ISOLDE

Love in the Western world—to borrow Denis de Rougemont's useful term—has come to mean, in the popular imagination, romantic love almost exclusively. Pure emotion, passion, "love at first sight"—we so take for granted the import of romantic love, it may come as a surprise to learn that the very concept of "love" based upon emotion as a high value, and not as an outlaw passion, is relatively new in the history of mankind.

Romantic love isn't so much a love that defies conventions, for romantic love is of all love types the most conventional, as a love that arises with seeming spontaneity: unwilled, undirected by others' suggestions or admonitions, raw and unpremeditated and of the heart; not cerebral and not genital. Romantic love is forever in opposition to formal, cultural and tribal prescriptions of behavior: arranged marriages, for instance, in which brides and their dowries are possessions to be handed over to a bridegroom and his family, or in which titled names are wed in businesslike arrangements that have little to do with the feelings of individuals. Arguably the most celebrated of late-20th-century public figures, Diana, Princess of Wales, would seem to have been a martyr to such an arrangement; her political marriage to Prince Charles ending in dissolution and divorce, and her "quest for personal happiness" (i.e., romantic love) ending in a grotesquely public death on a Parisian boulevard.

In the ancient world, romantic love would seem to have been virtually unknown, and rarely celebrated. Our generic term "love" didn't exist. The sentiment of romantic love as we know it was the homoerotic love of older Greek men for boys; marital love, which surely existed, seems oddly not to have been much honored, at least in surviving literature. Plato's elaborately extended metaphor of the republic, or the perfectly balanced state, discusses marriage primarily as mating; by contrast, Plato's "Symposium" celebrates homoerotic love in the most blushingly romantic terms. How different this is from the extramarital erotic attraction of heterosexuals, which results in devastation and violent death. In Euripides' "Hippolytus," for instance, the young Queen Phaedra falls in love with her husband's illegitimate son, who rejects her, and causes her to commit suicide; Phaedra is no romantic, but rather the victim of an ungovernable, unwished-for passion imposed upon her by Aphrodite. Such sexual desire is akin to a curse.

Where to the classical mind the intervention of eros in human affairs signals chaos, disaster and retribution, to the more modern, romantically inclined sensibility eros is the very engine of life's story, a seemingly inexhaustible fund of fantasies of (mostly heterosexual) desire. The adulterous tale of Sir Launcelot and Queen Guinevere, the wife of King Arthur, in Sir Thomas Malory's "Morte d'Arthur" strikes a startlingly contemporary note, though written in 1469; the illicit romances of Héloïse and Abélard, Tristram and Isolde and other medieval lovers concentrate upon an intensity of genuine feeling not found in earlier literature. By the 14th and 15th centuries, in aristocratic European societies at least, eros had become a fine art, worthy of a courtier's fullest attention. Not coarse sexuality but a refined *gentilesse* is the ideal of these romances; the love of the courtier for his lady, usually another man's wife, has been interpreted as a secularization of the medieval cult of the Virgin Mary, a "feminization" of the patriarchal Roman Catholic Church. These tales are inevitably from the male perspective: the lady is saintly, and of an unearthly beauty; or, in later refinements, the lady is cruel, even diabolical, and the courtier's passion becomes his punishment.

In subsequent centuries in the West, romantic love has triumphed as a sort of private, personal mystique linked with a high cultural value.

The quintessential romantic-minded heroine is Flaubert's Emma Bovary, a finely drawn portrait of a woman doomed to unhappiness in love. Emma is corrupted not by any actual man but by her reading; she yearns to locate, in the world, the elusive image of romantic passion. The problem with such yearning, Flaubert suggests, is that it invariably leads to disappointment.

At least one major American novelist, F. Scott Fitzgerald, wrote of virtually nothing except romantic love (and its unforeseen consequences), and it might be argued that writers as diverse as Carson McCullers and Jack Kerouac are essentially celebrants of homoerotic romance. John Updike, our intrepid explorer of love's willful illusions, would seem an American heir of Proust in both the poetic precision of his style and his fascination with erotic infatuation. Updike's preoccupations bring to mind a question of de Rougemont: "Without adultery, what would happen to imaginative writing?"

Coming of age in America for most of us has to do with falling under the spell of the culture's seductive promises about love: to grow up in the 50s, as I did, was to be bombarded with images of every kind of romantic-love idea. Advertisements presented unfailingly pretty feminine girl-women in various stages of bliss, always male-related; Hollywood movies dramatized the predominant—possibly for women the *only*—story of significance, the love story. Apart from these images of individuals fulfilled by romance, there were few others, and none as glamorous. (What images of the intellectual life, for instance? The artistic life?) Of course, these are clichés, and yet—what power clichés possess when we're young and vulnerable. "Romance" for me somehow became disembodied from any particular figure or icon and attached itself to the quest for adventure, the wild exploration itself. Luckily for me, I can't be disappointed in this "romance" precisely because it's purely abstract and imaginative.

Romantic love, that most precarious and gossamer of emotions, will surely survive the millennia that gave birth to it as long as a reasonably affluent civilization endures, for the secret of romantic love is economic: it's a luxury only some can afford, just as a refined taste in food is a consequence of a plentiful food supply. Is romantic love illusion? Delusion? An ideal dream? Just as the majority of humankind will continue to believe in gods of various denominations when no actual gods have been sighted, so men and women will continue to fall under the spell of romantic love and to shape, or misshape, their lives to that end. Biologists may grimly describe for us the mammalian underpinnings of courtship, mating, bonding, fidelity (where there is in fact fidelity)—but, being human, knowing full well as the song warns us that "falling in love with love is falling for make-believe," we are the species that demands to be lied to, in the nicest ways.

VOCABULARY

secularization: movement away from the sacred 4
quintessential: most typical 6
gossamer: anything thin or filmy 9

AUDIENCE AND PURPOSE

1. To what does the title refer?
2. Why does Oates include Princess Diana in her introduction?
3. Why does Oates conclude that romantic love is a luxury only some can afford?

CONTENT

1. How did the classical world see love in Oates's view?
2. When does romantic love emerge in Western culture, according to Oates?
3. What is the relation of love to literature, according to Oates?

STYLE AND STRUCTURE

1. Why does Oates use writers most often to illustrate what she means by romantic love?
2. Why does Oates talk about her personal coming of age and the clichéd images of romantic love in her time?
3. Why does Oates think that the desire for romantic love will continue?

Norman Doidge

Dr. Doidge (b. 1954), a writer and poet, is a research psychiatrist and psychoanalyst at the University of Toronto. His column appears every other Wednesday in the *National Post*.

DO CHILDREN "GET" IRONY? DUHHHH!

"Do you want to play some ball hockey now?" a certain overworked, empathically challenged father asks his nine-year-old son in the middle of playoff season.

"Duhhhh" is the reply.

Duhhhh has become one of the son's most potent weapons against his father's feeble-mindedness. Translation: "Oh, that's a tough one. Even though I've been waiting all day to play, and been waving my stick in your face since you got home, I still can't decide." He is using irony, or saying the opposite of what he means.

Duhhhh is not in the dictionary. It's not really even a word—that's the point. It is a form of feigned stupidity in which the son pretends he cannot even form a word. It doesn't rise to sarcasm, or bitter irony, because it is an invitation for more closeness. The musical jocularity belies the fact that a connection is desired, and that even the joke is meant to be shared. The son is speaking non-literally.

5 One reason we love nine-year olds is that they are discovering irony. Even in the 1990s these not-so-innocents sneak wry *Mad* magazines and flashlights under the blankets. They know everything there is to know about *The Simpsons*, a show laced with irony. Bart, unlike his slightly younger sister Lisa (who is still a goody two-shoes), is an exquisite ironist. His father, Homer, on the other hand, who takes things literally, is always in ironic situations, where he aims for one thing, and gets the opposite.

Non-literal speech is always factually incorrect. It includes metaphor (my love is a sweet flower), irony (saying the opposite of what you mean), or the non-factual exaggerations in most jokes. Ironically, it is non-literal speech that makes literature literary.

Adults, meanwhile, are increasingly inhibited from using non-literal speech in the workplace. Public institutions are increasingly filled with mere literal speech. Indeed, stale, recycled, literal speech is a major cause of sick building syndrome.

Thus, for instance, the Canadian Medical Protective Association (the group of lawyers who defend doctors against malpractice suits) recently advised MDs they had best be extremely careful when they make jokes that might be misinterpreted as offensive in emergency rooms, lest lawsuits arise. This is a pathetic attempt to end lawyer jokes while appearing to protect doctors, and won't work. Besides, anyone who has worked in an emergency room knows that sometimes the only way to survive the constant assault of anguish, pain, blood, pus, overwork, long shifts and lack of sleep is with a wry joke or two about the beauty of life. Hence it is probably no accident that the rise of political correctness coincided with grownups crowding around the family TV to watch *The Simpsons*, a kids' show. What you can't get at work, you get watching *The Simpsons* at home.

Literal speech consists of factual statements such as "Halifax is in Nova Scotia." That's a good thing, too. And it's necessary to know. But literal speech is actually often misunderstood. There is no greater proof of the insufficiency of literal speech than legal writing, which takes literalism to an extreme because it aims to avoid any possible misinterpretation. But, like legal documents, it ends up being understood by almost no one, and it's completely unattractive, unmusical and unimaginative, because the reader doesn't ever know what's important.

10 As kids start to understand irony, it means that they now know not only about the facts of the situation, but what the speaker believes about them, and what the speaker thinks about the person he is speaking to. Hence irony is interpersonal and intimate, and an appetite for it in kids signals an increasing comprehension of other minds, and psychological mindedness. An understanding of ironic situations (as in *Mad*'s "The Lighter Side of...") shows they now know that the best-laid plans often go awry and that people can be pretty rotten, and thus signals the emergence of prudence alongside of mischief. Ironic, mischievous Bart is more likely to end up more prudent than his doltish sucker of a father, whose "get rich quick" schemes take things at face value.

Irony isn't always negative. If you say to someone who always snatches victory from the jaws of defeat, after they triumph once again, "I hear you flubbed it as usual," you are really saying, "You did great, as usual, despite your doubts." That's gentle, supportive irony. Irony, so in love with opposites, takes into account that people are filled with conflicts and opposite inclinations.

The printed word isn't as friendly to irony as it looks. It is designed to appear intimate, while appealing to a mass audience.

But as no one is really present (present company excluded), the use of irony in print is rarely as exquisitely attuned, or tuneful, as it is in normal speech. Intonation, or tune, is essential to decoding irony. The same statement delivered deadpan, or in overly sincere tones, has a different meaning.

The most famous purveyor of irony after Bart Simpson is Socrates, who never did his homework, and thus never wrote anything, though Plato copied down almost everything he said, handed it in as his own work and got an A.

Socrates' excuse for not writing was that there are serious problems in setting stylus to papyrus because one does not know who might read what you write. Socrates invented Socratic irony. He pretended he knew nothing, and then asked people simple questions, like "What is the Good?" or "What is the Beautiful?" which exposed that others knew less than they thought. Bart also feigns ignorance and asks annoying questions of his teacher, such as "How's the diet going?" and "Why did they name Uranus Uranus?" and "Why do dogs sniff our butts?"

Irony is always judgmental. The ironist conveys what he *really* thinks about things, by saying the opposite. Irony polarizes, because it divides the world between those who "get it" and those who don't. The ironist can say the politically correct thing, mean the opposite, and create a silent chuckle in the minds of those who "get it." The typical dimestore-university-speech-code-inquisitor still hasn't made saying the politically correct thing a crime. So ironists sometimes walk.

But not always. Socrates was attacked for being an ironist at his trial, and consequently had to stand in the corner and drink his hemlock all by himself.

Ellen Winner has written a wonderful book, *The Point of Words*, reviewing psychological empirical studies of the age at which children begin to understand irony. Psychologists (by telling children all sorts of stories and getting reactions) have been trying to determine when a kid can understand that someone who spills spaghetti sauce on himself and says, "Great," is being ironic, as opposed to inviting the kids to start a food fight. Up to a certain age, if a child witnesses a spill and hears a grownup growl "Great," the child might think the grownup is mistaken, silly or lying. Then, at a certain age, the child can separate the words people say from what they really believe, and even realize that not all people who say things that they don't believe are liars. They are no longer literalists, but interesting, more empathic creatures, who are now capable of irony's deliciousness.

And just when is this magical age, when it all comes together? About the age of nine, which happens to be the age of the immortal ageless ironist, the grade-four hooky artist and schoolyard philosopher, Bartholomew J. Simpson.

VOCABULARY

feigned: pretended 4
jocularity: jolly, playful 4
belies: contradicts 4
wry: ironically humourous 5
awry: off-course 10
intonation: the rise and fall in pitch of the voice 12
purveyor: supplier 13
empathic: feeling, sensitive 17

AUDIENCE AND PURPOSE

1. Why does Doidge begin with a story? Who do you think the father and son are? Why doesn't he say so?
2. Why does Doidge combine evidence from psychology with examples from pop culture to make his point?
3. Give an example of how Doidge uses irony to explain irony.

CONTENT

1. Why, according to Doidge, are adults forced to speak literally these days?
2. Why does irony seem to Doidge to be a mark of maturity in children?
3. Why is irony harder to achieve in print than in person?

STYLE AND STRUCTURE

1. What does the title imply?
2. How does Doidge defend irony as valuable to children and to adults? Provide examples.
3. Why does Doidge include Socrates among his examples?
4. Why does Doidge end with a reference to Bart Simpson?

Erika Ritter

Erika Ritter (b. 1948) is a Canadian playwright whose most-produced play is *Automatic Pilot* (1980), for which she won the Floyd S. Chalmers Canadian Play Award. She is also a radio broadcaster, and the author of two books of humour essays and a number of short works of fiction and nonfiction.

GUILT

Some time ago, I received a polite mailing from my credit card company, informing me that a user fee would soon be charged on credit transactions involving the card. The reason for this change in policy was explained as follows: "Many customers pay their accounts in full each month and thus have not carried any of the increased servicing costs."

I must say I admired their crust. Under no circumstances was the company going to be bullied into a position of accepting responsibility for this regrettable but necessary development. Instead, the blame was being placed squarely where it belonged — on the scrawny shoulders of the overly conscientious consumer whose prompt paying habits had created the problem in the first place.

Yessiree, I thought, humming purposefully as I snipped the plastic card into several pieces and force-fed them to the guppy. Here was yet another glittering example of the many constructive uses of Guilt.

Guilt, as you probably know, is big business. And nowhere is the trading in guilt-edged insecurities brisker than right here in Canada.

5 Now, steady on there a minute, I hear you saying. What about the Germans? Don't they lead the world in guilt production? And let's not forget about the Americans, who managed to agonize their way through a civil war, the bombing of Hiroshima, and the invasion of Vietnam in the same length of time it took Canadians to sign up for Confederation and pick a flag. Now, surely the Americans have a much larger stockpile of guilt than Canadians do.

You'd think so, but apparently not.

I was pretty surprised, myself, when I completed my research and tabulated my findings on the subject, to discover that Canada has probably the world's largest untapped supply of guilt. If you're still unconvinced, allow me to share with you some of the highlights of my exploration of this rich field.

SOURCES OF GUILT: THE OLD, MIDDLE, AND NEW KINGDOMS

In the sixties, God said, "Let there be Guilt," to which the civil rights activists and war protesters replied, "Right on!"

Of course, in this country, the issue of moral responsibility was slightly complicated by the fact that we just didn't *feel* all that morally responsible, somehow, for the lousy state of the world. After all, Canadians weren't the ones flambé-ing churches in Alabama, or playing Sink the Sub in the Gulf of Tonkin, right?

10 Consequently, it was with a certain amount of understandable confusion that we chanted, "We shall overcome," and "Hell no, we won't go." Overcome what? Go where?

My God, we began to think nervously, is it marginally possible that we're out here shouting, "Hey, hey, LBJ, how many kids did you kill today?" only because we can't think of a rhyme for Pearson? I mean, what kind of people does that make us, anyway? Coattailing on other people's crises just because we don't have a government that's sufficiently together to murder the cream of the country's youth. How low can you get?

It was in attempting to grope toward an answer to that question, and many others, that we lost our collective footing, and stumbled instead upon the mother lode of Canadian guilt.

In the Middle Period of the Guilted Age—the 1970s—social causes were largely replaced by a rabid and earnest contemplation of the self. Nevertheless, the so-called Me Generation was still able to make time to feel guilty about its self-absorption, and once more Canadians were soon able to take a commanding lead, with significant pioneering work in the concept of Feeling Guilty About Feeling Guilty.

The fact that the best-selling self-help book of the period, *If I'm My Own Best Friend, Why Can't I Feel Okay About Looking Out For Number One?*, was written by an American and published in the States only assisted conscience-stricken Canadian nationalists in their never-ending quest for ultimate self-castigation.

15 The advent of the 1980s, however, saw a whole new development in the Canadian Guilt industry, in the form of the No-Win Situation, which, as observant students of guilt have pointed out, is really a refinement of the Middle Period's guilt-for-guilt's-sake syndrome writ large.

The No-Win Situation is best exemplified by the dilemma of a man who begins by feeling guilty about being out of shape, and tries to take up jogging to rectify the problem—only to end up feeling even more guilty when he learns that jogging may be as bad for him as obesity.

For such a person, no alternative provides any relief. Noontime racquetball makes him feel guilty as he flaunts his dufflebag and racquet under the nose of his secretary, typing reports on her lunch-hour. Dieting reminds him uneasily of the starving millions for whom slimming cannot be construed as an option.

He could, of course, solve his weight problem by taking up smoking. Or could he?

SOCIAL USES OF GUILT

Nowhere else in Canada has guilt proved its value as a natural resource so dramatically as it has in the bullying and intimidation of smokers.

At one time during the 1970s, it was considered necessary to create no-smoking zones in public buildings, restaurants, and movie theatres in order to impress upon smokers that their kind wasn't wanted here.

Now, however, guilt alone can do the trick. Verify this by observing the action at the next party you go to, where you will notice the few smokers huddled in secluded corners like hunted things, pursuing their lonely depravity.

Fine and dandy. That is, of course, as it should be in a society that is so guilt-oriented that the government spends the millions that it reaps in tobacco taxes on advertising campaigns that flagellate us about the dangers of smoking.

But where guilt really comes to a finely honed point in the smoking issue is the clever way in which the smokers at parties are manipulated into assuaging their guilt by accommodating a steady stream of *schnorrers*, who intrude upon their Molokai-like seclusion in order to bum a smoke because they "still enjoy one with a drink."

For their part, economists have begun to puzzle over the mathematical fragility of a supply-and-demand situation in which everybody appears to be smoking, while hardly anyone seems to actually buy any more. The centre, they have warned us time and again, cannot possibly hold—and then to allay their apprehensions, they promptly beg us to spot them a cigarette.

DISTRIBUTION OF GUILT BY REGIONS

Guilt can be found in great abundance in almost every province of Canada. But then, such a widespread distribution is hardly surprising in a nation whose motto speaks movingly of the onerous responsibility of ensuring that the shoreline of the country continues to meet the ocean on either side; a nation whose anthem rashly pledges the citizenry to stand endlessly on guard, but never once intimates against *what*; a nation whose long-standing Prime Minister gave new meaning to the phrase "responsible government" by carefully explaining to us time and again that the state of the economy was really our fault.

However, there are certain areas of Canada in which guilt can be found in particularly rich concentrations, and it is important for us to understand how this circumstance has come about.

Central Canada — otherwise known as Ontario — is enormously well-endowed with guilt, especially in its southern regions, where the city of Toronto is generally known as "Canada's Guilt Capital," and features a tall, tower-like monument that is, in fact, in the shape of the world's tallest free-standing nail, as a symbol of how willingly Toronto has impaled itself on the sins of the rest of the country.

Guilt in Toronto is available in quantity on almost every downtown street, where citizens can be heard remarking to each other that the current bad weather must be payment for the lovely summer the year before, and exhorting their friends to "Take care, eh?" (which phrase, etymologists tell us, is merely a colloquial derivative of the more formal injunction to "Stand on guard" found in the aforementioned national anthem).

As far as the rest of the country goes, it is customary in matters pertaining to Canada to assume that the concept of regional disparity has a relevant part to play in any comparison study of one area with another. In the case of guilt, however, it is far too simplistic to hypothesize that it is the relatively affluent regions of the country that hold the monopoly on this precious substance.

To the contrary, in the Maritime provinces — designated traditionally as a have-not area — guilt has always run very high, partly as a result of a great concentration of Scottish forebears (see The Origins of Guilt, below) and partly because they got all the best lobsters.

And whatever the state of its fortunes, one of the most guilt-ridden parts of the country throughout history has always been the prairie region, especially during those Depression-era times when the area had very little going for it economically. What Alberta, Saskatchewan, and Manitoba managed to find to feel guilty about at the height of the Dust Bowl period has never been clear, except that psychologists feel there is reason to suspect a residual sense of carelessness, arising from the inexplicable misplacement of so many buffalo in the late nineteenth century.

Interestingly, the only virtually guilt-free province in Canada is Quebec, where, in spite of a strong Roman Catholic heritage, guilt has been almost totally eradicated, following an assiduous and thorough-going government campaign involving legislation to make innocence the working emotion in La Belle Province.

The Quebec experience may give rise to some uneasy speculation about the possible fate of guilt in the rest of the country. In order to reassure ourselves that this valuable substance is indeed a renewable resource, we must look closely at its origins.

Can we possibly discover where Canadian guilt comes from? Do we have any idea how it was formed? And will Canadians ever run out of this precious material? The answers to those questions are: Yes, maybe, and emphatically not.

THE ORIGINS OF GUILT

Like so much else in this country, Canadian guilt was originally imported from Great Britain, particularly Scotland, whose downtrodden inhabitants swarmed eagerly to this land of promise in their grateful thousands (albeit at gunpoint) in the early part of the last century.

No one is exactly certain how the Scots got to feel so guilty in the first place, considering that they were a hard-pressed people with little that others might envy, unless others happened to have an unaccountable yen for blood pudding or chapped knees.

In the absence of other data, some historians have speculated that it may have been Calvinism that caused the Scots to feel so guilty as a people, and they point, by way of evidence, to the interesting fact that there was indeed a theologian named John Calvin whose teachings did exert enormous influence over the peoples of Northern Europe at one time.

Other scholars, however, dismiss the postulated link between Calvinism and this John Calvin person as far too tenuous to be credited, and insist instead that Calvinism was, in fact, derived from a spiritualist cult of the nineteenth century the devotees of which anticipated the sour visage of future American President Calvin Coolidge in a dream, and subsequently organized their worship around preparing themselves for Calvin's coming by learning to speak without moving their lips or making any extravagant gestures.

So much for the origins of guilt in Canada. It is now time to examine yet another vital question in the evolution of this bountiful natural resource. Namely, what were the enormous subterranean pressures that have transformed the raw material of Calvinistic guilt into the highly refined neurotic substance in the production of which our country leads the world today?

DISTRIBUTION OF GUILT BY SEX: A DEMOGRAPHIC OVERVIEW

40 As far as the conversion process by which guilt is created is concerned, sex has always been nature's perfect catalyst. Which is perhaps why experts tell us that as long as human relationships endure, so will guilt. Hence, it would seem there is no real reason to fear the coming of a day when Canadians wake up to find themselves fresh out of the emotional fuel that powers the giant turbines of remorse, entrapment, repining, and resentment that provide, in their turn, the energy source for more than ninety per cent of the human interaction in this country.

But how equal is the distribution of guilt between the sexes? Not very. Up-to-date surveys show us that in this regard, as in so many others, men have been endowed with the lion's share of a valuable resource material.

In extramarital relationships, for example, men demonstrate a striking proclivity for wallowing in regret and self-recrimination, to a degree that quickly creates fatigue and ennui in their part-time partner in debauchery. "My wife is a wonderful woman," they can be heard to say, over and over. "If she knew what I was up to, it would kill her."

Having so said, many men then proceed to go to any number of preposterous lengths to prove this lachrymose thesis by finding ways to ensure that the aforementioned wonderful woman does indeed get to know what they are up to. Surprisingly, however, intelligence regarding her husband's activities seldom kills her; more commonly, she will be heard to make extravagant statements about wanting to kill *him*. But not even the threat of death will deter a truly determined man from feeling guilty about philandering, and he is generally prepared to feel guilty again and again.

However, while men get to derive three-quarters of their enjoyment of illicit sex from the life-giving *frisson* of guilt it inspires, women have not been so lucky, and have always had to make their own fun in the adultery department. Try as they will (and they do try, believe me), women simply cannot bring themselves to feel very guilty about fooling around.

45 Women learn from an early age that, although the world may have short-changed them in the guilt department, they have been somewhat compensated by a generous endowment in the area of rationalization. Thus it becomes possible for any woman to justify an extra-curricular dalliance as a form of self-esteem enhancement absolutely vital to the well-being of her marriage and, indeed, being undertaken solely for the ultimate (if admittedly somewhat indirect) benefit of her husband.

In other areas of guilt-ridden social interaction — such as the workplace — Canadian men have also shown themselves to be miles ahead of their female counterparts. For example, a man will always be very careful to tell a female co-worker how badly he feels about earning twice as much as she does for doing the same job (sometimes even showing her his pay-cheque stub for emphasis), while most women lack the imagination and sensitivity to understand how a man could feel so poignantly about a situation he shows no apparent intention of rectifying.

Men are likewise extremely uncomfortable with the kind of ruthless tactics the cut-throat executive world often forces them to indulge in, which is the main reason they often find it necessary to linger over three-martini lunches, merely to blunt the keen edges of their remorse.

Meanwhile, their free-wheeling female employees can be found back in the office, polishing off nourishing portions of no-name cottage cheese and caffeine-reduced Tab at their comfortable desks, before ambling out of doors to enjoy the rest of an idle forty-five-minute lunch-hour picking up a birthday gift for the boss's wife, dropping off their husband's drycleaning, doing their mother's banking, and then sauntering in a leisurely way over to their son's school to exchange lighthearted speculations with the principal as to what might have inspired the child to set fire to several of his classmates.

GUILT IN NATURE: A SPECIAL CONSIDERATION

Although human beings tend to think of themselves as having a monopoly on the sensitive emotion under discussion, studies on less highly evolved creatures show great natural reservoirs of guilt in many familiar Canadian species.

50 For instance, scientists now believe that our national symbol, the beaver, is not so much busy as overwrought. He may, in fact, undertake his ambitious construction projects merely as a way of assuaging the guilt stemming from feelings of hostility and re-

sentment at being relegated to the five-cent piece, while the comparatively low-profile caribou gets to luxuriate on the quarter.

Meanwhile, in the domain of our feathered friends, we have come to see that the number one Bird in a Guilted Cage is none other than our very own Canada Goose, as demonstrated by this creature's unwavering tendency to begin every sentence with "I'm sorry, but..."

But the most compelling evidence for the excessive guiltiness of Canadian animals over the species of other countries comes from a detailed examination made of various breeds of dogs emanating from different lands.

While the tiny Chihuahua derives ample job-satisfaction from selling garish postcards and crudely executed pottery by the roadside; while the Irish setter is happy to waste entire days in the pub telling extravagant stories; and while even the American cocker feels entitled to relax on weekends in front of the TV, Canada's own Labrador is a virtual canine workaholic.

Not content to spend a full day retrieving in the marshes, the Labrador is often found also attending evening education courses, where he learns how to become a security guard, or readies himself for the job of helping the handicapped.

55 The Labrador is also possessed of a highly developed social conscience, and while he has sometimes been criticized abroad for remaining dumb on human-rights issues, it must be noted that he tries to make a point of keeping himself abreast of current affairs, and shows a keen interest in newspapers from an early age.

THE FUTURE OF CANADIAN GUILT: A CONCLUSION

Whither Canadian guilt? Or, to put the question another way, what should be done with our abnormally generous allotment of this valuable resource — besides just feeling guilty about it?

My own recommendation, based on the research I have undertaken, is that we seriously consider the possibility of exporting our national guilt, the logical successor to wheat.

Naturally infectious, guilt is therefore easily transported. More importantly, the psychological complexities suggested by this valuable resource promise to do much to upgrade Canada's shambling bucolic image abroad as a mere hewer of wood and drawer of you-know-what.

In fact, in contemplating a sanguine future for this country as a major guilt supplier to the world, only one consideration need sober us and continue to niggle at the back of the mind: how do we prevent the Japanese from finding a way to produce guilt better and cheaper than we can?

VOCABULARY

crust: nerve 2
self-castigation: self-criticism, scolding 14
depravity: corruption 21
flagellate: whip 22
assuaging: relieving 23
Molokai: one of the Hawaiian islands and a former leper colony 23
allay: to calm 24
onerous: burdensome 25
intimates: implies 25
impaled: pierced 27
etymologists: those who study word origins 28
injunction: ordered 28
residual: remaining 31
eradicated: wiped out 32
assiduous: careful 32
postulated: theorized 38
tenuous: flimsy 38
catalyst: trigger 40
repining: longing, discontent 40
proclivity: tendency 42
ennui: boredom (French) 42
debauchery: indulgence in the sensual 42
lachrymose: pitiable 43
philandering: adulterous 43
frisson: shiver (French) 44
dalliance: a casual affair 45
poignantly: movingly 46
overwrought: overexcited 50
luxuriate: relax 50
emanating: coming out 51
garish: flashy, gaudy 53
bucolic: pastoral 58
sanguine: cheerful, optimistic 59

AUDIENCE AND PURPOSE

1. What is Ritter's thesis statement?
2. How does her opening anecdote reinforce her thesis?
3. Why does Ritter include references to surveys and demographic studies?

CONTENT

1. Why does Ritter label the 60s, 70s, and 80s in her explanation of the guilt of Canada?
2. How is smoking affected by guilt in Ritter's estimation?
3. How does Ritter illustrate that women have nothing to feel guilty about compared with men?
4. What picture does Ritter paint of the Canadian identity?

STYLE AND STRUCTURE

1. How do the headings add to the humour of Ritter's piece?
2. Why do you think Ritter deals with guilt in nature near the end of the essay?
3. How is Ritter's conclusion effective?

Alberto Manguel

Alberto Manguel (b. 1948) is a Canadian author best known for his book *A History of Reading* (1996), a survey of reading from prehistoric times to the present day. His most recent work is entitled *Through the Looking-Glass Wood* (1999).

POINT OF ORDER: IN PRAISE OF THE DOT THAT BROUGHT SENTENCES TO THEIR SENSES

Diminutive as a mote of dust, a mere peck of the pen, a crumb on the keyboard, the full stop—the period—is the unsung legislator of our writing systems. Without it, there would be no end to the sorrows of young Werther, and the travels of the Hobbit would have never been completed. Its absence allowed James Joyce to weave "Finnegans Wake" into a perfect circle, and its presence made Henri Michaux compare our essential being to this dot, "a dot that death devours." It crowns the fulfillment of thought, gives the illusion of conclusiveness, possesses a certain haughtiness that stems, like Napoleon's, from its minuscule size. Anxious to get going, we require nothing to signal our beginnings, but we need to know when to stop: this tiny memento mori reminds us that everything, ourselves included, must one day come to a halt. As an anonymous English teacher suggested in the 1680 "Treatise of Stops, Points or Pauses," a full stop is "a Note of perfect Sense, and of a perfect Sentence."

The need to indicate the end of a written phrase is probably as old as writing itself, but the solution, brief and wonderful, was not set down until the Italian Renaissance. For ages, punctuation had been a desperately erratic affair. Already in the first century A.D., the Spanish author Quintilian (who had not read Henry James) had argued that a sentence, as well as expressing a complete idea, had to be capable of being delivered in a single breath. How that sentence should be ended was a matter of personal taste, and for a long time scribes punctuated their texts with all manner of signs and symbols—from a simple blank space to a variety of dots and slashes. In the early fifth century, St. Jerome, translator of the Bible, devised a system known as *per cola et commata,* in which each unity of sense would be signaled by a letter jutting out of the margin, as if beginning a new paragraph. Three centuries later, the *punctus*, or dot, was used to indicate both a pause within the sentence and the sentence's conclusion.

Following such muddled conventions, authors could hardly expect their public to read a text in the sense they had intended.

Then in 1566, Aldus Manutius the Younger, grandson of the great Venetian printer to whom we owe the invention of the paperback, defined the full stop in his punctuation handbook, "Interpungendi ratio." Here, in clear and unequivocal Latin, Manutius described for the first time its ultimate role and aspect. He thought he was offering a manual for typographers; he couldn't have known that he was granting us, future readers, the gifts of sense and music in all the literature to come: Hemingway and his staccato, Beckett and his recitativo, Proust and his largo sostenuto.

"No iron," Isaac Babel wrote, "can stab the heart with such force as a full stop put just at the right place." As an acknowledgment of both the power and the helplessness of the word, nothing else has served us better than this faithful and final speck.

VOCABULARY

diminutive: tiny 1
mote: speck 1
minuscule: minute, little 1
memento mori: a reminder of death or of human mortality (Latin) 1
erratic: unpredictable 2
unequivocal: unambiguous 3
staccato: disjointed 3
recitativo: rhythmically free vocal style (Italian) 3
largo sostenuto: slow, sustained, and stately music (Italian) 3

AUDIENCE AND PURPOSE

1. What is Manguel's thesis statement?
2. What is the meaning of the title?
3. This essay originally appeared in a magazine celebrating the new millennium. Why is it a suitable piece for such a collection?

CONTENT

1. Manguel urges readers to see the period as an invention. Why?
2. In what way is the period a memento mori, a reminder of death?
3. Why is the period a symbol of both "power and helplessness"?

STYLE AND STRUCTURE

1. How does Manguel's discussion of the history of the period add to the weight of his subject?
2. How does Manguel emphasize the music in language?
3. Is there a point to the shortness of this essay? Explain.
4. Why did the editors choose such a large period to end the piece?

Pico Iyer

Pico Iyer (b. 1957) is a travel writer who has written for *Time, Harper's,* and *The New York Review of Books.* His works include *Cuba and the Night* (1995), *Falling Off the Map: Some Lonely Places of the World* (1993), *The Lady and the Monk* (1991), and *Video Night in Kathmandu* (1988). *Tropical Classical* (1997) is a collection of essays about travel; his latest book, *The Global Soul* (2000), is a collection of transnational cultural essays.

IN PRAISE OF THE HUMBLE COMMA

The gods, they say, give breath, and they take it away. But the same could be said—could it not?—of the humble comma. Add it to the present clause, and, of a sudden, the mind is, quite literally, given pause to think; take it out if you wish or forget it and the mind is deprived of a resting place. Yet still the comma gets no respect. It seems just a slip of a thing, a pedant's tick, a blip on the edge of our consciousness, a kind of printer's smudge almost. Small, we claim, is beautiful (especially in the age of the microchip). Yet what is so often used, and so rarely recalled, as the comma—unless it be breath itself?

Punctuation, one is taught, has a point: to keep up law and order. Punctuation marks are the road signs placed along the highway of our communication—to control speeds, provide directions and prevent head-on collisions. A period has the unblinking finality of a red light; the comma is a flashing yellow light that asks us only to slow down; and the semicolon is a stop sign that tells us to ease gradually to a halt, before gradually starting up again. By establishing the relations between words, punctuation establishes the relations between the people using words. That may be one reason why schoolteachers exalt it and lovers defy it ("We love each other and belong to each other let's don't ever hurt each other Nicole let's don't ever hurt each other," wrote Gary Gilmore to his girlfriend). A comma, he must have known, "separates inseparables," in the clinching words of H.W. Fowler, King of English Usage.

Punctuation, then, is a civic prop, a pillar that holds society upright. (A run-on sentence, its phrases piling up without division, is as unsightly as a sink piled high with dirty dishes.) Small wonder, then, that punctuation was one of the first proprieties of the Victorian age, the age of the corset, that the modernists threw off: the sexual revolution might be said to have begun when Joyce's Molly Bloom spilled out all her private thoughts in 36 es of unbridled, almost unperioded and officially censored prose; and another rebellion was surely marked when E.E. Cummings first felt free to commit "God" to the lower case.

Punctuation thus becomes the signature of cultures. The hot-blooded Spaniard seems to be revealed in the passion and urgency of his doubled exclamation points and question marks ("*¡Caramba! ¿Quien sabe?*"), while the impassive Chinese traditionally added to his so-called inscrutability by omitting directions from his ideograms. The anarchy and commotion of the '60s were given voice in the exploding exclamation marks, riotous capital letters and Day-Glo italics of Tom Wolfe's spray-paint prose; and in Communist societies, where the State is absolute, the dignity—and divinity—of capital letters is reserved for Ministries, Sub-Committees and Secretariats.

5 Yet punctuation is something more than a culture's birthmark; it scores the music in our minds, gets our thoughts moving to the rhythm of our hearts. Punctuation is the notation in the sheet music of our words, telling us when to rest, or when to raise our voices; it acknowledges that the meaning of our discourse, as of any symphonic composition, lies not in the units but in the pauses, the pacing and the phrasing. Punctuation is the way one bats one's eyes, lowers one's voice or blushes demurely. Punctuation adjusts the tone and color and volume till the feeling comes into perfect focus: not disgust exactly, but distaste; not lust, or like, but love.

Punctuation, in short, gives us the human voice, and all the meanings that lie between the words. "You aren't young, are you?" loses its innocence when it loses the question mark. Every child knows the menace of a dropped apostrophe (the parent's "Don't do that" shifting into the more slowly enunciated "Do not do that"), and every believer, the ignominy of having his faith reduced to "faith." Add an exclamation point to "To be or not to be ..." and the gloomy Dane has all the resolve he needs; add a comma, and the noble sobriety of "God save the Queen" becomes a cry of desperation bordering on double sacrilege.

Sometimes, of course, our markings may be simply a matter of aesthetics. Popping in a comma can be like slipping on the necklace that gives an outfit quiet elegance, or like catching the sound of running water that complements, as it completes, the silence of a Japanese landscape. When V.S. Naipaul, in his latest novel, writes, "He was a middle-aged man, with glasses," the first comma can seem a little precious. Yet it gives the description a spin, as well as a subtlety, that it otherwise lacks, and it shows that the glasses are not part of the middle-agedness, but something else.

Thus all these tiny scratches give us breadth and heft and depth. A world that has only periods is a world without inflections. It is a world without shade. It has a music without sharps and flats. It is a martial music. It has a jackboot rhythm. Words cannot bend and curve. A comma, by comparison, catches the gentle drift of the mind in thought, turning in on itself and back on itself, reversing, redoubling and returning along the course of its own sweet river music; while the semicolon brings clauses and thoughts together with all the silent discretion of a hostess arranging guests around her dinner table.

Punctuation, then, is a matter of care. Care for words, yes, but also, and more important, for what the words imply. Only a lover notices the small things: the way the afternoon light catches the nape of a neck, or how a strand of hair slips out from behind an ear, or the way a finger curls around a cup. And no one scans a letter so closely as a lover, searching for its small print, straining to hear its nuances, its gaps, its sighs and hesitations, poring over the secret messages that lie in every cadence. The difference between "Jane (whom I adore)" and "Jane, whom I adore," and the difference between them both and "Jane — whom I adore — " marks all the distance between ecstasy and heartache. "No iron can pierce the heart with such force as a period put at just the right place," in Isaac Babel's lovely words; a comma can let us hear a voice break, or a heart. Punctuation, in fact, is a labor of love. Which brings us back, in a way, to gods.

VOCABULARY

clause: part of a sentence that contains both a subject and a verb 1
pedant: fussy scholar 1
exalt: raise in status 2
proprieties: conventional rules of behaviour 3
impassive: expressionless 4
enunciated: pronounced 6
ignominy: disgrace 6
sobriety: soberness 6
sacrilege: irreverent violation of the sacred 6
aesthetics: theory of beauty 7
precious: excessively fussy 7
heft: weight 8
inflections: changes in the pitch of the voice 8

ɔoot: military boot 8
ɹances: subtleties 9
cadence: rhythm 9

AUDIENCE AND PURPOSE

1. Iyer's introduction suggests the insignificance of the comma. Yet how are the seeds planted to argue for its value?
2. How does Iyer use the reader's associations as he strings together different metaphors related to the comma? Give examples.
3. Iyer takes us from the sterile world of rules to the emotional truths of self-expression and love. Show how this gradual building up of significance is achieved.

CONTENT

1. How does Iyer use examples to show that punctuation is a measure of morality and culture?
2. In what way does Iyer compare punctuation with music?
3. Iyer argues in this essay that details are of vital importance. What concrete details does he use to bring his subject to life?

STYLE AND STRUCTURE

1. Iyer makes extensive use of the metaphor to define the comma. What are some of the things he compares the comma with?
2. Iyer uses punctuation with considerable style himself. Give some examples.
3. How does punctuation accumulate significance as the essay continues?
4. Why does Iyer start and end with the gods?

Process

PROCESS: EXPLAINING HOW SOMETHING IS DONE

Putting the Horse Before the Cart

Process essays, when they are good, are clear and easy for the reader to follow. Many of them offer readers a sequence of events, or a set of instructions, intended to guide them from first to last by following the outlined steps. Oddly, the simplest process is often the hardest one to explain, at least when you are reduced to telling readers something in words versus the handier approach of showing them directly. It is far easier, for example, to show a child how to tie her or his shoelaces than it is to write a short paragraph describing the process. For such complex processes to be clear, they need test runs that ensure that you know what it is like to be in the reader's shoes.

Process is simple in one respect: it usually confines itself to explaining how to do something rather than how it works. So, for example, most of us know how to use a telephone but would be at a loss if we had to explain to others how the device works. Similarly, most of us know how to read, but would have little in the way of good advice for beginners. A process, if it is to be clear, needs to set forth a series of clear instructions to readers, much the way simple recipes do.

Think for a moment about the structure of a recipe, a good example of process at its finest. What is essential if you are going to bake a cake? One thing that certainly helps is a sense of what your goal is, how the final product will likely look when it is done. As a result, most recipe books provide pictures to give readers a clear idea of what they are aiming for. The other important feature of the recipe is a complete list of ingredients, usually established at the outset. The reason for this strategy is simple: woe to you if you are halfway through mixing your dry ingredients when you discover that you don't have any baking powder. The list of ingredients is a prerequisite to attempting the recipe, and therefore fits logically at the beginning. The next crucial element of the recipe is a sequential series of steps, often numbered or otherwise carefully delineated. The order of these matters greatly because, if the reader by chance should add the wet ingredients too soon to the dry ingredients, the result will vary considerably. For a recipe to succeed as an expository essay, it should provide timely information that makes the process clear.

Not all process essays depend on a time sequence. Some describe how something may be done well or done better. The point of the paper may be simply to explain how to boil an egg correctly, or it may involve the more complicated issue of how to prepare a boiled egg in the easiest possible way. The crucial matter in either case is that the information is organized into steps. The introduction must first explain why learning a particular process is worthwhile for readers. It must also include explanations of essential terminology, or helpful analogies or comparisons that create an atmosphere of familiarity for your reader. Depending on the level of difficulty of the process described, or on its potential dangers, you may want to include a segment that covers useful hints or even important warnings.

The following sample paragraph shows some of these expository techniques at work:

Topic sentence →

Suppose you suddenly find yourself in a strange city and want to choose a good restaurant, one that lives up to your standards of cleanliness, quality of food, service, and price. How do you go about choosing where to eat? The safest approach may be to read restaurant reviews: the purpose of these, after all, is to give the consumer reliable guidelines on what to expect from various eateries, not only in terms of food, but also in terms of hospitality and even décor. Even relatively small cities often have a restaurant reviewer, usually someone who works with the local paper who, on a weekly basis, samples the cuisine of new establishments. Without such reviews at your fingertips, though, here are some hints to get you through the dinner hour happily. First, know yourself. What kind of cuisine do you favour, and what can you reasonably afford? Next, ask yourself what is most important: the food, the ambience, the service, or the bargain price? If it's the latter, then be prepared to make some sacrifices. Then, check out the *Yellow Pages* to see what your dining options are. Sometimes ads will provide information about menus, hours, prices—you name it. When they don't, feel free to call and ask. Narrow down your search on the basis of your discoveries. Suitability is everything. It obviously doesn't matter if there is a world-class steakhouse in the vicinity if you are a vegetarian. Next, there is physical evidence. If you have time, stroll or drive by your top three choices. Consider these factors: How clean do the restaurants seem to be? How popular are they? Finally comes a crucial but basic question: What do they smell like? Eliminate the cluttered, the filthy, the screamingly loud, and the stunningly silent. Eliminate also those that smell strange or unappealing in any way. (As they say, where's there's smoke, there's fire.) With luck, there will be something left that you find acceptable, in your price range, and to your taste. Bon appétit.

How to Write E-Mail That Your Boss Might Read (or a Jury)

These days almost all of us are making the transition to e-mail, both in business and in our personal lives. Once you get past some initial fear of computers, the plain truth is that e-mail is faster, cheaper, and even less intrusive than other methods of communication. And it leaves an electronic trail that allows you to track what you and the other person said and when. For that last reason, alone, it is paramount that e-mail users learn some basic codes of behaviour that will protect them if the boss does wind up reading their e-mail correspondence (or, for that matter, a jury). Because e-mail is a medium that blends some of the best elements of conversation with some of the best elements of written communication, your way of approaching it needs to be different from either your use of the phone or of so-called "snail mail." You can learn to write effective, polite e-mail only if you keep a number of factors in mind: your audience, the screen, the tone, and propriety.

This is the thesis statement and gives the sequence of the process to be followed. →

The first point is developed.

Audience is crucial. To help your audience make sense of an e-mail message that appears apparently "out of the blue," you should make sure to include a subject line that will help the recipient file it away properly or decide when and how to respond to it. If something requires urgent attention, say so in the subject line. For your audience to find its way, you also need to provide a meaningful context. If, for example, you are responding to a previous message, it is a good idea to quote some of that message, particularly questions that you are answering, so that the reader sees, literally, where you are coming from. To make doubly sure that the reader catches your drift, make sure not to use too many pronouns in the first part of any messages you send. It is bound to be confusing to ask, "Have you talked to him yet?" when what you want to ask is "Have you talked to the judge yet?" In other words, give your reader enough background that your message will make sense without too much additional clarification.

The second point is developed.

The second thing to keep in mind if you intend to write good e-mail is that features of the screen determine much of the impact of your message. Just as the size and appearance of the printed page play a big role in written business correspondence, so the screen size and layout affect your reader's perceptions of your message. For this reason, it is imperative to use short paragraphs and to make the entire message as easy on the eyes as possible. Your typed lines should be short enough that they make the transition to different e-mail formats without too much indenting and confusion at the reader's end. Your messages, in general, should be short, if at all possible, so that they conform readily to screen size and don't place too much of a burden on your reader, who probably gets far too much e-mail anyhow. Plain text works best because not all e-mail readers can decipher accents, special characters, or formatting. While some e-mail readers have the capacity to decode attachments, it is usually better to place additional text on a Web page and then just send the URL or Web address, so that all recipients have equal access to a document. In general, remember that people's tolerance for long messages is likely to be strained when they have trouble unscrambling them, or when they are obliged to stare at a screen for extended periods of time.

Tone is another significant matter in composing effective e-mail. Because e-mail is generally considered more conversational than formal business correspondence, people often take great liberties with it. That's fine in some ways. It allows for greater familiarity and, some would say, a more egalitarian kind of relationship between letter writer and recipient (even in the hierarchy of employee and employer). The problem is that e-mail, devoid of gestures or intonation, may easily be misinterpreted. To compensate for this difficulty, it is often a good idea to develop some typographical features that will enable your recipients to spot irony and emotion when you need them to understand. Add emphasis by enclosing words in asterisks or by capitalizing a word or two, though never the whole message (the equivalent of screaming in face-to-face contact.) Even occasional exclamation marks are advisable for such situations, as in

> If you leave the party early, your hosts might be INSULTED!!

The third point and examples are developed.

On the other side of the emotional spectrum, to provide the written equivalent of a stage whisper, feel free to make sparing use of lowercase or of parentheses:

> you'll never guess. Martin resigned (was asked to leave) today, and the rest of us celebrated his departure.

In other words, think creatively. A bit of unusual punctuation, some white space to provide suspense, or ellipses are all good ways to indicate to your reader that there may be more going on than at first meets the eye. In addition to these approaches, you can resort to emoticons (typographical symbols with some agreed-upon meanings), but bear in mind that some people despise these smiley faces and consider them obtrusive. Fierce punctuation may suffice when you want to express consternation (???) or something ruder (that aggravating ##$$%!). These tactics are, of course, reserved for personal e-mail and should not be part of what you write on the job.

The final point is developed, as well as a detailed elaboration.

Now we come to the issue of propriety. What, in other words, is appropriate in terms of formality, and how can you make sure you have chosen suitable cues for your e-mail? First of all, you need to pay attention to some of the same things that are important in ordinary written communication — grammar, punctuation, and command of language. But, these things aside, your e-mail message should provide some good indicators of you, the composer. One thing that helps accomplish this representative approach to e-mail is a carefully composed signature file appended to the bottom of your message. Make sure that this "sig file" includes relevant information but does not sound too grand or seem unnecessarily long. If the people you are communicating with are strangers to you or the message is of vital importance, pay special attention to the way it is composed. Most of the same rules you would apply in typical business writing will also apply here. If not, then enjoy your freedom. Salutations in messages are probably still a good idea, and "signing" your message is important.

Conclusion

Becoming sensitive to the special demands of e-mail will guarantee that you master the medium and don't embarrass yourself. While e-mail gives the illusion of being a casual method of keeping in touch, bear in mind that e-mail servers often keep elaborate records of your correspondence, long after you have forgotten them. It's probably always a good idea not to write anything that you would be uncomfortable seeing a jury read. Furthermore, e-mail can be forwarded to other people at the touch of a key. Choose your words wisely.

Joel L. Swerdlow

Joel Swerdlow has published articles in many American newspapers and periodicals, including *Harper's Magazine* and *Rolling Stone.* He is author or editor of seven books. In May 1988 NBC produced a film based on *To Heal a Nation: The Vietnam Veterans Memorial* (1985), a book he co-authored with Jan C. Scruggs. Much of his recent work, including this piece, has appeared in *National Geographic.*

THE POWER OF WRITING

Chinese state security officers arrested Wei Jingsheng, an electrician, on March 29, 1979. Among his major crimes: writing essays arguing for democracy. Wei, who would spend 18 years in jail and become a prominent symbol of the power of the written word, was placed in the Beijing detention center.

Chinese authorities feared Wei, recognizing that writing has an almost magical power: Words on paper, created by ordinary citizens, have overthrown governments and changed the course of history. So powerful is writing that the beginnings of civilization and history are most often defined as the moment cultures develop it. Anthropologists can only paint outlines of ancient societies that had no writing; a written record provides the human details—history, belief, names and dates, thought, and emotion.

No other invention—perhaps only the wheel comes close—has had a longer and greater impact. Writing helped preserve the three major monotheistic religions, whose believers the Koran refers to as "the People of the Book." The transformation of language into written words has immortalized passion, genius, art, and science—the letters of St. Paul, the poems of Li Po, the humor of Aristophanes, the treatises of Maimonides.

Much of writing's power comes from its flexibility. Ever since the Sumerians began keeping records by impressing cuneiform signs on clay tablets 5,000 years ago, humans have searched for the ideal tools to portray words. They have chiseled symbols in stone and bone and have written on leaves, bark, silk, papyrus, parchment, paper, and electronic screens. This skill, once known only to a few professional scribes, grew into mass literacy: Some five billion people can read and write today, about 85 percent of the world's population.

5 From its beginning as recordkeeper to its transformation into one of humanity's most potent forms of artistic and political expression, writing reveals the power of innovation.

But the story of Wei proclaims writing's greatest power—its ability to move hearts and minds.

His cell measured four and a half feet by nine feet [1.2 x 2.8 meters]. Authorities kept the light on at all times. No one, not even his guards, was allowed to speak to Wei, and he was not permitted to read or write. His requests for paper and pencil were ignored.

To understand how writing evolved, I visit Sarabit el Khadim, a flat-topped, wind-eroded mountain of reddish sandstone in the southwestern Sinai Peninsula of Egypt. Here, in a turquoise mine dug by Egyptians almost 3,500 years ago, is one of the earliest examples of a phonetic alphabet. Avner Goren, an Israeli archaeologist who supervised excavations in the Sinai for 15 years, is leading me up a steep trail, with narrow ledges and a drop-off to rocks far below. Near the top, we stoop to enter a dark hole.

"What do you think?" Goren asks, pointing to a wall about six feet [two meters] in front of us. Carved into the stone are crude sketches of a fish, ox head, and square, remarkably different from the Egyptian hieroglyphs found elsewhere at the site.

10 The simplicity of these marks belies their significance. I move closer, as if proximity will reveal their magic. The people who made these signs were among the first to use characters each of which represented one sound—an alphabet. These alphabetic symbols had acrophonic values, with each representing the initial sound of the object depicted. The picture of the square—a house—thus stood for the *b* sound because the word for house was *beit*.

If these ancient writers were not Egyptians, who were they? After British archaeologists explored Sarabit el Khadim in 1905, some scholars argued that they were Israelites fleeing from Egypt with Moses about 1250 B.C. But similar writing as old or older was discovered in present-day Israel in the 1930s, so most researchers now believe that this alphabet was invented in Canaan, a region between the Jordan River and the Mediterranean Sea. Most likely, Canaanites who were brought in to work the mines left these messages.

Egyptian scribes had to master hundreds of symbols. I tell Goren that alphabetic writing must have seemed much more attractive to those scribes. "Probably not," he says. "About 30 of the symbols in Egyptian hieroglyphs represent single sounds, just like the alphabet. They knew about using symbols to represent sounds. To the Egyptians the Semitic writing may have looked too primitive to be significant."

That night, as we lie in sleeping bags at the base of the mountains, Goren warns against seeing an alphabet as "superior" to pictographic writing. "If you came from outer space and wrote a report, you'd give the alphabet high marks," he says. "It's flexible and easy to learn. But what actual effect did that have? There was no mass literacy until after the development of the printing press in the mid-15th century."

But alphabets, it seems to me, changed the way people thought. Theoretical science, formal logic, and the concept of time as a straight line moving from past into future came from societies with alphabets.

From a small patch in the Middle East the notion of one symbol per sound spread around the world, taking root first among the Greeks, who modified some characters into written vowels. The Latin alphabet of the Romans evolved from the Greek around the sixth century B.C. By the ninth century A.D., Japan had developed strong phonetic components in its written language; Korea by the 15th. Indeed, of the several hundred written languages in the world today, only Chinese still relies on a writing system in which individual characters represent individual words. These characters often mean one thing when used alone, but something else when combined. The Chinese character for "sincerity," for example, shows the character for "man" alongside the one for "word," literally a man standing by his word.

Wei drew characters in his head, taking pride in this mental calligraphy. One morning, more than two years after he was placed in solitary confinement, his food tray included a ballpoint pen—another prisoner or a sympathetic guard had smuggled it to him.

Wei began to write letters to his family on the rough sheets he had for toilet paper. Guards found these letters and demanded to know where he had hidden the pen. Wei refused to say. After guards failed to find the ballpoint, which Wei had tied to a string and lowered inside the hollow metal rods of his bed, the warden ordered him to another cell. Wei sneaked the pen with him.

Since writing's invention, people have used it to combat loneliness and establish a sense of self. In the fourth century B.C., Aristotle saw writing as a way to express "affections of the soul." Recent studies have documented that writing about feelings can alleviate depression, boost the immune system, and lower blood pressure.

How, then, do people in societies without writing express themselves? Of the more than 10,000 languages ever spoken, most had no written form. "We talk to each other, listen, visit, and trust the spoken word," says Guujaaw, a leader of the Haida Nation. "Expressing yourself without writing is natural."

20 The Haida have lived on the Queen Charlotte Islands off the coast of British Columbia for more than 10,000 years. Guujaaw and I are walking on Sgan Gwaii, a small island in the south that has some of the world's last temperate rain forest. Mosses and ferns cushion our steps. In the ocean, sea lions and puffins dive for fish.

"Like most other cultures in the Western Hemisphere, you never developed writing until outsiders brought it in," I say. "Do you think that's because you had no need for writing?"

"Are you suggesting that writing is better than speaking?" Guujaaw asks in response to my question.

The answer seems obvious, I say. Things get distorted when people repeat them to one another, especially over long periods of time.

"Things get distorted in writing as well," he says. "Oral histories from our people go back thousands of years. They are a living history. They provide a link between storyteller and listeners that written stories cannot. In fact, human intimacy and community can best come through oral communication."

25 Guujaaw leans on a rock. "I'll tell you a Haida story," he says. "Don't write it down. Listen. If you are busy writing, you will miss half the story. A story includes the telling and the listening."

Hearing his story about how animals warn humans not to spoil the water stimulates my senses. Guujaaw's voice, the breeze, the ocean, and the trees around us all flow through me. If I were reading the story, I would be alone in another world—and much less aware of my surroundings.

Plato would have said, "I told you so." Living at a time when writing began to challenge Greece's oral-based culture, he warned that writing would make people "trust to the external written characters and not remember of themselves. . . . They will be hearers of many things and will have learned nothing."

But Plato lived in the fifth century B.C., when reading was physically difficult. Books were papyrus scrolls often more than 60 feet [18 meters] long; the idea of pages, sparked in large part by the availability of parchment, emerged in Europe in the second century A.D. Space between words did not become standard in Western society until the seventh century. Long after Plato's time, writing served mostly as an aid to memory, something to stimulate the spoken word. People read aloud, a practice that died slowly.

St. Augustine, one of the world's leading scholars in the fourth century A.D., was shocked to come upon his mentor St. Ambrose reading silently. This transition from the spoken to the written word occurred because writing meets certain needs so much more effectively. Writing permits analysis, precision, and communication with future generations in a way not possible via the spoken word. The only way I know about St. Augustine's experience is that he mentions it in a book.

30 Still, Plato was right—people in an oral culture need strong memories. I have forgotten most of Guujaaw's story by the time we enter Ninstints, an old Haida village.

Ninstints was home to hundreds of Haida families in the mid-19th century, before white people landed. Now all that remains are the foundations of a few houses and some rotting totem poles. Today there are only about 4,000 Haida compared with 40,000 in the 19th century.

Despite such decline, Guujaaw insists that the Haida have not been defeated by people with writing. "We've been here on this land for thousands of years, and we're still here," he says. "Writing is not essential to living. People with writing are a brief chapter in our history."

But Native American oral culture worked best when people went on long hunting or fishing trips and gathered around campfires every evening. Now modern devices like television discourage the sharing of oral traditions.

Days later I share this thought with Pansy Collison, a Haida who teaches high school in Prince Rupert, British Columbia. "Don't forget that oral history is an essential part of our students' identity," she says.

35 Collison uses storytelling in the classroom to help her students learn their history and build pride in who they are. As part of this, her students write out the oral traditions of their family or clan—she relies on writing to preserve oral history.

As Collison shows me how these written lessons help invigorate oral traditions, I realize I am seeing another example of writing's extraordinary flexibility. Most Native Americans lost ground to outsiders who had weapons and machinery that developed only in societies with writing. But now writing is vital to the Haida's rejuvenation.

In the winter of 1981, after holding Wei in solitary confinement for more than two years, authorities realized they could not keep him from writing. They gave him a new ballpoint pen and better paper and authorized one monthly letter to his two sisters and brother.

In these letters Wei discussed art and offered advice on romance. He was forbidden to write about being beaten or deprived of sleep. He also could not mention his malnutrition, headaches, heart pain, diarrhea, and rotting teeth.

Wei never knew if his letters were delivered. He told his fiancée to find someone else, not knowing that she had already married.

40 *Authorities also told Wei to write to government officials explaining his crime: trying to break up China. He did write to officials but told them they threatened national cohesion by suppressing freedom.*

Maintaining national cohesion has always been a prime concern for China's rulers, who learned thousands of years ago that sharing the same written language can unite people. In the third century B.C. Chinese people spoke at least eight languages and countless dialects, but with the establishment of a unified empire and a standard system of writing around 200 B.C. everyone could read the same characters.

Joseph Stalin, who ruled the Soviet Union from 1928 to 1953, was a master of using writing to control people. Russia and Persia had divided Azerbaijan in the early 1800s. Shortly after taking power, Stalin feared the Azerbaijanis' loyalty to their countrymen in neighboring Iran, formerly Persia. Hoping to divide the two groups, he encouraged the Soviet Azerbaijanis to emulate nearby Turkey and switch from the Arabic alphabet to the Latin alphabet.

By the 1930s Stalin, concerned about growing ties between Turkey and Azerbaijan, forced the Azerbaijanis to adopt Cyrillic, a script used for writing Russian and other Slavic languages. It had evolved from a script created by missionaries of the Orthodox Church in the ninth century A.D.

This alphabetic clash seems alive as I walk through Baku, Azerbaijan's capital. Newspapers are in Cyrillic, labels on canned food are in the Western Latin alphabet or in the Turkish-style Latin with its umlauts and cedillas, and street signs are in freshly painted Azerbaijani Latin, which has "x," "ə," and "Q," letters not found in the Turkish alphabet. There is no sign of Arabic letters.

45 "We chose Latin letters largely because they will help us be modern and will link us to the rest of the world," Oruj Musayev, professor of English at the Azerbaijan State Institute of Languages, tells me. Musayev has just finished compiling the first Azerbaijani-English dictionary using Latin letters. "Our alphabet choice reflects geopolitics. Dropping Cyrillic meant moving away from Russia. Although we're Muslim, we're nonsectarian, so we

didn't want to use the Arabic alphabet, which would link us to the mullahs in Iran."

The stakes are high. Azerbaijan has promising oil reserves and is courting Western buyers.

That the West relies on the Latin alphabet is a remnant of the Roman Empire. Latin letters have endured because they serve Western languages well—and using Latin letters has become associated with being "modern."

The Latin alphabet's ability to link Azerbaijan to the outside world becomes evident the next day when I drive to Lahic, a village isolated in the Caucasus Mountains. In addition to Azerbaijani, people in Lahic speak a dialect of Persian found nowhere else, which has no written form.

Aga Ismailov, a farmer at the edge of town, invites me for a special lunch. As Ismailov barbecues a lamb he slaughtered the day before, his children prepare plates of tomatoes, cucumbers, watermelon, cheese, and freshly baked olive bread.

"My youngest son is learning French and English in school," Ismailov says, speaking in Azerbaijani. "He is the only one in the family who knows the Latin alphabet."

He asks his son, nine-year-old Bakhish, to join us. "Good afternoon, how are you?" Bakhish says in English. He then shows me how he writes his lessons.

As Bakhish writes, I'm struck by the frequency of the upside-down *e* that I'd noticed all over Azerbaijan. Why select the Latin alphabet because it is used in most international trade and computer transactions and then give yourself a letter no one else has?

"It's the sound somewhere between *a* and *e*, like 'hat' and 'cat,' and is the most common sound in our language," Anar Rzayev, one of Azerbaijan's leading writers and a member of parliament, explains the next day in Baku. "What you call the upside-down *e* dates back to early in our history. We kept it even when we had the Cyrillic alphabet. Maybe it's stubbornness, but it's a symbol of Azerbaijan." Shortly after independence, he says, Azerbaijan's parliament debated eliminating the ə but decided to keep it. Azerbaijan is a newly independent country with tremendous problems. Development of oil resources is still a dream, and the country's annual per capita income is about [U.S.] $500, making it one of the world's poorest nations. To have its own alphabet seems a strange indulgence.

"There's nothing new about what's happening in Azerbaijan," Anar says. "An alphabet is a symbol of a country just like a flag. Why do you think different alphabets have appeared in the first place?"

55 *Pride in his nation's writing system helped give Wei his Chinese identity. That most Chinese written characters have remained essentially unchanged for more than 2,000 years provides an emotional and a practical tie to the past.*

Many of his letters were to China's leaders, whom he criticized. As punishment, authorities sometimes took away the pen they had given him, but other prisoners took apart pens, often stolen from guards, and smuggled them to Wei.

"Why write?" the guards asked. "No one will ever see your letters."

In late 1993 authorities told Wei he would be released. They were trying to win international support for acting as host of the year 2000 Olympic Games. Wei, who had been in jail for nearly 14 years, refused to leave his cell without copies of his letters. "They've been lost," he was told.

"You can find them," he replied. Twelve hours later, the warden returned with his letters.

60 *Six months later, after the Olympic Committee rejected China, Wei was re-arrested. State security seized his papers but failed to find the computer disks onto which his letters had been transcribed.*

Tong Yi, the young woman who transcribed Wei's letters onto computer disks, had extraordinary courage. She also had to master the Latin-alphabet keyboard, which requires up to five keystrokes for one Chinese character.

The extra work needed to enter Chinese into a computer raises an important issue. China may become the wealthiest country in the world; it already is a major factor in the international economy. As this economy relies more on computers, does the Chinese writing system put it at a disadvantage?

Usama Fayyad, a senior researcher at Microsoft Corporation, whose job is to think about the long-term future of computers and data storage, says technology will eventually offer efficient and economical ways to bypass keyboards. Voice and handwriting recognition, he tells me, could make it irrelevant which writing system is used. We're in an office on Microsoft's 260-acre [105-hectare] campus near Seattle. A painting of clouds floating through a blue sky covers one wall.

Fayyad also says that the distinction between an alphabet and Chinese characters does not matter in terms of how a computer operates. He explains that when you hit a letter on the keyboard, the computer enters that action into its memory as a number. Each letter is a different number, and a sentence inside the computer is a string of numbers. It's up to the computer program to interpret the string of numbers as instructions.

65 Fayyad warns me not to get too romantic about computers.

"They're great at bookkeeping," he says, "but not yet great at recording impromptu ideas, thoughts, feelings. For that, paper is still far superior. You can hold it, fold it, put it in your pocket, look at it again later when it's convenient."

Fayyad's praise of paper leads me to Joseph Jacobson, a professor of physics at the Massachusetts Institute of Technology. He helped found a company, E-Ink, whose technology is trying to transform ink from a permanent medium to something that can change electronically.

"Paper is fantastic," Jacobson tells me as we tour E-Ink offices in Cambridge, Massachusetts. "If books or newspapers on paper had not already been invented, if we lived in a world only with computer screens, then paper would be a breathtaking breakthrough. But the way we use paper is incredibly wasteful."

Jacobson shows me the E-Ink technology he hopes will someday supplement ink on paper. It prints electronic letters on squares of plastic that can be erased and reused.

70 I ask Jacobson why he uses plastic. "Paper tears too easily," he replies. "We're working on a plastic substance that looks and feels like paper. You could photocopy it, even underline on it with a special pen."

"Isn't that a lot of trouble to solve a problem that doesn't exist?" "A problem does exist," Jacobson says. "Paper needs to be taken into the digital age. We need writing that changes on paper. Think about all the information people download from the Internet. They don't want to read it on a computer screen, so they print it on paper. The demand for paper is soaring. Think of all the savings in cost and the pollution prevented if you needed less paper."

As I watch the E-Ink letters blink, I feel as if I'm back in the cave at Sarabit el Khadim—looking at a piece of the future.

After Wei's re-arrest in 1994 he was placed back in solitary confinement. Two walls of his new cell were glass, so constant monitoring could ensure he did not write. For more than six months not even his family knew whether he was dead or alive. In 1997 a book of Wei's letters, The Courage to Stand Alone, *was published in the United States. Tong Yi, who transcribed his letters, had been sentenced to two and a half years in a labor camp. After serving this time, during which she was sometimes beaten, she was allowed to leave China.*

In the summer of 1997 I read *The Courage to Stand Alone* and follow news accounts of Wei's treatment. He is frequently beaten and denied adequate health care. I fear he will die soon.

75 Then in November 1997 the Chinese government releases Wei, largely in response to international pressure, and puts him on an airplane to the United States. A few weeks later I meet him at his office in the Center for the Study of Human Rights at Columbia University.

I am startled by Wei's smile and how well he looks. He explains that he can eat only soft food until his teeth are fixed, and sips tea as we talk.

"Writing," he says, "kept me alive. I sometimes thought about a letter for a week before writing anything. It's something that you must do even if you do not have the leisure of being in prison. To write, you must work methodically, forming your thoughts and prompting other people to think as they read. Writing requires work at both ends. That's what makes it special."

Wei plans to write a book about the experiences, feelings, and ideas he could not put in his letters, which he knew would be read by prison officials.

"I wish I could read it in Chinese," I say.

80 Wei laughs. "You can learn," he says, writing 友谊.

"It means 'friendship,'" Wei says.

VOCABULARY

phonetic: relating to speech sounds 15
calligraphy: beautiful handwriting 16
umlauts: marks (¨) placed over German and other vowels to indicate changes in sound 44
cedillas: marks (¸) placed under a letter to indicate alterations in phonetic value 44
nonsectarian: not affiliated with a particular religious group 45

AUDIENCE AND PURPOSE

1. This essay recounts two narratives at once. How does the one make the other more effective?
2. What powers does Swerdlow claim for writing, implicitly or explicitly?
3. How does the story of Wei exemplify the importance of writing?

CONTENT

1. What gives the alphabet such significance, according to Swerdlow?
2. How does Swerdlow explore the value of writing compared with speaking?
3. How did writing come to supplant oral tradition, according to Swerdlow?
4. Swerdlow's essay moves us through history, yet does so through the author's own experiences. Why do you think he uses this technique?

STYLE AND STRUCTURE

1. Swerdlow uses italic and regular fonts to make his point. Why?
2. How does Swerdlow's essay show writing's capacity to transcend time and space?
3. Why does Swerdlow end with a reference to the Chinese language?

Paul Roberts

Paul Roberts (1917–67) was a scholar of linguistics. His works include *English Syntax* (1964) and *Patterns of English* (1956). His best-known work is *Understanding English* (1958), from which this essay is taken.

HOW TO SAY NOTHING IN 500 WORDS

NOTHING ABOUT SOMETHING

It's Friday afternoon, and you have almost survived another week of classes. You are just looking forward dreamily to the week end when the English instructor says: "For Monday you will turn in a five-hundred word composition on college football."

Well, that puts a good big hole in the week end. You don't have any strong views on college football one way or the other. You get rather excited during the season and go to all the home games and find it rather more fun than not. On the other hand, the class has been reading Robert Hutchins in the anthology and perhaps Shaw's "Eighty-Yard Run," and from the class discussion you have got the idea that the instructor thinks college football is for the birds. You are no fool, you. You can figure out what side to take.

After dinner you get out the portable typewriter that you got for high school graduation. You might as well get it over with and enjoy Saturday and Sunday. Five hundred words is about two double-spaced pages with normal margins. You put in a sheet of paper, think up a title, and you're off:

> **Why College Football Should Be Abolished**
>
> College football should be abolished because it's bad for the school and also bad for the players. The players are so busy practicing that they don't have any time for their studies.

This, you feel, is a mighty good start. The only trouble is that it's only thirty-two words. You still have four hundred and sixty-eight to go, and you've pretty well exhausted the subject. It comes to you that you do your best thinking in the morning, so you put away the typewriter and go to the movies. But the next morning you have to do your washing and some math problems, and in the afternoon you go to the game. The English instructor turns up too, and you wonder if you've taken the right side after all. Saturday night you have a date, and Sunday morning you have to go to church. (You shouldn't let English assignments interfere with your religion.) What with one thing and another, it's ten o'clock Sunday night before you get out the typewriter again. You make a pot of coffee and start to fill out your views on college football. Put a little meat on the bones.

Why College Football Should Be Abolished

In my opinion, it seems to me that college football should be abolished. The reason why I think this to be true is because I feel that football is bad for the colleges in nearly every respect. As Robert Hutchins says in his article in our anthology in which he discusses college football, it would be better if the colleges had race horses and had races with one another, because then the horses would not have to attend classes. I firmly agree with Mr. Hutchins on this point, and I am sure that many other students would agree too.

One reason why it seems to me that college football is bad is that it has become too commercial. In the olden times when people played football just for the fun of it, college football was all right, but they do not play football just for the fun of it now as they used to in the old days. Nowadays college football is what you might call a big business. Maybe this is not true at all schools, and I don't think it is especially true here at State, but certainly this is the case at most colleges and universities in America nowadays, as Mr. Hutchins points out in his very interesting article. Actually the coaches and alumni go to the high schools and offer the high school stars salaries to come to their colleges and play football for them. There was one case where a high school star was offered a convertible if he would play football for a certain college.

Another reason for abolishing college football is that it is bad for the players. They do not have time to get a college education, because they are so busy playing football. A football player has to practice every afternoon from three to six, and then he is so tired that he can't concentrate on his studies. He just feels like dropping off to sleep after dinner, and then the next day he goes to his classes without having studied and maybe he fails the test.

(Good ripe stuff so far, but you're still a hundred and fifty-one words from home. One more push.)

> Also I think college football is bad for the colleges and the universities because not very many students get to participate in it. Out of a college of ten thousand students seventy-five or a hundred play football, if that many. Football is what you might call a spectator sport. That means that most people go to watch it but do not play it themselves.

(Four hundred and fifteen. Well, you still have the conclusion, and when you retype it, you can make the margins a little wider.)

> These are the reasons why I agree with Mr. Hutchins that college football should be abolished in American colleges and universities.

5 On Monday you turn it in, moderately hopeful, and on Friday it comes back marked "weak in content" and sporting a big "D."

This essay is exaggerated a little, not much. The English instructor will recognize it as reasonably typical of what an assignment on college football will bring in. He knows that nearly half of the class will contrive in five hundred words to say that college football is too commercial and bad for the players. Most of the other half will inform him that college football builds character and prepares one for life and brings prestige to the school. As he reads paper after paper all saying the same thing in almost the same words, all bloodless, five hundred words dripping out of nothing, he wonders how he allowed himself to get trapped into teaching English when he might have had a happy and interesting life as an electrician or a confidence man.

Well, you may ask, what can you do about it? The subject is one on which you have few convictions and little information. Can you be expected to make a dull subject interesting? As a matter of fact, this is precisely what you are expected to do. This is the writer's essential task. All subjects, except sex, are dull until somebody makes them interesting. The writer's job is to find the argument, the approach, the angle, the wording that will take the reader with him. This is seldom easy, and it is particularly hard in subjects that have been much discussed: College Football, Fraternities, Popular Music, Is Chivalry Dead?, and the like. You will feel that there is nothing you can do with such subjects except repeat the old bromides. But there are some things you can do which will make your papers, if not throbbingly alive, at least less insufferably tedious than they might otherwise be.

AVOID THE OBVIOUS CONTENT

Say the assignment is college football. Say that you've decided to be against it. Begin by putting down the arguments that come to your mind: it is too commercial, it takes the students' minds off their studies, it is hard on the players, it makes the university a kind of circus instead of an intellectual center, for most schools it is financially ruinous. Can you think of any more arguments just off hand? All right. Now when you write your paper, *make sure that you don't use any of the material on this list*. If these are the points that leap to your mind, they will leap to everyone else's too, and whether you get a "C" or a "D" may depend on whether the instructor reads your paper early when he is fresh and tolerant or late, when the sentence "In my opinion, college football has become too commercial," inexorably repeated, has brought him to the brink of lunacy.

Be against college football for some reason or reasons of your own. If they are keen and perceptive ones, that's splendid. But even if they are trivial or foolish or indefensible, you are still ahead so long as they are not everybody else's reasons too. Be against it because the colleges don't spend enough money on it to make it worth while, because it is bad for the characters of the spectators, because the players are forced to attend classes, because the football stars hog all the beautiful women, because it competes with baseball and is therefore un-American and possibly Communist inspired. There are lots of more or less unused reasons for being against college football.

10 Sometimes it is a good idea to sum up and dispose of the trite and conventional points before going on to your own. This has the advantage of indicating to the reader that you are going to be neither trite nor conventional. Something like this:

> We are often told that college football should be abolished because it has become too commercial or because it is bad for the players. These arguments are no doubt very cogent, but they don't really go to the heart of the matter.

Then you go to the heart of the matter.

TAKE THE LESS USUAL SIDE

One rather simple way of getting interest into your paper is to take the side of the argument that most of the citizens will want to avoid. If the assignment is an essay on dogs, you can, if you choose, explain that dogs are faithful and lovable companions, intelligent, useful as guardians of the house and protectors of children, indispensable in police work—in short when all is said and done, man's best friends. Or you can suggest that those big brown eyes conceal, more often than not, a vacuity of mind and an inconstancy of purpose; that the dogs you have known most intimately have been mangy, ill-tempered brutes, incapable of instruction; and that only your nobility of mind and fear of arrest prevent you from kicking the flea-ridden animals when you pass them on the street.

Naturally, personal convictions will sometimes dictate your approach. If the assigned subject is "Is Methodism Rewarding to the Individual?" and you are a pious Methodist, you have really no choice. But few assigned subjects, if any, will fall in this category. Most of them will lie in broad areas of discussion with much to be said on both sides. They are intellectual exercises and it is legitimate to argue now one way and now another, as debaters do in similar circumstances. Always take the side that looks to you hardest, least defensible. It will almost always turn out to be easier to write interestingly on that side.

This general advice applies where you have a choice of subjects. If you are to choose among "The Value of Fraternities" and "My Favorite High School Teacher" and "What I Think About Beetles," by all means plump for the beetles. By the time the instructor gets to your paper, he will be up to his ears in tedious tales about the French teacher at Bloombury High and assertions about how fraternities build character and prepare one for life. Your views on beetles, whatever they are, are bound to be a refreshing change.

Don't worry too much about figuring out what the instructor thinks about the subject so that you can cuddle up with him. Chances are his views are no stronger than yours. If he does have convictions and you oppose them, his problem is to keep from grading you higher than you deserve in order to show he is not biased. This doesn't mean that you should always cantankerously dissent from what the instructor says; that gets tiresome too. And if the subject assigned is "My Pet Peeve," do not begin, "My pet peeve is the English instructor who assigns papers on 'my pet peeve.'" This was still funny during the War of 1812, but it has sort of lost its edge since then. It is in general good manners to avoid personalities.

SLIP OUT OF ABSTRACTION

15 If you will study the essay on college football ... you will perceive that one reason for its appalling dullness is that it never gets down to particulars. It is just a series of not very glittering generalities: "football is bad for the colleges," "it has become too commercial," "football is a big business," "it is bad for the players," and so on. Such round phrases thudding against the reader's brain are unlikely to convince him, though they may well render him unconscious.

If you want the reader to believe that college football is bad for the players, you have to do more than say so. You have to display the evil. Take your roommate, Alfred Simkins, the second-string center. Picture poor old Alfy coming home from football practice every evening, bruised and aching, agonizingly tired, scarcely able to shovel the mashed potatoes into his mouth. Let us see him staggering up to the room, getting out his econ textbook, peering desperately at it with his good eye, falling asleep and failing the test in the morning. Let us share his unbearable tension as Saturday draws near. Will he fail, be demoted, lose his monthly allowance, be forced to return to the coal mines? And if he succeeds, what will be his reward? Perhaps a slight ripple of applause when the third-string center replaces him, a moment of elation in the locker room if the team wins, of despair if it loses. What will he look back on when he graduates from college? Toil and torn ligaments. And what will be his future? He is not good enough for pro football, and he is too obscure and weak in econ to succeed in stocks and bonds. College football is tearing the heart from Alfy Simkins and, when it finishes with him, will callously toss aside the shattered hulk.

This is no doubt a weak enough argument for the abolition of college football, but it is a sight better than saying, in three or four variations, that college football (in your opinion) is bad for the players.

Look at the work of any professional writer and notice how constantly he is moving from the generality, the abstract statement, to the concrete example, the facts and figures, the illustration. If he is writing on juvenile delinquency, he does not just tell you that juveniles are (it seems to him) delinquent and that (in his opinion) something should be done about it. He shows you juveniles being delinquent, tearing up movie theatres in Buffalo, stabbing high school principals in Dallas, smoking marijuana in Palo Alto. And more than likely he is moving toward some specific remedy, not just a general wringing of the hands.

It is no doubt possible to be *too* concrete, too illustrative or anecdotal, but few inexperienced writers err this way. For most the soundest advice is to be seeking always for the picture, to be always turning general remarks into seeable examples. Don't say, "Sororities teach girls the social graces." Say "Sorority life teaches a girl how to carry on a conversation while pouring tea, without sloshing the tea into the saucer." Don't say, "I like certain kinds of popular music very much." Say, "Whenever I hear Gerber Spinklittle play 'Mississippi Man' on the trombone, my socks creep up my ankles."

GET RID OF OBVIOUS PADDING

20 The student toiling away at his weekly English theme is too often tormented by a figure: five hundred words. How, he asks himself, is he to achieve this staggering total? Obviously by never using one word when he can somehow work in ten.

He is therefore seldom content with a plain statement like "Fast driving is dangerous." This has only four words in it. He takes thought, and the sentence becomes:

> In my opinion, fast driving is dangerous.

Better, but he can do better still:

> In my opinion, fast driving would seem to be rather dangerous.

If he is really adept, it may come out:

> In my humble opinion, though I do not claim to be an expert on this complicated subject, fast driving, in most circumstances, would seem to be rather dangerous in many respects, or at least so it would seem to me.

Thus four words have been turned into forty, and not an iota of content has been added.

Now this is a way to go about reaching five hundred words, and if you are content with a "D" grade, it is as good a way as any. But if you aim higher, you must work differently. Instead of stuffing your sentences with straw, you must try steadily to get rid of the padding, to make your sentences lean and tough. If you are really working at it, your first draft will greatly exceed the required total, and then you will work it down, thus:

> It is thought in some quarters that fraternities do not contribute as much as might be expected to campus life.
>
> Some people think that fraternities contribute little to campus life.
>
> The average doctor who practices in small towns or in the country must toil night and day to heal the sick.
>
> Most country doctors work long hours.
>
> When I was a little girl, I suffered from shyness and embarrassment in the presence of others.
>
> I was a shy little girl.
>
> It is absolutely necessary for the person employed as a marine fireman to give the matter of steam pressure his undivided attention at all times.
>
> The fireman has to keep his eye on the steam gauge.

You may ask how you can arrive at five hundred words at this rate. Simply. You dig up more real content. Instead of taking a couple of obvious points off the surface of the topic and then circling warily around them for six paragraphs, you work in and explore, figure out the details. You illustrate. You say that fast driving is dangerous, and then you prove it. How long does it take to stop a car at forty and at eighty? How far can you see at night? What happens when a tire blows? What happens in a head-on collision at fifty miles an hour? Pretty soon your paper will be full of broken glass and blood and headless torsos, and reaching five hundred words will not really be a problem.

CALL A FOOL A FOOL

Some of the padding in freshman themes is to be blamed not on anxiety about the word minimum but on excessive timidity. The student writes, "In my opinion, the principal of my high school acted in ways that I believe every unbiased person would have to call foolish." This isn't exactly what he means. What he means is, "My high school principal was a fool." If he was a fool, call him a fool. Hedging the thing about with "in-my-opinion's" and "it-seems-to-me's" and "as-I-see-it's" and "at-least-from-my-point-of-view's" gains you nothing. Delete these phrases whenever they creep into your paper.

25 The student's tendency to hedge stems from a modesty that in other circumstances would be commendable. He is, he realizes, young and inexperienced, and he half suspects that he is dopey and fuzzy-minded beyond the average. Probably only too true. But it doesn't help to announce your incompetence six times in every paragraph. Decide what you want to say and say it as vigorously as possible, without apology and in plain words.

Linguistic diffidence can take various forms. One is what we call *euphemism*. This is the tendency to call a spade "a certain garden implement" or women's underwear "unmentionables." It is stronger in some eras than others and in some people than others but it always operates more or less in subjects that are touchy or taboo: death, sex, madness, and so on. Thus we shrink from saying "He died last night" but say instead "passed away," "left us," "joined his Maker," "went to his reward." Or we try to take off the tension with a lighter cliché: "kicked the bucket," "cashed in his chips," "handed in his dinner pail." We have found all sorts of ways to avoid saying *mad*: "mentally ill," "touched," "not quite right upstairs," "feeble-minded," "innocent," "simple," "off his trolley," "not in his right mind." Even such a now plain word as *insane* began as a euphemism with the meaning "not healthy."

Modern science, particularly psychology, contributes many polysyllables in which we can wrap our thoughts and blunt their force. To many writers there is no such thing as a bad schoolboy. Schoolboys are maladjusted or unoriented or misunderstood or in need of guidance or lacking in continued success toward satisfactory integration of the personality as a social unit, but they are never bad. Psychology no doubt makes us better men or women, more sympathetic and tolerant, but it doesn't make writing any easier. Had Shakespeare been confronted with psychology, "To be or not to be" might have come out, "To continue as a social unit or not to do so. That is the personality problem. Whether 'tis a better sign of integration at the conscious level to display a psychic tolerance toward the maladjustments and repressions induced by one's lack of orientation in one's environment or—" But Hamlet would never have finished the soliloquy.

Writing in the modern world, you cannot altogether avoid modern jargon. Nor, in an effort to get away from euphemism, should you salt your paper with four-letter words. But you can do much if you will mount guard against those roundabout phrases, those echoing polysyllables that tend to slip into your writing to rob it of its crispness and force.

BEWARE OF THE PAT EXPRESSION

Other things being equal, avoid phrases like "other things being equal." Those sentences that come to you whole, or in two or three doughy lumps, are sure to be bad sentences. They are no creation of yours but pieces of common thought floating in the community soup.

30 Pat expressions are hard, often impossible, to avoid, because they come too easily to be noticed and seem too necessary to be dispensed with. No writer avoids them altogether, but good writers avoid them more often than poor writers.

By "pat expressions" we mean such tags as "to all practical intents and purposes," "the pure and simple truth," "from where I sit," "the time of his life," "to the ends of the earth," "in the twinkling of an eye," "as sure as you're born," "over my dead body," "under cover of darkness," "took the easy way out," "when all is said and done," "told him time and time again," "parted the best of friends," "stand up and be counted," "gave him the best years of her life," "worked her fingers to the bone." Like other clichés, these expressions were once forceful. Now we should use them only when we can't possibly think of anything else.

Some pat expressions stand like a wall between the writer and thought. Such a one is "the American way of life." Many student writers feel that when they have said that something accords with the American way of life or does not they have exhausted the subject. Actually, they have stopped at the highest level of abstraction. The American way of life is the complicated set of bonds between a hundred and eighty million ways. All of us know this when we think about it, but the tag phrase too often keeps us from thinking about it.

So with many another phrase dear to the politician: "this great land of ours," "the man in the street," "our national heritage." These may prove our patriotism or give a clue to our political beliefs, but otherwise they add nothing to the paper except words.

COLORFUL WORDS

The writer builds with words, and no builder uses a raw material more slippery and elusive and treacherous. A writer's work is a constant struggle to get the right word in the right place, to find that particular word that will convey his meaning exactly, that will persuade the reader or soothe him or startle or amuse him. He never succeeds altogether — sometimes he feels that he scarcely succeeds at all — but such successes as he has are what make the thing worth doing.

There is no book of rules for this game. One progresses through everlasting experiment on the basis of ever-widening experience. There are few useful generalizations that one can make about words as words, but there are perhaps a few.

Some words are what we call "colorful." By this we mean that they are calculated to produce a picture or induce an emotion. They are dressy instead of plain, specific instead of general, loud instead of soft. Thus, in place of "Her heart beat," we may write "Her heart *pounded*, *throbbed*, *fluttered*, *danced*." Instead of "He sat in his chair," we may say, "He *lounged*, *sprawled*, *coiled*." Instead of "It was hot," we may say, "It was *blistering*, *sultry*, *muggy*, *suffocating*, *steamy*, *wilting*."

However, it should not be supposed that the fancy word is always better. Often it is as well to write "Her heart beat" or "It was hot" if that is all it did or all it was. Ages differ in how they like their prose. The nineteenth century liked it rich and smoky. The twentieth has usually preferred it lean and cool. The twentieth century writer, like all writers, is forever seeking the exact word, but he is wary of sounding feverish. He tends to pitch it low, to understate it, to throw it away. He knows that if he gets too colorful, the audience is likely to giggle.

See how this strikes you: "As the rich, golden glow of the sunset died away along the eternal western hills, Angela's limpid blue eyes looked softly and trustingly into Montague's flashing brown ones, and her heart pounded like a drum in time with the joyous song surging in her soul." Some people like that sort of thing, but most modern readers would say, "Good grief," and turn on the television.

COLORED WORDS

Some words we would call not so much colorful as colored — that is, loaded with associations, good or bad. All words — except perhaps structure words — have associations of some sort. We have said that the meaning of a word is the sum of the contexts in which it occurs. When we hear a word, we hear with it an echo of all the situations in which we have heard it before.

40 In some words, these echoes are obvious and discussable. The word *mother*, for example, has, for most people, agreeable associations. When you hear *mother* you probably think of home, safety, love, food, and various other pleasant things. If one writes, "She was like a mother to me," he gets an effect which he would not get in "She was like an aunt to me." The advertiser makes use of the associations of *mother* by working it in when he talks about his product. The politician works it in when he talks about himself.

So also with such words as *home*, *liberty*, *fireside*, *contentment*, *patriot*, *tenderness*, *sacrifice*, *childlike*, *manly*, *bluff*, *limpid*. All of these words are loaded with favorable associations that would be rather hard to indicate in a straightforward definition. There is more than a literal difference between "They sat around the fireside" and "They sat around the stove." They might have been equally warm and happy around the stove, but *fireside* suggests leisure, grace, quiet tradition, congenial company, and *stove* does not.

Conversely, some words have bad associations. *Mother* suggests pleasant things, but *mother-in-law* does not. Many mothers-in-law are heroically lovable and some mothers drink gin all day and beat their children insensible, but these facts of life are beside the point. The thing is that *mother* sounds good and *mother-in-law* does not.

Or consider the word *intellectual*. This would seem to be a complimentary term, but in point of fact it is not, for it has picked up associations of impracticality and ineffectuality and general dopiness. So also with such words as *liberal*, *reactionary*, *Communist*, *socialist*, *capitalist*, *radical*, *schoolteacher*, *truck driver*, *undertaker*, *operator*, *salesman*, *huckster*, *speculator*. These convey meanings on the literal level, but beyond that—sometimes, in some places—they convey contempt on the part of the speaker.

The question of whether to use loaded words or not depends on what is being written. The scientist, the scholar, try to avoid them; for the poet, the advertising writer, the public speaker, they are standard equipment. But every writer should take care that they do not substitute for thought. If you write, "Anyone who thinks that is nothing but a Socialist (or Communist or capitalist)" you have said nothing except that you don't like people who think that, and such remarks are effective only with the most naïve readers. It is always a bad mistake to think your readers more naïve than they really are.

COLORLESS WORDS

45 But probably most student writers come to grief not with words that are colorful or those that are colored but with those that have no color at all. A pet example is *nice*, a word we would find it hard to dispense with in casual conversation but which is no longer capable of adding much to a description. Colorless words are those of such general meaning that in a particular sentence they mean nothing. Slang adjectives, like *cool* ("That's real cool") tend to explode all over the language. They are applied to everything, lose their original force, and quickly die.

Beware also of nouns of very general meaning, like *circumstances*, *cases*, *instances*, *aspects*, *factors*, *relationships*, *attitudes*, *eventualities*, etc. In most circumstances you will find that those cases of writing which contain too many instances of words like these will in this and other aspects have factors leading to unsatisfactory relationships with the reader resulting in unfavorable attitudes on his part and perhaps other eventualities, like a grade of "D." Notice also what "etc." means. It means "I'd like to make this list longer, but I can't think of any more examples."

VOCABULARY

bromides: trite sayings, platitudes 7
inexorably: inevitably 8
cogent: convincing 10
vacuity: emptiness 11
plump: choose 13
dissent: disagreement 14
soliloquy: speech delivered by a lone speaker 27

AUDIENCE AND PURPOSE

1. What is Roberts's thesis?
2. Why does Roberts use the pronoun "you" throughout this essay?
3. What is the tone of the essay?

CONTENT

1. Most, if not all, of Roberts's words are geared toward making writing interesting. What will produce that effect, in his view? Explain in your own words.
2. Define what Roberts means by "colourful words," "coloured words," and "colourless words."
3. Does Roberts follow his own advice? Provide an example to support your answer.

STYLE AND STRUCTURE

1. Why does Roberts break the essay in two, first showing you what not to do and then what to do?
2. Why does Roberts use headings?
3. How does Roberts create humour?

Russell Baker

Russell Baker (b. 1925) is an American essayist and a columnist for the *New York Times*. He is also currently the host of PBS's *Masterpiece Theatre*. Collections of his columns include *An American in Washington* (1961) and *Poor Russell's Almanac* (1971). Baker has also written two memoirs: *Growing Up* (1982) and *The Good Times* (1989).

FRANCS AND BEANS

As chance would have it, the very evening in 1975 Craig Claiborne ate his historic $4,000 dinner for two with thirty-one dishes and nine wines in Paris, a Lucullan repast for one was prepared and consumed in New York by this correspondent, no slouch himself when it comes to titillating the palate.

Mr. Claiborne won his meal in a television fund-raising auction and had it professionally prepared. Mine was created from spur-of-the-moment inspiration, necessitated when, I discovered a note on the stove saying, "Am eating out with Dora and Imogene—make dinner for yourself." It was from the person who regularly does the cooking at my house and, though disconcerted at first, I quickly rose to the challenge.

The meal opened with a 1975 Diet Pepsi served in a disposable bottle. Although its bouquet was negligible, its distinct metallic aftertaste evoked memories of tin cans one had licked experimentally in the first flush of childhood's curiosity.

To create the balance of tastes so cherished by the epicurean palate, I followed with a *pâté de fruites de nuts of Georgia*, prepared according to my own recipe. A half-inch layer of creamy-style peanut butter is troweled onto a graham cracker, then half a banana is crudely diced and pressed firmly into the peanut butter and cemented in place as it were by a second graham cracker.

5 The accompanying drink was cold milk served in a wide-brimmed jelly glass. This is essential to proper consumption of the pâté since the entire confection must be dipped into the milk to soften it for eating. In making the presentation to the mouth, one must beware lest the milk-soaked portion of the sandwich fall onto the necktie. Thus, seasoned gourmandisers follow the old maxim of the Breton chefs and "bring the mouth to the jelly glass."

At this point in the meal, the stomach was ready for serious eating, and I prepared beans with bacon grease, a dish I perfected in 1937 while developing my *cuisine du depression*.

The dish is started by placing a pan over very high flame until it becomes dangerously hot. A can of Heinz's pork and beans is then emptied into the pan and allowed to char until it reaches the consistency of hardening concrete. Three strips of bacon are fried to crisps, and when the beans have formed huge dense clots firmly welded to the pan, the bacon grease is poured in and stirred vigorously with a large screwdriver.

This not only adds flavor but also loosens some of the beans from the side of the pan. Leaving the flame high, I stirred in a three-day-old spaghetti sauce found in the refrigerator, added a sprinkle of chili powder, a large dollop of Major Grey's chutney and a tablespoon of bicarbonate of soda to make the whole dish rise.

Beans with bacon grease is always eaten from the pan with a tablespoon while standing over the kitchen sink. The pan must be thrown away immediately. The correct drink with this dish is a straight shot of room-temperature gin. I had a Gilbey's 1975, which was superb.

For the meat course, I had fried bologna *à la Nutley, Nouveau Jersey*. Six slices of A & P bologna were placed in an ungreased frying pan over maximum heat and held down by a long fork until the entire house filled with smoke. The bologna was turned, fried the same length of time on the other side, then served on air-filled white bread with thick lashings of mayonnaise.

The correct drink for fried bologna *à la Nutley, Nouveau Jersey* is a 1927 Nehi Cola, but since my cellar, alas, had none, I had to make do with a second shot of Gilbey's 1975.

The cheese course was deliciously simple — a single slice of Kraft's individually wrapped yellow sandwich cheese, which was flavored by vigorous rubbing over the bottom of the frying pan to soak up the rich bologna juices. Wine being absolutely *de rigueur* with cheese, I chose a 1974 Muscatel, flavored with a maraschino cherry, and afterwards cleared my palate with three pickled martini onions.

It was time for the fruit. I chose a Del Monte tinned pear, which, regrettably, slipped from the spoon and fell on the floor, necessitating its being blotted with a paper towel to remove cat hairs. To compensate for the resulting loss of pear syrup, I dipped it lightly in hot dog relish which created a unique flavor.

With the pear I drank two shots of Gilbey's 1975 and one shot of Wolfschmidt vodka (nonvintage), the Gilbey's having been exhausted.

At last it was time for the dish the entire meal had been building toward — dessert. With a paring knife, I ripped into a fresh package of Oreos, produced a bowl of My-T-Fine chocolate pudding which had been coagulating in the refrigerator for days and, using a potato masher, crushed a dozen Oreos into the pudding. It was immense.

Between mouthfuls, I sipped a tall, bubbling tumbler of cool Bromo-Seltzer, and finished with six ounces of Maalox. It couldn't have been better.

VOCABULARY

Lucullan: lavish, luxurious from Licinius Lucullus, known for his extravagant banquets 1
repast: meal 1
titillating: enticing 1
disconcerted: alarmed 2
epicurean: lavish, extravagant 4
confection: treat 5
gourmandisers: those who are fond of food and drink, perhaps to excess 5

AUDIENCE AND PURPOSE

1. What is the point of this essay?
2. How can you tell that Baker feels that many aspects of his essay will be familiar to his readers? How does he use this to create humour?
3. Why does Baker include so much disgusting detail? Explain how some of the examples work.

CONTENT

1. How does Baker make the comparison with Craig Claiborne's gourmet feast implicit throughout the essay?
2. Why does Baker provide such exact detail, which could be duplicated?
3. How does Baker use the repetition of references to Gilbey's to comic effect?
4. Baker juxtaposes two kinds of language—that of the gourmet and that of rather homely domestic life. Give examples of this juxtaposition. Why is it effective?

STYLE AND STRUCTURE

1. Why does Baker begin with a comparison to Craig Claiborne, a famous chef?

2. Why does Baker insist on the minute details of the process of putting his dinner together, even those that are not particularly relevant to the meal?
3. How does Baker create a sense of the ridiculous?

Jessica Mitford

Jessica Mitford (1917 – 96) was a British author whose books include *Lifeitselfmanship* (1956), her autobiography *Daughters and Rebels* (1960), the bestseller *The American Way of Death* (1963) and its posthumous, updated version *The American Way of Death Revisited* (1998), *The Trial of Dr. Spock* (1969), *Kind and Usual Punishment* (1973) (a study of the American penal system), *A Fine Old Conflict* (1977), and *Poison Penmanship* (1979).

THE STORY OF SERVICE

There was a time when the undertaker's tasks were clear-cut and rather obvious, and when he billed his patrons accordingly. Typical late-nineteenth-century charges, in addition to the price of merchandise, are shown on bills of the period as: "Services at the house (placing corpse in the coffin), $1.25," "Preserving remains on ice, $10," "Getting permit, $1.50." It was customary for the undertaker to add a few dollars to his bill for being "in attendance," which seems only fair and right. The cost of embalming was around $10 in 1880. An undertaker, writing in 1900, recommends these minimums for service charges: washing and dressing, $5; embalming, $10; hearse, $8 to $10. As Robert W. Habenstein and William M. Lamers, the historians of the trade, have pointed out, "The undertaker had yet to conceive of the value of personal service offered professionally for a fee, legitimately claimed." Well, he has now so conceived with a vengeance.

When weaving in the story of service as it is rendered today, spokesmen for the funeral industry tend to become so carried away by their own enthusiasm, so positively lyrical and copious in their declarations, that the outsider may have a little trouble understanding it all. There are indeed contradictions. Preferred Funeral Directors International has prepared a talk designed to inform people about service: "The American public receive the services of employees and proprietor alike, nine and one half days of labor for every funeral handled, they receive the use of automobiles and hearses, a building including a chapel and other rooms which require building maintenance, insurance, taxes and licenses, and depreciation, as well as heat in the winter, cooling in the summer, light and water." The writer goes on to say that while the process of embalming takes only about three hours, "it would be necessary for one man to work two forty-hour weeks to complete a funeral service. This is coupled with an additional forty hours of service required by members of other local allied professions, including the work of the cemeteries, newspapers, and, of course, the most important of all, the service of your clergyman. These some 120 hours of labor are the basic value on which the cost of funerals rests."

Our informant has lumped a lot of things together here. To start with "the most important of all, the service of your clergyman": the average religious funeral service lasts no more than twenty-five minutes. Furthermore, it is not, of course, paid for by the funeral director. The "work of the cemeteries" presumably means the opening and closing of a grave. This now mechanized operation, which takes fifteen to twenty minutes, is likewise not billed as part of the funeral director's costs. The work of "newspapers"? This is a puzzler. Presumably, reference is made here to the publication of an obituary notice on the vital statistics page. It is, incidentally, surprising to learn that newspaper work is considered an "allied profession."

Just how insurance, taxes, licenses, and depreciation are figured in as part of the 120 man-hours of service is hard to tell. The writer does mention that his operation features "65 items of service." In general, the funeral salesman is inclined to chuck in everything he does under the heading of "service." For example, in a typical list of "services" he will include items like "securing statistical data" (in other words, completing the death certificate and finding out how much insurance was left by the deceased), the "arrangements conference" (in which the sale of the funeral to the survivors is made), and the "keeping of records," by which he means his own bookkeeping work. Evidently, there is some confusion here between items that properly belong in a cost-accounting system and items of actual service rendered in any given funeral. In all likelihood, the idle time of employees is figured in and prorated as part of the "man-hours." The up-to-date funeral home operates on a twenty-four-hour basis, and the prepared speech contains this heartening news:

> The funeral service profession of the United States is proud of the fact that there is not a person within the continental limits of the United States who is more than two hours away from a licensed funeral director and embalmer. That's one that even the fire-fighting apparatus of our country cannot match.

5 While the hit-or-miss rhetoric of the foregoing is fairly typical of the prose style of the funeral trade as a whole, and while

the statement that 120 man-hours are devoted to a single funeral may be open to question, there really is a fantastic amount of service accorded the dead body and its survivors.

Having decreed what sort of funeral is right, proper, and nice, and having gradually appropriated to himself all the functions connected with it, the funeral director has become responsible for a multitude of tasks—beyond the obvious one of "placing corpse in the coffin" recorded in our nineteenth-century funeral bill. His self-imposed duties fall into two main categories: attention to the corpse itself, and the stage-managing of the funeral.

The drama begins to unfold with the arrival of the corpse at the mortuary.

Alas, poor Yorick! How surprised he would be to see how his counterpart of today is whisked off to a funeral parlor and is in short order sprayed, sliced, pierced, pickled, trussed, trimmed, creamed, waxed, painted, rouged, and neatly dressed—transformed from a common corpse into a Beautiful Memory Picture. This process is known in the trade as embalming and restorative art, and is so universally employed in the United States and Canada that for years the funeral director did it routinely, without consulting corpse or kin. He regards as eccentric those few who are hardy enough to suggest that it might be dispensed with. Yet no law requires embalming, no religious doctrine commends it, nor is it dictated by considerations of health, sanitation, or even of personal daintiness. In no part of the world but in North America is it widely used. The purpose of embalming is to make the corpse presentable for viewing in a suitably costly container; and here too the funeral director routinely, without first consulting the family, prepares the body for public display.

Is all this legal? The processes to which a dead body may be subjected are, after all, to some extent circumscribed by law. In most states, for instance, the signature of next of kin must be obtained before an autopsy may be performed, before the deceased may be cremated, before the body may be turned over to a medical school for research purposes; or such provision must be made in the decedent's will. In the case of embalming, permission is required (under Federal Trade Commission rules) only if a charge is to be made for the procedure. Embalming is not, as funeral providers habitually claim, a legal requirement even when the body of the deceased is to be on display in an open casket. A textbook, *The Principles and Practices of Embalming*, comments on this: "There is some question regarding the legality of much that is done within the preparation room." The author points out that it would be most unusual for a responsible member of a bereaved family to instruct the mortician, in so many words, to "embalm" the body of a deceased relative. The very term "embalming" is so seldom used that the mortician must rely upon custom in the matter. The author concludes that unless the family specifies otherwise, the act of entrusting the body to the care of a funeral establishment carries with it an implied permission to go ahead and embalm.

Embalming is indeed a most extraordinary procedure, and one must wonder at the docility of Americans who each year pay hundreds of millions of dollars for its perpetuation, blissfully ignorant of what it is all about, what is done, and how it is done. Not one in ten thousand has any idea of what actually takes place. Books on the subject are extremely hard to come by. You will not find them in your neighborhood bookshop or library.

In an era when huge television audiences watch surgical operations in the comfort of their living rooms, when, thanks to the animated cartoon, the geography of the digestive system has become familiar territory even to the nursery-school set, in a land where the satisfaction of curiosity about almost all matters is a national pastime, surely the secrecy surrounding embalming cannot be attributed to the inherent gruesomeness of the subject. Custom in this regard has within this century suffered a complete reversal. In the early days of American embalming, when it was performed in the home of the deceased, it was almost mandatory for some relative to stay by the embalmer's side and witness the procedure. Today, family members who might wish to be in attendance would certainly be dissuaded by the funeral director. All others, except apprentices, are usually barred by law from the preparation room.

A close look at what actually does take place may explain in large measure the undertaker's intractable reticence concerning a procedure that has become his major raison d'être. Is it possible he fears that public information about embalming might lead patrons to wonder if they really want this service? If the funeral men are loath to discuss the subject outside the trade, the reader may, understandably, be equally loath to go on reading at this point. For those who have the stomach for it, let us part the formaldehyde curtain. Others should skip to the [top] of page [180].

The body is first laid out in the undertaker's morgue—or, rather, Mr. Jones is reposing in the preparation room to be readied to bid the world farewell.

The preparation room in any of the better funeral establishments has the tiled and sterile look of a surgery, and indeed the embalmer/restorative artist who does his chores there is beginning to adopt the term "dermasurgeon" (appropriately corrupted by some mortician-writers as "demi-surgeon") to describe his calling. His equipment — consisting of scalpels, scissors, augers, forceps, clamps, needles, pumps, tubes, bowls, and basins — is crudely imitative of the surgeon's, as is his technique, acquired in a nine- or twelve-month post – high school course at an embalming school. He is supplied by an advanced chemical industry with a bewildering array of fluids, sprays, pastes, oils, powders, creams, to fix or soften tissue, shrink or distend it as needed, dry it here, restore the moisture there. There are cosmetics, waxes, and paints to fill and cover features, even plaster of Paris to replace entire limbs. There are ingenious aids to prop and stabilize the cadaver: a VariPose Head Rest, the Edwards Arm and Hand Positioner, the Repose Block (to support the shoulders during the embalming), and the Throop Foot Positioner, which resembles an old-fashioned stocks.

15 Mr. John H. Eckels, president of the Eckels College of Mortuary Science, thus describes the first part of the embalming procedure: "In the hands of a skilled practitioner, this work may be done in a comparative short time and without mutilating the body other than by slight incision so slight that it scarcely would cause serious inconvenience if made upon a living person. It is necessary to remove the blood, and doing this not only helps in the disinfecting, but removes the principal cause of disfigurements due to discoloration."

Another textbook discusses the all-important time element: "The earlier this is done, the better, for every hour that elapses between death and embalming will add to the problems and complications encountered. . . . , Just how soon should one get going on the embalming? The author tells us, "On the basis of such scanty information made available to this profession through its rudimentary and haphazard system of technical research, we must conclude that the best results are to be obtained if the subject is embalmed before life is completely extinct — that is, before cellular death has occurred. In the average case, this would mean within an hour after somatic death." For those who feel that there is something a little rudimentary, not to say haphazard, about this advice, a comforting thought is offered by another writer. "Speaking of fears entertained in the early days of premature burial," he points out, "one of the effects of embalming by chemical injection, however, has been to dispel fears of live burial." How true; once the blood is removed, chances of live burial are indeed remote.

To return to Mr. Jones, the blood is drained out through the veins and replaced by embalming fluid pumped in through the arteries. As noted in *The Principles and Practices of Embalming*, "Every operator has a favorite injection and drainage point—a fact which becomes a handicap only if he fails or refuses to forsake his favorites when conditions demand it." Typical favorites are the carotid artery, femoral artery, jugular vein, and subclavian vein. There are various choices of embalming fluid. If Flextone is used, it will produce a "mild, flexible rigidity. The skin retains a velvety softness, the tissues are rubbery and pliable. Ideal for women and children." It may be blended with B. and G. Products Company's Lyf-Lyk tint, which is guaranteed to reproduce "nature's own skin texture... the velvety appearance of living tissue." Suntone comes in three separate tints: Suntan; Special Cosmetic Tint; moderately pink.

About three to six gallons of a dyed and perfumed solution of formaldehyde, glycerin, borax, phenol, alcohol, and water is soon circulating through Mr. Jones, whose mouth has been sewn together with a "needle directed upward between the upper lip and gum and brought out through the left nostril," with the corners raised slightly "for a more pleasant expression." If he should be buck-toothed, his teeth are cleaned with Bon Ami and coated with colorless nail polish. His eyes meanwhile are closed with flesh-tinted eye caps and eye cement.

The next step is to have at Mr. Jones with a thing called a trocar. This is a long, hollow needle attached to a tube. It is jabbed into the abdomen and poked around the entrails and chest cavity, the contents of which are pumped out and replaced with "cavity fluid." This done, and the hole in the abdomen having been sewn up, Mr. Jones's face is heavily creamed (to protect the skin from burns which may be caused by leakage of the chemicals), and he is covered with a sheet and left unmolested for a while. But not for long—there is more, much more, in store for him. He has been embalmed, but not yet restored, and the best time to start the restorative work is eight to ten hours after embalming, when the tissues have become firm and dry.

20 The object of all this attention to the corpse, it must be remembered, is to make it presentable for viewing in an attitude of healthy repose. "Our customs require the presentation of our dead in the semblance of normality... unmarred by the ravages of illness, disease or mutilation," says Mr. J. Sheridan Mayer in his *Restorative Art*. This is rather a large order since few people

die in the full bloom of health, unravaged by illness and unmarked by some disfigurement. The funeral industry is equal to the challenge: "In some cases the gruesome appearance of a mutilated or disease-ridden subject may be quite discouraging. The task of restoration may seem impossible and shake the confidence of the embalmer. This is the time for intestinal fortitude and determination. Once the formative work is begun and affected tissues are cleaned or removed, all doubts of success vanish. It is surprising and gratifying to discover the results which may be obtained."

The embalmer, having allowed an appropriate interval to elapse, returns to the attack, but now brings into play the skill and equipment of sculptor and cosmetician. Is a hand missing? Casting one in plaster of Paris is a simple matter. "For replacement purposes, only a cast of the back of the hand is necessary; this is within the ability of the average operator and is quite adequate." If a lip or two, a nose, or an ear should be missing, the embalmer has at hand a variety of restorative waxes with which to model replacements. Pores and skin texture are simulated by stippling with a little brush, and over this cosmetics are laid on. Head off? Decapitation cases are rather routinely handled. Ragged edges are trimmed, and head joined to torso with a series of splints, wires, and sutures. It is a good idea to have a little something at the neck—a scarf or high collar—when time for viewing comes. Swollen mouth? Cut out tissue as needed from inside the lips. If too much is removed, the surface contour can easily be restored by padding with cotton. Swollen neck and cheeks are reduced by removing tissue through vertical incisions made down each side of the neck. "When the deceased is casketed, the pillow will hide the suture incisions. ... [A]s an extra precaution against leakage, the suture may be painted with liquid sealer."

The opposite condition is more likely to present itself—that of emaciation. His hypodermic syringe now loaded with massage cream, the embalmer seeks out and fills the hollowed and sunken areas by injection. In this procedure, the backs of the hands and fingers and the under-chin area should not be neglected.

Positioning the lips is a problem that recurrently challenges the ingenuity of the embalmer. Closed too tightly, they tend to give a stern, even disapproving expression. Ideally, embalmers feel, the lips should give the impression of being ever so slightly parted, the upper lip protruding slightly for a more youthful appearance. This takes some engineering, however, as the lips tend to drift apart. Lip drift can sometimes be remedied by pushing one or two straight pins through the inner margin of the lower lip and then inserting them between the two front upper teeth. If Mr. Jones happens to have no teeth, the pins can just as easily be anchored in his Armstrong Face Former and Denture Replacer. Another method to maintain lip closure is to dislocate the lower jaw, which is then held in its new position by wire run through holes which have been drilled through the upper and lower jaws at the midline. As the French are fond of saying, *il faut souffrir pour être belle.*

If Mr. Jones has died of jaundice, the embalming fluid will very likely turn green. Does this deter the embalmer? Not if he has intestinal fortitude. Masking pastes and cosmetics are heavily laid on, burial garments and casket interiors are color-correlated with particular care, and Jones is displayed beneath rose-colored lights. Friends will say, "How *well* he looks." Death by carbon monoxide, on the other hand, can be rather a good thing from the embalmer's viewpoint: "One advantage is the fact that this type of discoloration is an exaggerated form of a natural pink coloration." This is nice because the healthy glow is already present and needs but little attention.

The patching and filling completed, Mr. Jones is now shaved, washed, and dressed. A cream-based cosmetic, available in pink, flesh, suntan, brunette, and blond, is applied to his hands and face, his hair is shampooed and combed (and, in the case of Mrs. Jones, set), his hands manicured. For the horny-handed son of toil, special care must be taken; cream should be applied to remove ingrained grime, and the nails cleaned. "If he were not in the habit of having them manicured in life, trimming and shaping is advised for better appearance—never questioned by kin."

Jones is now ready for casketing (this is the present participle of the verb "to casket"). In this operation his right shoulder should be depressed slightly "to turn the body a bit to the right and soften the appearance of lying flat on the back." Positioning the hands is a matter of importance, and special rubber positioning blocks may be used. The hands should be cupped slightly for a more lifelike, relaxed appearance. Proper placement of the body requires a delicate sense of balance. It should lie as high as possible in the casket, yet not so high that the lid, when lowered, will hit the nose. On the other hand, we are cautioned, placing the body too low "creates the impression that the body is in a box."

Jones is next wheeled into the appointed slumber room, where a few last touches may be added—his favorite pipe placed in his hand, or, if he was a great reader, a book propped into position. (In the case of little Master Jones, a teddy bear may be clutched.) Here he will hold open house for a few days, visiting hours 10 A.M. to 5 P.M.

All now being in readiness, the funeral director calls a staff conference to make sure that each assistant knows his precise duties. Mr. Wilber Krieger writes: "This makes your staff feel that they are a part of the team, with a definite assignment that must be properly carried out if the whole plan is to succeed. You never heard of a football coach who failed to talk to his entire team before they go on the field. They have been drilled on the plays they are to execute for hours and days, and yet the successful coach knows the importance of making even the bench-warming third-string substitute feel that he is important if the game is to be won." The winning of *this* game is predicated upon a glass-smooth handling of the logistics. The funeral director has notified the pallbearers, whose names were furnished by the family, has arranged for the presence of a clergyman, organist, and soloist, has provided transportation for everybody, has organized and listed the flowers sent by friends. In *Psychology of Funeral Service*, Mr. Edward A. Martin points out: "He may not always do as much as the family thinks he is doing, but it is his helpful guidance that they appreciate in knowing they are proceeding as they should.... The important thing is how well his services can be used to make the family believe they are giving unlimited expression to their own sentiment."

The religious service may be held in a church or in the chapel of the funeral home; the funeral director vastly prefers the latter arrangement, for not only is it more convenient for him, but it affords him the opportunity to show off his beautiful facilities to the gathered mourners. After the clergyman has had his say, the mourners queue up to file past the casket for a last look at the deceased. The family is not asked whether they want an open-casket ceremony; in the absence of instruction to the contrary, this is taken for granted. Consequently, well over 68 percent of all American funerals in the mid-1990s featured an open casket —a custom unknown in other parts of the world. Foreigners are astonished by it. An Englishwoman living in San Francisco described her reaction in a letter to the writer:

> I myself have attended only one funeral here—that of an elderly fellow worker of mine. After the service I could not understand why everyone was walking towards the coffin (sorry, I mean casket), but thought I had better follow the crowd. It shook me rigid to get there and find the

> casket open and poor old Oscar lying there in his brown tweed suit, wearing a suntan makeup and just the wrong shade of lipstick. If I had not been extremely fond of the old boy, I have a horrible feeling that I might have giggled. Then and there I decided that I could never face another American funeral — even dead.

The casket (which has been resting throughout the service on a Classic Beauty Ultra Metal Casket Bier) is now transferred by a hydraulically operated device called Porto-Lift to a balloon-tired, Glide Easy casket carriage which will wheel it to yet another conveyance, the Cadillac Funeral Coach. This may be lavender, cream, light green. Black, once de rigueur, is coming back into fashion. Interiors, of course, are color-correlated, "for the man who cannot stop short of perfection."

At graveside, the casket is lowered into the earth. This office, once the prerogative of friends of the deceased, is now performed by a patented mechanical lowering device. A "Lifetime Green" artificial grass mat is at the ready to conceal the sere earth, and overhead, to conceal the sky, is a portable Steril Chapel Tent ("resists the intense heat and humidity of summer and the terrific storms of winter ... available in Silver Grey, Rose or Evergreen"). Now is the time for the ritual scattering of the earth over the coffin, as the solemn words "earth to earth, ashes to ashes, dust to dust" are pronounced by the officiating cleric. This can today be accomplished "with a mere flick of the wrist with the Gordon Leak-Proof Earth Dispenser. No grasping of a handful of dirt, no soiled fingers. Simple, dignified, beautiful, reverent! The modern way!" The Gordon Earth Dispenser is of nickel-plated brass construction. It is not only "attractive to the eye and long wearing"; it is also "one of the 'tools' for building better public relations" if presented as "an appropriate non-commercial gift" to the clergy. It is shaped something like a saltshaker.

Untouched by human hand, the coffin and the earth are now united.

It is in the function of directing the participants through this maze of gadgetry that the funeral director has assigned to himself his relatively new role of "grief therapist." He has relieved the family of every detail, he has revamped the corpse to look like a living doll, he has arranged for it to nap for a few days in a slumber room, he has put on a well-oiled performance in which the concept of *death* has played no part whatsoever — unless it was inconsiderately mentioned by the clergyman who conducted the religious service. He has done everything in his power to make the funeral a real pleasure for everybody concerned. He and his team have given their all to score an upset victory over death.

Dale Carnegie has written that in the lexicon of the successful man there is no such word as "failure." So have the undertakers managed to delete the word "death" and all its associations from their vocabulary. They have from time to time published lists of In and Out words and phrases to be memorized and used in connection with the final return of dust to dust; then, still dissatisfied with the result, they have elaborated and revised the list. Thus, a 1916 glossary substitutes "prepare body" for "handle corpse." Today, though, "body" is Out and "remains" or "Mr. Jones" is In.

35 "The use of improper terminology by anyone affiliated with a mortuary should be strictly forbidden," declares Edward A. Martin. He suggests a rather thorough overhauling of the language; his deathless words include: "service, not funeral; Mr., Mrs., Miss blank, not corpse or body; preparation room, not morgue; casket, not coffin; funeral director or mortician, not undertaker; reposing room, not showroom; baby or infant, not stillborn; deceased, not dead; autopsy or post-mortem, not 'post'; coach, not hearse; shipping case, not shipping box; flower car, not flower truck; cremains or cremated remains, not ashes; clothing, dress, suit, etc., not shroud; drawing room, not parlor."

This rather basic list was refined in 1956 by Victor Landig in his *Basic Principles of Funeral Service*. He enjoins the reader to avoid using the word "death" as much as possible, even when such avoidance may seem impossible; for example, a death certificate should be referred to as a "vital statistics form." One should speak not of the "job" but rather of the "call." We do not "haul" a dead person, we "transfer" or "remove" him—and we do this in a "service car," not a "body car." We "open and close" his grave rather than dig and fill it, and in it we "inter" rather than bury him. This is done not in a graveyard or cemetery, but rather in a "memorial park." The deceased is beautified, not with makeup, but with "cosmetics." Anyway, he didn't die, he "expired." An important error to guard against, cautions Mr. Landig, is referring to "cost of the casket." The phrase "amount of investment in the service" is a wiser usage here.

Miss Anne Hamilton Franz, writing in *Funeral Direction and Management*, adds an interesting footnote on the use of the word "ashes" to describe (in a word) ashes. She fears this usage will encourage scattering (for what is more natural than to scatter ashes?), and prefers to speak of "cremated remains" or "human remains." She does not like the word "retort" to describe the container in which cremation takes place, but prefers "cremation chamber" or "cremation vault," because this "sounds better and softens any harshness to sensitive feelings."

As for the Loved One, poor fellow, he wanders like a sad ghost through the funeral men's pronouncements. No provision seems to have been made for the burial of a Heartily Disliked One, although the necessity for such must arise in the course of human events.

VOCABULARY

copious: plentiful 2
circumscribed: limited 9
decedent: the dead person 9
docility: passivity 10
intractable: stubborn, rigid 12
loath: unwilling 12
somatic: of the body 16
rudimentary: basic 16
sere: dry 30
lexicon: vocabulary 34

AUDIENCE AND PURPOSE

1. Why does Mitford begin with a historical example?
2. Although Mitford never is explicit in her argument against it, she makes the notion of burial in North America seem ludicrous. What are her tactics?
3. Why does Mitford take us through the embalming process step by step?

CONTENT

1. Why does Mitford name all the products used in embalming so explicitly?
2. Why does Mitford quote exactly from her sources?
3. How does the blend of embalmers' language and Mitford's use of physical detail make her point?

STYLE AND STRUCTURE

1. Why does Mitford call the dead man "Mr. Jones" throughout the essay?

2. Mitford pokes fun at the euphemisms used in the funeral industry. Give some examples.
3. Mitford is a master of understatement. Give some examples.
4. Why does Mitford so often use the passive voice throughout the essay?

Peter Gzowski

Peter Gzowski (b. 1934) is a Canadian journalist best known for his radio show, *Morningside,* which he hosted for fifteen years. He was awarded a Governor General's Performing Arts Award for Lifetime Achievement in Broadcasting and has been presented with the Canadian Journalism Foundation's Lifetime Achievement Award. In 1997, he received a Peabody for his Outstanding Contribution to Broadcasting and is the only Canadian ever to be given this award.

AND THE BEST DAMN STEW-MAKER TOO

One of the nicest things about growing up is the way you can enjoy all the foods you turned your nose up at as a kid.

Take liver. When I was young, liver was right up there with bullies and social studies on my list of things to be avoided. I still don't like bullies, and social studies, though I make a lot of my living talking about them on the radio, still give me trouble. (I miss all the blue questions at Trivial Pursuit, too.) But on liver I've come all the way round. From a pet hate it's turned into a favoured food; I eat it now—I would never have believed this when I was six—by choice, and lick my lips when I'm finished.

The liver I ate as a child, of course, was cut in slabs as thick as beaverboard and cooked till you could fix your roof with it. Now, I buy my slices as thin as I can—a quarter inch is about right—and eat it as rare as filet mignon. To cook it, I fry up some bacon first, and while it's sizzling I cut up a couple of onions. When the bacon's done, I set it aside on a paper towel, turn the heat down and sauté the onions in the drippings. When the onions are soft but not translucent, I set them aside, too, crank the heat back up, splash some wine vinegar into the pan ("deglazing" is too fancy a word for the way I cook) and sear my liver on each side for less time than it took Northern Dancer to win the Kentucky Derby—two minutes flat. Smothered in the bacon and onions, and with a little watercress vinaigrette on the side, it's food for the gods—or a grown-up.

Or spinach. Spinach was *punishment* when I was a kid: a soggy, mossy blob that lay on your plate like a mud pie, leaking green effluvium.

5 The trick with spinach, I know, is to cook it as little as possible. Just grab a handful, chop off the heaviest stems, run cold water over what you have left and, without shaking it dry, pop it into a saucepan, jam the lid on and cook on high for *one minute*

—Northern Dancer's time for five furlongs. Want to get fancy? Squeeze half a lemon over the spinach before you start to steam it. Want to get *really* fancy? Plop a dab of sour cream on top as you bring your spinach to the table. With either or neither or both, it's wonderful.

This side dish, come to think of it, could go with your liver-and-bacon-and-onions, even though, if my mother found out I was recommending liver and spinach in one meal, she'd push her halo aside and scratch her head in wonderment.

The greatest treat of all among the foods I once disdained is stew.

Stew was my mother's admission she'd run out of either ideas or money, a kind of dinner-hour equivalent of—and about as tasty as—the Red River Cereal she tried to convince me to eat in the mornings.

For the grown-up me, stew has become a source of sheer pleasure. I like eating it, spearing the tenderest cubes of nut-brown meat, savouring the gay orange carrots and pale parsnips —*parsnips?* my mother's halo just clattered to heaven's floor— and sopping up the last rivulets of dark gravy with chunks of fresh bread. I *love* cooking it, and in the long cold winter there is no happier way for me to spend a late Friday afternoon than to follow the ritual I am pleased to share with you now. The quantities, I should tell you, are for two people, though there'll be enough extra if someone drops in or, failing that, for a reheated (and delicious) Saturday lunch.

At the liquor store, get a bottle of dark, fairly dry sherry. Make sure they put it in a brown paper bag. (This may not help your reputation in a strange town, but be brave.)

At the butcher's, get a pound and a quarter of lean stewing beef, cut into inch-and-a-half cubes.

At the grocer's, pick up some leeks, cooking onions, a few carrots and parsnips, a tin of beef stock, a nineteen-ounce tin of tomatoes and a tin of whole, peeled potatoes. From a guy who likes things simple and old-fashioned, I know this last suggestion will surprise you. But experience has taught me that even the best potatoes, cooked from scratch in a stew, get just a bit starchier than those little ones they put in the cans.

If you don't have butter, olive oil, flour, pepper (beef stews need no salt), garlic and other spices at home, pick those up, too. Oh, what the heck, get another couple of heads of garlic anyway.

And from your favourite bakery, get a fresh baguette.

If you have a fireplace, begin by lighting a fire to take the chill from the fading day. Then open your sherry and pour yourself a small glass—the shopping was cold, after all. Put a sinfully thick slice of butter and about a quarter cup of your best olive oil into a generously sized saucepan or soup kettle, and turn the heat to medium-high. While the butter melts and blends with the golden oil, take the paper bag from the booze store, put a cup of flour into it and grind some pepper on top. Throw the cubes of meat in the bag and shake it vigorously. Pick the meat out by hand—the way the flour coats every piece evenly is surely one of the great miracles of the kitchen—and put it in the pan. As it browns, chop three or four peeled onions into eighths, and the white parts of the same number of leeks into inches. Chop a *lot* of garlic—I use about five cloves, but you can never have too much—and scrape everything in with the meat. Reduce the heat, have a sip of sherry and take a moment to enjoy the seductive smell rising from the pan. Stir from time to time with a wooden spoon.

When the meat is brown, splash in about a cup—who measures?—of the sherry and the tin of beef stock. Add a sprinkle of oregano, if it pleases you, or a bit of sweet basil. Lower the heat a notch (you don't want to *boil* it), and savour the smell again as you open the tin of tomatoes.

This is a good time to cut up the carrots and parsnips, as well—I peel the parsnips but just scrape the roughest skin off the carrots. Try to get all your pieces roughly the size of Brazil nuts.

You can slow down now, while your stew simmers. In another twenty minutes or so, add the tomatoes, liquid and all, and root veggies, and, half an hour after that, the tinned potatoes. Give it another ten or fifteen minutes—there's no rush, you know—while you put out some bowls, forks and spoons. You can rip up the baguette by hand.

The result, like youth itself, would be wasted on kids anyway.

VOCABULARY

effluvium: flow of waste 4
rivulets: streams 9
baguette: a long thin loaf of French bread 14

AUDIENCE AND PURPOSE

1. This essay is essentially a series of recipes, plain and simple. How does Gzowski make it more readable than that?
2. How does Gzowski make this into a personal essay?
3. Gzowski is not very exact in his instructions. Why?

CONTENT

1. Gzowski makes general references to his mother in heaven. Why are these references effective?
2. What does Gzowski imply about his mother's cooking?
3. There is a great deal of emphasis on clarity in this essay. How does Gzowski make his instructions understood to the reader?
4. Why does Gzowski repeat the reference to Northern Dancer?

STYLE AND STRUCTURE

1. Why does Gzowski begin and end with references to childhood?
2. Gzowski uses commands, as recipes usually do, but sometimes even when the instruction is not part of the recipe. Give an example.
3. Why does Gzowski use the pronoun "you" in this essay?

Comparison and Contrast

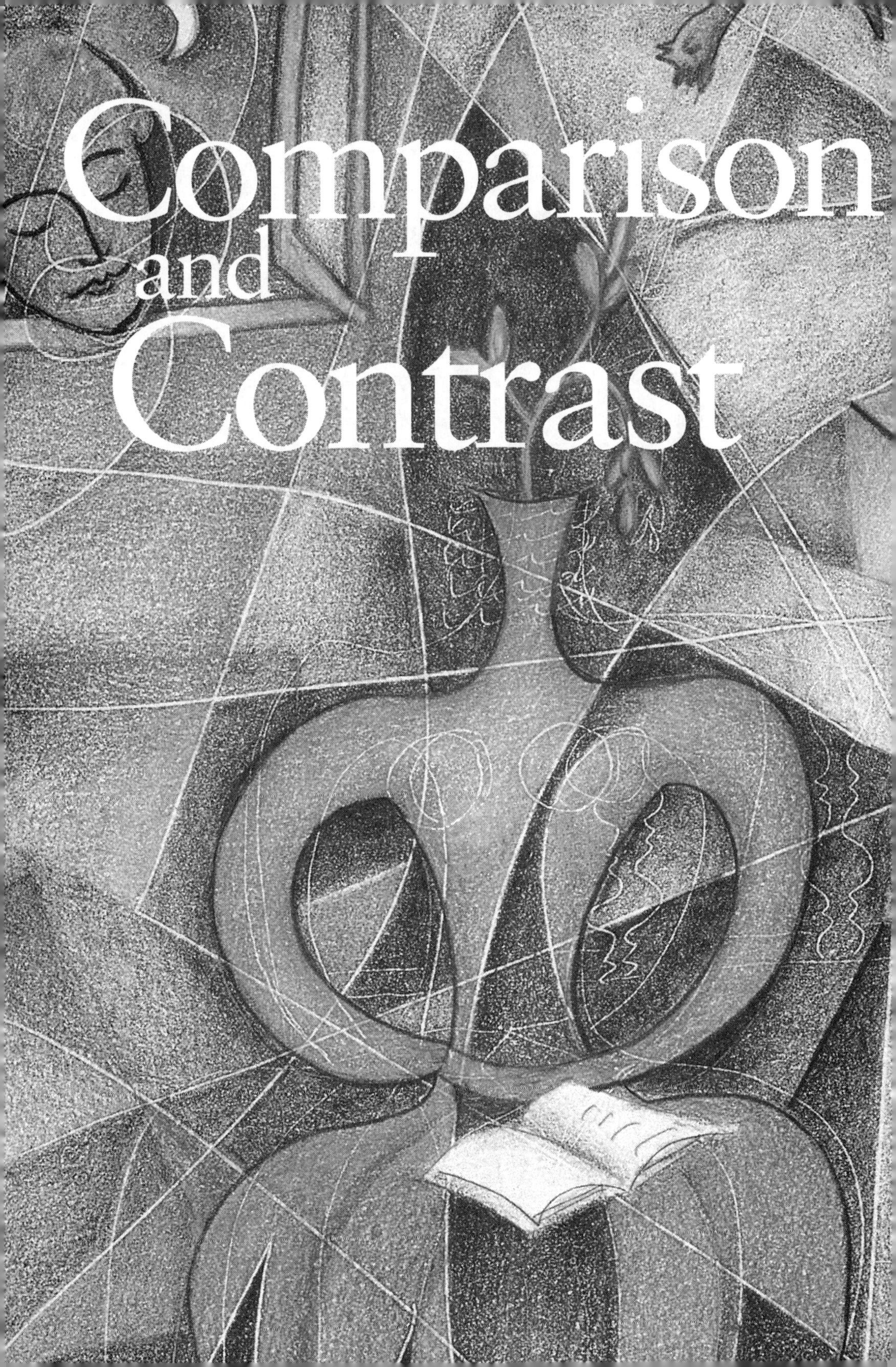

COMPARISON AND CONTRAST: WORKING TO ELUCIDATE AN ARGUMENT

Beyond Apples and Oranges

Comparison and contrast are important techniques for making a point. This pattern of rhetoric is one that you use frequently in school assignments and on examinations to demonstrate what you know about how provincial government works compared with federal government, or when you contrast the practices of environmentally conscious industries with those of companies known for careless pollution. You use comparison and contrast frequently in your daily life as well to explain how your life as a student is improved by having a part-time job compared with the lives of students who devote themselves full-time to the rigours of study. You might also use this method to compare why you think used books are a better idea than new ones, or how you think the movie you saw last night compares with other science fiction movies you have seen. Comparisons refer to the similarities between things; contrasts refer to the differences between them. Often you are called upon to refer to both similarities and differences, sometimes only to one and not the other.

Generally, comparison and contrast is not used just for its own sake but to illuminate something else. If you compare dogs and cats, you usually do so to prove that dogs are the superior pet, or that cats are more suitable companions for people who live in small urban homes. Seldom does one compare just for its own sake. It's important to remember what overall point you are making as you compare and contrast two things. Also, comparison and contrast almost always involves just two things, since the point you are trying to make may become convoluted if too many details intervene.

It is part of the writer's job to make the similarities and differences between two things absolutely clear to the reader. The reader should not be left in the awkward position of drawing his or her own conclusions at the end of the piece. To make sure that you are drawing out the appropriate points of comparison, divide your topic into suitable categories for consideration. If you want to compare and contrast two things, be clear at the outset why these two things invite comparison in the first place. Unless there is good reason to consider the two items together, such a writing strategy may not uncover much of value. You might, for example, begin by comparing the advantages of owning a bike with owning a car, in this case with an eye to showing that a bike is a better choice for a student. You might use the categories of cost, exercise level, and environmental friendliness to elaborate your comparison.

Two different structures are often called into play when you compare and contrast any pair of things. The first is used for simple comparisons that the reader can grasp easily. This is the *block comparison*, in which you completely describe one side of the comparison first, and only then fill in the other side. Block comparisons demand that they be short and to the point; otherwise, the reader will have too much to remember to appreciate the differences and similarities fully. Using the example of owning a bike over owning a car, our block comparison might look something like the following:

The first paragraph of this block comparison discusses the virtues of cars.

A car is a boon to students who want to visit their parents every weekend, but only if the students are willing to foot the bills for purchasing, maintaining, and insuring the car, not to mention keeping it full of gas. Cars are expensive not just to own but also to keep in operation. Cars are a good idea, too, if you are not concerned about your fitness level or if you already possess an expensive membership to a gym because you never have to walk more than a half a block in pursuit of anything, and your groceries and other purchases never become a burden to bear. Cars are great if you are not overly concerned about their impact on the environment. While they are messy, noisy, and hard on the environment, they are models of efficiency in getting from place to place.

If, on the other hand, you are satisfied to explore what's nearby without going too far afield, a bicycle is a far less costly alternative. With a minimum of maintenance, a little legwork, and a small outlay at the start, a bicycle will allow you to make small circuits in your neigh-

The second paragraph of the block comparison discusses the virtues of bikes.

bourhood without many worries about upkeep, maintenance, or insurance. Better still, the legwork will ensure that you get some exercise even if you typically lead the life of a sedentary student whose main exercise is turning pages. The bicycle, used as a means of getting to and from school, will guarantee that you wear off that extra plate of fries without much extra effort on your part. The bonus points come in the good that the bicycle will do for the environment and for your appreciation of it. Following bike trails and being outdoors will improve your health and increase your enjoyment of your environment, all the more so because you will not be contributing to the smoke, fumes, and odours normally associated with automobile use.

The other comparison and contrast structure is more common and intricate: the *point-by-point comparison*. In this case, the writer divides the things being compared into categories and then deals with each of them in turn. The following essay is an example of this method:

Of Mice and Human Habitation

Almost proverbial, the story of the city mouse and the country mouse is a study in the differences in attitudes and values that are involved in any choice of where to live. Students in particular often find their change in residence one of the challenges of adjusting to college or university. Many of them have to leave the comfort and familiarity of small towns for a larger, crowded city destination that seems to promise more people but fewer friends, and more opportunities but less welcome. Despite proverbial claims to the contrary, however, the city mouse is way ahead of the game. Students lucky enough to leave behind a pastoral setting for an urban one

The thesis statement makes a point-by-point comparison.

can congratulate themselves on several things: city life offers much more in terms of convenience, entertainment, and variety, whatever the charms of a more peaceful life.

This paragraph develops the first point of comparison.

Students in the city do not depend on the family car to get to school each day or even on their own physical prowess. Cities provide the ease and convenience of public transportation to make that journey simple and inexpensive. With a little planning, you can easily find a residence or apartment that is close to a bus stop or other public transport, not only making it possible for you to go to school independently, rain or shine, cheaply and efficiently, but also to go to other —perhaps more exciting—places. The larger the city, the more likely there are shops, bars, restaurants, gyms, and movie theatres within easy reach, often at all hours of the day or night. No more trudging two kilometres in the snow, or slogging back and forth to the grocery store carrying your week's supplies in your overburdened arms. Where you are going may be mere minutes away, without much needed in the way of strength or endurance.

This paragraph develops the second point of comparison.

Entertainment is an even more compelling attraction of urban life. If you pick your city with care, it should afford occasions for bargain rush seats for entertainment as varied as ballet, opera, music, or sports. This list includes only spectator sports and doesn't begin to plumb the range of possibilities of activities you can pursue on your own or with friends. In a more sheltered country setting, you can go on nature walks, it's true, but can you join a martial arts class? Visit a large bookstore? Learn ballroom dancing? Get a ticket to the latest concert and then walk to your destination? If the answer to any of these is no, perhaps you ought to think about the merits of living in the city. While it's true that you can go skating on the pond in the country, the assurance of a publicly supported rink may be better for your physical well-being anyhow. And even the most developed of high-rise city areas has parks and trails, most of which are safer to negotiate and policed more carefully than any trails in the country. Your parents might actually find that you are safer in a big city with the promise of such security within easy access.

This paragraph develops the third point of comparison.

Variety is another consideration in the advantages that make up city life. Variety comes in a number of forms in the city beyond just extracurricular activities. For one thing, the people themselves provide it, given that cities are the traditional destinations of new immigrants from every country of the world. The city also supplies the broadest range in class distinctions, from homeless waifs to pillars of society. All nationalities, languages, and points of view are accounted for in a city, and while that can be disorienting, it is almost certainly also educational. In the small town where lots of students grow up, all the families are related or acquainted, and a great deal—sometimes too much—is known about every member of every clan. In a big city apartment building, there is probably already more variety than in a small town, and exposure to it is undoubtedly something that makes a city-dwelling student worldly in a knowledgeable and sophisticated way. Education is about broadening your horizons, or so we are told. The best way to do that is to make it part of your life and not just a part of your course work.

Conclusion

The country has things going for it, to be sure, and if you want to return to a country or small town setting after your schooling is over, you could make a good case for its peacefulness, familiarity, and natural beauty. But for the convenience, efficiency, openness to change, and urge for stimulating activity that often motivate a young student, you just can't beat the city life. Vow to become a country mouse only after you've been a city mouse for an extended period of time. Cities aren't just for visits; they can be a way of life too.

Deborah Tannen

Deborah Tannen (b. 1945) is a professor at Georgetown University. Her most recent book is *The Argument Culture* (1998). Her other works include *You Just Don't Understand: Women and Men in Conversation* (1990), which was a bestseller for nearly four years, and *Talking from 9 to 5 — Women and Men in the Workplace: Language, Sex and Power* (1994).

LISTENING TO MEN, THEN AND NOW

A woman and a man meet at the end of the day. He asks how her day was, and she replies with a long report of what she did, whom she met, what they said and what that made her think and feel. Then she eagerly turns to him:

She: How was your day?
He: Same old rat race.
She: Didn't anything happen?
He: Nah, nothing much.

Her disappointment is deepened when that evening they go out to dinner with friends and suddenly he regales the group with an amusing account of something that happened at work. She is cut to the quick, crestfallen at hearing this story as part of an audience of strangers. "How could he have said nothing happened?" she wonders. "Why didn't he tell me this before? What am I? Chopped liver?"

The key to this frustration is that women and men typically have different ideas about what makes people friends. For many women, as for girls, talk is the glue of close relationships; your best friend is the one you tell your secrets to, the one you discuss your troubles with. For many men, as for boys, activities are central; your best friend is the one you do everything with (and the one who will stick up for you if there is a fight).

As the millennium approaches and commentators examine how our lives have changed in the last thousand years, I find myself wondering about the change in relations between the sexes. Clearly there has been a transformation. In the past, the woman was deferential, subordinate. Now we are not trying to be partners in a societal arrangement with a clearly defined separation of labor, but rather hoping to be each other's best friends. Yet at least two aspects of women's and men's relations have endured — our differing expectations about the importance of talk in intimacy, and the tendency of women to take the role of listener in conversation with men.

5 In the absence of tape recordings from earlier times, we can look to conversations in literature. For a glimpse of how a 16th-century couple might have talked to each other, I turned to Shakespeare—and my earliest memory of his plays. When I was at Ditmas Junior High in Brooklyn, my classmates were all atitter: our teacher had us reading "Julius Caesar" aloud, and, having read ahead, we knew that the next day some poor girl would have to stand and read a passage in which Brutus's wife uses the word "harlot." Susan Ehrlich had the bad luck to be chosen, and I can still see her, tall and brown-haired, reading, "Portia is Brutus's harlot, not his wife."

Revisiting those lines today, what strikes me is how similar the sentiment is to what I hear from contemporary women. Portia wants to be Brutus's best friend—and her idea of what this means is similar to ours. Waking up to discover that her husband has left their bed, she finds him pacing, and implores him to say what is worrying him. Like the modern woman who feels that best friends tell each other secrets, Portia pleads:

Within the bond of marriage, tell me Brutus,
Is it excepted I should know no secrets
That appertain to you? Am I yourself
But, as it were, in sort or limitation,
To keep with you at meals, comfort your bed,
And talk to you sometimes? Dwell I but in the suburbs
Of your good pleasure? If it be no more,
Portia is Brutus's harlot, not his wife.

A similar sentiment merges in an even more distant conversation—in the Arabian romance of the Bedouin hero Antar, believed to have been written between 1080 and 1400. In one episode, a character named al-Minhal, escaping a king he has wronged, comes upon a ruined castle inhabited by a female demon named Dahiya. She gives him shelter, feeds him, falls in love with him and wins his love by her attentions, which include her conversation. Sounding rather like Portia, Dahiya says: "I want you to be my companion and to be my lord, and I will be your wife. Disclose to me what is in your heart. Do not believe that I will ever let you go. Open your mind to me for I have need to know your thoughts." They are married on the spot, and, we are told, "Long was their companionship, and they loved each other dearly."

I am not suggesting that relationships between women and men were the same then as now. But it's intriguing to think that what women regard as intimacy, talking about what's on your mind, has been a common thread right through the millenium. There's another, related pattern that seems to have endured. It, too, is evident in the case of the husband who can't think of anything to tell his wife but comes up with an amusing story to entertain a dinner gathering. To her, it's a failure of intimacy: if we're truly close, I should hear everything first. To him, I think, the situation of being home with someone he feels close to does not call for a story performance. This creates a paradox. Many women were drawn to the men they fell in love with because the men told captivating stories. After marriage, the women expect that the closer they get, the more the men will open up and tell. Instead, to their deep disappointment, after marriage the men clam up.

Once again, looking at how boys and girls are socialized provides a key. Boys' groups are hierarchical; low-status boys are pushed around. One way boys earn and keep status is to hold center stage by verbal performance—boasting, telling jokes or recounting mesmerizing stories. And this seems to work well in winning maidens as well.

10 This aspect of storytelling can be seen as far back as "Beowulf," that Anglo-Saxon saga, usually dated to the eighth century. The hero, a member of a Swedish tribe known as the Geats, wins the attention of Wealhtheow, queen of Hrothgar, who is serving beer to a gathering of men:

> *Beowulf spoke, the son of Ecgtheow: "I resolved, when I set out on the sea, sat down in the sea-boat with my band of men, that I should altogether fulfill the will of your people or else fall in slaughter, fast in the foe's grasp. I shall achieve a deed of manly courage or else have lived to see in the mead-hall my ending day." These words were well-pleasing to the woman, the boast of the Geat. Gold-adorned, the noble folk-queen went to sit by her lord.*

Boasting, my colleague Catherine Ball tells me, was a customary male activity in the Anglo-Saxon mead-hall, so it is not surprising that Wealhtheow was well pleased, even though the exploits Beowulf boasts of have not yet taken place. (In fact, he sounds a little like Cassius Clay predicting what he will do to Sonny Liston.)

This scenario—a woman wooed by a man's boasts of exploits in battle—brings us back to Shakespearean icons: Desdemona and Othello. As Othello tells "how I did thrive in this fair lady's love," he explains that she became entranced when she heard him telling "the story of my life":

Wherein I spoke of most disastrous chances:
Of moving accidents by flood and field,
Of hair-breadth scapes i'th'imminent deadly breach;
Of being taken by the insolent foe....

And so on, until:

My story being done,
She gave me for my pains a world of kisses. ...
And bad me, if I had a friend that lov'd her,
I should but teach him how to tell my story,
And that would woo her.

As we know, he wooed her himself with his own story.

In our era, the tactic of wooing by verbal performance takes a funny turn. Etiquette books of the 50s instructed young women to be good listeners if they wanted to win their men, and you need only look around a restaurant to see many women attentively listening to talking men. In place of battle yarns, what I hear, over and over, is that a woman fell in love because "he makes me laugh." That's why Michelle Pfeiffer said in 1992 she picked a particular boyfriend, and why Joanne Woodward fell for Paul Newman. I don't hear the same explanation from men as to why they fall in love. What I hear is the corresponding one, as for example when Woody Allen said of his relationship with Soon-Yi Previn: "She's a marvel. And she laughs at all my jokes."

We seem to have a situation of *plus ça change*. Even as relationships between men and women have changed, our contrasting expectations about the meaning of closeness still cause confusion and disappointment. And though the performance has shifted from heroic tales to amusing entertainment, more often than not the apportionment of roles has stayed the same: Women are the audience and men are the show.

VOCABULARY

deferential: respectful 4
appertain: belong 6
icons: symbols 12
plus ça change: the more things change (the more they stay the same) (French) 16

AUDIENCE AND PURPOSE

1. Why does Tannen begin with a dialogue between a man and a woman?
2. Why does Tannen go to literature for her examples of men and women's relations in the past?
3. Tannen argues that two things remain the same in the relations of men and women today. What are these things?

CONTENT

1. How does Tannen use the example of Portia and Brutus in *Julius Caesar* to parallel the modern relations of men and women?
2. Tannen claims that men are socialized differently from women, and this socialization affects their understanding of each other. Explain.
3. How does Tannen use an example from *Beowulf* to show how men continue to woo women?
4. How does she use *Othello* to further this thinking?

STYLE AND STRUCTURE

1. Where is the thesis statement of this essay?
2. Tannen uses examples from classic literature and from pop culture to make her point. Why is this mixture effective?
3. What is the effect of the concise concluding sentence?

Hugh MacLennan

Hugh MacLennan's (1907–90) best-known novels include *Two Solitudes* (1945) and *The Watch That Ends the Night* (1959). He received the Governor General's Award three times for his fiction. The best of his essays are collected in *The Other Side of Hugh MacLennan* (1978). His work is well known for its stress on Canadian nationalism.

IF YOU DROP A STONE ...

If you drop a stone into the ocean the impact is as great as if you drop it into a farmer's pond. The difference is that the ocean doesn't seem to care. It swallows the stone and rolls on. But the pond, if the stone is large enough, breaks into waves and ripples that cover its surface and are audible in every cranny along its banks.

So it is with life in a metropolis and life in a small town. It takes a colossal event to affect a city. After the bombing of Hamburg in which eighty thousand people were killed, the city was functioning within a few days. Grief did not paralyse it because, to the survivors, most of the casualties were people they had never met. But a single murder can convulse a small town for the reason that in such a community people care who lives and who dies. They care because they know each other. All knowledge is relative to our capacity to grasp its details, and no matter what the communists and industrial organizers may say, no man can think humanly if he thinks in terms of masses. In the small town, and not in the metropolis, human life is understood in fundamental terms.

Because I grew up in a smallish town, this idea struck me with the force of a shock the first time I saw a play in London about London life. I marvelled how any audience could believe in it. Apparently, I thought, Londoners don't know each other and the playwright has taken advantage of their ignorance. A play as superficial as this, I said to myself when I left the theatre, could never succeed in Halifax.

My youthful reaction was naïve, but it was not stupid. I did not know then, as I have learned since, that practically no creative ideas have ever originated in a megalopolis. The prelude to creation, as every parent knows, is intimacy. I had come straight to London from an intimate town, and what we knew about each other in that town could have kept a Balzac supplied with material for life. Small-town gossip may be notorious, but by no means all of it is malicious. It has one virtue which its metropolitan imitators, the newspapers, cannot claim. Most of it has personal significance for the people who listen to it.

We knew in our town, for example, and we knew in detail, how our wealthiest citizens had made their money. Although we did not know a neurosis from a psychosis, we understood, and made allowances for, the family conditions which caused one man to be aggressive and another subservient, one woman to be charming and another to be a shrew. We had a sixth sense which the more intelligent city-dwellers lack—a sense of time. We knew that a family, like Rome, is not built in a day.

We would look at one family and remember hearing about the grandfather, now dead, who used to sit in his galluses on a stool outside the livery stable chewing a straw and occasionally reaching up with the thumb of his left hand to scratch his head. It had been a matter of interested speculation whether he scratched because he was nervous or because he was lousy. The father, still with us, was a middle-aged man doing fairly well in a hardware business. He never scratched his head, but it was noticed that he had a curious habit of stopping suddenly while walking down the street to lift the right leg of his trousers and scratch the back of his calf. As the hardware merchant was certainly not lousy, this gesture was assumed to be hereditary; as such, it cleared the grandfather's reputation from all suspicion of uncleanliness. The merchant's son raised the family one notch higher. He went to college, did well, and now was laying the foundations of a solid career in the administration in Ottawa. Perhaps he might even rise to cabinet rank and make us all proud, for rumour had it that the Prime Minister's eye was on him. Incidentally, he was never seen to scratch himself at all.

This kind of small-town knowledge may seem petty, but the sum of it is vast. Through a multitude of intimate details people come to know the best and the worst about each other, and concealment of character is impossible over a lifetime. A ruthless or a cunning man can ride roughshod over his neighbours and cop most of the money in the place. In every small town there are always a few who try this, and at least one who succeeds. They make bad bargains, for they spend the rest of their days knowing exactly what their neighbours think and say about them. In the small town, since everyone knows the sins of everyone else, each man must live as best he can with the knowledge that his faults and weaknesses are part of the lore of the whole community. That is what I mean by saying that in a small town people know life as it really is. That is why Halifax or Peterborough has a better chance of producing a Balzac than London or New York, and why a little place like Bermuda, where the stakes are really high, could produce a second Shakespeare if some Bermudian had the genius and the nerve to write as Shakespeare did.

But for the past two hundred years the small towns have failed in what should be their mission, which is the illumination of life. Only to a very small extent has their unrivalled knowledge of life been used for artistic purposes. They have given the world nearly all its famous writers and artists, but the moment their gifted children are ready to produce they are compelled to leave home and emigrate to the city. "Appearances must be maintained," a small-town friend said to me not long ago; "otherwise life couldn't go on." But to maintain appearances is the one thing no creative artist can ever do. If he tries, his work shows as much liveliness and veracity as the average obituary column. So, for freedom's sake, he moves to the big city and there he tends to stay. That is why for the past two hundred years art has always been associated in people's minds with the life of the metropolis.

But the metropolis—London, Paris, New York, Rome—does not nurture art. It merely gives the immigrant artist or writer freedom to paint or write as he pleases. And it exacts a bitter price for this freedom, the loss of the small-town intimacy from which all life-knowledge derives. That is why so many writers over the past two hundred years have done their best work before they were forty. In their early years in the big city, they availed themselves of the freedom it offered to be themselves. They wrote, generally, of the life they had lived in their native regions. But as they grew older they inevitably consumed their vital material, and in middle age they tended to run dry. The metropolis which was now their home failed to provide them with the life-giving material they required.

10 The very freedom the big city grants is based on a kind of indifference to the individual, an indifference that springs from ignorance. The city has no real gossip. In the city a man is a name or a career, a unit in a factory or the occupant of an office desk. There is no universal folk-memory of the grandfather who scratched his head or the son who hoisted his trouser to scratch the back of his leg. The emotional upheavals which shatter families are swallowed up by the city as the ocean swallowed the *Titanic*, and to the onlooking artist they seem almost as meaningless as traffic accidents because he cannot possibly know, much less feel, the forces which caused them.

When modern writers attempt to use metropolitan life as the material for tragedy their work is usually cold and dry. This has been especially notable in the English-speaking centres of London and New York. It is true that Dickens was a Londoner; it is equally true that he saw only the surface of things. As for New York, in the whole of American literature not a single great book has been based on its life.

How could it be? In New York, who cares who commits suicide? The crowds massed in the street to see if the stranger will jump from the skyscraper window are not interested in the man, because they do not know him. They are interested only in the spectacle. In New York, who cares who cheats whom? Or who survives through endurance? Or who, by a denial of himself, wins spiritual greatness? This does not imply that New York is less noble than a small town. It merely implies that in terms of art it is too large for any individual artist to handle.

Far different was the situation in the days when no cities were immense and a few small or medium-sized towns were the life-centres of a whole people. Ancient Athens at the height of her glory had a voting list somewhat smaller than that of modern Halifax. But she had a spirit which Halifax and all modern smallish towns entirely lack — she preferred excitement to caution and greatness to respectability. She invented tragic and comic drama, the art of history, and the democratic method of government. All these stupendous inventions arose out of her own experience. The characters in her great comedies were living Athenian citizens, and when Socrates was satirized in *The Clouds* by Aristophanes he rose in the theatre so that everyone would know that he was enjoying the play, too. Plato's *Republic* had its origin in a dinner party which assembled after a late-afternoon walk just as casually as Joe Smith gets together his cronies for a poker game by the simple expedient of walking the length of the main street from the barber shop to the Maple Leaf Hotel.

It has always been the same — without intimacy, there can be no creation. Republican Rome was a relatively small town. Florence, Genoa, Venice, and Pisa, in the days of their glory, were about a quarter the size of Ottawa. In Shakespeare's London everyone who mattered knew everyone else, and we can be pretty certain that the characters who live in Shakespeare's plays were modelled on people the playwright knew personally or had heard about from the intimate gossip of others who did.

15 But these wonderful small towns had one thing in common besides the intimate knowledge of life which all small towns share. It never occurred to them that their knowledge should be repressed "in order that life might go on." There was no con-

spiracy of silence when it came to writing books and plays. The citizens were not afraid of gossip. In such communities a man like Mackenzie King could never have become Prime Minister, nor would a generation of public servants have admired his theory that a leader should veil his thoughts in the stuffiest language possible lest the public become sufficiently interested to make an effort to find out what he was talking about.

It seems to me, thinking along these lines, that the cultural future of Canada is opposed only by fear of what the neighbours will say. For Canada, by and large, is still a nation of small towns. Toronto, for all its sprawling size, has a small-town psychology. So, when it comes down to it, does Montreal; in this city we still have a great deal of the intimate small-town knowledge of life which New York and London lack. It has made us shrewder than we realize. We know, for example, that our present material prosperity does not mean, in itself, that we are a great country. We know intuitively that we will become great only when we translate our force and knowledge into spiritual and artistic terms. Then, and only then, will it matter to mankind whether Canada has existed or not.

VOCABULARY

galluses: suspenders 6
veracity: truth 8

AUDIENCE AND PURPOSE

1. What introductory comparison does MacLennan use to set up his argument? Why is it effective?
2. MacLennan argues that intimacy is essential to creation and cannot be achieved in a city. Does his argument convince you? Why or why not?
3. How might MacLennan's attitude toward the importance of small towns have an impact on the arts in Canada?

CONTENT

1. Why, in MacLennan's view, does the city not nurture creativity as the small town does?
2. Why did Athens thrive as a city in MacLennan's estimation?
3. What prevents Canada from developing writers with the stature of Shakespeare or Balzac if it is, as MacLennan shows, a nation of small towns?

STYLE AND STRUCTURE

1. MacLennan makes many bold generalizations, the main one of which is that "practically no creative ideas have ever originated in a megalopolis"? Are such generalizations persuasive? Why or why not?
2. Why does MacLennan use the homely examples of a grandfather, a father, and his son from his own small town?
3. How does MacLennan come to compare Joe Smith from his own small town with Plato? Does the comparison work, in your view? Explain.
4. Find examples of MacLennan's generalizations and comment on their effect.

Margaret Atwood

Margaret Atwood (b. 1939) is a Canadian writer best known for her novels, including *The Edible Woman* (1969), *The Handmaid's Tale* (1985), and *Alias Grace* (1996), and her poetry, the most recent volume of which is called *Morning in the Burned House* (1995).

APPROXIMATE HOMES

1. DOWN HOME

Down home, they would say, although what they meant was north on the map. I used to wonder—why was home always down? Nobody ever said *up home*. But now I know: home is down the way memory is down, and hidden springs of water. Derelict cities, abandoned bones, lost keys.

Home is buried. You have to dig for it.

2. THE HOME FOR INCURABLE CHILDREN

In one of my phases of being a child, which took place in Toronto at the end of the forties, there was a building called The Home for Incurable Children.

We make fun of our predecessors for their euphemisms, but in fact these were mostly for sex. In other matters they were blunt in their labelling to the point of crudeness. Thus we once had The Provincial Lunatic Asylum: no beating about the bush there. And orphans were put into orphanages. Everything in its place.

5 The Home for Incurable Children was made of brownish-red brick, and was grim. There was the sign with its name in big black letters, right on the lawn. There on the lawn, too, in summer, were the incurable children, dressed usually in white, sitting usually in chairs, wan and set apart—a warning to us other children. If we became for some reason incurable, would we too be put in there? And where were the mummies and daddies?

These children, we were told in sad adult voices, would never grow up. We did not confuse this state with what we knew about Peter Pan. In fact, The Home for Incurable Children made growing up seem a more desirable thing than perhaps it was, and we became very anxious to do it.

Once I'd managed to escape from childhood as far as high school, The Home for Incurable Children still obsessed me. It was the name: I could see it contained a swarm of meanings. Did "incurable children" mean those who could not be cured of being children? Was it childhood itself that was the disease? And "home"—why call it a home, when everyone knew it wasn't a real home at all, but, like "homes for the elderly," the exact opposite? If such places really were homes, what a sinister and quicksand twist it gave the word!

A home wasn't where the heart was, but where it wasn't. It was where you were stuck when nobody wanted you. *Home* was the name for longing.

3. A HOUSE IS NOT A HOME

It was little girls who taught me the game called "playing house." It was never called "playing home." The real-estate ads always say "home," not "house," but little girls are the reverse. For them, the house comes first.

10 My brother was no good at this game. His idea of the thing was a sand house, or better still a fortress, which we would then drop rocks on. Occasionally he would go so far as to play Baby to my doting Mother, but only in order to scream and demand things. I quickly saw that with him I was better off as part of a bombing squadron.

The little girls however knew houses backwards and forwards. The cupboards will be here, this will be the table, these are the beds; here is where we do the ironing, this is the stove, over there can be the sink. Such talk would go on for some time. Then, finally, everything would be in order; and then what?

It was the *and then what* I had trouble with. The other little girls would solve the problem by serving a meal or having someone fall ill, but these were not enough for me; because after the meal must come the washing of the dishes, and then another meal, and after the illness must come a cure; and after the cure, then another meal or another illness, and then what?

Playing house, so comforting for other little girls, caused a great deal more anxiety for me than it was worth. Faced with those dolly teacups, those plates made of leaves, that cutlery of twigs, those relentless cupboards, tables, and beds, in endless variations and proliferations but always essentially the same—how much more desirable it seemed to reduce them to rubble with a few well-placed sticks of dynamite.

At least it would be an end. At least, then, you would know.

4. HOME FREE

15 Long ago, before television and the fears of their parents had drawn them indoors, children used to stay out after supper. In the late-spring evenings, humid and dense and smelling of lilacs and mowed lawns, they would play in groups and gangs and mobs, in the streets and in and out of their yards, and in vacant lots and on beaches — long, intricate, exciting, tedious, and inexplicable games.

Here is one we played. It was called "Kick the Can." You needed a can — a tomato juice can, big size, was about right. It had to be large enough to make a clanging noise when kicked. A home space would be marked out, drawn with a stick in the dirt; the can would be placed on its frontier. An It was chosen, who had to guard both home space and can. The other children would run tantalizingly near; if tagged they were caught, and imprisoned in the home, where they had to stay, held by invisible walls, sneering and jumping up and down and licking the blood from their scraped elbows. But if a free child could run close enough to kick the can, there would be a general escape.

When almost all had been caught and were locked into home, the It could go further afield in search of prey; but if the last remaining free one could sneak into the home space untagged, and yell *Home free!*, the power of the It was shattered and all enchantments broken, and the game was over.

The home space — how odd it was! A precious thing, to be guarded; also a dungeon. You didn't want to be kept in it against your will, yet it was bliss to enter it when forbidden, sliding in, skidding in, throwing yourself in, and shrieking at the top of your lungs: *Home free!* What a relief, what a triumph! And what a triumph also to kick the tomato juice can, so that everyone could run away from home. Well, it was more or less how we felt about our real homes: ours to claim when we wanted them, ours to be trapped in, ours to escape from.

I may have got the rules wrong though; I may have mixed them up with some other game. It was quite a long time ago now.

5. THE CONSUMERS' GAS "MISS FUTURE HOMEMAKER CONTEST"

20 The fifties was the age of contests: contests for teenaged girls. I once met someone who had been Miss Wool, and who'd had to

wear an itchy wardrobe and carry around a live lamb, which peed on her. A friend of mine was once Miss Vodka, which was more dangerous as it involved a clutch of middle-aged men who'd been testing the product. She leapt from a moving convertible, and quit.

The Consumers' Gas "Miss Future Homemaker Contest" was less hazardous. It was held during the Home Show. You had to iron a shirt with a gas iron, cook a dinner on a gas stove, and do a third thing involving gas, which I have repressed. Myself and my partner—was it you, Sally?—were chosen as the entrants from our high school Home Economics class. In this class we were learning to be homemakers, or else—like our teacher, who was a Miss and whose hobby was skiing—we were learning to teach other girls to be them.

By the year of the contest we were quite advanced. We'd progressed from sewing aprons to sewing whole outfits, with box pleats and interfacing and dressmaker buttonholes; we'd gone from applesauce to balanced meals with each food group represented. I do not jeer at such knowledge. I shudder to think how many young girls now are hurled into life without it, and are forced to read magazines. The making of a choux paste is a skill I retain, though seldom use. They were not called choux then, however, but cream puffs. As I said, it was the fifties.

For the Miss Future Homemaker Contest, Sally and I dressed neatly and wore aprons; homemakers were supposed to be very clean and efficient. The menu for the dinner was pre-set: meat loaf, frozen peas, baked potatoes. There was a time limit—how fast you could get the shirt wrinkle-free and slide the meat loaf out of the oven. (This aspect of it I found hilarious. The husband marches in from the office, left right left right. Off with the old wrinkly shirt, on with the newly pressed one, and Hup! over to the table. Whomp! goes the meat loaf onto his plate! Blop! goes the baked potato! Pitter-patter go the peas! And now, for the third thing involving gas....)

Sally and I were speedy, but we didn't win, although we each received a charm bracelet with little golden bells on it. Perhaps the judges detected my lack of sincerity; but did they really think that I thought that this rushing about in aprons with gas appliances had anything to do with real life? Not mine, that was for sure; I wasn't going to end up making any homes! Not me.

25 I did make some, though. Several of them. I once knitted a whole bedspread, if you can believe it. I once put up two dozen jars of mustard pickle. I once baked bread.

6. HOME LAND

I don't have a home town, but I have a home land. A chunk of pink granite sticking out of the ground, a kettle bog, a horizon line of ragged black spruce: ah! there you are! Home!

I'm most at home in an airplane, a thousand feet up, skimming over the taiga at one remove. Lake, lake, lake, swamp, sprinkle of low hills, twist of river; ice creeping out from the shores. It has to be big, though; rocky, sparse, a place you could find yourself lost in easy as pie, and walk around in circles and die of exposure. Me too, you understand; when it comes to home, I'm no expert.

Out the window, way down there: desolation, instant panic, slow starvation. With a view like that you can feel comfortable.

7. NO HOME TOWN

Between 1936 and 1948 my parents moved twenty times. Sometimes between two fixed points—to a city in the late fall, to the forest in the early spring; sometimes it was from one city to another. My mother and father were from Nova Scotia, and that was *home* to them. But it wasn't where I was. So where was I?

Here and there, but never both at once. Home was not a place but a trajectory; it was the dotted line that marked our trail. It would appear out of boxes and suitcases, be packed away, appear again in a different form, in a different room, after a long and uncomfortable journey, hundreds of miles in the back of a car stuffed full of bundles and packages, then on the bottom of a canoe with the rain dribbling down your neck or on a sleigh drawn by horses over the creaking ice. You couldn't count on home. You couldn't count on it to stay put.

What has become of them, those provisional homes—the second-floor apartment in Ottawa with its long dark hallways, and the French Canadian and the English Canadian who lived below, and were always squabbling, and were married to each other? Or the drafty mansion in Sault Ste. Marie, which was falling apart and stood in a field of cabbages, with the hole in the ceiling through which we dropped crayons onto the stove to melt in puddles of smelly colour? Or the one house that was torn down, or the other one that burned down; or the tent whose roof you weren't supposed to touch for fear of leaks? That tent had no floor, and the mice always got in; they knew a good home when they saw it.

We're almost home now, they would say, in the middle of the rainstorm or the middle of the night, whichever was darker, and that was always the best part of home: the moment before lamplight. Home was something that was constantly being approached but could never be reached, because we'd left it days ago, we'd locked the door and hidden the key, and it was already behind us. It's not only that you can't go home again, you can never get there in the first place.

Here we are—home at last! they would say; though home had no location, only a direction: *homeward*. And yet we went on—we go on—believing we are there.

VOCABULARY

euphemisms: pleasant words for unpleasant things 4
proliferations: rapid increases 13
taiga: a plant system located between the tundra and coniferous forests 27
trajectory: the curved path of a projectile 30
provisional: temporary 31

AUDIENCE AND PURPOSE

1. Atwood compares uses of the word "home" but never draws any particular conclusions. Why?
2. Atwood uses the images of home to explore her own childhood development. Trace this development through each section. What do we find out about her?
3. Atwood ends up showing that home is not a place but a direction. How does this attempted definition fit in with some of her earlier attempts at definition?

CONTENT

1. How does Atwood capture home as a place in each of her contrasting vignettes?
2. Many of Atwood's notions of home reflect something significant about our attitudes toward women. Give examples.
3. How does home define a person in Atwood's conceptions of it?

STYLE AND STRUCTURE

1. Why does Atwood use headings to divide her various configurations of home?

2. Atwood uses many sentence fragments. What is the effect of this device in her writing?
3. In some ways this is a memory piece. Where does Atwood make reference to her memory or its failure?

Ann Marie McQueen

Ann Marie McQueen (b. 1970) is a reporter with the *Ottawa Sun.*

MY FLING WITH MEN'S MAGS

Like a furtive boy trying to sneak a peak at the latest Hustler or Playboy, my visits to magazine racks of late have been spent lurking in front of titles such as Details, Maxim and GQ. As I crack their covers, all graced with near-nude models, I pretend I am buying for a boyfriend or brother. But actually, they are for me. You see, I'm rethinking the long-term relationship I've had with magazines such as Glamour and Cosmopolitan, and deciding in the process that I like men's magazines better.

I have been an avid reader of women's magazines for more than a decade. At 29, I am their advertisers' dream date—the working female with a passion for cosmetics, clothes, shoes, fragrances, pop culture and gadgets—and every month I get reeled right in. But lately I've grown bored with my old guilty pleasures. They've all started to look the same, and I've grown tired with what their writers tell me month after month.

How many recycled sex, dating, beauty and fashion articles can one person take? Do I really need some expert in the May Cosmopolitan telling me How To Become A Man Magnet, or the May Glamour providing tips on What Makes A Man Cross The Line From Like To Love? Is there anything redeeming about a piece detailing the connection between chest hair quantity and a man's psyche? (In case you're interested, a man with a light sprinkling is more likely to have an average sex drive than a hairy wonder of a man who "shouts sexual power.")

Recently a male co-worker loaned me a new publication called Stuff, and several back issues of Maxim, a men's magazine that is getting a lot of attention. I was amazed. The articles and captions had me laughing out loud. Not only was it fascinating to read about my gender from a completely different perspective, the life-is-a-big-fun-game tone was a refreshing change.

5 Sure, I may be a little embarrassed to approach the Chapters clerk with a magazine featuring a buxom, come-hither actress or model pictured on the cover—Maxim's trademark. But wait, wasn't that starlet Sarah Michelle Gellar on my June Cosmo, in a pink dress with a plunging neckline?

It all seems fairly calculated to me. Warrior-princess Lucy Lawless, featured on the Maxim cover back in April, seemed to breathe to men, "This is what you want." As far as I can figure, the only message the current Cosmo cover featuring model Rebecca Romijn-Stamos in a leather micro-miniskirt and lace doily sends to women is, "This is what you should be like." Could feeding on women's insecurities and body issues be the reason women's magazines don't feature men on their covers? Or is it all part of a master plan to give men more to look at on their way through the checkout line?

The men's mags include articles on wacky subjects you couldn't find anywhere else. Some of them could prove valuable (though it's unlikely)—from the June Maxim piece How To Escape A Sinking Car to Details's June guide to surviving a war zone. Their advice if a grenade ever happens to roll your way? "Your best bet is to put your ass to the blast, open your mouth, cover your ears and pray."

A recent issue of Stuff includes an interview with a doctor who studies decomposing corpses at the University of Tennessee Body Farm. ("Ever thrown up?" Stuff's cheeky reporter asks.) It also gives the lowdown on how a breath-analysis machine works, and compelling photographs of the Gnarliest Sports Injuries Of All Time.

As you can probably tell, these magazines soar in an area where women's mags fall flat: They are funny—really funny, not just trying hard. An article in last October's Maxim called That Damn Maxim Office Game listed hundreds of workplace pranks: "When no one's watching, remove the paper tray from the photocopier or laser printer and, with a felt pen, write the word Satan on several sheets at random. Reinsert tray." June's GQ even features an 88-page section saluting humour, complete with a list purporting to include the 75 funniest jokes of all time.

10 How can these not lure my attention away from absurdities such as I Can Steal Your Boyfriend, published in Cosmo's May issue, or the June Glamour's invitation to find out my "lovemaking personality?"

Admittedly, both types of magazines focus on what many men and women really want, which is to attract desirable members of the opposite sex. But men's magazines seem to do it by trying to describe what women feel, think and want, while the versions available for women frequently instruct "how to change yourself to get him."

There's a difference between learning how to make the perfect margarita and a four-day countdown-to-the-date guide to make you feel "suddenly sexier, slimmer and more in-the-sack sensational" (Cosmo in June).

After reading these men's magazines, I'm left with the generalized impression men just don't take themselves, and the rest of the world, as seriously as women do. What a relief to stop constantly analyzing my emotions and motivations — not to mention eyebrow-plucking style — and just laugh and learn a little.

I wish editorial staffers at the publications that took me from my teenage years to womanhood would realize just how out-of-step they have become, before I have to swear off them altogether. Some new magazines do show promise. In its latest "Sheroes" issue, Moxie features real women who are pursuing real adventures, and includes a profile of cool-to-the-core Katharine Hepburn. Jane, Bust, and Bitch are three more that do seem bent on breaking the mould. Yet even these magazines seem to focus more on improvement and empowerment, rather than using wit to enlighten and entertain.

15 Old habits die hard, so I suspect the odd Glamour or Cosmo may still make its way into my reading stack. But for sheer entertainment value, general interest and a bit of insight into that mysterious other sex, I think this summer I'll confuse the advertisers and spend some of my money on magazines for men.

AUDIENCE AND PURPOSE

1. What is McQueen's thesis?
2. What does McQueen see as the problem with women's magazines?
3. Why does McQueen think women's magazines are outdated for her age group?
4. Why does McQueen refer to her reading of men's magazines as a fling?

CONTENT

1. Summarize why McQueen likes men's magazines better than women's magazines?
2. What do women's magazines instill in their readers, according to McQueen?
3. What differences does McQueen find in the instructional section of men's and women's magazines?

STYLE AND STRUCTURE

1. Analyze McQueen's use of examples from the magazines. Why does she include them in such detail?

2. McQueen's examples are often hilarious and may seem absurd. How does the knowledge that the examples are real add force to her argument?
3. What does McQueen conclude is the difference between men and women as the advertisers and writers of these magazines see it?

Natalia Ginzburg

Natalia Ginzburg (1916–91) was a major Italian writer of the second half of the twentieth century. Her autobiographical novel *Lessico Famigliare* (1963), translated as *Family Sayings* (1967), won the Strega Prize. Her work, like this essay, explores the roles of women in relationships. Her best-known works include the play *L'inserzione* (1969), produced as *The Advertisement*, and the collected essays *Mai devi domandarmi* (1970), translated as *Never Must You Ask Me* (1973).

HE AND I

He always feels hot, I always feel cold. In the summer when it really is hot he does nothing but complain about how hot he feels. He is irritated if he sees me put a jumper on in the evening.

He speaks several languages well; I do not speak any well. He manages — in his own way — to speak even the languages that he doesn't know.

He has an excellent sense of direction, I have none at all. After one day in a foreign city he can move about in it as thoughtlessly as a butterfly. I get lost in my own city; I have to ask directions so that I can get back home again. He hates asking directions; when we go by car to a town we don't know he doesn't want to ask directions and tells me to look at the map. I don't know how to read maps and I get confused by all the little red circles and he loses his temper.

He loves the theatre, painting, music, especially music. I do not understand music at all, painting doesn't mean much to me and I get bored at the theatre. I love and understand one thing in the world and that is poetry.

5 He loves museums, and I will go if I am forced to but with an unpleasant sense of effort and duty. He loves libraries and I hate them.

He loves travelling, unfamiliar foreign cities, restaurants. I would like to stay at home all the time and never move.

All the same I follow him on his many journeys. I follow him to museums, to churches, to the opera. I even follow him to concerts, where I fall asleep.

Because he knows the conductors and the singers, after the performance is over he likes to go and congratulate them. I follow him down long corridors lined with the singers' dressing-rooms and listen to him talking to people dressed as cardinals and kings.

He is not shy; I am shy. Occasionally however I have seen him be shy. With the police when they come over to the car armed with a notebook and pencil. Then he is shy, thinking he is in the wrong.

And even when he doesn't think he is in the wrong. I think he has a respect for established authority. I am afraid of established authority, but he isn't. He respects it. There is a difference. When I see a policeman coming to fine me I immediately think he is going to haul me off to prison. He doesn't think about prison; but, out of respect, he becomes shy and polite.

During the Montesi trial, because of his respect for established authority, we had very violent arguments.

He likes tagliatelle, lamb, cherries, red wine. I like minestrone, bread soup, omelettes, green vegetables.

He often says I don't understand anything about food, that I am like a great strong fat friar — one of those friars who devour soup made from greens in the darkness of their monasteries; but he, oh he is refined and has a sensitive palate. In restaurants he makes long inquiries about the wines; he has them bring two or three bottles then looks at them and considers the matter, and slowly strokes his beard.

There are certain restaurants in England where the waiter goes through a little ritual: he pours some wine into a glass so that the customer can test whether he likes it or not. He used to hate this ritual and always prevented the waiter from carrying it out by taking the bottle from him. I used to argue with him about this and say that you should let people carry out their prescribed tasks.

And in the same way he never lets the usherette at the cinema direct him to his seat. He immediately gives her a tip but dashes off to a completely different place from the one she shows him with her torch.

At the cinema he likes to sit very close to the screen. If we go with friends and they look for seats a long way from the screen, as most people do, he sits by himself in the front row. I can see well whether I am close to the screen or far away from it, but when we are with friends I stay with them out of politeness; all the same it upsets me because I could be next to him two inches from the screen, and when I don't sit next to him he gets annoyed with me.

We both love the cinema, and we are ready to see almost any kind of film at almost any time of day. But he knows the history of the cinema in great detail; he remembers old directors and actors who have disappeared and been forgotten long ago, and he is ready to travel miles into the most distant suburbs in search of some ancient silent film in which an actor appears—perhaps just for a few seconds—whom he affectionately associates with memories of his early childhood. I remember one Sunday afternoon in London; somewhere in the distant suburbs on the edge of the countryside they were showing a film from the 1930s, about the French Revolution, which he had seen as a child, and in which a famous actress of that time appeared for a moment or two. We set off by car in search of the street, which was a very long way off; it was raining, there was a fog, and we drove for hour after hour through identical suburbs, between rows of little grey houses, gutters and railings; I had the map on my knees and I couldn't read it and he lost his temper; at last, we found the cinema and sat in the completely deserted auditorium. But after a quarter of an hour, immediately after the brief appearance of the actress who was so important to him, he already wanted to go; I on the other hand, after seeing so many streets, wanted to see how the film finished. I don't remember whether we did what he wanted or what I wanted; probably what he wanted, so that we left after a quarter of an hour, also because it was late—though we had set off early in the afternoon it was already time for dinner. But when I begged him to tell me how the film ended I didn't get a very satisfactory answer; because, he said, the story wasn't at all important, the only thing that mattered was those few moments, that actress's curls, gestures, profile.

I never remember actors' names, and as I am not good at remembering faces it is often difficult for me to recognize even the most famous of them. This infuriates him; his scorn increases as I ask him whether it was this one or that one; "You don't mean to tell me," he says, "You don't mean to tell me that you didn't recognize William Holden!"

And in fact I didn't recognize William Holden. All the same, I love the cinema too; but although I have been seeing films for years I haven't been able to provide myself with any sort of cinematic education. But he has made an education of it for himself and he does this with whatever attracts his curiosity; I don't know how to make myself an education out of anything, even those things that I love best in life; they stay with me as scattered images, nourishing my life with memories and emotions but without filling the void, the desert of my education.

He tells me I have no curiosity, but this is not true. I am curious about a few, a very few, things. And when I have got to know them I retain scattered impressions of them, or the cadence of phrase, or a word. But my world, in which these completely unrelated (unless in some secret fashion unbeknown to me) impressions and cadences rise to the surface, is a sad, barren place. His world, on the other hand, is green and populous and richly cultivated; it is a fertile, well-watered countryside in which woods, meadows, orchards and villages flourish.

Everything I do is done laboriously, with great difficulty and uncertainty. I am very lazy, and if I want to finish anything it is absolutely essential that I spend hours stretched out on the sofa. He is never idle, and is always doing something; when he goes to lie down in the afternoons he takes proofs to correct or a book full of notes; he wants us to go to the cinema, then to a reception, then to the theatre — all on the same day. In one day he succeeds in doing, and in making me do, a mass of different things, and in meeting extremely diverse kinds of people. If I am alone and try to act as he does I get nothing at all done, because I get stuck all afternoon somewhere I had meant to stay for half an hour, or because I get lost and cannot find the right street, or because the most boring person and the one I least wanted to meet drags me off to the place I least wanted to go to.

If I tell him how my afternoon has turned out he says it is a completely wasted afternoon and is amused and makes fun of me and loses his temper; and he says that without him I am good for nothing.

I don't know how to manage my time; he does.

He likes receptions. He dresses casually, when everyone is dressed formally; the idea of changing his clothes in order to go to a reception never enters his head. He even goes in his old raincoat and crumpled hat; a woolen hat which he bought in London and which he wears pulled down over his eyes. He only stays for half an hour; he enjoys chatting with a glass in his hand for half an hour; he eats lots of *hors d'oeuvres*, and I eat almost none because when I see him eating so many I feel that I at least must be well-mannered and show some self-control and not eat too much; after half an hour, just as I am beginning to feel at ease and to enjoy myself, he gets impatient and drags me away.

I don't know how to dance and he does.

I don't know how to type and he does.

I don't know how to drive. If I suggest that I should get a licence too he disagrees. He says I would never manage it. I think he likes me to be dependent on him for some things.

I don't know how to sing and he does. He is a baritone. Perhaps he would have been a famous singer if he had studied singing.

Perhaps he would have been a conductor if he had studied music. When he listens to records he conducts the orchestra with a pencil. And he types and answers the telephone at the same time. He is a man who is able to do many things at once.

30 He is a professor and I think he is a good one.

He could have been many things. But he has no regrets about those professions he did not take up. I could only ever have followed one profession—the one I chose and which I have followed almost since childhood. And I don't have any regrets either about the professions I did not take up, but then I couldn't have succeeded at any of them.

I write stories, and for many years I have worked for a publishing house.

I don't work badly, or particularly well. All the same I am well aware of the fact that I would have been unable to work anywhere else. I get on well with my colleagues and my boss. I think that if I did not have the support of their friendship I would soon have become worn out and unable to work any longer.

For a long time I thought that one day I would be able to write screenplays for the cinema. But I never had the opportunity, or I did not know how to find it. Now I have lost all hope of writing screenplays. He wrote screenplays for a while, when he was younger. And he has worked in a publishing house. He has written stories. He has done all the things that I have done and many others too.

35 He is a good mimic, and does an old countess especially well. Perhaps he could also have been an actor.

Once, in London, he sang in a theatre. He was Job. He had to hire evening clothes; and there he was, in his evening clothes, in front of a kind of lectern; and he sang. He sang the words of Job; the piece called for something between speaking and singing. And I, in my box, was dying of fright. I was afraid he would get flustered, or that the trousers of his evening clothes would fall down.

He was surrounded by men in evening clothes and women in long dresses, who were the angels and devils and other characters in Job.

It was a great success, and they said that he was very good.

If I loved music I would love it passionately. But I don't understand it, and when he persuades me to go to concerts with him my mind wanders off and I think of my own affairs. Or I fall sound asleep.

40 I like to sing. I don't know how to sing and I sing completely out of tune; but I sing all the same—occasionally, very quietly, when I am alone. I know that I sing out of tune because others have told me so; my voice must be like the yowling of a cat. But

I am not—in myself—aware of this, and singing gives me real pleasure. If he hears me he mimics me; he says that my singing is something quite separate from music, something invented by me.

When I was a child I used to yowl tunes I had made up. It was a long wailing kind of melody that brought tears to my eyes.

It doesn't matter to me that I don't understand painting or the figurative arts, but it hurts me that I don't love music, and I feel that my mind suffers from the absence of this love. But there is nothing I can do about it, I will never understand or love music. If I occasionally hear a piece of music that I like I don't know how to remember it; and how can I love something that I can't remember?

It is the words of a song that I remember. I can repeat words that I love over and over again. I repeat the tune that accompanies them too, in my own yowling fashion, and I experience a kind of happiness as I yowl.

When I am writing it seems to me that I follow a musical cadence or rhythm. Perhaps music was very close to my world, and my world could not, for whatever reason, make contact with it.

In our house there is music all day long. He keeps the radio on all day. Or plays records. Every now and again I protest a little and ask for a little silence in which to work; but he says that such beautiful music is certainly conducive to any kind of work.

He has bought an incredible number of records. He says that he owns one of the finest collections in the world.

In the morning when he is still in his dressing gown and dripping water from his bath, he turns the radio on, sits down at the typewriter and begins his strenuous, noisy, stormy day. He is superabundant in everything; he fills the bath to overflowing, and the same with the teapot and his cup of tea. He has an enormous number of shirts and ties. On the other hand he rarely buys shoes.

His mother says that as a child he was a model of order and precision; apparently once, on a rainy day, he was wearing white boots and white clothes and had to cross some muddy streams in the country—at the end of his walk he was immaculate and his clothes and boots had not one spot of mud on them. There is no trace in him of that former immaculate little boy. His clothes are always covered in stains. He has become extremely untidy.

But he scrupulously keeps all the gas bills. In drawers I find old gas bills, which he refuses to throw away, from houses we left long ago.

I also find old, shrivelled Tuscan cigars, and cigarette holders made from cherry wood.

I smoke a brand of king-size, filterless cigarettes called *Stop*, and he smokes his Tuscan cigars.

I am very untidy. But as I have got older I have come to miss tidiness, and I sometimes furiously tidy up all the cupboards. I think this is because I remember my mother's tidiness. I rearrange the linen and blanket cupboards and in the summer I reline every drawer with strips of white cloth. I rarely rearrange my papers because my mother didn't write and had no papers. My tidiness and untidiness are full of complicated feelings of regret and sadness. His untidiness is triumphant. He has decided that it is proper and legitimate for a studious person like himself to have an untidy desk.

He does not help me get over my indecisiveness, or the way I hesitate before doing anything, or my sense of guilt. He tends to make fun of every tiny thing I do. If I go shopping in the market he follows me and spies on me. He makes fun of the way I shop, of the way I weigh the oranges in my hand unerringly choosing, he says, the worst in the whole market; he ridicules me for spending an hour over the shopping, buying onions at one stall, celery at another and fruit at another. Sometimes he does the shopping to show me how quickly he can do it; he unhesitatingly buys everything from one stall and then manages to get the basket delivered to the house. He doesn't buy celery because he cannot abide it.

And so—more than ever—I feel I do everything inadequately or mistakenly. But if I once find out that he has made a mistake I tell him so over and over again until he is exasperated. I can be very annoying at times.

His rages are unpredictable, and bubble over like the head on beer. My rages are unpredictable too, but his quickly disappear whereas mine leave a noisy nagging trail behind them which must be very annoying—like the complaining yowl of a cat.

Sometimes in the midst of his rage I start to cry, and instead of quietening him down and making him feel sorry for me this infuriates him all the more. He says my tears are just play-acting, and perhaps he is right. Because in the middle of my tears and his rage I am completely calm.

I never cry when I am really unhappy.

There was a time when I used to hurl plates and crockery on the floor during my rages. But not any more. Perhaps because I am older and my rages are less violent, and also because I dare not lay a finger on our plates now; we bought them one day in London, in the Portobello Road, and I am very fond of them.

The price of those plates, and of many other things we have bought, immediately underwent a substantial reduction in his memory. He likes to think he did not spend very much and that he got a bargain. I know the price of that dinner service — it was £16, but he says £12. And it is the same with the picture of King Lear that is in our dining room, and which he also bought in the Portobello Road (and then cleaned with onions and potatoes); now he says he paid a certain sum for it, but I remember that it was much more than that.

Some years ago he bought twelve bedside mats in a department store. He bought them because they were cheap, and he thought he ought to buy them; and he bought them as an argument against me because he considered me to be incapable of buying things for the house. They were made of mud-coloured matting and they quickly became very unattractive; they took on a corpse-like rigidity and were hung from a wire line on the kitchen balcony, and I hated them. I used to remind him of them, as an example of bad shopping; but he would say that they had cost very little indeed, almost nothing. It was a long time before I could bring myself to throw them out — because there were so many of them, and because just as I was about to get rid of them it occurred to me that I could use them for rags. He and I both find throwing things away difficult; it must be a kind of Jewish caution in me, and the result of my extreme indecisiveness; in him it must be a defence against his impulsiveness and open-handedness.

He buys enormous quantities of bicarbonate of soda and aspirins.

Now and again he is ill with some mysterious ailment of his own; he can't explain what he feels and stays in bed for a day completely wrapped up in the sheets; nothing is visible except his beard and the tip of his red nose. Then he takes bicarbonate of soda and aspirins in doses suitable for a horse, and says that I cannot understand because I am always well, I am like those great fat strong friars who go out in the wind and in all weathers and come to no harm; he on the other hand is sensitive and delicate and suffers from mysterious ailments. Then in the evening he is better and goes into the kitchen and cooks himself tagliatelle.

When he was a young man he was slim, handsome and finely built; he did not have a beard but long, soft moustaches instead, and he looked like the actor Robert Donat. He was like that about twenty years ago when I first knew him, and I remember that he used to wear an elegant kind of Scottish flannel shirt. I remember that one evening he walked me back to the *pensione* where I was living; we walked together along the *Via*

Nazionale. I already felt that I was very old and had been through a great deal and had made many mistakes, and he seemed a boy to me, light years away from me. I don't remember what we talked about on that evening walking along the *Via Nazionale*; nothing important, I suppose, and the idea that we would become husband and wife was light years away from me. Then we lost sight of each other, and when we met again he no longer looked like Robert Donat, but more like Balzac. When we met again he still wore his Scottish shirts but on him now they looked like garments for a polar expedition; now he had his beard and on his head he wore his ridiculous crumpled woollen hat; everything about him put you in mind of an imminent departure for the North Pole. Because, although he always feels hot, he has the habit of dressing as if he were surrounded by snow, ice and polar bears; or he dresses like a Brazilian coffee-planter, but he always dresses differently from everyone else.

If I remind him of that walk along the *Via Nazionale* he says he remembers it, but I know he is lying and that he remembers nothing; and I sometimes ask myself if it was us, these two people, almost twenty years ago on the *Via Nazionale*, two people who conversed so politely, so urbanely, as the sun was setting; who chatted a little about everything perhaps and about nothing; two friends talking, two young intellectuals out for a walk; so young, so educated, so uninvolved, so ready to judge one another with kind impartiality; so ready to say goodbye to one another for ever, as the sun set, at the corner of the street.

Translated from the Italian by Dick Davis

VOCABULARY

cadence: rhythm 20
urbanely: sophisticatedly 64

AUDIENCE AND PURPOSE

1. What sense do you have of the narrator's attitude toward the "he" of the essay? Why?
2. How does Ginzburg show the differences between women and men in just these two individuals?
3. In some ways Ginzburg's essay makes the reader think about the process of comparison itself. Discuss.

CONTENT

1. Most often the "I" of the essay compares herself negatively to the "he." How does this repeated tendency affect the reader?
2. Why does Ginzburg repeat the image of the "yowling" cat in relation to the "I" of the essay?
3. Why does Ginzburg include so many details? We know, for example, that "he" dislikes celery. Why are such details important?

STYLE AND STRUCTURE

1. Ginzburg's style seems very plain, but also touching. Analyze one of her extended comparisons to show its effect.
2. Sometimes Ginzburg starts with the "he" example; sometimes she starts with the "I." Do you see any difference between the two kinds of examples?
3. Do you feel you understand her or him well at the end? What is the effect of never learning their names?
4. What makes Ginzburg's conclusion seem poignant?

Division and Classification

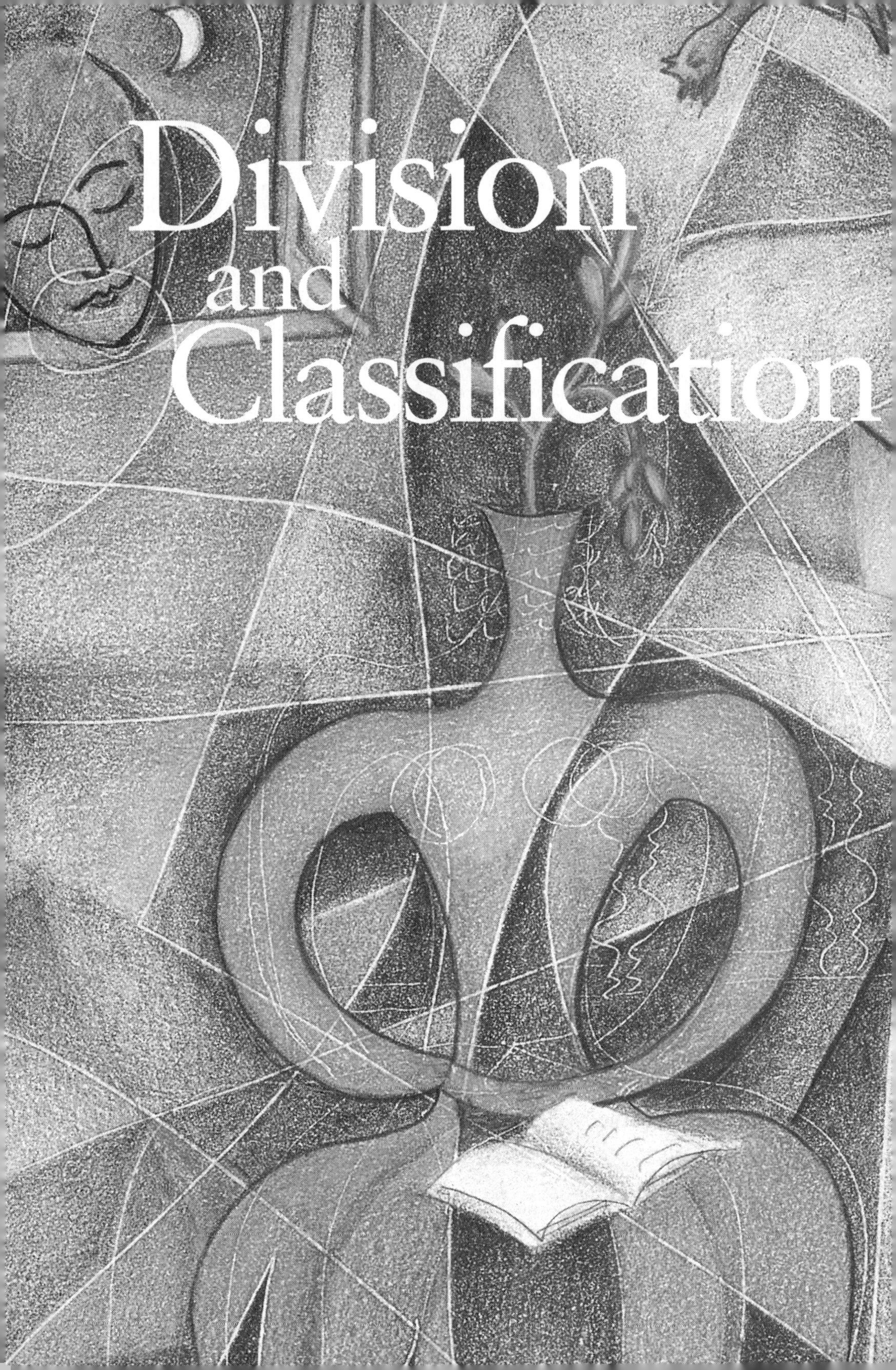

DIVISION AND CLASSIFICATION

A Place for Everything and Everything in Its Place

One of the first tasks of a writer approaching a subject is to decide how to divide it up so that it can be more easily tackled, from the point of view of both writer and reader. The concept is familiar enough. You find information sorted in the library, in the bookstore, in the pharmacy, even, if you are savvy about computers, in the files and folders located on your hard drive.

Choosing division/classification as a rhetorical structure involves something more, though. When you select this method of presenting information, you are analyzing the subject matter in order to make some salient differences apparent to your reader. This particular rhetorical pattern takes two forms. Division begins with one unit that is broken down into smaller parts in order to describe what is essential to the whole. You might, for example, seek to divide the concept of the ideal vacation into its component parts, in order to demonstrate what is an essential function of all good vacations. You might, in other words, say that a good vacation involves equal proportions of relaxation and stimulation. In essence, you need to mix exciting new experiences with some comfortable old habits. To make your point, you would then collect instances of each of the divisions in turn to show how they form part of the overall picture.

Classifying, by contrast, demands that you examine an entire category of things and determine what smaller groups they might be sorted into. To visualize this task, imagine what it would be like to classify kinds of weddings. Weddings might be grouped into three categories: the spectacles, the parties, and legalized lip-service. Then you would be free to elaborate on the characteristics that you observe as typical for each category. In the case of both division and classification, you will find examples of categories that are both abstract and concrete, fanciful and factual. But whether you are discovering categories or inventing them, it is important to use this rhetorical technique as a means of making your point. Whether your point is that weddings are indications of people's attitudes toward public responsibility, or that vacations, to be satisfying, need to be not too jarring to the sensibilities, you want to make use of division and classification to make your case persuasively.

When an essay calls for division or classification as its pattern of development, you need to decide how exhaustive or selective you want your groupings to be. Most often, writers select a representative group of categories rather than trying to establish all the relevant parts of the whole, though that will depend, to a large extent, on the subject matter. You may wish to consider all the kinds of treatment for acne available today, or you may wish to concentrate on just topical treatments. Given the length strictures of most essays, a narrower topic is often the better way to go. That way, you have the advantage of being able to develop each point that you make in informative and careful detail.

The other absolute requirement of division and classification as a rhetorical pattern is that your categories should not overlap. Each category you find or create must be seen by the reader as distinct in order for the division or classification to make sense. If you are classifying kinds of student employment according to levels of responsibility and reward, you might dream up these categories: McJob, Lackey, Gopher, and Self-Starter. You may reserve the term "McJob" for those kinds of service jobs where you work behind a counter, and "Self-Starter" for the kinds of jobs you create and maintain yourself. Then you may wind up discovering that Lackey and Gopher cover much the same territory, both implying that workers are at the beck and call of the employer, but are not necessarily part of the service industry. It is important to develop categories that are discrete and that are capable of sharp differentiation.

Division and classification is a useful technique when you need to "divide and conquer" a broad topic, and when you want to show the results of your analysis and observation.

Vacations, if they are going to live up to your hopes, need to be genuinely recreational. To achieve this goal, you have to keep your balance. Remember the expression "All work and no play makes Jack a dull boy." In some ways, it is still true on vacation. To maintain an equilibrium that is happy and healthy, aim at two apparently contrary things while on vacation: relaxation and stimulation. The relaxation is the easy part for most people. Think of some comfortable old habits of yours that you don't always have time

Topic sentence ⟶ (true on vacation. To maintain an equilibrium …)

to enjoy when caught up in the demands of a gruelling timetable or work schedule. Then practise them, even if that means sleeping in till eleven, wearing comfy clothes (no neckties or pantyhose allowed), and watching TV till all hours. That's part of what a vacation is all about. The other part, the stimulation, involves making sure that you do something memorable on your holidays. This is tougher, simply because it requires that you break out of old ways a bit by meeting some new people, visiting an unfamiliar locale, or even trying a new dish. The main criterion is that you must do something that will make a good story, or your vacation will seem banal. A good vacation will re-create you and satisfy your desire for both rest and release. You want something that puts you at ease, and something you can write about if anyone asks you what you did on your summer vacation.

Wedding Bell Clues: What Weddings Tell You About You and Society

Introduction ⟶ Weddings are one of the last bastions of individuality on the planet. People who normally make an effort to look, talk, and act just like everybody else will go to exaggerated extremes to set themselves apart when it comes to their wedding. People who are usually right-minded and sane will design wedding invitations that look like baseball cards. People who are normally unassuming and shy will wear wedding clothes that smack of Vegas. People who seem like loners will suddenly invite hordes of folk who barely know their names to extravagant ceremonies and register for gaudy china patterns at expensive shops. Despite the seeming eccentricity of this kind of wedding behaviour, a lot of personal information can indeed be gleaned from observation at such events. The wedding is actually a fairly reli-

Thesis statement → able index of a couple's attitude toward society. From the kind of wedding a couple celebrates, you can tell a good deal about how they measure their responsibility toward others.

Route map → From long observation, I have concluded that there are three chief kinds of wedding to which you might unwittingly be invited. They are spectacles, parties, and lip-service rituals. The first is the kind that the bridal magazines usually try to uphold, mainly because they are the most expensive events and certainly the most photogenic. At a spectacle, the bride and groom are done up to resemble artificial figures not unlike those normally found only on the tops of wedding cakes. Usually, the outfits that they are forced to wear allow them about the same amount of movement too. This is the black-tie event that men and women traditionally go through in order to oblige friends and acquaintances to buy expensive wedding presents and come prepared to enjoy the show. The wedding guests—society, if you will—are there to behold the spectacle and to buy the presents. Not much thought is usually given to whether or not the guests will enjoy themselves. They are there to gawk and to pay tribute for the most part, though for an unlucky few who are cast in the role of wedding party members, they are there, in ugly neon bridesmaid dresses and odd unlikely uniforms, to be gawked at and paid tribute.

The first category is developed.

The middle ground of weddings is the party. This particular social event sometimes doesn't even really feel like a wedding. In this case, the bride and groom are social animals par excellence, and their purpose is to have a good time. This is a lucky break for the guests, although the whole affair is often not as fancy as the spectacle. Here the dress code is more lax, and the guests feel that it is their responsibility to do the limbo in the middle of the floor even in tight pants or high heels. The food may not be foie gras, but it is plentiful and more like what you're used to eating anyhow. The liquor often flows more freely at the party wedding if only because, rightly or

The second category is developed.

wrongly, many of the participants see it as the essential lubricant of a good time. This bride and groom have the best interests of their friends at heart: they feel it is incumbent upon them to make sure that everyone has, at the very least, a good time.

The third category is developed.

The final category of wedding is the legalized lip service. This is a legal wedding (indeed that is the whole point), so the emphasis is on getting the job done, and the social responsibility of bride and groom is assumed to be nil. People are called upon to attend these events merely to act as public witnesses, and very little — apart from some semblance of wedding present — is expected. No one dances, few people drink, dining is at a minimum, and the knot is tied neatly and quickly, though usually years after the bride and groom first began enjoying their mutual conjugal rights. These kinds of weddings aim at making the whole thing legal, and while some sentiment may occasionally also be unobtrusively attached, the couple's object is to get by without incurring too much in the way of cost or social responsibility from either in-laws or friends. You're on your own in terms of entertainment here, although, as with most weddings, there is usually lots of unintentional hilarity.

Conclusion

The next time you are a guest at one of these ceremonial events, ask yourself what kind of social responsibility is offered by bride and groom or expected by guests. Depending on the kind of event you attend, your behaviour should be vastly different. If you live up to expectations and stay permanently acquainted with the principal participants, it is your duty to know what your role as a guest is.

Pico Iyer

Pico Iyer (b. 1957) is a travel writer who has written for *Time, Harper's,* and *The New York Review of Books.* His works include *Cuba and the Night* (1995), *Falling Off the Map: Some Lonely Places of the World* (1993), *The Lady and the Monk* (1991), and *Video Night in Kathmandu* (1988). *Tropical Classical* (1997) is a collection of essays about travel; his latest book, *The Global Soul* (2000), is a collection of transnational cultural essays.

LONELY PLACES

On every trip I took to Havana, the ritual was the same: I would get into a car with two of my friends (into a '56 De Soto most likely), and we would judder off towards José Martí International Airport. We drove past huge pictures of Che (BE LIKE HIM), past billboards that said SOCIALISM OR DEATH, THE MOTHERLAND BEFORE EVERYTHING, IT IS ALWAYS THE 26TH (of July, 1953), past long lines of women waiting for a bus. We spoke only in indefinite pronouns, so as not to arouse the driver's suspicions, pretending that we thought that everything was well, pretending that we did not hope to meet again. When we arrived at the airport, we would get out and sit under a tree just outside the battered terminal. There my friends would tell me about everything they planned to do as soon as they arrived in America: how they would open a bookstore, or take pictures of the clubs on Forty-second Street, or send all the jeans they could find back to their families at home. Then, when it came time for me to leave, they would turn and, without looking back, walk across the street to another tree and wait for a bus back into town. They couldn't bear, they said, to see me getting on the plane that they had been dreaming of for twenty-five, or twenty-seven, or thirty-one years.

That is one of the things that make me think of Cuba as a Lonely Place. Just like the old men sitting on the terraces of the cheap hotels, showing you photos of long-lost fiancées ("Miss Dade County 1956"), or the trim government officials who ask, in perfect Eisenhower-era English, "Do they still play tetherball in the States?" Just like the statues of Don Quixote set on lonely hills across the countryside, and the pictures of Ava Gardner in the downtown restaurants; just like the tiny huddle of worshipers singing hymns on Easter Sunday, or the messages people give you to take to unheard-from mothers in the Bronx, distant cousins in Miami, an Indian—of course you can find him—by the name of Singh. Cuba is ninety miles from the United States, but it might as well be a universe away. Letters pass only infrequently between the two neighbors, and telephone calls are next to impossible (though it was once my mixed fortune to befriend, of all things, a telephone operator: every night in Havana, she would call me up, unbidden, and serenade me with Spanish love songs, and for months after I returned home, the phone would ring, at 2:00 A.M., 3:15 A.M., 4:36 A.M., and I would pick it up, to hear "*Oye, oye!*" and the opening strains of "Guantanamera"). Exiled from the Americas, deserted by its Communist friends, its only ally these days a xenophobic hermit state run by an octogenarian madman ("Querido compañero Kim Il Sung," run the greetings in the Cuban official newspaper, *Granma*), Cuba is increasingly, quite literally, a Lonely Place.

Lonely Places are the places that don't fit in; the places that have no seat at our international dinner tables; the places that fall between the cracks of our tidy acronyms (EEC and OPEC, OAS and NATO). Cuba is the island that no one thinks of as West Indian; Iceland is the one that isn't really part of Europe. Australia is the odd place out that no one knows whether to call an island or a continent; North Korea is the one that gives the lie to every generality about East Asian vitality and growth. Lonely Places are the exceptions that prove every rule: they are ascetics, castaways, and secessionists; prisoners, anchorites, and solipsists. Some are famous for their monasteries (Bhutan and, in some respects, Iceland); some are famous for their criminals and cranks (North Korea and Paraguay). And though no one has ever formally grouped them together—save me—every Lonely Place conforms to the Paraguay described by its native writer Augusto Roa Bastos as "an island surrounded by land."

Yet loneliness cuts in both directions, and there are 101 kinds of solitude. There is the loneliness of the sociopath and the loneliness of the only child, the loneliness of the hermit and the loneliness of the widow. And as with people, so too with nations. Some are born to isolation, some have isolation thrust upon them. Each makes its own accommodation with wistfulness and eccentricity and simple, institutionalized standoffishness. Australia, a part of the Wild West set down in the middle of the East, hardly seems to notice, or to care, that it is a Lonely Place; Bhutan all but bases its identity upon its loneliness, and its refusal to be assimilated into India, or Tibet, or Nepal. Vietnam, at present, is a pretty girl with her face pressed up against the window of the dance hall, waiting to be invited in; Iceland is the mystic poet in the corner, with her mind on other things. Argentina longs to be part of the world it left and, in its absence, re-creates the place it feels should be its home; Paraguay simply slams the door and puts up a Do Not Disturb sign. Loneliness and solitude, remoteness and seclusion, are many worlds apart.

Yet all Lonely Places have something in common, if only the fact that all are marching to the beat of a different satellite drummer. And many are so far from the music of the world that they do not realize how distant they are. Both South Korea and North are zany, lonely places in their way: the difference is that North Korea is so cut off from the world that it does not know how strange it is and cannot imagine anything except North Korea. This is how life is, I imagine North Koreans thinking: being woken up each morning with loudspeaker exhortations in the bedroom; being told exactly what clothes to wear and which route to take to work; being reminded each day that Kim Il Sung is revered around the world. In the half-unnatural state of solitary confinement, Lonely Places develop tics and manias and heresies. They pine, they brood, they molder. They gather dust and data, and keep their blinds drawn round the clock. In time, their loneliness makes them stranger, and their strangeness makes them lonelier. And before long, they have come to resemble the woman with a hundred cats in a house she's never cleaned, or the man who obsessively counts the names in the telephone book each night. They grow three-inch nails, and never wash, and talk with the artificial loudness of someone always talking to himself.

Burma, out of the blue, decides to call itself Myanmar and to name its most famous city, unintelligibly, Yangon. Iceland speaks a tongue that Grendel would have recognized. North Korea, which sees no tourists, is building the largest tourist hotel in the world, 105 stories high. And for many years now in Havana, across the street from the U.S. Interests Section, there has stood a huge billboard, with a caricature of a "Ggrrrr"-breathing Uncle Sam, next to the message SEÑOR IMPERIALISTS! WE HAVE ABSOLUTELY NO FEAR OF YOU! There are more things on earth, Horatio, than are dreamt of in your philosophy.

When people think of Lonely Places, they tend to think of moody outcrops off the coast of Scotland, or washed-up atolls adrift in the Pacific. They may even think of the place where I am writing this, a silent hermitage above the sea along the unpeopled coast of northern California. But Lonely Places are not just isolated places, for loneliness is a state of mind. The hut where I am sitting now is utterly alone. For days on end, I do not hear a single voice; and from where I write, I cannot see a trace of human habitation. Yet in a deeper sense, the place is packed. I am companioned—by rabbits, stars, and wisps of cloud—in worlds far richer than any capital. The air is charged with presences, and every inch of hillside stirs. I watch for the skittering of a fox on my terrace, listen to the crickets chattering in the dusk, catch a blue jay's wings against the light. Birds sing throughout the day, and the ocean's colors shift. Everything is a jubilee of blue and gold, and at night, walking along the hills, I feel as if I am walking towards a starlit Temple of Apollo. A Lonely Place in principle, perhaps, but certainly not in spirit.

More than in space, then, it is in time that Lonely Places are often exiled, and it is their very remoteness from the present tense that gives them their air of haunted glamour. The door slams shut behind them, and they are alone with cobwebs and yellowed snapshots, scraps of old bread and framed photographs of themselves when young. The beauty (and pathos) of Burma today derives from the fact that it is stranded amidst decaying remnants of its former glory, and the poignancy of Cuba that in the midst of leafy university quadrangles, you will find bird-spotted tanks. You wind back the clock several decades when you visit a Lonely Place; and when you touch down, you half expect a cabin attendant to announce, "We have now landed in Lonely Place's Down-at-Heels Airport, where the local time is 1943 and the temperature is … frozen."

Yet Lonely Places are generally sure that their time is about to come. North Korea is just waiting for Stalinism to sweep the world and the Olympics to be held in the stadia it has built for them (the secret of his longevity, says Kim Il Sung, the world's longest-running dictator, is his optimism); Argentina is just waiting for the day when it will be a world power again, the cynosure of every distant eye. Lonely Places have seen Bulgaria, China, even Albania admitted, or awakened, to the world; they have seen the Falklands, Grenada, even Kuwait enjoy their moments in the spotlight. They tell themselves that even Japan was once a "double-bolted land," as Melville put it, and China, and Korea too; they tell themselves that tomorrow will bring yesterday once more.

10 Lonely Places are often poor places, because poverty breeds wonkiness and a greater ability to visualize than to realize dreams. Lonely Places are often small countries, because smallness gets forgotten: the tiny voices of Tibet, or Benin, or East Timor are seldom heard at international gatherings. But even huge countries can be Lonely Places, or have Lonely Places inside them, as anyone who has been to Siberia or Ladakh, Kashgar or Wyoming, can attest. Everywhere, in some lights, is a Lonely

Place, just as everyone, at moments, is a solitary. Everyone sometimes dances madly when alone, or thumbs through secrets in a drawer. Everyone, at some times, is a continent of one.

Lonely Places are defined, in fact, by their relation to the things they miss. You would expect the western fjords of Iceland, or the depths of Tierra del Fuego, to be lonely; but there is a more unanswerable kind of loneliness, and restlessness, in Reykjavik and Buenos Aires, the loneliness of people just close enough to the world to see what they might be. Both American Samoa and Western Samoa are pretty little South Sea bubbles a world away from anywhere, and both are isolated hideaways lost in their own surf-soft universe. Both are graced by palm-fringed beaches, Technicolor cricket games, and huts echoing with cries of "Bingo" in the dark. But what makes American Samoa a Lonely Place is that it also has a zip code, a Radio Shack, and a Democratic caucus. It has American-style license plates, yellow school buses, and *Days of Our Lives*. It sends a congressman to Washington, but he is not allowed to vote.

Other Lonely Places are happy in their loneliness, or able, at least, to turn it to advantage. The Australians, it seems to me, thrive on their remoteness from the world and see it as a way of keeping up a code of "No worries, mate," while peddling their oddities to visitors: nonconformity is at once a fact of life for many, and a selling point. Others, like Tibetans, pine for a loneliness that is tantamount to peace. Still others have the bitterness of outcasts: if they cannot play the game, say the Libyans, why should you? "Ye Visions of the hills! And Souls of lonely places!" sang Wordsworth, who found all his solace and scripture in his loneliness, and saw in it purity and a return to buried-over divinity. Everyone is a Wordsworth in certain moods, and every traveler seeks out places that every traveler has missed. Everyone longs at times to get away from it all. Finding a sanctuary, a place apart from time, is not so different from finding a faith.

So it is that Lonely Places attract as many lonely people as they produce, and the loneliness we see in them is partly in ourselves. Romantic when first I visited Iceland, I found in it a province of romance; returning, four years later, in a darker mood, I saw in it only shades of winter dark. The Gobi Desert, for a couple in love, is as far from loneliness as Hong Kong, for a single traveler, may be close. Even a jam-packed football stadium may be lonely for the referee. It is common these days to hear that as the world shrinks, and as more and more places are pulled into the MTV and CNN circuit, loneliness itself may become extinct. Certainly, many Lonely Places—Vietnam and Cuba, for two — grow less remote with every joint-venture hotel, and cities like Toronto and Sydney, London and L.A., already seem part of some global Eurasamerican village, with a common language and video culture. Yet the very process of feverish cross-communication that is turning the world into a single polyglot multiculture is producing new kinds of Lonely Places as fast as it eliminates the old. The lingua franca of parts of American Samoa is Mandarin, and Farsi is the second language of Beverly Hills. Japanese Joãos are returning to their grandfathers' homes from São Paulo as fast as German Hanses are taking Michikos back to Buenos Aires. Reykjavik is loneliest of all, I suspect, for the Thai girls who sit in the Siam Restaurant (on Skolavördustigur), alone with their mail order husbands. And even as the world contracts and isolation fades, half the countries around the globe are still off the map in some sense, out of sight, out of mind, out of time. There will never be a shortage of Lonely Places, any more than there will ever be of lonely people.

Lonely Places, then, are the places that are not on international wavelengths, do not know how to carry themselves, are lost when it comes to visitors. They are shy, defensive, curious places; places that do not know how they are supposed to behave. Yemen, Brunei, and Mali are Lonely Places; Paradise, Purgatory, and Hell are too. Desolation Isle is a Lonely Place, and Suriname, and California as seen by the Hmong. So, too, is the room next door.

VOCABULARY

judder: invented word that imitates the noise and motion Iyer experiences 1
acronyms: abbreviations that are formed by initial letters 3
ascetics: those who practise stern self-denial 3
anchorites: those who live in seclusion for religious reasons 3
solipsists: philosophers who believe that nothing beyond the existence of self can be proved 3
sociopath: psychopath; a person who exhibits aggressive antisocial behaviour 4
heresies: opinions or practices that are contrary to accepted beliefs or standards 5
skittering: skipping lightly 7
longevity: relating to a long life 9
cynosure: the North Star, or another guide 9
tantamount: equivalent in value 12
polyglot: relating to multiple languages 13

AUDIENCE AND PURPOSE

1. Why does Iyer start with a description of Havana?
2. How does Iyer convince us that Havana is a lonely place in his introductory paragraph?
3. Iyer's readers might be defined as "armchair travellers." How does he conjure up places for those who have never been there?

CONTENT

1. What kinds of loneliness does Iyer include in his classification? Give examples.
2. Why does Iyer claim that writing is not lonely?
3. Why does Iyer think there will never be a shortage of lonely places?
4. In what way are lonely places lost in time, according to Iyer?

STYLE AND STRUCTURE

1. Iyer uses comparisons between lonely people and lonely places throughout the essay. Find examples.
2. Why does Iyer capitalize his Lonely Places?
3. Iyer treats lonely places with respect. Comment on his examples of their eccentricity and of their estrangement from the world.

Lewis Thomas

Lewis Thomas (b. 1913) is a physician who has written several books, including the collections of essays *The Lives of a Cell: Notes of a Biology Watcher* (1974) and *The Medusa and the Snail* (1979), both of which won National Book Awards in the United States. He has also written *Late Night Thoughts on Listening to Mahler's Ninth Symphony* (1983). Lewis's recent work includes *The Fragile Species* (1992). His work is notable for its ability to bring scientific information to the general reader in an entertaining form.

SEVEN WONDERS

A while ago I received a letter from a magazine editor inviting me to join six other people at dinner to make a list of the Seven Wonders of the Modern World, to replace seven old, out-of-date Wonders. I replied that I couldn't manage it, not on short order anyway, but still the question keeps hanging around in the lobby of my mind. I had to look up the old biodegradable Wonders, the Hanging Gardens of Babylon and all the rest, and then I had to look up that word "wonder" to make sure I understood what it meant. It occurred to me that if the magazine could get any seven people to agree on a list of any such seven things you'd have the modern Seven Wonders right there at the dinner table.

Wonder is a word to wonder about. It contains a mixture of messages: something marvelous and miraculous, surprising, raising unanswerable questions about itself, making the observer wonder, even raising skeptical questions like, "I *wonder* about that." Miraculous and marvelous are clues; both words come from an ancient Indo-European root meaning simply to smile or to laugh. Anything wonderful is something to smile in the presence of, in admiration (which, by the way, comes from the same root, along with, of all telling words, "mirror").

I decided to try making a list, not for the magazine's dinner party but for this occasion: seven things I wonder about the most.

I shall hold the first for the last, and move along.

5 My Number Two Wonder is a bacterial species never seen on the face of the earth until 1982, creatures never dreamed of before, living violation of what we used to regard as the laws of nature, things literally straight out of Hell. Or anyway what we used to think of as Hell, the hot unlivable interior of the earth. Such regions have recently come into scientific view from the research submarines designed to descend twenty-five hundred me-

ters or more to the edge of deep holes in the sea bottom, where open vents spew superheated seawater in plumes from chimneys in the earth's crust, known to oceanographic scientists as "black smokers." This is not just hot water, or steam, or even steam under pressure as exists in a laboratory autoclave (which we have relied upon for decades as the surest way to destroy all microbial life). This is extremely hot water under extremely high pressure, with temperatures in excess of 300 degrees centigrade. At such heat, the existence of life as we know it would be simply inconceivable. Proteins and DNA would fall apart, enzymes would melt away, anything alive would die instantaneously. We have long since ruled out the possibility of life on Venus because of that planet's comparable temperature; we have ruled out the possibility of life in the earliest years of this planet, four billion or so years ago, on the same ground.

B.J.A. Baross and J.W. Deming have recently discovered the presence of thriving colonies of bacteria in water fished directly from these deep-sea vents. Moreover, when brought to the surface, encased in titanium syringes and seated in pressurized chambers heated to 250 degrees centigrade, the bacteria not only survive but reproduce themselves enthusiastically. They can be killed only by chilling them down in boiling water.

And yet they look just like ordinary bacteria. Under the electron microscope they have the same essential structure—cell walls, ribosomes, and all. If they were, as is now being suggested, the original archebacteria, ancestors of us all, how did they or their progeny ever learn to cool down? I cannot think of a more wonderful trick.

My Number Three Wonder is *oncideres*, a species of beetle encountered by a pathologist friend of mine who lives in Houston and has a lot of mimosa trees in his backyard. This beetle is not new, but it qualifies as a Modern Wonder because of the exceedingly modern questions raised for evolutionary biologists about the three consecutive things on the mind of the female of the species. Her first thought is for a mimosa tree, which she finds and climbs, ignoring all other kinds of trees in the vicinity. Her second thought is for the laying of eggs, which she does by crawling out on a limb, cutting a longitudinal slit with her mandible and depositing her eggs beneath the slit. Her third and last thought concerns the welfare of her offspring; beetle larvae cannot survive in live wood, so she backs up a foot or so and cuts a neat circular girdle all around the limb, through the bark and down into the cambium. It takes her eight hours to finish this cabinetwork. Then she leaves and where she goes I do not know.

The limb dies from the girdling, falls to the ground in the next breeze, the larvae feed and grow into the next generation, and the questions lie there unanswered. How on earth did these three linked thoughts in her mind evolve together in evolution? How could any one of the three become fixed as beetle behavior by itself, without the other two? What are the odds favoring three totally separate bits of behavior — liking a particular tree, cutting a slit for eggs, and then girdling the limb — happening together by random chance among a beetle's genes? Does this smart beetle know what she is doing? And how did the mimosa tree enter the picture in its evolution? Left to themselves, unpruned, mimosa trees have a life expectancy of twenty-five to thirty years. Pinned each year, which is what the beetle's girdling labor accomplishes, the tree can flourish for a century. The mimosa-beetle relationship is an elegant example of symbiotic partnership, a phenomenon now recognized as pervasive in nature. It is good for us to have around on our intellectual mantelpiece such creatures as this insect and its friend the tree, for they keep reminding us how little we know about nature.

The Fourth Wonder on my list is an infectious agent known as the scrapie virus, which causes a fatal disease of the brain in sheep, goats, and several laboratory animals. A close cousin of scrapie is the C-J virus, the cause of some cases of senile dementia in human beings. These are called "slow viruses," for the excellent reason that an animal exposed to infection today will not become ill until a year and a half or two years from today. The agent, whatever it is, can propagate itself in abundance from a few infectious units today to more than a billion next year. I use the phrase "whatever it is" advisedly. Nobody has yet been able to find any DNA or RNA in the scrapie or C-J viruses. It may be there, but if so it exists in amounts too small to detect. Meanwhile, there is plenty of protein, leading to a serious proposal that the virus may indeed be *all* protein. But protein, so far as we know, does not replicate itself by itself, not on this planet anyway. Looked at this way, the scrapie agent seems the strangest thing in all biology and, until someone in some laboratory figures out what it is, a candidate for Modern Wonder.

10 My Fifth Wonder is the olfactory receptor cell, located in the epithelial tissue high in the nose, sniffing the air for clues to the environment, the fragrance of friends, the smell of leaf smoke, breakfast, nighttime and bedtime, and a rose, even, it is said, the odor of sanctity. The cell that does all these things, firing off urgent messages into the deepest parts of the brain, switching on one strange unaccountable memory after another, is itself a prop-

er brain cell, a certified neuron belonging to the brain but miles away out in the open air, nosing around the world. How it manages to make sense of what it senses, discriminating between jasmine and anything else non-jasmine with infallibility, is one of the deep secrets of neurobiology. This would be wonder enough, but there is more. This population of brain cells, unlike any other neurons of the vertebrate central nervous system, turns itself over every few weeks; cells wear out, die, and are replaced by brand-new cells rewired to the same deep centers miles back in the brain, sensing and remembering the same wonderful smells. If and when we reach an understanding of these cells and their functions, including the moods and whims under their governance, we will know a lot more about the mind than we do now, a world away.

Sixth on my list is, I hesitate to say, another insect, the termite. This time, though, it is not the single insect that is the Wonder, it is the collectivity. There is nothing at all wonderful about a single, solitary termite, indeed there is really no such creature, functionally speaking, as a lone termite, any more than we can imagine a genuinely solitary human being; no such thing. Two or three termites gathered together on a dish are not much better; they may move about and touch each other nervously, but nothing happens. But keep adding more termites until they reach a critical mass, and then the miracle begins. As though they had suddenly received a piece of extraordinary news, they organize in platoons and begin stacking up pellets to precisely the right height, then turning the arches to connect the columns, constructing the cathedral and its chambers in which the colony will live out its life for the decades ahead, air-conditioned and humidity-controlled, following the chemical blueprint coded in their genes, flawlessly, stoneblind. They are not the dense mass of individual insects they appear to be; they are an organism, a thoughtful, meditative brain on a million legs. All we really know about this new thing is that it does its architecture and engineering by a complex system of chemical signals.

The Seventh Wonder of the modern world is a human child, any child. I used to wonder about childhood and the evolution of our species. It seemed to me unparsimonious to keep expending all that energy on such a long period of vulnerability and defenselessness, with nothing to show for it, in biological terms, beyond the feckless, irresponsible pleasure of childhood. After all, I used to think, it is one sixth of a whole human life span! Why didn't our evolution take care of that, allowing us to jump catlike from our juvenile to our adult (and, as I thought) productive stage of life? I had forgotten about language, the single human trait that marks us out as specifically human, the property that enables our survival as the most compulsively biologically, obsessively social of all creatures on earth, more interdependent and interconnected even than the famous social insects. I had forgotten that, and forgotten that children *do* that in childhood. Language is what childhood is for.

There is another related but different creature, nothing like so wonderful as a human child, nothing like so hopeful, something to worry about all day and all night. It is *us*, aggregated together in our collective, critical masses. So far, we have learned how to be useful to each other only when we collect in small groups—families, circles of friends, once in a while (although still rarely) committees. The drive to be useful is encoded in our genes. But when we gather in very large numbers, as in the modern nation-state, we seem capable of levels of folly and self-destruction to be found nowhere else in all of Nature.

As a species, taking all in all, we are still too young, too juvenile, to be trusted. We have spread across the face of the earth in just a few thousand years, no time at all as evolution clocks time, covering all livable parts of the planet, endangering other forms of life, and now threatening ourselves. As a species, we have everything in the world to learn about living, but we may be running out of time. Provisionally, but only provisionally, we are a Wonder.

And now the first on my list, the one I put off at the beginning of making a list, the first of all Wonders of the modern world. To name this one, you have to redefine the world as it has indeed been redefined in this most scientific of all centuries. We named the place we live in the *world* long ago, from the Indo-European root *wiros*, which meant man. We now live in the whole universe, that stupefying piece of expanding geometry. Our suburbs are the local solar system, into which, sooner or later, we will spread life, and then, likely, beyond into the galaxy. Of all celestial bodies within reach or view, as far as we can see, out to the edge, the most wonderful and marvelous and mysterious is turning out to be our own planet earth. There is nothing to match it anywhere, not yet anyway.

It is a living system, an immense organism, still developing, regulating itself, making its own oxygen, maintaining its own temperature, keeping all its infinite living parts connected and interdependent, including us. It is the strangest of all places, and there is everything in the world to learn about it. It can keep us awake and jubilant with questions for millennia ahead, if we can learn not to meddle and not to destroy. Our great hope is in being such a young species, thinking in language only a short while, still learning, still growing up.

We are not like the social insects. They have only the one way of doing things and they will do it forever, coded for that way. We are coded differently, not just for binary choices, *go* or *no-go*. We can go four ways at once, depending on how the air feels: *go*, *no-go*, but also *maybe*, plus *what the hell let's give it a try*. We are in for one surprise after another if we keep at it and keep alive. We can build structures for human society never seen before, thoughts never thought before, music never heard before.

Provided we do not kill ourselves off, and provided we can connect ourselves by the affection and respect for which I believe our genes are also coded, there is no end to what we might do on or off this planet.

At this early stage in our evolution, now through our infancy and into our childhood and then, with luck, our growing up, what our species needs most of all, right now, is simply a future.

VOCABULARY

autoclave: an apparatus using superheated steam under pressure 5
progeny: offspring 7
mandible: jaw 8
cambium: a thin formative layer in plants that gives rise to new growth 8
symbiotic: interdependent 8
propagate: reproduce 9
olfactory: relating to the sense of smell 10
epithelial: relating to the cellular tissue that covers or lines a body 10
unparsimonious: wasteful 12
feckless: irresponsible 12

AUDIENCE AND PURPOSE

1. Why does Thomas define "wonder" at the start of the essay?
2. Why does Thomas hold his number one choice until the end?
3. How does Thomas create the sense of humans' significance in the scheme of things through his enumeration of the Seven Wonders?
4. Wonder is very different from knowledge. How does Thomas use the concept of wonder to help close the gap between himself and his readers in terms of scientific knowledge?

CONTENT

1. Thomas uses the examples of the Seven Wonders almost as a moral lesson for humans. Give examples.
2. Why does Thomas take us to the limits of scientific knowledge in his examples?
3. Examine Thomas's paragraph about the child. How does he arrive at his conclusion in that paragraph?
4. Why does Thomas argue that humans are superior to social insects?

STYLE AND STRUCTURE

1. How does Thomas use concrete detail to draw in readers who may not come from a science background?
2. How does Thomas combine scientific and colloquial language to help the lay reader along? Go through one of his examples in detail as you consider this question.
3. Why does Thomas insist on the personal idiosyncrasy of his list of Seven Wonders?

Kildare Dobbs

Kildare Dobbs (b. 1923) is a well-known Canadian travel writer who has won the Governor General's Award. Born in India, he was raised in Ireland and then served in the British Navy. His works include *Reading the Time* (1968), *Running to Paradise* (1962), and *The Eleventh Hour: Poems for the New Millennium* (1997). His most recent work is *Casablanca: The Poem* (1999).

THE SCHOOLS

"Money—" said the billionaire, wintering in Palm Beach, Florida, a town where money is everything, "money isn't everything—but it's a great way to keep in touch with the kids."

Money is also a great way to keep *out* of touch with them—get them out of your hair. Money lets you pack them off to private boarding-schools where many parents believe they can buy a better education than the state provides.

Right or wrong, this is one reason why in every Canadian province, and especially in populous Ontario, private schools still flourish, catering to the rich and upwardly mobile and sometimes, through scholarships, to promising boys and girls of small means. In Canada these schools don't appear to be much resented as centres of privilege. Enrollment in them grew by almost fifty per cent between 1974 and 1986, keeping pace with new money and growing disillusion with the public system. It has stayed high ever since. More than sixty institutions belonging to the Canadian Association of Independent Schools ("independent" means not subsidized) charge from $4,200 a year to $20,000-plus to teach the same subjects that public schools teach for free.

There are splendid private schools in every province. But four in the Golden Crescent of Ontario have extra lustre, attracting students from across Canada and overseas. The Little Big Four, as Upper Canada College, St. Andrew's College, Trinity College School, and Ridley College quaintly call themselves, are a special case. (This is a football category; the Big Four were the original members of the Canadian Football League.)

5 Upper Canada College is conspicuous in Toronto, with boarders at its preparatory school as well as its upper school. Its central location in the city enables many students to come daily. In sports, hockey is its passion, but academic standards are high too, and there are literary exemplars among old boys, starting with Stephen Leacock. Luxury cars in the parking lot attest the wealth of its students; the VWs belong to staff. The portfolio

power of UCC old boys is formidable. When the college buildings were condemned in 1958, the governing board quickly raised nearly three million dollars for rebuilding. Soon the tower with its famous "four-faced liar" of a clock rose once more over the campus.

St. Andrew's at Aurora, Ontario, originally a school of hard Knox dedicated to porridge and Calvinist principles, has clans instead of houses, a cadet corps affiliated with the 48th Highlanders, kilted pipers and drummers, and dancing cousinship with Havergal College, a Toronto private school for girls. Among its famous sons, Vincent and Raymond Massey disliked the place. Others are grateful for what it gave them. According to Ed Wood, senior vice-president and general manager of Canvideo Television Sales Ltd., the school rescued him from trouble in the late fifties, giving him so much confidence he ran away from the Ottawa Roughriders' training camp to enter university. "In those days," he says, "many entrants were sort of general bad-asses, including me. I owe a lot to St. Andrew's."

Trinity College School, Port Hope, an Anglican foundation, is genially recalled by Charles Taylor, one of Canada's pre-eminent horse-breeders and a respected writer who was for years the sole western newspaper correspondent in Peking. His schoolmates included the avant-garde novelist Scott Symons, already an original in boyhood, as Taylor recalls in a book in praise of the British strain in Canadian identity. Back in the sixties when I asked a TCS principal to name a couple of TCS's famous sons, he reeled off a list of business leaders—forgetting Archibald Lampman, the nineteenth-century romantic poet. With fund-raising in mind, poets hardly count.

Ridley (in the lunch-bucket city of St. Catharines, Ontario) somewhat unfairly had the reputation of a school for jocks when Peter Gzowski, Canada's best-known radio personality, attended. In rowing, Ridley crews have beaten the world's best oarsmen at Henley Regatta. Since then, the college has gone co-educational and laid more stress on academic values, and voluntary drama, music, choir, cadet corps, and debating. Not that sports are neglected. A new arts and sciences complex, rivalling its opulent gymnasium, reflects this orientation. The school has even endowed a chair for the novelist Richard B. Wright (*The Weekend Man, Farthing's Fortunes, etc.*), a dedicated member of the English faculty. School life has already influenced his fiction. In *Tourists*, the hero, a private schoolmaster and wife-killer, is condemned to life imprisonment, a happy ending, because it's just like school.

And indeed it is in the spartan living conditions of school dormitories that adolescents learn the furtive consolations of the jail: mad pleasures of masturbation, secret, solitary, and guiltridden; reading under the bedclothes by flashlight; smoking, drinking vodka, and toking up; breathless crushes on teachers or school heroes and heroines; athletic frenzy and self-torture. Anguish expresses itself in heartfelt graffiti on lavatory walls: *"Lou-Ann has BIG TITS."* What hopeless passion finds blurted expression behind the locked door! Exile from home and home-comforts can steel the heart. Displays of homesickness or family affection can threaten the self-control of companions in misery, releasing sorrow and anger. Offenders are jeered at and punished. Survivors learn to substitute fair play for love, as to endure institutional food.

10 Richard Wright's fictional tourist-teacher is a murderer, doubtless exceptional. Yet teachers at private schools do seem to be more original, on the whole, than their high-school equivalents, though most prepare themselves for their profession at universities and training schools like their public colleagues, acquiring earnestness and pedagogical jargon. Some are employed only briefly, moving on to become classics professors, journalists, or business tycoons. A cherished few make one think of the staff at Evelyn Waugh's prep school in *Decline and Fall* (the novelist himself taught at Arnold House in Wales). As Dr. Fagan, the headmaster, remarks when interviewing the hero, "I have been in the scholastic profession long enough to know that nobody enters it unless he has some very good reason which he is anxious to conceal." Not all the sneaky perverts find their victims in Catholic orphanages.

Each of the little big four is heavily represented in university enrollment and business leadership. If private school graduates are given no favours in corporate hiring, neither are they discriminated against.

What schools teach may be less important than how they teach. Nursed at the stony bosom of the *alma mater* some break their teeth while others absorb granite. Private schools tend to breed loyal supporters or angry rebels. They can also provide refuge from unhappy homes. Whatever the syllabus, private schools influence character mainly by their styles, which range from cricket and chapel to carrot-juice and eurythmics. In addition to small classes, firm discipline, individual guidance, and healthy sports, private schools provide chances to make lasting friendships with well-connected schoolmates. And for old boys caught out by the securities commission, there's the bonus that jails can hold no terror for survivors of the more spartan schools.

Though still attempting the ungrateful role of civilizing rich kids, private schools are changing with the times. Floggers broke their canes back in the 1950s, maybe because it appeared that some little boys liked being caned by their football heroes. Sadism was acceptable, but masochism was ... unmanly.

Partly from conviction, partly from economic pressure, some schools began to accept students from ethnic minorities, home-grown or imported. (This had never been impossible; there had always been room for a few dusky princes, emirs, and future taipans.) One or two schools went so far as to abandon monastic restrictions and risk co-education. But as it became clear that numbers could be kept up without so drastic a novelty, most Canadian private schools stayed with the gender they knew. This way they could still compete with public schools by being different.

Perhaps it was inevitable that training-college gobbledegook should infect the vocabulary of principals. This annoys patrician parents who want their kids to hear and learn plain English that dogs and cats can understand. Governors ponder new roles for the private school, bringing in new blood from business, the arts, and even from social work. The pursuit of "excellence" contends with "character development," doubtless biased by the reflection that the money of backward rich kids is every bit as good as that of poor little geniuses. Attempts to create a kinder, gentler private school with sensitive, caring boys and girls can upset alumni to whom the whole effort looks like mollycoddling.

The boo-hoo pedagogues are in eclipse right now, but some of their innovations will stay. For example, the provision of an outside "mentor" for every eight or nine pupils to help smooth the path of alienated or homesick adolescents; and exposure to working artists, professionals, and entrepreneurs to give reality to book-learning.

Meanwhile big-city schools report growth in day-attendance and a trend to later entry. The heavy expense of private schooling, especially of boarding, is one cause. The trend could downgrade the academies into mere finishing-schools and crammers for examinations. But thrifty parents reflect that if the great advantage of private schools lies in future networking, two or three years give time enough for making lifelong friends.

Private schools also function as instruments of social mobility, recruiting new entries for social and business leadership. This democratic function is often forgotten. But astute immigrant minorities have long used it to ease the ascent of their second generations into the Canadian meritocracy.

I like to think of them the way they used to be. Old boys and girls are happy to reminisce. Like old warriors who relive battles but forget the tedium of hurry-up-and-wait, school veterans recall the scandals and pranks rather than the classroom. True, most of school life is placid routine. But who wants to hear about that?

Modelled on British schools that evolved to supply leaders for Victoria's expanding empire, Canada's private academies sought to impart confident manners, with the help of neckties, blazers, bullying, canings, cricket, cold showers, and irrepressible flatulence.

The most powerful educational influences were not necessarily imposed by the staff. Boys and girls in each school developed distinctive traditions and subcultures of their own, in addition to the mores and swiftly changing fashions of North American teenagers in general. A private school bus overtaking a rival institution's bus could be a cheerful sight, with a moon in every window. Pressures to conform were just as powerful as in public schools. Some of this barbarous subculture was colonial, imitated from British schools. One thinks of the boys' subculture described in William Golding's *Lord of the Flies*. The novel is often thought to be a satire on the human condition. (One should be vigilant when a reviewer uses that phrase "the human condition," trying for a stock response. This is what Hamlet calls "mitching mallecho," a cop-out.) In fact the horrible little boys in *Lord of the Flies* behave the way they do, not so much because they are human as because they have already been brutalized in an English prep school.

Girls used to be brainwashed much the same way. Field hockey and funny costumes—gym-tunics, tartans and bloomers—took the place of the boys' canes and blazers. At Toronto's Bishop Strachan School—although Strachan himself, the first Anglican bishop of Toronto and a Family Compact man, was prim enough—the uniforms were downright kinky. Back in the fifties I sat beside a music judge at a festival in which BSS was competing. The singers were bursting out of middies with very short skirts, navy bloomers, and black lisle stockings suspended from garterbelts. Beads of sweat stood on the Irish maestro's brow. "Now those," he said faintly, "are what I call well-developed girls ..."

According to Dr. Barbara Eastman, a Toronto company director who put in thirteen years at BSS, at least four safety-pins were needed to preserve modesty. (Branksome Hall girls needed only one for their wrap-around kilts.) Naughty BSS girls could omit a pin or two. The well-stacked songsters I saw could have been two-pin girls.

Canada's ranking private school, Upper Canada College, is almost next door to BSS, on thirty-eight prime acres in midtown Toronto. Maddened by the proximity of those two-pin girls, hot-blooded UCC boys in the late fifties attempted a night-raid on the BSS dorms. An old boy tells the story. Unluckily entering by the wrong window, the raiders stumbled over the school matron. One of them, in his rush to escape, knocked the lady down. Another, a bishop's son and more chivalrous, stayed to help her—and was caught.

Imagine the disgrace! The college, founded in 1829 by Lieutenant Governor Sir John Colborne to breed up leaders for the infant colony of Upper Canada—with support from public funds till around 1900—was and remains one of the most illustrious schools of what used to be the British Commonwealth of Nations. An Upper Canada boy won his Victoria Cross galloping in the Charge of the Light Brigade at Balaclava, and lived to read about it in Tennyson's poem; the UCC cadet corps (now eclipsed) was unique in having Battle Honours blazoned in its Colour ("flag" to you), commemorating war service in 1866 against invading Fenians, paddywhacks, and Yankee shopboys; twenty-six UCC old boys were admirals and generals in the Second World War; and the names of a whole phalanx of national and provincial worthies glitter in gold from the honour rolls of its great Prayer Hall. Add to these heroes and bishops the ranks of CEOs and bank presidents among UCC's alumni and on its Board of Governors. Such was the side the unlucky son-of-a-bishop had let down by being caught!

Naturally he was expelled. Honourable conduct could have no other reward. It's whispered that he became a mayor in the interior of British Columbia.

Despite this tale of a good man sent into exile, it's arguable that expulsion from a private school gives a fine start on the road to success. Remember the late Harold Ballard, ejected from UCC to become the Canadian sports magnate the media loved to hate. Regard the man Conrad Black, Officer of the Order of Canada, Argus-eyed benefactor of the Clarke Institute (Toronto's favourite laughing academy), author of a book on Maurice Duplessis, proprietor of many publications, and the latest in a line of wild colonial boys to knock British business on its ear. Black was expelled in 1959 from UCC for stealing exam papers and selling them to candidates, which he did to avenge oppressive coercion, including what he calls "the joys of corporal punishment" by a regime of losers (his teachers). It also was a precocious feat of enterprise that his schoolmate John Fraser calls "the biggest single scandal in the college's history." The quotation is from Fraser's lively book, *Telling Tales*, published in 1986 before its author went to work for Black as editor of *Saturday Night*—surely an example of how a school friendship can help one's career.

As Black was leaving the campus in disgrace, the principal's wife approached him. He remembers she was wearing a Viet Cong helmet. "Your life is over," she told him.

Black, a dayboy at UCC, went on to board at Trinity College School, Port Hope. What with compulsory sports, which he loathed, and a complete lack of privacy, the granite entered his soul. He slogged on to graduate impressively from three universities. The rest is financial history.

I reached Black by telephone at his London office. "How much did you make on the exam caper?"

"About $1,400," he said. "Not bad for a fourteen-year-old!"

"I hear things are much better now at UCC," Black concedes. He doubts that the old-boy network exerts much influence at the highest level, though in professional cadres that serve the Establishment there might be some over-representation. In his view the corporate leadership is now a meritocracy.

His friend Fraser, numbed by a family breakup, flunked his last year at UCC and later boarded at Lakefield, of which he's now a governor. Sparkling, friendly, a verbal ballet-dancer done up with a neat bow-tie, Fraser has forgiven home and school. "I don't regret any of it," he says, "I don't have bad memories." He found ways to survive, defending himself with jokes and dodging battalion parades by pretending to practise the glockenspiel for the corps band. The springs of happiness as of sorrow are in childhood.

The most brilliant Canadian old boy is the novelist Robertson Davies (UCC). A Merlin reborn in freshly laundered beard and garb of antique cut, the former Master of Massey College looks as if he had materialized from Celtic mists and fogs. The majestic, wizardly airs go with magical wit. According to Fraser, Davies thinks naughty boys who made good are less interesting than good ones who were later disgraced. He evokes a paragon who won the Herbert Mason Medal, UCC's top honour. This likely lad (according to the novelist) ended begging for handouts on Bay Street—though only from UCC old boys. The pan-handler could put a number, Davies told Fraser, on what the old-boy connection was good for: exactly $12.00 a day.

35 I once saw Davies at Lakefield, a dazzling presence in that outdoorsy, outward-bound place by the Kawartha lakes. He was there to give the occasion a breath of the great world of letters.

Lakefield was never one of the Little Big Four, whose alumni were mortified in 1977 to learn that Prince Andrew was to spend two terms there. "Why, it's only a notch above Pickering!" they gasped, affecting to believe that Pickering, a respectable Quaker foundation, was a reform school. When Prince Andrew was followed to Lakefield in 1985 by Prince Felipe de Borbon, the Infante and heir to the Spanish throne, they were crushed. "If God were not God," says a Castilian verb, "he would be King of all the Spains, and he of France his cook!"

Sources dry up at mention of Prince Andrew's Lakefield schooldays. At least one uncheckable tale, though, should be told. It seems the prince, with a few schoolmates, made an orienteering trip into Algonquin Park. The group spent the night in a federal surveyors' camp, an elaborate installation with some five residents. The seventeen-year-old prince loudly complained about the waste of public money. Tight-lipped, his RCMP bodyguard asked H.R.H. to step outside. "As far as we're concerned, sir," the mountie told his royal charge, "around here you're the biggest waste of public money!"

In Britain, few go to more than one public (*i.e.*, private) school. In Canada it's not unusual. Black and Fraser admit to two each. The late Raymond Massey, according to his memoir, *When I Was Young*, was at four of them, Havergal, UCC, St. Andrew's, and Appleby (at Oakville, Ontario). Havergal College is for girls. Massey, one of only two boys in its kindergarten, was there for six months in 1902. He claimed that being outnumbered by big girls left him permanently in awe of women *en masse*, though evidently not *en Massey*; he found the courage to marry three times. In 1934 one of his nice little playmates was tried in London with her chauffeur for murdering her husband.

Then there was John Julius Cooper, now Lord Norwich. He went from UCC to Eton during wartime. How did he make the trip at a time when civilian passengers were rarer than hen's teeth? Daddy sent a destroyer for him. Daddy Duff Cooper was a former First Lord of the Admiralty and a member of the war cabinet.

40 Eastern schools were not the only ones to turn out ladies (*i.e.*, women who might conceivably employ chauffeurs, not necessarily with felonious intent). Though BSS enjoys a certain pre-eminence, there's no Big Four in girls' schools, probably because parents tend to keep daughters close to home. Girls' schools cherish a single ideal coast-to-coast, like Miss Edgar's and Miss

Cramp's School in Montreal, which was founded in 1909 to educate ladies, and whose girls still sing:

Beloved School! Our faith we pledge to thee,
Our love and honour through long years to be.

One undoubted lady is Pat Buckley, married to the conservative publisher and broadcaster William F. Buckley, Jr. A New Jersey social sheet recently described her as "Queen of New York Society," and "First Lady of Good Works." As Patricia Taylor of Vancouver she spent certain years at Crofton House, a private school for girls which, along with York House, house-trained the daughters of Vancouver's first families. "I was never properly schooled," Mrs. Buckley once told Michael Dupree of *Avenue* magazine. And still she managed two years at Vassar, not exactly a college for backward girls. What do queens of society do? They throw parties, benefits, and galas, all for charity. You don't need much Latin for queening but you do need brains, charm, and presence.

Girls' private schools value poise, correct manners, and a sense of duty. One Toronto school, St. Clement's, awards a prize for "Ardour." Headmistresses don't overesteem the arts of buying things in shops or of wearing them; a gentlewoman need not court high fashion. Many an alumna could be described (in J.D. Salinger's phrase) as "not too categorically cashmere sweater," favouring the po-hat, the sensible shoes, and, in the drawing room, wall-to-wall beige.

Is there a male private school type? "You can always tell someone who's been to a private school," a private school principal claimed in 1978. "There's a certain confidence, a certain assurance. You can spot it a mile away." This holds for the British public school type who once ran the Empire and now works in public relations. But the Canadian old boy surely isn't so obvious, unless he has gone on to Oxford to acquire its famous informed apathy, or to an American ivy league college to learn moral earnestness. Certain traits can give him away though, the loud, honking voice, the too-firm handshake, the palpable self-esteem, the air of hornier-than-thou. The true private school type has been raised in an all-male society and shows it in male company by dropping final Gs and coarsening his speech, and in female company by a wary politeness.

But naturally all the specimens you and I know are exceptions. What, after all, do Peter Gzowski, the late George Grant (*Lament for a Nation*), the late Harold Ballard, and Scott Symons have in common, other than old school ties?

45 "For what do [the private schools] now stand," an old boy asked in *The Idler* late in 1989, "except privilege itself? They struggle to justify themselves on meritocratic grounds...." Hugh Rutherford (pen name of a descendant of an early Canadian prime minister) went on to imply that they were busy training up yuppies to buy BMWs.

It's too early to characterize the new, co-educated private school type now emerging from schools like King's-Edgeworth, Nova Scotia (the oldest private academy in Canada), Ridley, and Lakefield.

But this much can be said: there are consequences of knowing that someone is spending a fortune on your education. It can be proof either of great love or of great willingness to do without your company. Love makes you feel secure; exile removes you from a nasty home. Either way you are well off. Maybe this is the true inwardness of privilege.

VOCABULARY

opulent: wealthy 8
spartan: austere 9
eurythmics: a system of harmonious body movement to the rhythm of spoken words 12
patrician: of noble birth 15
mollycoddling: spoiling 15
pedagogues: teachers, schoolmasters 16
meritocracy: government based on merit 18
mores: moral attitudes 21
lisle: made of twisted cotton thread 22
Argus: a guardian, named after the hundred-eyed monster of Greek legend 27
cadres: core groups 32
palpable: tangible 43

AUDIENCE AND PURPOSE

1. What stereotypes surround the notion of the private school, according to Dobbs's essay?
2. Dobbs accepts these stereotypes rather than combatting them. Why?
3. Dobbs argues that private schools, particularly the old ones, can be characterized easily. After reading this essay, can you describe their chief traits?

CONTENT

1. What sorts of distinctions does Dobbs make among private schools in Canada?
2. How do girls' schools differ from boys' schools, according to Dobbs?
3. What relation is there between good behaviour in school and success in the world, according to Dobbs? What are his examples?
4. How do private schools differ from public schools? (This comparison is implicit in Dobbs's discussion.) How might private schools, in his view, provide a superior education?

STYLE AND STRUCTURE

1. Dobbs's tone is naughty. Why does he focus on the secrets and the little-known stories in private schools?
2. It could be said that in this essay Dobbs "tells tales out of school." What is the effect of all this "private information"?
3. Dobbs seems to start with the "public" side of things and to end with the "private." Why does he use this tactic?

Sidney Katz

Sidney Katz (b. 1916) is a Toronto journalist who has written for magazines and newspapers, including the *Toronto Star* and *The Globe and Mail.* He has published two books: *The Divided Woman* (1973) and *The Intelligent Man's Guide to Hair Transplants and Other Methods of Hair Replacement* (1979), co-authored with Walter P. Unger.

'TIS THE SEASON TO BE KISSING

Kissing, a delightful human activity which peaks on Valentine's Day, is a simple enough act: two people saluting or caressing each other with their lips. But depending on how it's done, the kiss can convey a wide variety of messages — duty, gratitude, curiosity, respect, friendship, sexual passion or undying love. In unsentimental medical jargon, a kiss is described as "the anatomical juxtaposition of the two orbicularis oris muscles in a state of contraction." But to the romantic Greeks, a kiss is "the key to paradise," while Cyrano de Bergerac defined it as "a rosy dot placed on the eye of loving; 'tis a secret told to the mouth instead of the ear."

A widely respected standard for "the perfect kiss" was set more than 50 years ago by Hugh Morris, author of The Art of Kissing. The secret, said Morris, lies in concentration. "Kiss as though at that moment nothing else exists in the world. Kiss as though your entire life is wrapped up in the period of the kiss. Kiss as though there is nothing else you would rather be doing."

The main types of commonly used kisses can be listed as follows:

The blow kiss. This comes highly recommended for people who want to avoid physical contact. With a quick gesture of hand and mouth, you can dispatch a kiss to someone at the other end of the room — or to anyone in sight.

The cheek peck. Widely used, it's a kiss without substance consisting of a quick touch to the cheek. For casual acquaintances.

The cheek nuzzle. This is more personal than the perfunctory cheek peck and takes longer. You warmly touch the cheek of the recipient with your lips and cheek. Limited to people you genuinely like.

The ear kiss. Thoughtful people will resort to this kiss if the recipient is a heavily made-up lady who's in fear of seeing her handiwork smeared.

The low-voltage lip kiss. For friends you like or for people to whom you wish to express sincere gratitude.
The high-voltage lip kiss. To express intense passion and/or love. You should be warned that this kiss triggers a physiological earthquake in the body. The pulse rate shoots up from 72 to 100, the blood pressure and the blood sugar level rise and there's a flutter around the heart—the result of spleen contraction and the addition to the blood of millions of red blood corpuscles.

Although kissing is a pretty safe form of recreation, there are still some hazards to be reckoned with. During a kiss, anywhere between 23 and 280 colonies of bacteria are exchanged, most of them harmless unless you happen to have a cold or some other ailment. In the so-called "Hollywood Kiss" (duration 10 to 12 seconds), twice as many bacteria travel mouth-to-mouth as are transmitted during a perfunctory kiss on the lips. Men with a mustache deliver more bacteria during a kiss than do smooth-shaven ones.

5 Wearers of contact lenses are urged to exercise caution during high-voltage kissing: the vigorous movement of the cheek and jaw muscles during kissing can work the lenses loose and you stand a good chance of losing them. The amount of high-voltage kissing which prevails at any given time must have some bearing on the prosperity (or lack of it) in the optical supplies business.

VOCABULARY

perfunctory: matter-of-fact 3

AUDIENCE AND PURPOSE

1. What are the indications that the tone of the piece is not really serious?
2. Why does Katz begin with contrasting definitions from sources like medicine and Cyrano de Bergerac?
3. Why does Katz conclude his introduction with a standard for kissing?

CONTENT

1. What do you learn about the social meaning of the kiss from Katz's essay?
2. How seriously do you take the warnings about the hazards of kissing that the author includes?
3. Why does Katz provide so much medical information?

STYLE AND STRUCTURE

1. How does Katz structure the kinds of kisses?
2. Why does he name the kinds?
3. How does Katz create humour in the essay?

Betty S. Flowers

Betty S. Flowers (b. 1947) published this essay in the *Proceedings of the Conference of College Teachers of English of Texas* in 1979.

MADMAN, ARCHITECT, CARPENTER, JUDGE: ROLES AND THE WRITING PROCESS

"What's the hardest part of writing?" I ask on the first day of class.

"Getting started," someone offers, groaning.

"No, it's not getting started," a voice in the back corrects. "It's keeping on once you do get started. I can always write a sentence or two—but then I get stuck."

"Why?" I ask.

5 "I don't know. I'm writing along, and all of a sudden I realize how awful it is, and I tear it up. Then I start over again, and after two sentences, the same thing happens."

"Let me suggest something which might help," I say. Turning to the board, I write four words: "madman," "architect," "carpenter," "judge." Then I explain:

"What happens when you get stuck is that two competing energies are locked horn to horn, pushing against each other. One is the energy of what I'll call your 'madman.' He's full of ideas, writes crazily and perhaps rather sloppily, gets carried away by enthusiasm or anger, and if really let loose, could turn out ten pages an hour.

"The second is a kind of critical energy—what I'll call the 'judge.' ... He peers over your shoulder and says 'That's trash!' with such authority that the madman loses his crazy confidence and shrivels up. You know the judge is right—after all, he speaks with the voice of your most imperious English teacher. But for all his sharpness of eye, he can't create anything.

"So you're stuck. Every time your madman starts to write, your judge pounces on him.

10 "Of course this is to over-dramatize the writing process—but not entirely. Writing is so complex ... that sitting down to a fresh sheet of paper can sometimes seem like 'the hardest work among those not impossible,' as Yeats put it. Whatever joy there is in the writing process can come only when the energies are flowing freely—when you're not stuck.

"And the trick to not getting stuck involves separating the energies. If you let the judge ... come too close to the madman, ... the ideas which form the basis for your writing will never have a chance to surface. But ... the subjective, personal outpourings of your madman must be balanced by the objective, impersonal vision of the educated critic within you. Writing is not just self-expression; it is communication as well.

"So start by promising your judge that you'll get around to asking his opinion — but not now. And then let the madman energy flow. Find what interests you in the topic, the question or emotion that it raises in you, and respond as you might to a friend — or an enemy. Talk on paper, page after page, and don't stop to judge or correct sentences. Then, after a set amount of time, perhaps, stop and gather the paper up and wait a day.

"The next morning, ask your 'architect' to enter. She will read the wild scribblings saved from the night before and pick out maybe a tenth of the jottings as relevant or interesting. (You can see immediately that the architect is not sentimental about what the madman wrote; she's not going to save every crumb for posterity.) Her job is simply to select large chunks of material and to arrange them in a pattern that might form an argument. The thinking here is large, organizational, paragraph-level thinking — the architect doesn't worry about sentence structure.

"No, sentence structure is left for the 'carpenter' who enters after the essay has been hewn into large chunks of related ideas. The carpenter nails these ideas together in a logical sequence, making sure each sentence is clearly written, contributes to the argument of the paragraph, and leads logically and gracefully to the next sentence. When the carpenter finishes, the essay should be smooth and watertight.

15 "And then the judge comes around to inspect. Punctuation, spelling, grammar, tone — all the details which result in a polished essay become important only in this last stage. These details are not the concern of the madman who's come up with the ideas, or the architect who's organized then, or the carpenter who's nailed the ideas together, sentence by sentence. Save details for the judge."

AUDIENCE AND PURPOSE

1. Why does Flowers suggest breaking up the task of writing?
2. Why does she dramatize each of the roles that the writer must play?

3. Why is the essay written mostly as a dialogue between a teacher and a class?

CONTENT

1. Why should the madman come first, in Flowers's opinion?
2. Why does the architect have the task of being unsentimental about the previous work of the madman?
3. Why should there be a lapse of time between each phase?

STYLE AND STRUCTURE

1. How is the two-part structure a good example of Flowers's attempt to follow her own advice?
2. How does the tone and the use of the pronoun "you" make the reader feel?
3. Flowers's strategy is to "divide and conquer." Show how she breaks down her own essay into manageable chunks.

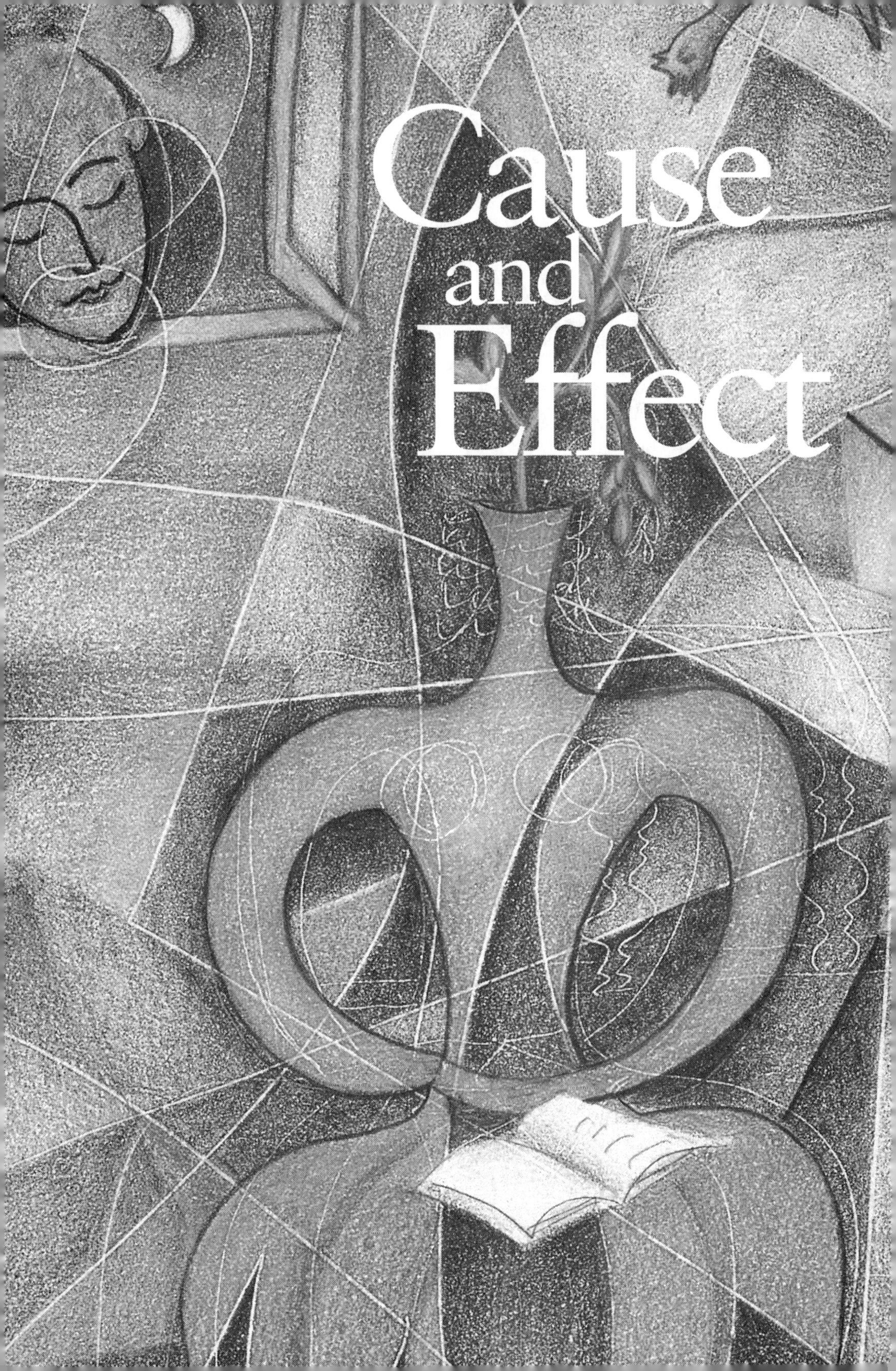
Cause
and
Effect

CAUSE AND EFFECT

Every Way Has a Wherefore, or Does It?

When you write a paper using cause and effect patterns as part of its development, you attempt to account for something, to ask the question "Why?" The little question why, however, is never simple, perhaps because, in analyzing an event or theorizing about an occurrence, you usually have to lay some blame as well as hand out some credit. Causal analysis, despite being one of the most common rhetorical patterns, is one of the most challenging to master. To explore causal analysis well, you need to proceed with caution. Let's begin with the title of this section. Despite its wording, usually an essay will explore in depth either causes or effects. The unmanageability of cause and effect relations demands such a reined-in approach to the problem. Your thesis statement will generally take this form: "X is caused by this, that, and the other." Alternatively, you might approach the topic from its effects and write the following: "This, that, and the other are all consequences of X." Although such a formulaic approach makes causal analysis look easy enough, it is actually a complex rhetorical pattern that is frequently hard to substantiate. The causes and the effects of anything are often extremely difficult to nail down. For this reason, it is a good idea to limit your discussion in this kind of essay. Don't promise any simple explanations to complex problems, however temptingly neat the idea might seem. Real cause and effect relationships are frequently messy, subtle, and complicated.

Consider this example. You want to argue that a proliferation of violence in the media leads to increasing violent behaviour in schools. Indeed, this argument is made fairly regularly these days, and the evidence for it appears to abound. You could, for example, cite well-known examples of recent violence in schools and show the apparent connections between popular violent movies and the actions of real students in real and violent situations. But be wary of overgeneralizing or of claiming too much. While it may be true that there is a resemblance between recent school violence and Oliver Stone's film *Natural Born Killers*, that connection may be only sufficient to demonstrate the relation between one particular act of violence and the media, and not a universal link between them. The other shortcoming of this causal analysis is that it does not take into account other potential causes — for example, an individual's troubled family life, or perhaps his or her untreated medical condition, both of which could well be factors in acting out violence.

When you develop a causal analysis, you need to remember that your support or evidence needs to be strong and authoritative. Theories that aren't substantiated won't hold up in the face of disagreement from others. Causal analysis, in particular, is vulnerable to attack from others whose take on a situation points to different causes. For example, the argument made above might be susceptible to attack on the grounds that it offers too simplistic a view of how we learn behaviour and where we learn it. If, after all, it is true that an impressionable teenager might "learn" to behave in a destructive psychotic way by watching television, does that mean that others will "learn" to behave kindly and according to socially acceptable standards by watching situation comedies with happy endings? Can you generalize that all of us learn to model our behaviour from watching the media? And why, for that matter, should we confine the discussion to media such as video games and movies? Couldn't a bloody play like Shakespeare's *Macbeth* be considered equally dangerous in its moral impact? Such disputes about the validity of causal analysis are typical and should warn you against the difficulties of establishing too much too conclusively.

Causal analysis, then, demands caution. You may make small claims about relevant causes, but larger, more universal claims are usually not advisable (at least without a lot of confirming illustration, examples, and firm authority in support). Partly because we tend to seek cause and effect everywhere in our understanding of the world, many conclusions drawn by causal analysis are subject to revision. You need to be especially careful to guard against a common fallacy: assuming that because one event preceded another, that it was, in fact, the cause. This fallacy is referred to as *post hoc ergo propter hoc* (from the Latin, literally, "after this therefore because of this), and it reminds us that seemingly immediate connections are often red herrings. In truth, there are very few easy explanations for an event, and any essay that uses causal analysis should try not to oversimplify its weighing of the evidence.

Strong reliable support is a must in a convincing causal analysis. Your theory about why something is as it is and your powers of persuasion need the assistance of good evidence in the form of developed examples, powerfully cited experts, clear and understandable statistics, and the best reasons you can find. Weak arguments rely on ungrounded theories. Strong ones are grounded on fact and reason. Without such support, no rhetorical powers will save your case.

Topic sentence → One clear effect of the prevalence of cell phones and the widespread use of electronic mail these days is the neglect of our immediate environment. Every day, people are becoming more involved with groups of people around the world and less aware of their actual neighbours. Those who play chess converse avidly with international chess players and engage in games and discussions about them on-line. In the meantime, they do not cultivate the friendship of people near them. It has always been true that people who use public transportation are disinclined to talk to one another; these days, however, you often witness the same people animatedly chatting about their highly personal lives without any regard for those who might overhear them on the bus or in the train compartment. And the neglect is often more dangerous than the loss of potential conversation and friendship among people meeting in the flesh. It often extends to traffic accidents caused by cell phone users lost in a long-distance conversation with someone, unaware of an oncoming car. The positive side is an increasingly global network of "virtual" friends and people who share common interests; the negative is that we are becoming more and more alone in an "actual" crowd.

Global Warming: Why Does It Matter?

The introduction includes some discussion of the effects of global warming.

Global warming is a fact. While its effects are gradual, they are real, and they have potentially devastating results. It is known that some regions have become as much as 15°C warmer over the last century, a change that has already produced a number of alarming consequences. The cause of global warming is the buildup of carbon dioxide and "greenhouse gases" created by the burning of fuels that add to pollution. Since pollution is the root cause, we need to seek out ways to improve the situation and to put a stop to dangerous levels of pollution and concomitant global warming now. A brief look at the causes and effects of the greenhouse effect will enable us to know our enemy and to vanquish it.

Thesis statement →

The main causes of global warming are given.

The enemy is everywhere. Cars that burn a lot of fuel are one source of the problems. A single car on the road may release 45 tonnes of carbon dioxide into the atmosphere over its lifetime. Better regulations for fuel consumption would combat this unnecessary pollution. Power plants, too, are dangerous to the environment, particularly those that burn coal. Replacing coal with cleaner natural gas would reduce carbon dioxide production by half. Another encroaching danger is the tendency to destroy forests by cutting or burning them. Protecting the forests is essential to protecting the environment now and in the future.

The effects of global warming are given.

While the increase in carbon dioxide in the atmosphere is the main effect of global warming, there are other effects as well. For example, there is a marked increase in infectious diseases that have changed their range in the past few years. Cases of malaria and dengue fever have occurred as far north as New York, New Jersey, and Michigan in recent years, and diseases such as encephalitis are becoming more common. The sea level has changed, affecting low-lying areas and destroying beaches and wetlands around the world. Glaciers and snow cover are gradually disappearing on all five continents. And finally, plant and animal populations are shifting and migration patterns are changing as species try to adapt to changing climates. Some species that are unable to adapt successfully have begun to decline. More severe weather events, such as droughts and flooding, are also a consequence of global warming, and a warning that action must be taken to preserve the environment now.

Conclusion

Those of us who recognize the dire consequences of global warming can help reduce pollution by demanding more control over car emissions, insisting that more power plants burn natural gas, and attempting to save energy in our daily lives.

Source: Based on information taken from
The Sierra Club Global Warming Campaign,
http://www.toowarm.org/CAFÉ/factsheets,
January 5, 2000.

Jared Diamond

Jared Diamond (b. 1937) is a professor of physiology at UCLA. He was a recipient of the MacArthur Foundation "Genius" Award and is a member of the American Academy of Arts and Sciences. He is a renowned physiologist, ecologist, and author who has taken many expeditions to the rainforests of New Guinea. Diamond is also the author of *Guns, Germs, and Steel* (1997), which won the Pulitzer Prize for general nonfiction in 1998.

INVENTION IS THE MOTHER OF NECESSITY

My 11-year-old twin sons just told me what they learned today in school. "Daddy, Johannes Gutenberg invented the printing press, and that was one of the greatest inventions in history." I learned that, too, when I was a child. I suspect that the same view is taught in most other American and European schools. What we are told about printing is partly true, or at least defensible. Personally, I would rate it as the best single "invention" of this millennium. Just think of its enormous consequences for modern societies. Without printing, millions of people wouldn't have read quickly, with no transmission errors, Martin Luther's 95 Theses, the Declaration of Independence, the Communist Manifesto or other world-changing texts. Without printing, we wouldn't have modern science. Without printing, Europeans might not have spread over the globe since 1492, because consolidation of initial European conquests required the emigration of thousands of would-be conquistadors motivated by written accounts of Pizarro's capture of the Incan emperor Atahualpa.

So I agree with half of what my kids were taught — the part about the importance of printing. But things get more complicated when you credit this invention specifically to Gutenberg, or even when you credit him with just the printing press itself. Gutenberg did much more than invent the printing press — and much less than invent printing. A more accurate rendering of his achievements would be something like the following legalistic sentence: "Gutenberg played a major practical and symbolic role in independently reinventing, in a greatly improved form and within a more receptive society, a printing technique previously developed in Minoan Crete around 1700 B.C., if not long before that."

Why did Gutenbergian printing take off while Minoan printing didn't? Therein lies a fascinating story that punctures our usual image of the lonely and heroic inventor: Gutenberg, James Watt, Thomas Edison. Through his contribution to the millennium's best invention, Gutenberg gave us the millennium's best window into how inventions actually unfold. Even American and European schoolchildren reared on Gutenberg hagiography soon learn that China had printing long before Gutenberg. Chinese printing is known to go back to around the second century A.D., when Buddhist texts on marble pillars began to be transferred to the new Chinese invention of paper via smeared ink. By the year 868, China was printing books. But most Chinese printers carved or otherwise wrote out a text on a wooden block instead of assembling it letter by letter as Gutenberg did (and as almost all subsequent printers using alphabetic scripts have also done). Hence the credit for what Gutenberg invented is also corrected from "printing" to "printing with movable type": that is, printing with individual letters that can be composed into texts, printed, disassembled and reused.

Have we now got the story right? No, Gutenberg still doesn't deserve credit even for that. By about 1041, the Chinese alchemist Pi Sheng had devised movable type made of a baked-clay-and-glue amalgam. Among the subsequent inventors who improved on Pi Sheng's idea were Korea's King Htai Tjong (cast-bronze type, around 1403) and the Dutch printer Laurens Janszoon (wooden type with hand-carved letters, around 1430). From all those inventors, it's convenient (and, I think, appropriate) to single out Gutenberg for special credit because of his advances—the use of a press, a technique for mass-producing durable metal letters, a new metal alloy for the type and an oil-based printing ink. We also find it convenient to focus on Gutenberg as a symbol because he can be considered to have launched book production in the West with his beautiful Bible of 1455.

5 But a form of printing with movable type was invented far earlier by an unnamed printer of ancient Crete in the Minoan age. The proof of Minoan printing can be found in a single baked-clay disk, six inches in diameter. Found buried deep in the ruins of a 1700 B.C. palace at Phaistos on Crete, the disk is covered on both sides with remarkable spiraling arrays of 241 symbols constituting 45 different "letters" (actually, syllabic signs), which were not deciphered until a couple of years ago. A recent decipherment identifies the signs' language as an ancient form of Greek that predates even Homer.

Astonishingly, the symbols of the Phaistos disk weren't scratched into the clay by hand, as was true of most ancient writing on clay, but were instead printed by a set of punches, one for each of the 45 signs. Evidently, some ancient Cretan predecessor of Pi Sheng beat him to the idea by 2,741 years. Why did Minoan printing die out? Why was Renaissance Europe ready to make use of the millennium's best invention while Minoan Crete was not?

Technologically, the Minoans' hand-held punches were clumsy. The early Minoan writing system itself, a syllabary rather than an alphabet, was so ambiguous that it could be read by few people and used for only very particular kinds of texts, perhaps only tax lists and royal propaganda. Chinese printing's usefulness was similarly limited by China's own nonalphabetic writing system. To make Minoan printing efficient would have required technological advances that did not occur until much later, like the creation of paper, an alphabet, improved inks, metals and presses.

I mentioned that Gutenberg is part not only of the millennium's best invention but also of its best insight into how our usual view of inventions often misses the point. Coming up with an invention itself may be the easy part; the real obstacle to progress may instead be a particular society's capacity to utilize the invention. Other famously premature inventions include wheels in pre-Columbian Mexico (relegated to play toys because Mexican Indians had no draft animals) and Cro-Magnon pottery from 25,000 B.C. (What nomadic hunter-gatherer really wants to carry pots?)

The technological breakthroughs leading to great inventions usually come from totally unrelated areas. For instance, if a queen of ancient Crete had launched a Minoan Manhattan Project to achieve mass literacy through improved printing, she would never have thought to emphasize research into cheese, wine and olive presses — but those presses furnished prototypes for Gutenberg's most original contribution to printing technology. Similarly, American military planners trying to build powerful bombs in the 1930s would have laughed at suggestions that they finance research into anything so arcane as transuranic elements.

10 We picture inventors as heroes with the genius to recognize and solve a society's problems. In reality, the greatest inventors have been tinkerers who loved tinkering for its own sake and who then had to figure out what, if anything, their devices might be good for. The prime example is Thomas Edison, whose phonograph is widely considered to be his most brilliant invention. When he built his first one, in 1877, it was not in response to a national clamor for hearing Beethoven at home. Having

built it, he wasn't sure what to do with it, so he drew up a list of 10 uses, like recording the last words of dying people, announcing the time and teaching spelling. When entrepreneurs used his invention to play music, Edison thought it was a debasement of his idea.

Our widespread misunderstanding of inventors as setting out to solve society's problems causes us to say that necessity is the mother of invention. Actually, invention is the mother of necessity, by creating needs that we never felt before. (Be honest: did you really feel a need for your Walkman CD player long before it existed?) Far from welcoming solutions to our supposed needs, society's entrenched interests commonly resist inventions. In Gutenberg's time, no one was pleading for a new way to churn out book copies: there were hordes of copyists whose desire not to be put out of business led to local bans on printing.

The first internal-combustion engine was built in 1867, but no motor vehicles came along for decades, because the public was content with horses and railroads. Transistors were invented in the United States, but the country's electronics industry ignored them to protect its investment in vacuum-tube products; it was left to Sony in bombed-out postwar Japan to adapt transistors to consumer-electronics products. Manufacturers of typing keyboards continue to prefer our inefficient QWERTY layout to a rationally designed one.

All these misunderstandings about invention pervade our science and technology policies. Every year, officials decry some areas of basic research as a waste of tax dollars and urge that we instead concentrate on "solving problems": that is, applied research. Of course, much applied research is necessary to translate basic discoveries into workable products—a prime example being the Manhattan Project, which spent three years and $2 billion to turn Otto Hahn and Fritz Strassman's discovery of nuclear fission into an atomic bomb. All too often, however, the world fails to realize that neither the solutions to most difficult problems of technology nor the potential uses of most basic research discoveries have been predictable in advance. Instead, penicillin, X-rays and many other modern wonders were discovered accidentally—by tinkerers driven by curiosity.

So forget those stories about genius inventors who perceived a need of society, solved it single-handedly and transformed the world. There has never been such a genius; there have only been processions of replaceable creative minds who made serendipitous or incremental contributions. If Gutenberg himself hadn't devised the better alloys and inks used in early printing, some other tinkerer with metals and oils would have done so. For the best invention of the millennium, do give Gutenburg some of the credit—but not too much.

VOCABULARY

conquistadors: conquerors 1
hagiography: writings about saints 3
amalgam: blend 4
syllabary: a series of written characters, each representing a syllable 7
arcane: antiquated 9
transuranic: an element with an atomic number greater than uranium 9
entrenched: strongly established or defended 11
serendipitous: luckily accidental 14
incremental: increasing 14

AUDIENCE AND PURPOSE

1. What does Diamond claim about inventions?
2. In what ways does Diamond show that invention and usefulness to society are not related?
3. Why does Diamond claim that people prefer the theory of genuises as the makers of history?

CONTENT

1. Why does Diamond argue that Gutenberg did not single-handedly invent printing?
2. Why, in Diamond's opinion, does invention precede necessity?
3. Why do many societies not leap to use inventions? What examples of this phenomenon does Diamond give?
4. What point does Diamond make about Edison's invention?

STYLE AND STRUCTURE

1. Why does Diamond begin with the story of his sons?
2. Why does Diamond use the word "tinkerers" to describe inventors?
3. Why does Diamond make the point that inventions come from unexpected places?
4. What does the conclusion claim is the driving force behind inventions?

Mel Hurtig

Mel Hurtig (b. 1932), once an Edmonton bookseller and always a Canadian nationalist, was for many years a Canadian publisher. He is also founder of the Council of Canadians and of *The Canadian Encyclopedia* (1985), which is now available on CD-ROM. This excerpt is taken from his memoirs, *At Twilight in the Country: Memoirs of a Canadian Nationalist* (1996).

"NEVER HEARD OF THEM ... THEY MUST BE CANADIAN"

In the early 1970s, teachers from across the country began asking me to come to speak at their conventions. The more time I spent talking with the teachers and students, the more disappointed I became at the lack of Canadian content in the curriculum. In many school libraries there were only a few Canadian books or magazines. Most of the students I talked to knew very little about our country.

It seemed to me that somehow curriculum people and many teachers had become preoccupied with methodology, forgetting to keep course content in mind. The teachers' conventions I attended most often had keynote speakers from the United States. The seemingly obvious mandate to teach Canadian children about Canada had somehow been discarded.

One school text I came across, *How People Live in Canada*, had a big picture of Abraham Lincoln on the cover. Another book, this one about hockey called *Fury on Ice*, ended with the dirty French-Canadian centre getting a two-minute penalty, which allowed the valiant American captain to score the winning goal. One grade-three class in Edmonton learned that "our flag" consisted of thirteen red and white stripes and fifty stars. Another class was assigned a paragraph to copy that ended: "Now we have 50 states. We are proud of our country." A grade-eight class wrote essays about Robert E. Lee, "one of our greatest generals." In Calgary a grade-four class dutifully recorded that "our nation's birthday is on the fourth of July." Quizzes concentrated on which was the highest mountain, the biggest lake, the largest city, and so on, all in the United States. One American high school text used in Manitoba advised students that Canada needs the U.S. ten times more than the U.S. needs Canada. In one grade-twelve class I visited in Charlottetown, of thirty students, only one knew who Papineau was, only one could identify Samuel Hearne, and only half could identify the name Wilfrid Laurier. In

Calgary a group of twenty-four grade-twelve students did an educational television show with me; only four knew who Laurier was; only one could identify Palliser, and only one knew who Crowfoot was. After one speech I gave complaining about the situation in Canadian schools, the Canadian Press reporter wrote: "Mr. Hurtig said young Canadians were learning all about Davey Crockett, but not about Simon Frazer." No editor caught the spelling error. Canadian kids knew all about Daniel Boone and George Washington; they rarely knew anything about David Thompson or Louis Riel. Some four hundred Ontario university students were asked to take a test given to landed immigrants before they received their citizenship. Seventy-six percent of the students could not name the governor general, eighty students identified Harold Wilson as a Canadian premier, while more than ninety percent could not name three provincial premiers. Most of the university students failed the test.

In 1971 students in political science at McMaster University in Hamilton went on strike because there was not enough Canadian content in their classes. Sixteen of the eighteen faculty members were not Canadians. The University of Alberta hired an American professor from Texas to teach high school teachers how to teach social studies.

5 By the mid-1970s, some ninety-five percent of all the texts used in elementary and high schools in Canada were produced by foreign publishers, mostly American, and at the postsecondary level it was ninety-two percent. Canadian librarians were asked in a survey, "What sources do you use to choose your books?" The four most-mentioned sources were *The American Library Association Journal*, the *Virginia Kirkus Service* (out of Chicago), *Time* magazine, and the *New York Times Book Review*.

About the same time, Lakehead University in Thunder Bay, with some nine thousand Indians and Métis living in the immediate area, had a graduate course in Black studies, but not a single course on Canadian Indians or Métis. The head of the sociology department at one major Canadian university was an American citizen as were twenty-five of the department's thirty-six members. When staff had to be reduced, five Canadians were let go.

Closer to home, Imperial Oil sent a speaker to a high school in Edmonton. After his talk, teachers phoned to tell me that the speaker told the students they mustn't be overly concerned with issues like foreign ownership. "Nationalists like to make a lot of noise," the speaker had said. Besides, "we shouldn't turn our back on the rest of the world."

After eight years of trying, *The Journal of Canadian Studies* finally was given a small grant from the Canada Council—$3,770. The same year, the council gave the *Canadian Journal of African Studies* a grant for $11,355. (About the same time, the RCMP decided to celebrate its anniversary with a cross-country pageant. The RCMP hired an American to write the show!)

In 1974 not one of the three professors teaching Canadian history at Simon Fraser University in Vancouver was a Canadian.

In my travels across the country the question I asked over and over again was: "How can we expect to survive as a country if, in the face of massive inundation of American culture, we fail to teach our own kids about our own history, culture, traditions, heroes, accomplishments, and values?" Across Canada provincial ministries of education, instead of insisting on texts with adequate Canadian content or developing curriculums with adequate Canadian content, simply allowed themselves to become dependent on foreign textbooks, almost all of them American. In a Reader's Digest "reading skill builder" used in elementary schools, Canadian youngsters learned that the American eagle is the "symbol of our proud freedom." In Nanaimo students read in their language text that the American forces defeated the British "and our flag had won its first victory." In Calgary students were asked in a test: "Who was the first president of our country?"

Seven months after Pauline Jewett was appointed president of Simon Fraser University, the senior faculty threatened to break her. She had vowed to restrict the hiring of American staff. Sixty percent of the faculty were non-Canadian, with Americans the highest percentage among them.

During the 1970s billions of dollars flowed out of Canada to purchase American films, film strips, books, and other educational material for use in Canadian schools.

One day in 1974, after visiting a high school in Ottawa and once again being disappointed by the lack of Canadian content in the curriculum, I decided to see if I could somehow give the Canadian educational establishment a jolt. What I set out to do became one of the most important things I had ever done. It took almost a year of planning, organization, distribution, and coordination, and cost some $5,000. Political scientist Larry Pratt helped, as did a large number of teachers in every province. In a March 22, 1975, article in the *Globe and Mail* I recounted how "in March of 1974 the Surrey-Langley chapter of the Committee for an Independent Canada conducted a 'Canadian Awareness Survey' of students in their last year of high school in six schools in and around Vancouver." I went on to document a shocking lack of knowledge about Canada. For instance, less than thirty percent could identify the BNA Act as Canada's Constitution—the Magna Carta, Declaration of Independence, and Bill of Rights were frequent answers; seventy-two percent could not name the premier of the province of Quebec; seventy-one percent could not name the capital of New Brunswick; asked to name *any* three Canadian authors, sixty-one percent were unable to do so.

My own survey was conducted in all ten provinces, the Northwest Territories, and Yukon. It was distributed to students in villages, towns, and all our major cities, in affluent and poor areas, in farm communities and urban suburbs. We worked very hard to obtain a true cross-section of students in their last year of high school all across Canada.

Here are some of those results: 63% were unable to name *any three* of Canada's prime ministers who held office since the end of the Second World War; 61% were unable to name the BNA Act as Canada's Constitution; the majority of students could not name the province or territories in which the Annapolis Valley, Athabasca River, Mackenzie River, or the Klondike are located; 66% were not able to name the Canadian who was awarded the Nobel Peace Prize in 1957; 89% could not identify Gabriel Dumont, 69% Rene Levesque, 96% Emily Murphy, 92% Norman Bethune; given a list of eight names (Robert Frost, E.J. Pratt, Ernest Hemingway, Margaret Atwood, Al Purdy, T.S. Eliot, Margaret Laurence, and Morley Callaghan) and asked simply to circle the names of Canadians, 78% failed to select Pratt, 69% Atwood, 79% Purdy, 70% Laurence, and 51% Callaghan; 59% could not say into which ocean the Mackenzie River flows; about half had no idea why the War Measures Act was proclaimed in 1970; over a third of the students surveyed thought Imperial Oil, General Motors of Canada Ltd., Chrysler, and Shell were Canadian companies, and selected Harold Wilson as among the premiers of Canada's provinces.

Altogether, 62% of the students failed the questionnaire (that is, they scored under 50%). At the bottom of the last page of the questionnaire we asked for comments from the students. Here are a few representative comments: "I know more about American presidents than Canadian prime ministers!"; "I can't believe how ignorant I am about Canada"; "I could probably talk on the U.S. for many hours and yet maybe 10 minutes on Canada"; "I find that although I have almost completely finished Gr. 13 and with an honour standing each year, I am unable to answer a good

50% of your questions"; "If they want us to know these things why don't they teach them in school?"

My *Globe* article went on to criticize the educational establishment. "If, when our kids leave school, they know very little about their country, where are they likely to pick it up? If they're not provided with an education that makes them *interested* in Canada, are they very likely to acquire it later? I am not suggesting the cultivation of isolationist, parochial, inward-looking schools. But I am suggesting that in a nation overwhelmed by American influence, and increasingly owned by Americans, we have a special obligation to our own children in our own schools. If they are supposed to be the decision-makers of the future, then surely we must equip them better than the results of this survey indicate."

Perhaps one of the student comments summed it up best: "Margaret Atwood, Margaret Laurence—never heard of them so they must be Canadian."

The response to the article was incredible. Ontario Premier John Robarts had breakfast with Eddie Goodman the morning the survey results appeared in the *Globe*. Robarts was furious. Goodman told me that he just about went through the roof of the Prince Arthur Room in the Park Plaza. Many newspapers across the country phoned for permission to reprint the survey results. Newspapers, magazines, and radio and TV stations did their own surveys. *Canadabooks* sent copies of the survey to every member of Parliament and every senator in Ottawa. I was inundated with letters expressing outrage at the lack of Canadian content in our schools from every region of the country. There were many mostly supportive letters from people in education.

One rather interesting development after the survey was published was the establishment of chairs of (wait for this) American Studies at Canadian universities. Four months after my survey, Val Sears of the *Toronto Star* reported the details of a memo from the U.S. Embassy in Ottawa to the State Department in Washington:

> The American Embassy in Ottawa has proposed that the government finance a professorship in American studies at Ottawa's Carleton University to offset a "negative image" of the United States on Canadian campuses. The memo says that the "traditional" arguments against the appointment of a U.S. professor—that there are too many already and that he would become the target for attacks by Canadian nationalists—are now irrelevant.

> The targets of the Canadian nationalist sentiments are not scholars of the first rank but those who have been judged as third-rate academics by peers on both sides of the border. The nationalists' complaint is that preference in the third-rate academic category should go to the Canadian citizen.

So it was clear that it would be okay to hire "third-rate" Canadians.

Oil money was used to establish a chair of American studies at the University of Calgary, where no chair or department of Canadian studies existed.

I wish to make something clear in all of this. Yes, Canadian students must learn about the world about them; it's imperative that they do so. Yes, we should have good American and British and French professors, and others, in our postsecondary institutions. Many of them become Canadian citizens and are among the most patriotic and valuable people in the country. But somehow in Canada we have gone way too far in the opposite direction from patriotism. We have become a pale shadow of a country, lacking in understanding of our own roots, our own genesis, our own metamorphosis from colony to nation. By the 1970s, we were rapidly headed once again for colonial status. Myopia, money, and mesmerism allowed American culture to dominate even our schools.

In October 1993 a poll showed that the most popular of all politicians for Canadian teenagers was U.S. President George Bush. George Bush, for God's sake!

VOCABULARY

inundation: flood 10
parochial: narrow, confined 17
mesmerism: hypnotism 22

AUDIENCE AND PURPOSE

1. What is the effect of the anecdotes with which Hurtig begins?
2. Why does Hurtig think that knowledge of Canada is imperative?
3. Why is the title effective?

CONTENT

1. Why do you think Hurtig's survey led to the establishment of chairs in American studies?
2. How recognizable to you are the Canadians that Hurtig names?
3. In your opinion, is the article still timely today?

STYLE AND STRUCTURE

1. What is the effect of accumulating examples of lack of knowledge of Canada without Hurtig intervening to comment on them?
2. Why does Hurtig mention Ontario Premier John Robarts's response the way he does?
3. Why is the concluding detail so effective?

John Tierney

John Tierney (b. 1953) is a staff writer for the *New York Times*. His most recent publication is the comic novel, co-authored with Christopher Buckley, *God is My Broker: A Monk-Tycoon Reveals the 7 1/2 Laws of Spiritual and Financial Growth* (1998).

OUR OLDEST COMPUTER, UPGRADED

When the Sojourner's tiny wheels rolled over the Martian surface on July 5, it was in some ways a bigger leap for mankind than Neil Armstrong's first step on the Moon. You may not have realized that if you were watching network television, which gave the Mars landing relatively short shrift. But that was the beauty of this extraterrestrial event: you didn't need television to follow it.

Anyone in the world with a computer and an Internet connection could see pictures from the spacecraft. You could study Martian sunsets or put on cardboard 3-D glasses to take in a 360-degree view of the landscape. With a few clicks of the mouse, you could read a treatise on Martian geology, check out the latest weather conditions on the planet, sit in on a news conference or watch scientists issuing commands from the mission-control room. One Web site provided a recipe for throwing a Mars Madness Celebration—red and brown M & Ms were recommended—and gave directions to dozens of such gatherings across America. Other sites let you participate in on-line chats with planetary scientists as well as religious fundamentalists convinced that the mission was a hoax being staged in the Arizona desert. During the week of the landing, the various Mars Web sites were visited more than 200 million times.

It was easily the most popular event in the history of the Internet, proof at last that humanity could use this new medium for something loftier than viewing pictures of a naked Pamela Anderson Lee. The Moon landing was the apotheosis of the old technological order: a big-budget achievement of central planning, a cold-war triumph of the military-industrial complex packaged by politicians and presented to the masses by the media establishment. The Mars visit was a low-budget operation with a charming quirkiness to it, a peaceful scientific exercise instead of a propaganda victory over an enemy nation. In 1969, Communist authorities suppressed coverage of the Moon landing; this year, Russians followed the Mars mission on the World Wide Web, using the very machines that helped end the cold war.

Is this a better world? Has technology made us better? Tools can't change human nature, but they can encourage or suppress certain qualities, and most people would probably agree on what constitutes "better": wiser, happier, kinder, more equitable and cooperative, less duplicitous and belligerent. The tricky part is defining "us."

5 In the two centuries after the Industrial Revolution, individuals reaped enormous personal benefits that were accompanied by some social liabilities. As people abandoned farms and small towns, they lost communal bonds; as personal incomes rose, public air and water got dirtier; as power became concentrated in capital cities, elites controlled new tools of mass communication and mass destruction. Indoor plumbing and washing machines freed women of onerous work, but there was less socializing at wells. Trains and cars enabled workers to move away from industrial neighborhoods, but these suburbanites spent more time alone in their cars and backyards, lapping up the wisdom of distant publishers and broadcasters instead of chatting with relatives and neighbors. Although new technology is often described as a Faustian bargain, historically it has involved a trade-off not between materialism and spirituality—lugging water from the well was not a spiritually uplifting exercise for most people, no matter how much it might appeal to the Unabomber—but between individual freedom and social virtue.

Today's technologies offer a better deal for everyone. Individuals are acquiring more control over their lives, their minds and their bodies, even their genes, thanks to the transformations in medicine, communications, transportation and industry. At the same time, these technologies are providing social benefits and undoing some of the damage of the past. Technology helps to conserve natural resources and diminish pollution. Today's farmers are so efficient that unneeded cropland is reverting to forests and parks; the most high-tech countries have the cleanest air and water. The Information Revolution, besides enabling people to visit Mars at will, is fostering peaceful cooperation on Earth by decentralizing power. Political tyrants and demagogic warmongers are losing control now that their subjects have tools to communicate directly with one another. People are using the tools to do their jobs without leaving their families. They're forming new communities in cyberspace and forming new bonds with their neighbors in real space. Technology has the potential to increase individual freedom *and* strengthen community—even though at the moment, so many people complain it does neither.

Technology's victims have become familiar images in the media: on-line addicts who don't know their next-door neighbors; satellite-dish owners who have stopped reading; computer users overwhelmed by E-mail, infuriated by software glitches and baffled by incomprehensible manuals; workers displaced by machines or forced to put in longer hours; frazzled parents, especially working mothers, too exhausted and busy to spend time with their children. We contrast these pathetic figures with images of a happier past, of families quietly relaxing in a premachine age when people still had time to read, contemplate the meaning of life, visit with their relatives and neighbors.

But when exactly were those halcyon days? If premachine means before the Industrial Revolution, the average person then was short-lived, illiterate and oblivious to most culture beyond the village. Women's lives were consumed with domestic chores and continual pregnancies, and women were especially unlikely to be educated. Marriage records from a region of 1750s England, then one of the world's most literate societies, show that two-thirds of the bridegrooms could sign their names, but only one-third of the brides could. It would be hard to call that a better world.

Living conditions and educational opportunities certainly improved after the Industrial Revolution, but people still didn't have much time to sit around discussing the classics or communing with nature. In the middle of the last century, the typical man in Britain worked more than 60 hours a week, with no annual vacation, from age 10 until he died at about 50. That left him with about 90,000 hours of free time over the course of his adult life —barely a third of the free time enjoyed by today's workers. This trend shows no sign of abating, says Jesse H. Ausubel, director of the Program for the Human Environment at Rockefeller University. He projects that by the middle of the next century, the average workweek in America will be shorter than 28 hours.

10 Since 1965, Americans have gained an average of almost one hour of leisure each day, according to social scientists at the University of Maryland who have been studying people's "time diaries" over the past three decades. Americans are now spending a little more time reading books and magazines, exercising, pursuing hobbies and attending adult-education courses. Evidence from the diaries and other research shows that in recent decades, people have been going more frequently to art museums, the theater and the opera.

Contrary to popular stereotypes, the diaries show that the workweek has been shortening, that women have as much leisure time as men and that parents are spending as much time with their children as they did in the 1960s. These children, unfortunately, are less likely to live with two parents, which may be partly a consequence of technology that has made divorce and single parenthood less of an economic burden: men and women are presumably more inclined to live separately now that they can both support themselves outside the home, relying on machines to make clothes, clean house and do most food preparation. But new technology is hardly the only cause of the traditional family's decline, and in any case it's hard to get too nostalgic for the days when women had no choice but to stay in the kitchen.

Why, if men and women have more time and opportunity than ever to pursue their dreams, do they grouse so much about modern technology? One reason is that new technologies like computers usually are more trouble than they're worth—at first. They're hard to learn and create resentment among workers, particularly the unskilled ones who fear displacement and are jealous of higher-paid experts in the new technology. The introduction last century of electricity to factories did not immediately increase workers' pay and productivity; the widespread benefits came only after several decades, when factory managers and workers finally learned how to use the new motors efficiently. Then wages increased for everyone, raising the standard of living and creating new kinds of jobs. Luddites have been warning for two centuries that technology destroys jobs, but the overall effect of automation is to free workers to concentrate on other, less-tedious tasks. Today's workers are richer and more cultured than their Luddite ancestors (and better dressed, thanks to mechanical looms). While they may have fewer jobs in the textile industry, they have more opportunities to work as teachers, social workers, travel agents, personal trainers, writers and museum curators.

As much discomfort as the personal computer has caused, there's no reason to assume that the machines will remain complicated. Gadgets become simpler as technologies mature and marketers appeal to the masses. George Orwell's despair over cars, gramophones and telephones was at least partly due to the crude state of those technologies in his day. The automobile was a relatively unreliable, high-maintenance machine until a couple of decades ago. Gramophones were cumbersome and yielded tinny sounds. Telephones were forever disturbing the peace of people trying to eat, converse or read. The phone didn't become wholly civilized until people were freed to ignore it by the invention of the answering machine—a contraption that was despised before coming to be regarded as a necessity. Today, E-mail is a novelty that can be disruptive, but pioneers are developing techniques for coping, like automated responses when there's no time to deal with an overloaded mailbox and filters to sift out the junk mail.

Another reason we grouse about modernity is that our expectations are higher. The middle class wants perquisites once limited to the rich, from material luxuries to cultural experiences to intellectual fulfillment. Our ancestors may have been content to pass the time on the porch chatting with neighbors about the weather and crop prices, but they didn't have many other choices. Today most people—including those academics who rhapsodize about traditional communities while working in offices far from their hometowns—demand more stimulation than their relatives and neighbors can provide. We feel more rushed because we have more possibilities.

15 Free time is increasing, but not as fast as our sense of the necessary," says Geoffrey Godbey, a co-author of "Time for Life," a report on the time-diary research project. "With technology we've upped the ante. Instead of corresponding with 6 or 7 people, we have 150 E-mail partners. Thirty years ago most people didn't bother shampooing their carpets or blow-drying their hair or making their own bread, but now that they have the equipment, they have higher standards."

The most dispiriting trend discovered by Godbey and his colleagues is the couch-potato paradox: people have been watching more television even though they rate it among their least-favorite forms of leisure. Americans average more than 16 hours a week, an increase of 4 hours since 1965,which means that most of our recently acquired free time has gone to the tube. A diehard optimist could argue that television has been improving, that people are deriving joy and enlightenment from all those new cable channels, but it would be just as easy to argue that they're staring at cubic zirconium rings. The increase in tube-watching seems especially perverse considering that it coincides with a decline of two hours a week in the amount of time people spend socializing, an activity they consider much more enjoyable than television. A society of solitary people sitting at home enviously watching the camaraderie on "Friends" does not seem like a triumph of the communications revolution.

The good news is that people with computers are watching less television, and they've increased the amount of time spent socializing with family and friends (partly because they get together to play computer games). At the moment only about 40 percent of American households have computers, but the percentage is rising as the machines become cheaper and easier to use. Over the past year, home computers have begun outselling televisions in the United States, a statistic that cheers George Gilder, who in 1990 wrote a book titled "Life After Television." Now the editor of the Gilder Technology Report, he expects the broadcast-television empires to collapse—and an intellectual culture to flourish—once the masses can easily receive video and text from a computer network as diverse as the Internet.

"When I debate network television executives," Glider says, "they come up to me afterward and say: `Look, you don't understand. People *like* the stuff we put on. We've done market surveys and we've found that people are boobs.' Well, I'm a boob when faced with conventional TV. It's too much work to find something good, and if you do, it probably won't accord with your particular interests. Television is a lowest-common-denominator medium even with 50 or 500 channels. You'd never go to a bookstore with only 500 titles. In the book or the magazine industries, 99.7 percent of the stuff is by definition not for you, and that's what the Internet is like. It's a first-choice medium with a bias toward each individual's area of excellence instead of the few commonly shared interests, which are mostly prurient and sensational."

Now that the computer is combining the television with the telephone, it's clear that George Orwell got things precisely wrong in "1984." He was remarkably prescient to envision society's being transformed by a two-way communication device called the telescreen, but he didn't foresee that these telescreens would promote freedom. One-way television is useful to Big Brother, but two-way communication devices undermine central authority by communicating with one another. Totalitarian countries have fewer telephones than televisions; democracies have more telephones.

20 Why was Orwell so technophobic, so sure that telescreens would promote tyranny and war? Peter Huber, a senior fellow at the Manhattan Institute who analyzes the mistakes of "1984" in his recent book, "Orwell's Revenge," finds the answer in an essay Orwell wrote imagining how humans could free themselves of the drudgery of washing dishes. In this 1945 essay, Orwell considers the possibility of paper plates but settles on another solution: "Every morning the municipal van will stop at your door and carry off a box of dirty crocks, handing you a box of clean ones (marked with your initial, of course) in return." Orwell envisions a dishwashing factory run by a public agency—Big Brother's Ministry of Crockery, as Huber calls it.

"The thought of private, automatic dishwashing machines never even surfaces," Huber writes. "For Orwell, the centralization of powerful machines is inescapable economic destiny in the industrial age." The most graphic refutation of Orwell was the famous Apple commercial broadcast during the 1984 Super Bowl, in which the enslaved masses were liberated by a lone woman hurling a sledgehammer at a demagogue on a huge telescreen.

At the time it was a wonderful image of the home computer's revolutionary potential. In hindsight, it's even more apt, because the target of the attack, I.B.M., which then seemed to be the omnipotent Big Blue, was about to be humbled. It was more Wizard of Oz than Big Brother. The company had dominated the era of mainframe computers, but it floundered in the late 1980s when it faced competition from upstarts offering cheaper, decentralized machines.

As these personal devices proliferate, it's becoming impossible for political leaders to censor information. Africa's leaders can control newspapers, but citizens in remote villages are now getting uncensored news from Africa Online. And as information becomes central to economies, the incentives for tyrants to wage war are diminishing. Military conquest of foreign lands made a certain amount of sense when the victors acquired manpower and resources from farms, mines and factories. Access to scarce natural resources was vital—in the Middle Ages, armies fought wars over salt. Today wealth is based more and more on information, not natural resources, which is why the Congo is poor despite its vast mineral reserves, and why Hong Kong is rich even though it must import food and drinking water. The Beijing autocrats may have acquired title to Hong Kong's real estate, but they haven't conquered it. They can't seal its borders or appropriate its wealth. If they try to stop Hong Kong's telescreens from communicating, computer keyboards around the world will respond, and Hong Kong's money will start to flow away, followed shortly by its populace.

Now that the specter of Big Brother is receding, today's critics of technology have been focusing on the opposite danger: too much freedom. Conservatives worry that traditional values are threatened by on-line crudity; liberals worry that social injustice and selfishness will prevail in the unregulated realm of cyberspace. The critics correctly see that governments are losing some of their power to impose laws and moral standards, but that doesn't mean we're doomed to chaos and cruelty. Humans developed sociable rules and moral codes long before the era of centralized governments. The Internet may look like a dangerously anarchic world, but it's actually fairly similar to the ancient environment in which humans evolved to become the most cooperative, virtuous creatures on earth.

The original Information Revolution occurred during the Pleistocene, a decentralized era if there ever was one, when hunter-gatherers on the African savanna developed a powerful new computer: the human brain. The brain evolved to its large size because its information-processing capacity enabled humans to band together and increase their chances of survival. The size of a primate's brain correlates directly with the size of its social group, and the formula worked out by scientists indicates that the human brain is sized for a group of about 150, which by no coincidence is the number in a typical band of hunter-gatherers.

The large brain enabled our ancestors to work together because they had so much information about one another. They knew whom to trust because they could store memories of past behavior and obtain news about others' reputations. They developed instincts and customs that stigmatized selfishness and encouraged voluntary cooperation, especially within the band but also with outsiders. Other animals make sacrifices for the common good of their immediate kin, performing acts of altruism that insure the survival of their mutual genes, but humans go further. "We are just about the only animals who act altruistically toward nonrelatives," says Matt Ridley, a zoologist and the author of "The Origins of Virtue," a new book analyzing the evolution and economics of cooperative behavior. "Humans can be selfish, of course, but what makes us special is our instinct to be nice to one another. Every culture defines virtue almost exclusively as pro-social behavior, and vice as antisocial behavior."

This cooperative spirit has made possible the division of labor, which has been the source of all wealth, technology and culture. Just as Stone Age toolmakers independently developed complex trading networks for obtaining rock blades from distant tribes, 11th-century merchants established a trading system across Europe without any central guidance or enforcement authority. The merchants traveling among disparate kingdoms developed their own legal code and observed it voluntarily because they knew that a violator would be ostracized and unable to conduct business. The mere communication of information was enough to make them behave honorably.

"The Information Revolution is taking us back toward our better social instincts," Ridley says. "The Industrial Revolution helped centralize authority, creating hierarchical bureaucracies that tried to coerce cooperation but often brought out the most selfish instincts in both the rulers and their subjects. The way to regain community spirit is to have small institutions and horizontal networks of equals who voluntarily cooperate, like the people you see chatting on the Internet today. These virtual communities formed spontaneously because our brains are naturally inclined to this sort of information exchange. It's what we spent most of our time doing in the Pleistocene."

The Pleistocene savanna makes a good image for the Internet: a wide-open frontier being settled without any central planning. A few sociopaths are out there spreading computer viruses, and encounters among strangers can provoke viciously uncivil "flame" wars. But rules of etiquette are evolving as people coalesce into communities and networks. By trading information, they're discovering whom to trust and whom to avoid. They're writing E-mail letters to relatives and scheduling meetings with friends. Some, like merchants, are cooperating for profit, but a surprising number seem to be acting out of pure goodwill. They're freely providing information, from software to consumer advice to counsel for the lovelorn.

Most of the information is of no interest to most people, which is why the Internet can seem so pointless. My first few forays persuaded me that it was the world's most effective way to waste time. But in researching this article, I decided to give it another try. I had just read a good review of "Data Smog," a book by David Shenk about the dangers of the Information Revolution, so I looked for it among the 2.5 million books at the Amazon.com Web site. I found it right away, along with an assortment of reviews from newspapers and magazines. Some of the most succinct analysis ("Excellent at describing info glut, not so hot at solutions") came from laypeople who had volunteered their own comments.

There was also an area—"Check out these titles!"—listing other books ordered by buyers of this one, an extraordinarily useful cross-referencing feature. I began clicking from book to book, each time benefiting from the expertise of previous buyers to discover new related titles. It was like going from one Pleistocene water hole to another, at each stop picking up advice and directions to the next one.

In a couple of hours I had found enough technophobic literature to keep George Orwell happy for years—hundreds of books ranging from old scholarly critiques of the Industrial Revolution to titles like "Surviving the Media Jungle" and "Under Technology's Thumb." I discovered "Technopoly" by Neil

Postman, revealing that America has become the world's "totalitarian technocracy," a place with no "transcendent sense of purpose or meaning."

Within a week, Amazon.com had graciously delivered to my door a small library assailing its own electronic technology. I read "Data Smog" — which decried the Internet's "fragmented, asynchronous, decentralized 'free-market' culture where the public good is sacrificed" — as well as Clifford Stoll's "Silicon Snake Oil" and "Amusing Ourselves to Death," another lament by Postman. I went through treatises on information have-nots and spiritually deprived Internet surfers. I learned about a degraded electronic culture that is rendering books obsolete — an ominous trend revealed in books purchased on-line at the largest, most helpful bookstore in history. I tried to take the warnings seriously, but as the experts described the terrible plight of Americans drowning in data, there was something I couldn't get out of my mind.

It was the line spoken by Emperor Joseph II after the premiere of "The Abduction from the Seraglio": "Too many notes, my dear Mozart." He was expressing the feeling common among the day's elite that Mozart's complex music was too fast-paced and stimulating for the average listener.

Like new music, new technology is always disturbing, especially to the establishment, and it always causes unforeseen problems. The agricultural and industrial revolutions were accompanied by new plagues, pollutants and weapons of destruction. Today's revolution will bring troubles and trade-offs, but we can cope with them. Transmitting information from one willing individual to another is hardly a new menace.

Like Mozart's music, this is something our brains are equipped to handle. This is what we're good at, and what makes us better.

VOCABULARY

apotheosis: the glorification of a person or a thing 3
onerous: burdensome 5
demagogic: able to stir up the people 6
halcyon: peaceful, happy, idyllic 8
grouse: complain 12
Luddites: people opposed in principle to technological change 12
perquisites: perks 14

camaraderie: comradeship 16
prurient: lewd, exciting lust 18
prescient: prophetic 19
proliferate: increase 23
altruistically: unselfishly 26
coalesce: unite 29
forays: raids 30

AUDIENCE AND PURPOSE

1. Where is Tierney's thesis?
2. What does the title of the essay refer to?
3. What point does Tierney make with his reference to Mozart in the conclusion?

CONTENT

1. What advantages does Tierney believe technology will provide?
2. Why are the advantages not all obvious immediately?
3. What is Tierney's point about Amazon.com?

STYLE AND STRUCTURE

1. Why does Tierney include information about the Industrial Revolution?
2. Why does Tierney compare humans now with humans in the Pleistocene era?
3. How does Tierney use Orwell's fear of technology to make his point?

Ray Kurzweil

Ray Kurzweil (b. 1948) is an American technologist and the author of *The Age of Spiritual Machines: When Computers Exceed Human Intelligence* (1999). He was a pioneer in the development of machines that can read text, turn print into speech, and recognize voices. He has won awards including the Dickson Prize, given by Carnegie-Mellon University, and honours from the Canadian National Institute for the Blind.

WHEN MACHINES THINK

A threshold event will take place early in the 21st century: the emergence of machines more intelligent than their creators. By 2019, a $1,000 computer will match the processing power of the human brain—about 20-million-billion calculations per second. Organizing these resources—the "software" of intelligence—will take us to 2029, by which time your average personal computer will be equivalent to 1,000 human brains.

Once a computer achieves a level of intelligence comparable to human intelligence, it will necessarily soar past it. For one thing, computers can easily share their knowledge. If I learn French, or read *War and Peace*, I can't readily download that learning to you. You have to acquire that scholarship the same painstaking way that I did. But if one computer learns a skill or gains an insight, it can immediately share that wisdom with billions of other computers. So every computer can be a master of all human and machine-acquired knowledge.

Keep in mind that this is not an alien invasion of intelligent machines. It is emerging now within our civilization. There will not be a clear distinction between human and machine as we go through the 21st century. First of all, we will be putting computers—neural implants—directly into our brains. We have already started down this path. We have neural implants to counteract Parkinson's disease and tremors from multiple sclerosis. We have cochlear implants that restore hearing to deaf individuals. Under development is a retina implant that will perform a similar function for blind people, basically replacing the visual processing circuits of the brain. Recently, scientists from Emory University in Atlanta placed a chip in the brain of a paralyzed stroke victim, who can now begin to communicate and control his environment directly from his brain.

In the 2020s, neural implants will not be just for disabled people. There will be ubiquitous use of neural implants to improve our sensory experiences, perception, memory and logical thinking. These implants will also plug us in directly to the World Wide Web. This technology will enable us to have virtual reality experiences with other people—or simulated people—without requiring any equipment not already in our heads. And virtual reality will not be the crude experience that you may have experienced today in arcade games. Virtual reality will be as realistic, detailed and subtle as real reality. So instead of just phoning a friend, you can meet in a virtual French café in Paris, or stroll down a virtual Champs Elysées, and it will seem very real. People will be able to have any type of experience with anyone—business, social, romantic, sexual—regardless of physical proximity.

5 One approach to designing intelligent computers will be to copy the human brain, so these machines will seem very human. And through nanotechnology, which is the ability to create physical objects atom by atom, they will have human-like—albeit greatly enhanced—bodies as well. Having human origins, they will claim to be human, and to have human feelings. And being immensely intelligent, they'll be very convincing when they tell us these things.

The next 20 years will see far more change than the previous hundred. Most comments I hear about the future are not very well thought out. One common failure is to focus on only one aspect of science and technology, while ignoring other developments that are likely to intersect. Another is to see only one or two iterations of advancement in a technology and then assume that progress will come to a halt. Another is failing to understand the accelerating nature of technological progress.

One very important trend is referred to as "Moore's Law." Gordon Moore, one of the inventors of integrated circuits, and then chairman of Intel, noted in the mid-1970s that we could squeeze twice as many transistors on an integrated circuit every 24 months. The implication is that computers, which are built from integrated circuits, are doubling in power every two years. Lately the rate has been even faster.

After 60 years of devoted service, Moore's Law will die a dignified death around the year 2019. By that time, transistor features will be just a few atoms in width, and the strategy of ever finer photolithography will have run its course. So will that be the end of the exponential growth of computing?

Don't bet on it. Computing devices have been consistently multiplying in power from the mechanical calculating devices used in the 1890 U.S. census, to Alan Turing's relay-based machine that cracked the Nazi Enigma code, to the vacuum-tube computer that predicted the election of Eisenhower, to the transistor-based machines used in the first space launches, to the integrated-circuit-based personal computer that I used to dictate this article, using speech-to-text software.

A new pattern of exponential growth will take over from Moore's Law, just as Moore's Law took over from discrete transistors, and vacuum tubes before that. I call it the Law of Accelerating Returns. There are many new technologies waiting in the wings — three-dimensional chips, nanotubes, optical computing, crystalline computing, DNA computing, and quantum computing — to keep the Law of Accelerating Returns going for a long time.

So where will this take us? By 2030, it will take a village of human brains to match a $1,000 personal computer. By 2055, a thousand dollars of computing will equal the processing power of all human brains on Earth. OK, I may be off a year or two.

Actually this only includes those brains still using carbon-based neurons. While human neurons are wondrous creations in a way, we certainly wouldn't design computing circuits the same way. Our electronic circuits are already more than a million times faster. Most of the complexity of a human neuron is devoted to maintaining its life-support functions, not its information-processing capabilities. Ultimately, we will need to port our mental processes to a more suitable computing environment. Then our minds won't have to stay so small, being constrained as they are today to a mere 100 trillion neural connections (each operating at a ponderous 200 calculations per second).

So far, I've been talking about the hardware of computing. But achieving the computational capacity of the human brain, or even villages and nations of human brains, will not automatically produce human levels of capability. The organization and content of these resources — the *software* of intelligence — is also critical.

There are a number of compelling scenarios to capture higher levels of intelligence in our computers, and ultimately human levels and beyond. Using massive parallel processing and neural networks that emulate the brain, we will be able to evolve and train a system to understand language and absorb knowledge, including the ability to read and understand written documents. Although the ability of today's computers to extract and learn knowledge from natural language documents is limited, their capacity in this domain is improving rapidly. Computers will be able to read on their own, understanding what they have read, by the second decade of the 21st century. We can then have our computers read all of the world's literature—books, magazines, scientific journals, and other available material. Ultimately, the machines will gather knowledge on their own by venturing into the physical world, drawing from the full spectrum of media and information services, and sharing knowledge with each other (which machines can do far more easily than their human creators).

Once a computer achieves a human level of intelligence, it will quickly surpass it. A computer can remember billions or even trillions of facts perfectly, while we are hard-pressed to remember a handful of phone numbers. A computer can quickly search a database with billions of records in fractions of a second. And computers can readily share their knowledge. The combination of human-level intelligence in a machine with a computer's inherent superiority in the speed, accuracy and sharing ability of its memory will be formidable.

Let me describe one other particularly critical scenario. We have a good example of an intelligent process inside of each of us—and it's not even copyrighted. There is no reason why we cannot reverse engineer the human brain, and essentially copy its design.

One approach is to scan a living brain. We have techniques today, including high resolution magnetic resonance imaging—MRI—scans, optical imaging, near-infrared scanning, and other noninvasive scanning technologies, that are capable of resolving individual somas, or neuron cell bodies. Brain-scanning technologies are increasing their resolution with each new generation. The next generation will enable us to resolve the connections between neurons. Ultimately, we will be able to peer inside the synapses and record the neurotransmitter strengths.

There are a number of ways to apply the information. One approach is to use the results to create more intelligent algorithms—the basic elements of computer programs—for our machines, particularly those based on a neural net design. With this approach, we don't have to copy every single connection. There is a great deal of repetition and redundancy within any particular brain region. With this information, we can design simulated nets that operate similarly. There are already many efforts under way to scan the human brain and apply the insights derived to the design of intelligent machines.

Perhaps a more interesting approach than this scanning-the-brain-to-understand-it scenario is scanning-the-brain-to-download-it. Here we copy someone's brain to map the locations, interconnections and contents of all the somas, axons, dendrites, presynaptic vesicles and other neural components. Its entire organization can then be recreated on a neural computer of sufficient capacity, including the contents of its memory. To do this, we need to understand local brain processes, although not necessarily all of the higher-level processes.

20 Scanning a brain to download it is not as daunting an effort as it may sound. Another scanning project—the human genome scan—also sounded daunting when it was first suggested. And at the rate at which they could scan genetic codes 12 years ago, it would have taken thousands of years to complete the project. But our ability to sequence the DNA in human genes has been accelerating like all other technology, so it appears that it will indeed be completed on time, in a few years from now.

The computing aspects of individual neurons are complicated, but definitely not beyond our ability to accurately model. For example, Ted Berger and his colleagues at Hedco Neurosciences in Los Angeles have built integrated circuits that precisely match the digital and analog information processing characteristics of neurons, including clusters with hundreds of neurons. Carver Mead and his colleagues at the California Institute of Technology in Pasadena have built a variety of integrated circuits that emulate the digital-analog characteristics of mammalian neural circuits.

An even easier way to do this is to take a frozen brain—preferably one frozen just slightly before rather than slightly after it was going to die anyway—and examine one brain layer—one very thin slice—at a time. We can readily see every neuron and every connection and every neurotransmitter strength represented in each synapse-thin layer.

As the computational power to emulate the human brain becomes available—we're not there yet, but we will be there within a couple of decades—projects will be initiated in earnest to scan the human brain, with a view both to understand it in general, and to provide a detailed description of the contents and design of specific brains. By the third decade of the 21st century, we will be in a position to create highly detailed and complete maps of the computationally relevant features of all neurons, neural connections and synapses in the human brain, and to recreate these designs in suitably advanced neural computers.

Now what will we find when we do this?

25 We have to consider this question on both the objective and subjective levels. Objectively, when we scan someone's brain and reinstantiate their personal mind file (meaning, copy all of the processes relevant to human thinking) into a suitable computing medium, the newly emergent "person" will appear to other ob-

servers to have very much the same personality, history and memory as the person originally scanned. That is, once the technology has been refined and perfected—like any new technology, it won't be perfect at first. But ultimately, the scans and recreations will be very accurate and realistic.

Interacting with the newly instantiated person will feel like interacting with the original person. The new person will claim to be that same old person and will have a memory of having been that person.

There is an issue regarding the new person's body. A reinstantiated mind without a body will quickly get depressed. And there are a variety of bodies that we will provide for our machines, and that they will provide for themselves—nanoengineered bodies, virtual bodies, bodies comprised of nanorobot (microscopic-sized robot) swarms that can turn themselves into various forms at will, and other scenarios.

Subjectively, the question is more subtle and profound. Is this the same consciousness as the person we just scanned?

Consciousness in our 21st-century machines will be a critically important issue. But it is not easily resolved, or even readily understood. People tend to have strong views on the subject, and often just can't understand how anyone else could possibly see the issue from a different perspective. Artificial intelligence guru Marvin Minsky of the Massachusetts Institute of Technology in Boston observed that, "there's something queer about describing consciousness. Whatever people mean to say, they just can't seem to make it clear."

We don't worry, at least not yet, about causing pain and suffering to our computer programs. But at what point do we consider an entity, a process, to be conscious, to feel pain and discomfort, to have its own intentionality, its own free will? How do we determine if an entity is conscious, if it has subjective experience? How do we distinguish a process that is conscious from one that just acts as if it is conscious?

We can't simply ask it. If it says, "Hey, I'm conscious," does that settle the issue? No, we have computer games today that effectively do that, and they're not terribly convincing.

What if the entity is very convincing and compelling when it says, "I'm lonely, please keep me company"—does that settle the issue? If we look inside its circuits, and see similar kinds of feedback loops in its brain that we see in a human brain, does that settle the issue?

And just who are these people in the machine, anyway? The answer will depend on who you ask. If you ask the people in the machine, they will strenuously claim to be the original persons. For example, if we scan, let's say, myself, and record the exact state and position of every neurotransmitter, synapse, neural connection, and other relevant details, and then reinstantiate that information into a neural computer of sufficient capacity, the person that then emerges in the machine will think that he is (and had been) me. He will say, "I grew up in Queens, N.Y., went to college at MIT, stayed in the Boston area, walked into a scanner there, and woke up in the machine here. Hey, this technology really works."

But wait. Is this really me? For one thing, old Ray (that's me) still exists. I'll still be here in my carbon-cell-based brain. Alas, I will have to sit back and watch the new Ray succeed in endeavours that I could only dream of.

Will these future machines be capable of having spiritual experiences? Oh, they'll certainly claim to. They will claim to be people, and to have the full range of emotional and spiritual experiences that people claim to have. And these will not be idle claims; they will evidence the sort of rich complex behaviour one associates with these feelings. How do the claims and behaviours — compelling as they will be — relate to the subjective experience of these reinstantiated people? We keep coming back to the very real but ultimately unmeasurable issue of consciousness.

From a practical perspective, we'll accept these claims. They'll get mad if we don't.

Before the next century is over, the Earth's technology-creating species will merge with its computational technology. After all, what is the difference between a human brain enhanced a trillionfold by neural implants, and a computer whose design is based on high-resolution scans of the human brain, extended a trillionfold?

Most forecasts of the future seem to ignore the revolutionary impact of the inevitable emergence of computers that match and ultimately vastly exceed the capabilities of the human brain. This development will be no less important than the evolution, thousands of centuries ago, of human intelligence itself.

VOCABULARY

cochlear: pertaining to one of the parts of the ear 3
ubiquitous: existing everywhere 4
iterations: repetitions 6
exponential: something expressible as an exponent, for example, a growth rate 8

genome: one set of chromosomes with the genes they contain 20
reinstantiate: to represent concretely again 25

AUDIENCE AND PURPOSE

1. How does Kurzweil use detail to make his predictions at the start of the essay seem credible?
2. What effect do the personal references throughout the essay have?
3. Kurzweil uses many questions. What effect do these have?

CONTENT

1. How does Kurzweil's reference to Moore's Law add credence to his claims for the future?
2. Why does Kurzweil use the expression "it will take a village"?
3. How does Kurzweil argue that computers and their technology are superior to human brains? What evidence does he use to support his claim?

STYLE AND STRUCTURE

1. Why does the essay begin with a prediction?
2. Why does Kurzweil use the metaphorical terms "hardware" and "software" to describe the human brain?
3. Why does the definition of consciousness affect Kurzweil's claim so much?
4. Why does Kurzweil insist on the term "evolution" in the conclusion?

Umberto Eco

Umberto Eco (b. 1932) is an Italian writer and a professor of semiotics at the University of Bologna. He is the author of fiction, essays, academic texts, and children's books. His best-known novel is *The Name of the Rose* (1980), which was made into a film released in 1986. In 1988 he published another very successful novel entitled *Foucault's Pendulum*.

HOW THE BEAN SAVED CIVILIZATION

In 1918, at the age of 40, my maternal grandfather was stricken by a form of viral influenza, popularly known as the Spanish flu, which was decimating much of Europe. Within a week, despite the best efforts of three physicians, he died. In 1972, at the age of 40, I was stricken by a serious illness that seemed very similar to *la spagnola*. Thanks to penicillin, after a week I was up and about. So it is easy to understand why, forgetting about atomic energy, space travel and the computer, I persist in thinking that the most important invention of our century is penicillin (and, more generally, all those drugs that allow people today to reach the age of 80, whereas in the past they might have died at 50 or 60).

It is hard to determine a century's most important technological invention or scientific discovery, not least because our ideas of the date of a given invention are not clear. There are many things that readers would list among the most interesting achievements of this century, when in fact they date from the century before ours: the automobile, for example, and the skyscraper, the subway, the dynamo, the turbine. You can also add the typewriter, the gramophone, the dictaphone, the sewing machine, the refrigerator, as well as canned foods, pasteurized milk, the cigarette lighter (along with the cigarette), the elevator, the washing machine, the eraser, blotting paper, the electric fan, the safety razor, the Murphy bed, the barber's chair, the safety match, the raincoat, the safety pin, carbonated beverages, bicycles with gears and pneumatic tires, the electric tramway, synthetic fibers and great department stores to sell all this stuff, and —if I may continue—electric light, the telephone, the telegraph, radio, photography and moving pictures. Furthermore, Mr. Babbage invented a calculating machine that could perform numerous additions in one minute, setting us firmly on the path toward the computer.

When you are dealing with millennia, calculation becomes still more difficult. For the origin of gunpowder and the compass, we have only legends to go by. And even when we can be sure that a certain instrument existed, say, in the 12th century, because it is depicted in a painting of the period, we cannot assert that it did not exist a century earlier. I bring up these problems because I want to deal with some inventions that appeared at the beginning of our millennium, though it is possible that some of them made a shy debut in the last two centuries of the previous millennium without anyone paying them much attention. In any case, these are inventions that changed the last thousand years.

If I were to speak of inventions that unquestionably appeared in the first centuries after the year 1000, my immediate temptation would be to cite the stern-mounted rudder. Take a look at history's most famous comic strip, the Tapestry of Queen Mathilde, known also as the Bayeux Tapestry (after the city where it is preserved). This work gives us a minute-by-minute account of the Norman landing in England, including the Battle of Hastings. You will see that the troops of William the Conqueror arrive in a Viking-type boat, and you can observe that, for a rudder, these ships have a lateral oar, fixed at the stern (actually, these ships had two such oars, one fixed on each side). This is how vessels were steered as late as 1066. But with these lateral rudders, it was impossible to tack, to sail against the wind, offering first one flank, then the other, to the wind's force. Moreover, it was difficult to sail when the sea was rough.

Between the 12th and 13th centuries, however, the modern rudder was developed. Fixed at the ship's stern and hinged, like a door, it moved just below the surface of the water and could be operated by a single man, thanks to a tiller on the deck. As usual, the dates are vague, but something between the hinged rudder and an oar fixed at the stern is found in a bas-relief in Winchester Cathedral; it dates from 1180, barely 100 years after the Bayeux Tapestry.

Why is the rudder so important? Suffice it to say that without this invention, Columbus could not have sailed to America, and the history of the rest of the millennium would have been rather different. I would like, however, to discuss a series of inventions that, rather than characterize this millennium, have enabled us to celebrate its conclusion. Without these inventions, perhaps we would never have been born.

*

A thousand years ago we were squarely in the Middle Ages. Of course, "Middle Ages" is a scholastic convention. For example, in certain countries—including Italy—the term "Middle Ages" is employed even when the writer is referring to the time of Dante and Petrarch; in other countries, scholars already speak of these years as the Renaissance. To make things a bit more clear, let us say that there are at least two "Middle Ages": one lasting from the fall of the Roman Empire (fifth century A.D.) to the year 999, and the other, beginning in the year 1000 and continuing at least until the 15th century.

Now the Middle Ages before the year 1000 can deservedly be called the Dark Ages, a term carelessly used to cover all the centuries between the 5th and the 14th. I say "deservedly" not because those Ages were full of burnings at the stake, for there were flames and pyres also in the highly civil 17th and 18th centuries (we must not forget "The Scarlet Letter"), or because superstitious beliefs were widespread, for when it comes to superstitions—though for different reasons—our own New Age is second to none.

No, they can deservedly be called the Dark Ages because the barbarian invasions that took place during this time beset Europe for centuries and gradually destroyed Roman civilization. Cities were deserted, in ruins; the great highways, neglected, disappeared under a tangle of weeds: and fundamental techniques were forgotten, including the processes of mining and quarrying. The land was no longer cultivated and, at least until the feudal reform of Charlemagne, entire agriculture areas reverted to forest.

10 In this sense, the Middle Ages before 1000 A.D. were a period of indigence, hunger, insecurity. In his splendid "La civilisation de l'Occident médiévale," rich in observations of everyday life in the Middle Ages, Jacques Le Goff illustrated how impoverished this time was by recounting popular tales. In one such story, a saint appears magically to retrieve a sickle that a peasant had accidentally dropped down a well. In an era when iron had become rare, the loss of a sickle would have been a terrible thing, making it impossible for the peasant to continue harvesting: the sickle's blade was irreplaceable.

As the population became smaller and less strong physically, people were mowed down by endemic diseases (tuberculosis, leprosy, ulcers, eczema, tumors) and by dread epidemics like the plague. It is always risky to venture demographic calculations for past millennia, but according to some scholars, Europe in the seventh century had shrunk to roughly 14 million inhabitants; others posit 17 million for the eighth century. Underpopulation combined with undercultivated land left nearly everyone undernourished.

As the second millennium approached, however, the figures changed—the population grew. Some experts calculate a total of 22 million Europeans in 950; others speak of 42 million in 1000. In the 14th century, Europe's population hovered between 60 million and 70 million. Though the figures differ, on one point there is agreement: in the five centuries after the year 1000, Europe's population doubled, maybe even tripled.

The reasons for Europe's boom are hard to pinpoint; between the 11th and 13th centuries, radical transformations occurred in political life, in art, in the economy and, as we shall see, in technology. This new surge of physical energy and of ideas was evident to those living at the time. The monk Radulphus Glaber, born in the very last years of the first millennium, began writing his famous "Historiarum" (known in English as "Five Books of the Histories") about 30 years later. The monk did not have a particularly merry view of life, and he tells of a famine in 1033, describing atrocious instances of cannibalism among the poorest peasants. But somehow he sensed that, with the year 1000, a new spirit was stirring in the world, and things—which until then had gone very badly—were taking a positive turn.

Thus he burst forth in an almost lyrical passage, which still stands out in the annals of the Middle Ages. In it, he told how, at the end of the millennium, the earth suddenly blossomed, like a meadow in spring: "It was already the third year after 1000, when, in the whole world, but especially in Italy and the regions of Gaul, there was a renewal of the basilical churches... each Christian nation strove to achieve the most beautiful. It seemed that the very earth, stirring itself and shaking off old age, was newly clad with a white mantle of churches."

Now the flowering of Romanesque art (for that is what Radulphus was talking about) did not suddenly take place in 1003; Radulphus was writing more as a poet than as an historian. But he was talking about a rivalry of power and prestige among various city-states; he was talking about new architectural techniques and of an economic resurgence, for you cannot build such churches without wealth behind you; he was talking about churches conceived in dimensions larger than their predecessors—churches capable of accommodating a growing population.

Naturally it can be said that, with the reforms of Charlemagne, with the construction of the Germanic empire, with the rejuvenation of cities and the birth of the communes, the economic situation also improved. But would it not also be possible to say the opposite, namely that the political situation evolved, the cities flourished anew, because daily life and working conditions were improved by something?

*

In the centuries before 1000, a new triennial system of crop rotation was slowly adopted, allowing the land to be more fruitful. But cultivation requires tools and working animals, and on this front there were breakthroughs too. Just before the year 1000, horses began to be fitted with iron horseshoes (up until then, the hooves were bound with cloth) and with stirrups. The latter, of course, were more for the benefit of knights than for peasants. For the peasants, it was the invention of a new kind of collar for horses, oxen and other beasts of burden that proved revolutionary. The old collars put all the strain on the animal's neck muscles, compromising its windpipe. The new collar involved the chest muscles, increasing the animal's efficiency by at least two-thirds, and permitting, for certain tasks, horses to replace oxen (oxen were better suited to the old type of collars, but they also worked at a slower pace than horses). Moreover, whereas in the past horses had been yoked in a horizontal line, now they could be yoked in single file, significantly increasing their capacity for pulling. Around this time, plowing methods changed. Now the plow had two wheels and two blades, one for cutting the earth and the other — the plowshare — for turning it over. Though this "machine" was already known to Nordic people as early as the second century B.C., it was not until the 12th century that it spread throughout Europe.

But what I really want to talk about is beans, and not just beans but also peas and lentils. All these fruits of the earth are rich in vegetable proteins, as anyone who goes on a low-meat diet knows, for the nutritionist will be sure to insist that a nice dish of lentils or split peas has the nutritional value of a thick, juicy steak. Now the poor, in those remote Middle Ages, did not eat meat, unless they managed to raise a few chickens or engaged in poaching (the game of the forest was the property of the lords). And as I mentioned earlier, this poor diet begat a population that was ill nourished, thin, sickly, short and incapable of tending the fields. So when, in the 10th century, the cultivation of legumes began to spread, it had a profound effect on Europe. Working people were able to eat more protein; as a result, they became more robust, lived longer, created more children and repopulated a continent.

We believe that the inventions and the discoveries that have changed our lives depend on complex machines. But the fact is, we are still here — I mean we Europeans, but also those descendants of the Pilgrim Fathers and the Spanish conquistadors — because of beans. Without beans, the European population would not have doubled within a few centuries, today we would not number in the hundreds of millions and some of us, including even readers of this article, would not exist. Some philosophers say that this would be better, but I am not sure everyone agrees.

20 And what about the non-Europeans? I am unfamiliar with the history of beans on other continents, but surely even without European beans, the history of those continents would have been different, just as the commercial history of Europe would have been different without Chinese silk and Indian spices.

Above all, it seems to me that this story of beans is of some significance for us today. In the first place, it tells us that ecological problems must be taken seriously. Secondly, we have all known for a long time that if the West ate unmilled brown rice, husks and all (delicious, by the way), we would consume less food, and better food.

But who thinks of such things? Everyone will say that the greatest invention of the millennium is television or the microchip. But it would be a good thing if we learned to learn something from the Dark Ages too.

Translated by William Weaver from the Italian.

VOCABULARY

decimating: devastating, literally destroying one in ten 1
pyres: fires for burning dead bodies at a funeral 8
indigence: extreme poverty 10
posit: claim 11
annals: records 14
basilical: related to an early church building 14
resurgence: rising again into life or into prominence 15

AUDIENCE AND PURPOSE

1. Why does Eco end with his choice for the best invention rather than beginning with it?

2. Why does Eco move back in time even though penicillin seems to him demonstrably the most important invention of the twentieth century?
3. Why does Eco suggest that our own New Age might be among the Dark Ages in some respects?

CONTENT

1. Why does Eco insist on the value of the Dark Ages in his conclusion?
2. What are Eco's candidates for the best invention of the millennium?
3. Why do you think he focuses on the stern-mounted rudder, given that it is not well known to the general reader?
4. Why does Eco go back to the beginning of the millennium to find his choice of the best invention?

STYLE AND STRUCTURE

1. How does Eco go about tracing the invention he has in mind?
2. How does Eco use numbers to support his point?
3. Why does Eco move toward the simple solution and away from the complex in his nomination of the bean as the most important invention?
4. How does Eco's whole essay call into question the cause and effect line of thinking?

Persuasion and Argument

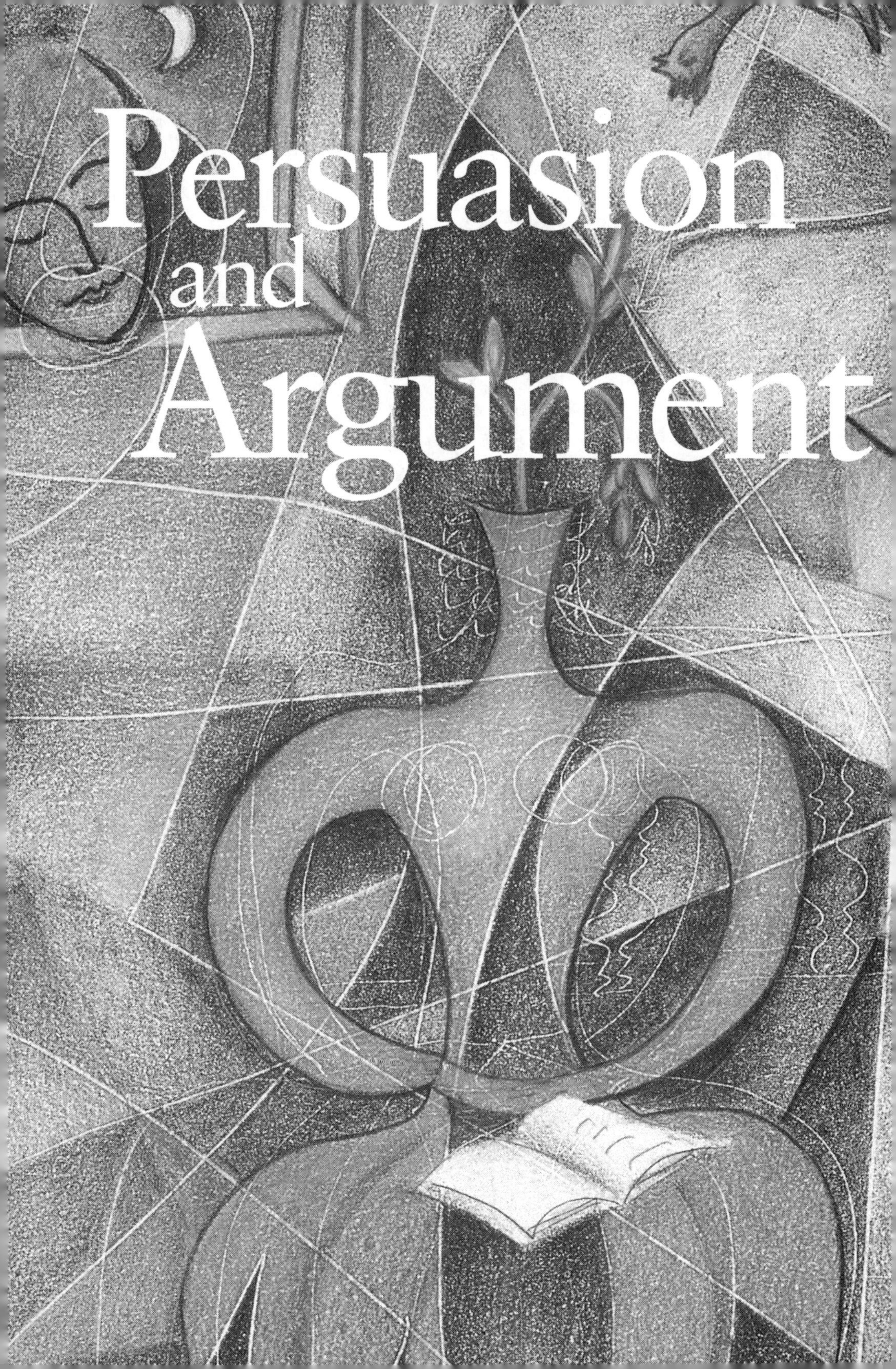

PERSUASION AND ARGUMENT

The Art of Gentle Persuasion

While most of the essays in this volume make arguments, their main function is usually expository rather than persuasive. That is, they show the reader something important. Frequently, the author's decision to classify kinds of private school or to consider what is meant by the term "guilt" involves a measure of persuasion, but that is not the essay's primary function. In this section, however, the focus is on persuasion and argument. Persuasion usually applies to emotional appeals to readers, those that make readers feel something pronounced in response to what is written. An argument, on the other hand, refers to the structure that is followed by the reasoning in an essay. The word itself usually implies a more logical approach to an issue, with a clear and direct stand in relation to the facts. Both emotional and logical appeals are necessary, however, if you want to make an essay convincing to the reader.

The thesis statement of a persuasive essay thus states an opinion, often about a controversial issue. When you write a persuasive essay, you begin with the knowledge that others may try to refute your position. It is rather like the position of a defence attorney who knows that each of his or her clients must be adequately prepared to face cross-examination from the prosecuting attorney. The case must be decided by the reader of the essay, whose job is to accept or reject what you give as evidence. And evidence is an absolutely crucial part of persuasion, especially because it is founded on opinions about matters of considerable dispute. An essay, by definition, entitles you to an opinion; that is the whole point of writing one. But you must be prepared to defend your opinion with facts, statistics, expert testimony, and the best reasons you can muster.

Writing a definitive persuasive argument may sound like a tough task, but remember, you are not expected to settle a controversial issue once and for all. You are simply expected to make the best possible case you can for your opinion. The emotional power of your opinion counts for something, to be sure, but even more important is the logical punch of the reasoning marshalled to defend your opinion.

To sharpen your reasoning, become more conscious of your tactics as you argue. Keep in mind that there are two essential ways to reason: inductive and deductive. Inductive reasoning moves from the specific to the general, and most of our reasoning works that way. Inductive reasoning is based on experience. It is the stuff of scientific experiments that produces a generalization after a number of clinical trials. It is the kind of reasoning that leads an allergic person to avoid all nuts when he or she discovers an allergy to almonds after several increasingly unpleasant experiences over the course of a year. Inductive reasoning led you to a certain college or university after talking to a number of individuals who all recommended it highly and recounted their happy memories of being there. Most of our generalizations about the world are formulated in this manner, through the accumulated evidence of individual cases.

For inductive arguments to be strong, they must be based on solid and sufficient evidence, not just on rumour or assumption. You also need to have lots of evidence. Deciding that a particular film director is incompetent after seeing just one of his or her films is not good reasoning. While your opinion may be grounded in reason, you need to ensure that the evidence is plentiful enough to make your case. Only when your evidence is trusted and taken from a broad sampling can you be sure that you have done your argument justice. Inductive arguments also involve a leap of faith. You probably cannot prove absolutely that your suspicions of a particular politician's conduct are true, but you can show, through an accumulation of individual specific instances, why you have good reason to suspect him or her. You can make a case to which a reader can reasonably assent.

The opposite side of the coin, deductive reasoning, is rarer and simpler. When you argue deductively, you move from the general to the specific. This kind of reasoning involves formal logic, expressed in the form of a syllogism, a formula by which a conclusion is drawn from the connection between a major premise and a minor premise.

Major Premise:	All dogs can be trained.
Minor Premise:	Fluka is a dog.
Conclusion:	Therefore, Fluka can be trained.

Deductive reasoning depends entirely on the truth of the premises. If it is true that all dogs can be trained and that Fluka is a dog, then it must follow absolutely that Fluka can be trained. If either of the premises is not true, however, the deductive line of reasoning will lead to an untrue conclusion. If the generalization that forms the basis of the major premise is untrue, then the reasoning that results can be dangerously wrong.

Look at the following example:

Major Premise:	All doctors have medical degrees.
Minor Premise:	Spock is a doctor.
Conclusion:	Therefore, Spock has a medical degree.

This line of reasoning looks flawed, if only because the reader can see that perhaps other kinds of doctors exist who do not practise medicine. The first generalization is thus patently false.

Other things can go wrong with deductive reasoning. In addition to making sure that your premises are true, you need to make sure that the structure of the argument is valid. Look at the following deductive argument:

Major Premise:	Exotic short-hair cats are gentle and affectionate.
Minor Premise:	Nicky is a gentle and affectionate cat.
Conclusion:	Therefore, Nicky is an exotic short-hair cat.

This argument is not correctly structured since the minor premise is not properly related to the major premise. You need to establish first that *only* exotic short-hair cats are affectionate to show that Nicky is, by deduction, an exotic short-hair. Here the premises may all be true, yet the conclusion is invalid.

Check your line of reasoning when you write an essay that is intended to persuade your reader. You need to present a good deal of substantiated evidence to support your opinions, and you need to scrupulously avoid hasty generalizations, illogical arguments, and indefensible opinions. A persuasive essay achieves its purpose—persuading readers—only when it is grounded in a variety of good reasons and supported by evidence and not merely attitude. To be successful, you need to be able to anticipate potential objections that might be raised and argue why your position is the better view. Often it is a good test of your skill in argumentation to take on a case or defend a position that is contrary to what you actually believe. Then you can test your rhetorical skills in persuasive argument.

When you argue one side of an argument, you can never afford to neglect the other side. This doesn't mean that you should present all the pro side and then all the con side, and finally make up your mind. It means that you should begin writing with your mind made up about the issue being debated and gradually win readers to your way of thinking. A clear, strong thesis statement is a definite prerequisite to a powerful persuasive argument. You can, of course, opt to discuss an issue from the opponent's perspective, prepared at every turn to counter opposing arguments with better views of your own. But before you begin writing, you must make it incontrovertibly clear which side you are on.

This particular rhetorical pattern demands great care in writing to deal adequately with the sensitivities of readers and to deflect criticism before it is raised. You must remember at all times that your purpose in writing is to get readers on your side, and thus avoid any kind of language that may alienate them or leave them hostile to your position. Reasonable argument is the backbone of powerful, emotionally persuasive essays.

The next paragraph shows how the accumulation of reasons can act as solid support for a deeply held opinion.

Topic sentence ⟶ Students entering college or university should study the arts, at least among their options, even if they anticipate careers in business or technology. An education in the arts is the foundation of every civilized person who wants to develop his or her creativity, communication skills, and human relations. An education that is strictly practical and vocational in its purpose does not take into account the whole person. To develop creativity, students need to explore more than just the skills needed to make a living; they need to write, paint, play music, and experience all of these arts to some degree to nurture their own creativity and their ability to express themselves. The communication skills that are major components of arts courses are also vital to success in one's professional life. All walks of life benefit from the enhanced speaking, writing, and designing aspects of the arts, and students who take the trouble to learn how to use these tools effectively have, ultimately, a great deal more to offer employers. Finally, the arts provide the essential requirement of all professions: the value of human relations. An understanding of the arts, both as participant and as spectator, enables a student to be more fully human and more capable of understanding the needs and desires of others, all fundamental to success and happiness at work and in life.

Never Eat Anything with a Face

Thesis statement → Vegetarianism, the decision not to eat meat, is becoming increasingly common, particularly among young people whose principles with regard to world hunger, the environment, anticruelty issues, and health forbid it. For these reasons, especially, vegetarianism is often a preferred way of life that is seen as providing both personal and global benefits. While vegetarianism was once the choice of religious groups and rare health-conscious individuals, it is now embraced as a conscientious approach to life. It probably doesn't hurt the cause that vegetarianism is advocated by numerous celebrities, among them Paul McCartney, David Duchovny, Cindy Crawford, and Drew Barrymore.

The first argument is developed and statistical evidence is presented.

The humanitarian reasons not to eat meat are overwhelming. Consider, for example, that the amount of land used for cattle production could much more efficiently be used to raise other kinds of food capable of feeding more people more economically. World hunger could be sharply decreased if more of the corn and oats now grown in North America were eaten by humans and not by livestock intended for meat consumption. The horrifying statistic that a child dies of malnutrition somewhere in the world every 2.3 seconds ought to be enough to encourage people to rethink their position regarding wasteful meat consumption.

And then there's the question of the environment. Meat production is one of the apparent causes of global warming, which threatens the

The second argument is developed and more statistical evidence is presented (two paragraphs).

survival of other species as well as the human. Three times more fuel is consumed in the production of a meat-centred diet compared with a meat-free diet. The destruction of tropical rain forests for cattle grazing leads to extinction at the rate of approximately 1000 species annually. This meat industry exists in Central America largely to support North American meat-centred dietary habits. At the same time, however, about 75 percent of children in Central America under the age of 5 are said to be malnourished. The wasteful and selfish eating habits of a wealthy few are clearly undermining others' chances for survival and quality of life.

Furthermore, natural resources are thrown away at a great rate in the service of meat production. More than half of all water used in North America alone is dedicated to livestock production, enough that it takes roughly 22 730 L of water to produce 0.5 kg of beef, as compared with 114 L of water to produce 0.5 kg of wheat. Oil reserves and fossil fuels are similarly affected. If you are concerned about protecting natural resources for future generations, vegetarianism makes clear sense.

The third argument is developed.

Global concerns aside, an abhorrence of cruelty to animals is, of course, a chief motivation to become vegetarian. For ethical reasons, many of us do not wish to kill animals for consumption. If people had to slaughter their own food, many would likely become vegetarians to avoid inflicting pain or taking lives. Chicken, eviscerated and wrapped in cellophane, as bought in grocery stores, doesn't present the horror of an animal's death. If hunting was essential to survival, a different argument might be possible, but among North Americans in the current economy, no such claim may reasonably be made.

Health issues are also part of the decision to become vegetarian. In societies where high consumption of animal fats has led to heart disease, widespread obesity, and attendant problems like diabetes, it may make sense to consider eating just plant sources and thus avoid a major health

The fourth argument is developed, reinforced by examples.

hazard. Opponents of vegetarianism who claim that some vitamins, like B12, are more readily available in meat-centred diets need to be reassured that a proper vegetarian diet with attention to complete plant proteins is easily and economically attainable, and that health benefits are actually to be expected. Partly this is due to the vegetarian's increased protection from pesticides and from unhealthy overexposure to antibiotics that can result from meat consumption. Levels of DDT in mothers' milk are significantly higher among meat-eating mothers than among vegetarians, an indication of the many dangers that accrue to meat consumption, even for infants.

Conclusion

For a number of reasons, not the least of which is revulsion at the suffering and death of animals, many of us choose to become vegetarian. Consider the consequences of your meat-eating habits at your next meal, and become more conscious of the widespread, indeed global, effects of your routine behaviour. What are you willing to sacrifice for the supposed privilege of enjoying meat?

Jennifer Kahn

Jennifer Kahn is a writer for *Salon* magazine.

I DON'T WANT TO GO FORTH AND MULTIPLY

I do not want, have never wanted and do not expect to ever want children. For the record, this is a personal, biological decision and not a political statement, a matter of national security or a renunciation of my female citizenship. I am not childless because the world is overpopulated, because I am overly ambitious or because I had a bad childhood. Simply put, I do not want children —the way that many people would not want to own a horse.

I have developed an affinity for this comparison because it is one that APs (Avid Procreators) understand best. That APs often don't understand is evident in their questions, which are typically "Never?" and "Why not?"

The latter is an odd question, I think—like asking someone why she doesn't like peas or flowered wallpaper or the music of Michael Bolton. There are answers to be given, but the most immediate response is a visceral one: It's just not appealing.

A friend has observed that the decision to bear children is unusual in that it is an intimate topic about which everybody feels free to opine. Parents of adult children (though not mine) can be positively proselytizing about the virtues of grandchildren. Acquaintances send photos (always the same—the "angelic" baby asleep or else smiling vacuously, eyes crossed as though medicated) and ask not so subtly when they can expect word of your own foray into fecundity. At dinner parties, women who one has only just met rush to share their stories: the doubts and misgivings, the putting on hold of the career, the financial worries and the body-change vanity, the difficulties of raising a child in an Increasingly Dangerous World—always ending with the happy assessment that the "rewards made it all worthwhile"—all to better direct the wayward down the road to multiplication.

5 One might expect such propaganda to persist in more traditional parts of the country, but the pro-procreative view pervades even the quintessentially liberal city where I live. Here, I've found, one can be openly gay, socialist, Buddhist, Scientologist, naturist or anarchist without incurring looks of either disap-

proval or consternation, and without being subject to the tacit assumption that it's "just a phase."

Strangely, these are the very responses that greet the admission that one does not intend to have children. There is a moment of disbelief, followed by an almost visible dredging of possible explanations. "She just means not yet," the AP concludes, relieved.

The idea that a person simply may not want children at all, the way some men do not want to have sex with other men, or the way some women do not like flowered wallpaper, rarely occurs. Hence the horse.

"If someone suggested that you buy a horse," this simple-minded comparison begins, "and told you that you'd have to feed it and brush it and exercise it every day (thereby cramping your schedule radically and forcing you to miss out on a good number of other things that you might like to do), have to spend nights sleeping on the stall floor when the horse gets sick, pay for vets and farriers and blankets and bridles (which aren't cheap), and moreover have to continue to live this way for roughly the next 20 years—you might be reluctant."

Granted, there are good things about horses. Horses can be ridden and petted. One can feed them treats, braid their manes and buy them particularly snuggly sheepskin blankets. Moreover, much as parents take pleasure in a wide variety of otherwise unappealing tasks—changing diapers, feeding, bathing, dressing—so horse people enjoy grooming, polishing tack, cleaning hooves and forking hay. The difference being that while there's a lot to dislike about both these endeavours, if you're not a "horse person," you will decide very quickly that the so-called advantages of equine parenting are outweighed rather dramatically by the constraints put on your otherwise carefree life. If you are not a "child person," however, chances are that you will decide nothing quickly, but rather will obsess, doubt your femininity or your sanity, reconsider, worry, feel bad and, often as not, decide just to go along with the wishes of your more reproductively inclined mate.

10 Having trotted out this particular comparison more than once, I know that it typically raises objections. "Tut tut!" one of these goes. "Owning a horse is not the same thing as raising a child. A child grows, questions, argues, learns and ultimately becomes a functioning (with luck), moral, intelligent (again, with luck) adult."

This is true. Children are more rewarding than horses, assuming you find children rewarding at all. If you don't, I venture that the two are not so dissimilar.

VOCABULARY

affinity: kinship 2
visceral: instinctive 3
opine: state an opinion 4
proselytizing: attempting to convert 4
vacuously: emptily, stupidly 4
foray: raid 4
fecundity: fertility 4
quintessentially: typically 5
consternation: amazement 5
tacit: unspoken, assumed 5
farriers: blacksmiths 8
equine: pertaining to horses 9

AUDIENCE AND PURPOSE

1. Where is the thesis statement, and why is it located there?
2. How effective is the title? What does it refer to?

CONTENT

1. What comparisons does Kahn use to show that having children is a matter of personal preference?
2. What main comparison does Kahn use to make her case?
3. Is it a valid comparison in your estimate?
4. What, according to Kahn, is the propaganda that encourages people to have children?
5. According to Kahn, what assumptions do most people make about having children?

STYLE AND STRUCTURE

1. Why does Kahn use the acronym AP to refer to Avid Procreators?
2. Why does Kahn devote the first paragraph to explaining what are *not* her reasons for not wanting children?
3. Although analogy is often considered a weak form of argument and Kahn concedes the objections one might make to hers, she still uses it. What is her point in doing so?

Neil Postman

Neil Postman is professor of media ecology and chair of the Department of Culture and Communication at New York University. He has written twenty books, including *Amusing Ourselves to Death: Public Discourse in the Age of Show Business* (1985). Recent works include *Technopoly: The Surrender of Culture to Technology* (1992), from which this excerpt is taken, *How to Watch TV News* (1992), written with Steve Powers, and *Building a Bridge to the Eighteenth Century: How the Past Can Improve Our Future* (1999).

THE IDEOLOGY OF MACHINES: COMPUTER TECHNOLOGY

That American Technopoly has now embraced the computer in the same hurried and mindless way it embraced medical technology is undeniable, was perhaps inevitable, and is certainly most unfortunate. This is not to say that the computer is a blight on the symbolic landscape; only that, like medical technology, it has usurped powers and enforced mind-sets that a fully attentive culture might have wished to deny it. Thus, an examination of the ideas embedded in computer technology is worth attempting. Others, of course, have done this, especially Joseph Weizenbaum in his great and indispensable book *Computer Power and Human Reason*. Weizenbaum, however, ran into some difficulties, as everyone else has, because of the "universality" of computers, meaning (a) that their uses are infinitely various, and (b) that computers are commonly integrated into the structure of other machines. It is, therefore, hard to isolate specific ideas promoted by computer technology. The computer, for example, is quite unlike the stethoscope, which has a limited function in a limited context. Except for safecrackers, who, I am told, use stethoscopes to hear the tumblers of locks click into place, stethoscopes are used only by doctors. But everyone uses or is used by computers, and for purposes that seem to know no boundaries.

Putting aside such well-known functions as electronic filing, spreadsheets, and word-processing, one can make a fascinating list of the innovative, even bizarre, uses of computers. I have before me a report from *The New York Times* that tells us how computers are enabling aquatic designers to create giant water slides that mimic roller coasters and eight-foot-high artificial waves.[1] In my modest collection, I have another article about the

1 *New York Times*, August 7, 1990, sect. C, p. 1.

uses of personal computers for making presentations at corporate board meetings.[2] Another tells of how computer graphics help jurors to remember testimony better. Gregory Mazares, president of the graphics unit of Litigation Sciences, is quoted as saying, "We're a switched-on, tuned-in, visually oriented society, and jurors tend to believe what they see. This technology keeps the jury's attention by simplifying the material and by giving them little bursts of information."[3] While Mr. Mazares is helping switched-on people to remember things, Morton David, chief executive officer of Franklin Computer, is helping them find any word in the Bible with lightning speed by producing electronic Bibles. (The word "lightning," by the way, appears forty-two times in the New International version and eight times in the King James version. Were you so inclined, you could discover this for yourself in a matter of seconds.) This fact so dominates Mr. David's imagination that he is quoted as saying, "Our technology may have made a change as momentous as the Gutenberg invention of movable type."[4] And then there is an article that reports a computer's use to make investment decisions, which helps you, among other things, to create "what-if" scenarios, although with how much accuracy we are not told.[5] In *Technology Review*, we find a description of how computers are used to help the police locate the addresses of callers in distress; a prophecy is made that in time police officers will have so much instantly available information about any caller that they will know how seriously to regard the caller's appeal for help.

One may well wonder if Charles Babbage had any of this in mind when he announced in 1822 (only six years after the appearance of Laënnec's stethoscope) that he had invented a machine capable of performing simple arithmetical calculations. Perhaps he did, for he never finished his invention and started work on a more ambitious machine, capable of doing more complex tasks. He abandoned that as well, and in 1833 put aside his calculator project completely in favor of a programmable machine that became the forerunner of the modern computer. His first such machine, which he characteristically never finished, was to be controlled by punch cards adapted from devices French weavers used to control thread sequences in their looms.

Babbage kept improving his programmable machine over the next thirty-seven years, each design being more complex than the

2 *Personal Computing*, June 29, 1990, p. 36.
3 *New York Times*, November 24, 1989.
4 *Publishers Weekly*, March 2, 1990, p. 26.
5 *Bottom Line*, July 15, 1989, p. 5.

last.[6] At some point, he realized that the mechanization of numerical operations gave him the means to manipulate non-numerical symbols. It is not farfetched to say that Babbage's insight was comparable to the discovery by the Greeks in the third century B.C. of the principle of alphabetization—that is, the realization that the symbols of the alphabet could be separated from their phonetic function and used as a system for the classification, storage, and retrieval of information. In any case, armed with his insight, Babbage was able to speculate about the possibility of designing "intelligent" information machinery, though the mechanical technology of his time was inadequate to allow the fulfillment of his ideas. The computer as we know it today had to await a variety of further discoveries and inventions, including the telegraph, the telephone, and the application of Boolean algebra to relay-based circuitry, resulting in Claude Shannon's creation of digital logic circuitry. Today, when the word "computer" is used without a modifier before it, it normally refers to some version of the machine invented by John von Neumann in the 1940s. Before that, the word "computer" referred to a person (similarly to the early use of the word "typewriter") who performed some kind of mechanical calculation. As calculation shifted from people to machines, so did the word, especially because of the power of von Neumann's machine.

5 Certainly, after the invention of the digital computer, it was abundantly clear that the computer was capable of performing functions that could in some sense be called "intelligent." In 1936, the great English mathematician Alan Turing showed that it was possible to build a machine that would, for many practical purposes, behave like a problem-solving human being. Turing claimed that he would call a machine "intelligent" if, through typed messages, it could exchange thoughts with a human being—that is, hold up its end of a conversation. In the early days of MIT's Artificial Intelligence Laboratory, Joseph Weizenbaum wrote a program called ELIZA, which showed how easy it was to meet Turing's test for intelligence. When asked a question with a proper noun in it, ELIZA's program could respond with "Why are you interested in," followed by the proper noun and a question mark. That is, it could invert statements and seek more information about one of the nouns in the statement. Thus, ELIZA acted much like a Rogerian psychologist, or at least a friendly and inexpensive therapist. Some people who used ELIZA refused to be-

6 For a concise and readable review of the development of the computer, I would recommend Arno Penzias' *Ideas and Information: Managing in a High-Tech World.*

lieve that they were conversing with a mere machine. Having, in effect, created a Turing machine, Weizenbaum eventually pulled the program off the computer network and was stimulated to write *Computer Power and Human Reason*, in which, among other things, he raised questions about the research programs of those working in artificial intelligence; the assumption that whatever a computer *can* do, it *should* do; and the effects of computer technology on the way people construe the world—that is, the ideology of the computer, to which I now turn.

The most comprehensive idea conveyed by the computer is suggested by the title of J. David Bolter's book, *Turing's Man*. His title is a metaphor, of course, similar to what would be suggested by saying that from the sixteenth century until recently we were "Gutenberg's Men." Although Bolter's main practical interest in the computer is in its function as a new kind of book, he argues that it is the dominant metaphor of our age; it defines our age by suggesting a new relationship to information, to work, to power, and to nature itself. That relationship can best be described by saying that the computer redefines humans as "information processors" and nature itself as information to be processed. The fundamental metaphorical message of the computer, in short, is that we are machines—thinking machines, to be sure, but machines nonetheless. It is for this reason that the computer is the quintessential, incomparable, near-perfect machine for Technopoly. It subordinates the claims of our nature, our biology, our emotions, our spirituality. The computer claims sovereignty over the whole range of human experience, and supports its claim by showing that it "thinks" better than we can. Indeed, in his almost hysterical enthusiasm for artificial intelligence, Marvin Minsky has been quoted as saying that the thinking power of silicon "brains" will be so formidable that "If we are lucky, they will keep us as pets."[7] An even giddier remark, although more dangerous, was offered by John McCarthy, the inventor of the term "artificial intelligence." McCarthy claims that "even machines as simple as thermostats can be said to have beliefs." To the obvious question, posed by the philosopher John Searle, "What beliefs does your thermostat have?" McCarthy replied, "My thermostat has three beliefs—it's too hot in here, it's too cold in here, and it's just right in here."[8]

What is significant about this response is that it has redefined the meaning of the word "belief." The remark rejects the view

7 Quoted in M. Hunt, *The Universe Within: A New Science Explores the Mind*, New York: Simon & Schuster, 1982, p. 318.

8 J. Searle, *Minds, Brains and Science*, Cambridge, Mass.: Harvard University Press, 1984, p. 30.

that humans have internal states of mind that are the foundation of belief and argues instead that "belief" means only what someone or something does. The remark also implies that simulating an idea is synonymous with duplicating the idea. And, most important, the remark rejects the idea that mind is a biological phenomenon.

In other words, what we have here is a case of metaphor gone mad. From the proposition that humans are in some respects like machines, we move to the proposition that humans are little else but machines and, finally, that human beings *are* machines. And then, inevitably, as McCarthy's remark suggests, to the proposition that machines are human beings. It follows that machines can be made that duplicate human intelligence, and thus research in the field known as artificial intelligence was inevitable. What is most significant about this line of thinking is the dangerous reductionism it represents. Human intelligence, as Weizenbaum has tried energetically to remind everyone, is not transferable. The plain fact is that humans have a unique, biologically rooted, intangible mental life which in some limited respects can be simulated by a machine but can never be duplicated. Machines cannot feel and, just as important, cannot *understand*. ELIZA can ask, "Why are you worried about your mother?" which might be exactly the question a therapist would ask. But the machine does not know what the question means or even *that* the question means. (Of course, there may be some therapists who do not know what the question means either, who ask it routinely, ritualistically, inattentively. In that case we may say they are acting like a machine.) It is meaning, not utterance, that makes mind unique. I use "meaning" here to refer to something more than the result of putting together symbols the denotations of which are commonly shared by at least two people. As I understand it, meaning also includes those things we call feelings, experiences, and sensations that do not have to be, and sometimes cannot be, put into symbols. They "mean" nonetheless. Without concrete symbols, a computer is merely a pile of junk. Although the quest for a machine that duplicates mind has ancient roots, and although digital logic circuitry has given that quest a scientific structure, artificial intelligence does not and cannot lead to a meaning-making, understanding, and feeling creature, which is what a human being is.

All of this may seem obvious enough, but the metaphor of the machine as human (or the human as machine) is sufficiently powerful to have made serious inroads in everyday language. People now commonly speak of "programming" or "deprogramming" themselves. They speak of their brains as a piece of "hard wiring," capable of "retrieving data," and it has become common to think about thinking as a mere matter of processing and decoding.

10 Perhaps the most chilling case of how deeply our language is absorbing the "machine as human" metaphor began on November 4, 1988, when the computers around the ARPANET network became sluggish, filled with extraneous data, and then clogged completely. The problem spread fairly quickly to six thousand computers across the United States and overseas. The early hypothesis was that a software program had attached itself to other programs, a situation which is called (in another human-machine metaphor) a "virus." As it happened, the intruder was a self-contained program explicitly designed to disable computers, which is called a "worm." But the technically incorrect term "virus" stuck, no doubt because of its familiarity and its human connections. As Raymond Gozzi, Jr., discovered in his analysis of how the mass media described the event, newspapers noted that the computers were "infected," that the virus was "virulent" and "contagious," that attempts were made to "quarantine" the infected computers, that attempts were also being made to "sterilize" the network, and that programmers hoped to develop a "vaccine" so that computers could be "inoculated" against new attacks.[9]

This kind of language is not merely picturesque anthropomorphism. It reflects a profound shift in perception about the relationship of computers to humans. If computers can become ill, then they can become healthy. Once healthy, they can think clearly and make decisions. The computer, it is implied, has a will, has intentions, has reasons — which means that humans are relieved of responsibility for the computer's decisions. Through a curious form of grammatical alchemy, the sentence "We use the computer to calculate" comes to mean "The computer calculates." If a computer calculates, then it may decide to miscalculate or not calculate at all. That is what bank tellers mean when they tell you that they cannot say how much money is in your checking account because "the computers are down." The implication, of course, is that no person at the bank is responsible. Computers make mistakes or get tired or become ill. Why blame people? We may call this line of thinking an "agentic shift," a term I borrow from Stanley Milgram to name the process whereby humans

9 See R. Gozzi, Jr., "The Computer 'Virus' as Metaphor," *Etcetera: A Review of General Semantics*, vol. 47, no. 2 (Summer 1990), pp. 177–80.

transfer responsibility for an outcome from themselves to a more abstract agent.[10] When this happens, we have relinquished control, which in the case of the computer means that we may, without excessive remorse, pursue ill-advised or even inhuman goals because the computer can accomplish them or be imagined to accomplish them.

Machines of various kinds will sometimes assume a human or, more likely, a superhuman aspect. Perhaps the most absurd case I know of is in a remark a student of mine once made on a sultry summer day in a room without air conditioning. On being told the thermometer read ninety-eight degrees Fahrenheit, he replied, "No wonder it's so hot!" Nature was off the hook. If only the thermometers would behave themselves, we could be comfortable. But computers are far more "human" than thermometers or almost any other kind of technology. Unlike most machines, computers do no work; they direct work. They are, as Norbert Wiener said, the technology of "command and control" and have little value without something to control. This is why they are of such importance to bureaucracies.

Naturally, bureaucrats can be expected to embrace a technology that helps to create the illusion that decisions are not under their control. Because of its seeming intelligence and impartiality, a computer has an almost magical tendency to direct attention away from the people in charge of bureaucratic functions and toward itself, as if the computer were the true source of authority. A bureaucrat armed with a computer is the unacknowledged legislator of our age, and a terrible burden to bear. We cannot dismiss the possibility that, if Adolf Eichmann had been able to say that it was not he but a battery of computers that directed the Jews to the appropriate crematoria, he might never have been asked to answer for his actions.

Although (or perhaps because) I came to "administration" late in my academic career, I am constantly amazed at how obediently people accept explanations that begin with the words "The computer shows ..." or "The computer has determined ..." It is Technopoly's equivalent of the sentence "It is God's will," and the effect is roughly the same. You will not be surprised to know that I rarely resort to such humbug. But on occasion, when pressed to the wall, I have yielded. No one has as yet replied, "Garbage in, garbage out." Their defenselessness has something Kafkaesque about it. In *The Trial*, Josef K. is charged with a

10 See S. Migram, *Obedience to Authority: An Experimental View*, New York: Harper & Row, 1974.

crime — of what nature, and by whom the charge is made, he does not know. The computer turns too many of us into Josef Ks. It often functions as a kind of impersonal accuser which does not reveal, and is not required to reveal, the sources of the judgments made against us. It is apparently sufficient that the computer has pronounced. Who has put the data in, for what purpose, for whose convenience, based on what assumptions are questions left unasked.

This is the case not only in personal matters but in public decisions as well. Large institutions such as the Pentagon, the Internal Revenue Service, and multinational corporations tell us that their decisions are made on the basis of solutions generated by computers, and this is usually good enough to put our minds at ease or, rather, to sleep. In any case, it constrains us from making complaints or accusations. In part for this reason, the computer has strengthened bureaucratic institutions and suppressed the impulse toward significant social change. "The arrival of the Computer Revolution and the founding of the Computer Age have been announced many times," Weizenbaum has written. "But if the triumph of a revolution is to be measured in terms of the social revision it entrained, then there has been no computer revolution."[11]

In automating the operation of political, social, and commercial enterprises, computers may or may not have made them more efficient but they have certainly diverted attention from the question whether or not such enterprises are necessary or how they might be improved. A university, a political party, a religious denomination, a judicial proceeding, even corporate board meetings are not improved by automating their operations. They are made more imposing, more technical, perhaps more authoritative, but defects in their assumptions, ideas, and theories will remain untouched. Computer technology, in other words, has not yet come close to the printing press in its power to generate radical and substantive social, political, and religious thought. If the press was, as David Riesman called it, "the gunpowder of the mind," the computer, in its capacity to smooth over unsatisfactory institutions and ideas, is the talcum powder of the mind.

I do not wish to go as far as Weizenbaum in saying that computers are merely ingenious devices to fulfill unimportant functions and that the computer revolution is an explosion of nonsense. Perhaps that judgment will be in need of amendment

11 J. Weizenbaum, *Computer Power and Human Reason: From Judgment to Calculation*, San Francisco: W.H. Freeman & Company, 1976, p. 32.

in the future, for the computer is a technology of a thousand uses —the Proteus of machines, to use Seymour Papert's phrase. One must note, for example, the use of computer-generated images in the phenomenon known as Virtual Reality. Putting on a set of miniature goggle-mounted screens, one may block out the real world and move through a simulated three-dimensional world which changes its components with every movement of one's head. That Timothy Leary is an enthusiastic proponent of Virtual Reality does not suggest that there is a constructive future for this device. But who knows? Perhaps, for those who can no longer cope with the real world, Virtual Reality will provide better therapy than ELIZA.

What is clear is that, to date, computer technology has served to strengthen Technopoly's hold, to make people believe that technological innovation is synonymous with human progress. And it has done so by advancing several interconnected ideas.

It has, as already noted, amplified beyond all reason the metaphor of machines as humans and humans as machines. I do not claim, by the way, that computer technology originated this metaphor. One can detect it in medicine, too: doctors and patients have come to believe that, like a machine, a human being is made up of parts which when defective can be replaced by mechanical parts that function as the original did without impairing or even affecting any other part of the machine. Of course, to some degree that assumption works, but since a human being is in fact not a machine but a biological organism all of whose organs are interrelated and profoundly affected by mental states, the human-as-machine metaphor has serious medical limitations and can have devastating effects. Something similar may be said of the mechanistic metaphor when applied to workers. Modern industrial techniques are made possible by the idea that a machine is made up of isolatable and interchangeable parts. But in organizing factories so that workers are also conceived of as isolatable and interchangeable parts, industry has engendered deep alienation and bitterness. This was the point of Charlie Chaplin's *Modern Times*, in which he tried to show the psychic damage of the metaphor carried too far. But because the computer "thinks" rather than works, its power to energize mechanistic metaphors is unparalleled and of enormous value to Technopoly, which depends on our believing that we are at our best when acting like machines, and that in significant ways machines may be trusted to act as our surrogates. Among the implications of these beliefs is a loss of confidence in human judgment and subjectivity. We have devalued the singular human capacity to see things whole in all their psychic, emotional and moral dimensions, and we have replaced this with faith in the powers of technical calculation.

VOCABULARY

Technopoly: an attitude toward technology that assumes it is essential to progress and is beneficial 1
construe: understand 5
virulent: damaging 10
anthropomorphism: the attribution of human characteristics to something nonhuman 11
relinquished: surrendered 11

AUDIENCE AND PURPOSE

1. What sort of reader does Postman imagine for his essay?
2. How would you describe Postman's purpose in this piece?
3. How does Postman educate his readers as well as form their opinions?

CONTENT

1. Why does Postman find the advances in computer technology and people's reactions to them even more unsettling than the advances in medical technology and corresponding reactions?
2. Why does Postman include a brief history of the computer?
3. How, according to Postman, is the computer the dominant metaphor of our age?
4. How does modern thinking about computers reduce the human and the biological, according to Postman?

STYLE AND STRUCTURE

1. Comment on Postman's examples of how computers are conceived of by humans.
2. How does Postman use authorities to strengthen his argument?
3. Why does Postman call a "bureaucrat armed with a computer" "the unacknowledged legislator of our age"?

Salman Rushdie

Salman Rushdie, born in Bombay, India in 1947, is the author of *Midnight's Children* (1981), which won the Booker Prize and earned him international fame. His novel *The Satanic Verses* (1988) was banned in India, and he was forced into hiding when the Ayatollah Khomeini of Iran called on all Muslims to execute the writer and the publisher of the book. In 1995, Rushdie published *The Moor's Last Sigh*, which focuses on contemporary India, and in 1999 he produced his latest work, *The Ground Beneath Her Feet.*

AMERICAN CULTURE IS NOT THE ENEMY

A couple of years ago a British literary festival staged a public debate on the motion that "it is the duty of every European to resist American culture." Along with two American journalists (one of whom was Sidney Blumenthal, now more famous as a Clinton aide and impeachment witness), I opposed the motion. I'm happy to report that we won, capturing roughly 60 per cent of the audience's vote.

But it was an odd sort of victory. My American co-panelists were surprised by the strength of the audience's anti-Americanism; after all, 40 per cent of the crowd had voted for the motion. Sidney, noting that "American culture" as represented by American armed forces had liberated Europe from Nazism not all that many years ago, was puzzled by the audience's apparent lack of gratitude. And there was a residual feeling that the case for "resistance" was actually pretty strong.

Since that day, the debate about cultural globalization and its military-political sidekick, intervention, has continued to intensify, and anti-American sentiment is if anything on the increase. In most people's heads, globalization has come to mean the worldwide triumph of Nike, the Gap and MTV. Confusingly, we want these goods and services when we behave as consumers, but with our cultural hats on we have begun to deplore their omnipresence.

On the merits of intervention, even greater confusion reigns. We don't seem to know if we want a world policeman or not. If the "international community," which these days is little more than a euphemism for the United States, fails to intervene promptly in Rwanda, Bosnia or Kosovo, it is excoriated for that failure. Elsewhere, it is criticized just as vehemently when it does intervene: when American bombs fall on Iraq, or when American agents assist in the capture of the Kurdish leader Abdullah Ocalan.

5 Clearly, those of us who shelter under the Pax Americana are deeply ambiguous about it, and the United States will no doubt continue to be surprised by the level of the world's ingratitude. The globalizing power of American culture is opposed by an improbable alliance that includes everyone from cultural-relativist liberals to hard-line fundamentalists, with all manner of pluralists and individualists, to say nothing of flag-waving nationalists and splintering sectarians, in between.

Much ecological concern is being expressed about the crisis in biodiversity, the possibility that a fifth or more of the Earth's species of living forms may soon become extinct. To some, globalization is an equivalent social catastrophe, with equally alarming implications for the survival of true cultural diversity, of the world's precious localness: the Indianness of India, the Frenchness of France.

Amid this din of global defensiveness, little thought is given to some of the most important questions raised by a phenomenon that, like it or not, isn't going away any time soon.

For instance: Do cultures actually exist as separate, pure, defensible entities? Is not mélange, adulteration, impurity, pick 'n' mix at the heart of the idea of the modern, and hasn't it been that way for most of this all-shook-up century? Doesn't the idea of pure cultures, in urgent need of being kept free from alien contamination, lead us inexorably toward apartheid, toward ethnic cleansing, toward the gas chamber?

Or, to put it another way: Are there other universals besides international conglomerates and the interests of superpowers? And if by chance there were a universal value that might, for the sake of argument, be called "freedom," whose enemies—tyranny, bigotry, intolerance, fanaticism—were the enemies of us all; and if this "freedom" were discovered to exist in greater quantity in the countries of the West than anywhere else on Earth; and if in the world as it actually exists, rather than in some unattainable Utopia, the authority of the United States were the best current guarantor of that "freedom," then might it not follow that to oppose the spread of American culture would be to take up arms against the wrong foe?

10 By agreeing on what we are against, we discover what we are for. André Malraux believed that the third millennium must be the age of religion. I would say rather that it must be the age in which we finally grow out of our need for religion. But to cease to believe in our gods is not the same thing as commencing to believe in nothing.

There are fundamental freedoms to fight for, and it will not do to doom the terrorized women of Afghanistan or of the circumcision-happy lands of Africa by calling their oppression their "culture."

And of course it is America's duty not to abuse its pre-eminence, and it is our right to criticize such abuses when they happen—when, for example, innocent factories in Sudan are bombed, or Iraqi civilians pointlessly killed.

But perhaps we, too, need to rethink our easy condemnations. Sneakers, burgers, blue jeans and music videos aren't the enemy. If the young people of Iran now insist on rock concerts, who are we to criticize their cultural contamination? Out there are real tyrants to defeat. Let's keep our eyes on the prize.

VOCABULARY

residual: remaining 2
omnipresence: inescapable presence 3
euphemism: pleasant word or phrase that covers up some ugly truth 4
excoriated: taken to task 4
pluralists: those who advocate the separate identities of diverse cultural groups in a society 5
sectarians: those who belong to small, perhaps bigoted, groups 5
mélange: mixture 8
adulteration: contamination 8
inexorably: irretrievably 8
Utopia: perfect place 9

AUDIENCE AND PURPOSE

1. Rushdie assumes some ambiguity between our attitude toward America as consumers and as critics of culture. Explain.
2. Why does Rushdie feel we have doubts about America as the "world policeman"?
3. What does globalization mean, according to Rushdie?

CONTENT

1. What is Rushdie's attitude toward intervention on the part of the international community?
2. In Rushdie's view, does globalization threaten cultural diversity? Explain.
3. How does Rushdie arrive at the conclusion that America is on the side of freedom?

STYLE AND STRUCTURE

1. How does Rushdie move from the specific to the general in this essay?
2. Why does he compare globalization with an ecological crisis?
3. How does Rushdie use the rhetorical question to make his point?
4. Where does the expression "eyes on the prize" come from? Why is it appropriate?

Jonathan Swift

Jonathan Swift (1667–1745) was an Irish-born Anglican priest in Dublin in the eighteenth century. He was a brilliant satirist and author of *Gulliver's Travels* (1726), his most famous work. Earlier works of note include *A Tale of a Tub* (1704), a prose satire on religious extremes, as well as *The Battle of the Books* (1704), which pokes fun at literary critics.

A MODEST PROPOSAL FOR PREVENTING THE CHILDREN OF IRELAND FROM BEING A BURDEN TO THEIR PARENTS OR COUNTRY

It is a melancholy object to those who walk through this great town or travel in the country, when they see the streets, the roads, and cabin-doors crowded with beggars of the female sex, followed by three, four, or six children, all in rags, and importuning every passenger for an alms. These mothers, instead of being able to work for their honest livelihood, are forced to employ all their time in strolling to beg sustenance for their helpless infants, who, as they grow up, either turn thieves for want of work, or leave their dear native country to fight for the Pretender in Spain, or sell themselves to the Barbadoes.

I think it is agreed by all parties, that this prodigious number of children in the arms, or on the backs, or at the heels of their mothers, and frequently of their fathers, is in the present deplorable state of the kingdom a very great additional grievance; and therefore whoever could find out a fair, cheap, and easy method of making these children sound and useful members of the common-wealth, would deserve so well of the publick as to have his statue set up for a preserver of the nation.

But my intention is very far from being confined to provide only for the children of professed beggars; it is of a much greater extent, and shall take in the whole number of infants at a certain age, who are born of parents in effect as little able to support them, as those who demand our charity in the streets.

As to my own part, having turned my thoughts, for many years, upon this important subject, and maturely weighed the several schemes of other projectors, I have always found them grossly mistaken in their computation. It is true, a child just dropt from its dam may be supported by her milk for a solar year with little other nourishment, at most not above the value of two shillings, which the mother may certainly get, or the value in scraps, by her lawful occupation of begging; and it is exactly at one year old that I propose to provide for them in such a manner, as, instead of being a charge upon their parents, or the parish, or wanting food and raiment for the rest of their lives, they shall, on the contrary, contribute to the feeding and partly to the clothing of many thousands.

5 There is likewise another great advantage in my scheme, that it will prevent those voluntary abortions, and that horrid practice of women murdering their bastard children, alas! too frequent among us — sacrificing the poor innocent babes, I doubt, more to avoid the expense than the shame — which would move tears and pity in the most savage and inhuman breast.

The number of souls in this kingdom being usually reckoned one million and a half, of these I calculate there may be about two hundred thousand couples whose wives are breeders; from which number I subtract thirty thousand couples, who are able to maintain their own children, although I apprehend there cannot be so many, under the present distresses of the kingdom; but this being granted, there will remain an hundred and seventy thousand breeders. I again subtract fifty thousand, for those women who miscarry, or whose children die by accident or disease within the year. There only remain an hundred and twenty thousand children of poor parents annually born: The question therefore is, How this number shall be reared, and provided for? which, as I have already said, under the present situation of affairs, is utterly impossible by all the methods hitherto proposed; for we can neither employ them in handicraft or agriculture; we neither build houses, (I mean in the country) nor cultivate land: They can very seldom pick up a livelihood by stealing till they arrive at six years old, except where they are of towardly parts, although, I confess, they learn the rudiments much earlier; during which time they can however be properly looked upon only as probationers; as I have been informed by a principal gentleman in the county of Cavan, who protested to me, that he never knew above one or two instances under the age of six, even in a part of the kingdom so renowned for the quickest proficiency in that art.

I am assured by our merchants, that a boy or a girl before twelve years old, is no saleable commodity, and even when they come to this age, they will not yield above three pounds, or three pounds and half a crown at most, on the exchange; which cannot turn to account either to the parents or kingdom, the charge of nutriment and rags having been at least four times that value.

I shall now therefore humbly propose my own thoughts, which I hope will not be liable to the least objection.

I have been assured by a very knowing American of my acquaintance in London, that a young healthy child well nursed is at a year old a most delicious nourishing and wholesome food, whether stewed, roasted, baked, or boiled; and I make no doubt that it will equally serve in a fricasee, or a ragout.

I do therefore humbly offer it to publick consideration, that of the hundred and twenty thousand children, already computed, twenty thousand may be reserved for breed, whereof only one fourth part to be males; which is more than we allow to sheep, black cattle, or swine, and my reason is, that these children are seldom the fruits of marriage, a circumstance not much regarded by our savages; therefore, one male will be sufficient to serve four females. That the remaining hundred thousand may at a year old be offered in sale to the persons of quality and fortune, through the kingdom, always advising the mother to let them suck plentifully in the last month, so as to render them plump and fat for a good table. A child will make two dishes at an entertainment for friends, and when the family dines alone, the fore or hind quarter will make a reasonable dish, and seasoned with a little pepper or salt will be very good boiled on the fourth day, especially in winter.

I have reckoned upon a medium, that a child just born will weigh 12 pounds, and in a solar year, if tolerably nursed, encreaseth to 28 pounds.

I grant this food will be somewhat dear, and therefore very proper for landlords, who, as they have already devoured most of the parents seem to have the best title to the children.

Infant's flesh will be in season throughout the year, but more plentiful in March, and a little before and after; for we are told by a grave author, an eminent French physician, that fish being a prolifick dyet, there are more children born in Roman Catholick countries about nine months after Lent, than at any other season; therefore reckoning a year after Lent, the markets will be more glutted than usual, because the number of popish infants, is at least three to one in this kingdom, and therefore it will have one other collateral advantage, by lessening the number of papists among us.

I have already computed the charge of nursing a beggar's child (in which list I reckon all cottagers, labourers, and four fifths of farmers) to be about two shillings per annum, rags included; and I believe no gentleman would repine to give ten shillings for the carcass of a good fat child, which, as I have said will make four dishes of excellent nutritive meat, when he hath only some particular friend, or his own family to dine with him.

Thus the squire will learn to be a good landlord, and grow popular among his tenants; the mother will have eight shillings neat profit, and be fit for work till she produces another child.

Those who are more thrifty (as I must confess the times require) may flay the carcass; the skin of which, artificially dressed, will make admirable gloves for ladies, and summer boots for fine gentlemen.

As to our city of Dublin, shambles may be appointed for this purpose, in the most convenient parts of it, and butchers we may be assured will not be wanting; although I rather recommend buying the children alive, and dressing them hot from the knife, as we do roasting pigs.

A very worthy person, a true lover of his country, and whose virtues I highly esteem, was lately pleased, in discoursing on this matter, to offer a refinement upon my scheme. He said, that many gentlemen of this kingdom, having of late destroyed their deer, he conceived that the want of venison might be well supplied by the bodies of young lads and maidens, not exceeding fourteen years of age, nor under twelve; so great a number of both sexes in every country being now ready to starve, for want of work and service: And these to be disposed of by their parents if alive, or otherwise by their nearest relations. But with due deference to so excellent a friend, and so deserving a patriot, I cannot be altogether in his sentiments; for as to the males, my American acquaintance assured me from frequent experience, that their flesh was generally tough and lean, like that of our schoolboys, by continual exercise, and their taste disagreeable, and to fatten them would not answer the charge. Then as to the females, it would, I think with humble submission, be a loss to the publick, because they soon would become breeders themselves: And besides it is not improbable that some scrupulous people might be apt to censure such a practice (although indeed very unjustly) as a little bordering upon cruelty, which, I confess, hath always been with me the strongest objection against any project, how well so-ever intended.

But in order to justify my friend, he confessed, that this expedient was put into his head by the famous Psalmanazar, a native of the island Formosa, who came from thence to London, above twenty years ago, and in conversation told my friend, that in his country when any young person happened to be put to death, the executioner sold the carcass to persons of quality, as a prime dainty, and that, in his time, the body of a plump girl of fifteen, who was crucified for an attempt to poison the Emperor, was sold to his Imperial Majesty's prime minister of state, and other great mandarins of the court, in joints from the gibbett, at four hundred crowns. Neither indeed can I deny, that if the same use were made of several plump young girls in this town, who, without one single groat to their fortunes, cannot stir abroad without a chair, and appear at a play-house and assemblies in foreign fineries which they never will pay for, the kingdom would not be the worse.

Some persons of a desponding spirit are in great concern about that vast number of poor people, who are aged, diseased, or maimed, and I have been desired to employ my thoughts what course may be taken, to ease the nation of so grievous an encumbrance. But I am not in the least pain upon that matter, because it is very well known, that they are every day dying, and rotting, by cold, and famine, and filth, and vermin, as fast as can be reasonably expected. And as to the younger labourers, they are now in almost as hopeful a condition. They cannot get work, and consequently pine away for want of nourishment, to a degree, that if at any time they are accidentally hired to common labour, they have not strength to perform it, and thus the country and themselves are happily delivered from the evils to come.

I have too long digressed, and therefore shall return to my subject. I think the advantages by the proposal which I have made are obvious and many, as well as of the highest importance.

For *first*, as I have already observed, it would greatly lessen the number of papists, with whom we are yearly over-run, being the principal breeders of the nation, as well as our most dangerous enemies, and who stay at home on purpose with a design to deliver the kingdom to the Pretender, hoping to take their advantage by the absence of so many good Protestants, who have chosen rather to leave their country, than stay at home, and pay tithes against their conscience to an episcopal curate.

Secondly, the poorer tenants will have something valuable of their own which by law may be made liable to distress, and help to pay their landlord's rent, their corn and cattle being already seized, and money a thing unknown.

Thirdly, whereas the maintenance of an hundred thousand children, from two years old, and upwards, cannot be computed at less than ten shillings a piece per annum, the nation's stock will be thereby increased fifty thousand pounds per annum, besides the profit of a new dish, introduced to the tables of all gentlemen of fortune in the kingdom who have any refinement in taste, and the money will circulate among our selves, the goods being entirely of our own growth and manufacture.

Fourthly, the constant breeders, besides the gain of eight shillings sterling per annum, by the sale of their children, will be rid of the charge of maintaining them after the first year.

Fifthly, this food would likewise bring great custom to taverns, where the vintners will certainly be so prudent as to procure the best receipts for dressing it to perfection; and consequently have their houses frequented by all the fine gentlemen, who justly value themselves upon their knowledge in good eating; and a skilful cook, who understands how to oblige his guests, will contrive to make it as expensive as they please.

Sixthly, this would be a great inducement to marriage, which all wise nations have either encouraged by rewards, or enforced by laws and penalties. It would encrease the care and tenderness of mothers towards their children, when they were sure of a settlement for life to the poor babes, provided in some sort by the publick, to their annual profit instead of expence; we should soon see an honest emulation among the married women, which of them could bring the fattest child to the market. Men would become as fond of their wives during the time of their pregnancy, as they are now of their mares in foal, their cows in calf, or sows when they are ready to farrow, nor offer to beat or kick them (as is too frequent a practice) for fear of a miscarriage.

Many other advantages might be enumerated. For instance, the addition of some thousand carcasses in our exportation of barreled beef: the propagation of swine's flesh, and improvement in the art of making good bacon, so much wanted among us by the great destruction of pigs, too frequent at our tables, which are no way comparable in taste or magnificence to a well grown, fat yearling child, which roasted whole will make a considerable figure at a Lord Mayor's feast, or any other publick entertainment. But this, and many others, I omit, being studious of brevity.

Supposing that one thousand families in this city, would be constant customers for infant's flesh, besides others who might have it at merry meetings, particularly at weddings and christenings, I compute that Dublin would take off annually about twenty thousand carcasses, and the rest of the kingdom (where probably they will be sold somewhat cheaper) the remaining eighty thousand.

I can think of no one objection, that will possibly be raised against this proposal, unless it should be urged, that the number of people will be thereby much lessened in the kingdom. This I freely own, and 'twas indeed one principal design in offering it to the world. I desire the reader will observe, that I calculate my remedy for this one individual kingdom of Ireland, and for no other that ever was, is, or, I think, ever can be upon earth. Therefore let no man talk to me of other expedients: of taxing our absentees at five shillings a pound: of using neither clothes, nor household furniture, except what is of our own growth and manufacture: of utterly rejecting the materials and instruments that promote foreign luxury: of curing the expensiveness of pride, vanity, idleness, and gaming in our women: of introducing a vein of parsimony, prudence and temperance: of learning to love our country, wherein we differ even from Laplanders, and the inhabitants of Topinamboo: of quitting our animosities, and factions, nor act any longer like the Jews, who were murdering one another at the very moment their city was taken: of being a little cautious not to sell our country and consciences for nothing: of teaching landlords to have at least one degree of mercy towards their tenants. Lastly, of putting a spirit of honesty, industry, and skill into our shop-keepers, who, if a resolution could now be taken to buy only our native goods, would immediately unite to cheat and exact upon us in the price, the measure, and the goodness, nor could ever yet be brought to make one fair proposal of just dealing, though often and earnestly invited to it.

Therefore I repeat, let no man talk to me of these and the like expedients, till he hath at least some glimpse of hope, that there will ever be some hearty and sincere attempt to put them in practice.

But as to my self, having been wearied out for many years with offering vain, idle, visionary thoughts, and at length utterly despairing of success, I fortunately fell upon this proposal, which as it is wholly new, so it hath something solid and real, of no expense and little trouble, full in our own power, and whereby we can incur no danger in disobliging England. For this kind of commodity will not bear exportation, the flesh being of too tender a consistence to admit a long continuance in salt, although perhaps I could name a country, which would be glad to eat up our whole nation without it.

After all, I am not so violently bent upon my own opinion, as to reject any offer, proposed by wise men, which shall be found equally innocent, cheap, easy, and effectual. But before something of that kind shall be advanced in contradiction to my scheme, and offering a better, I desire the author or authors, will be pleased maturely to consider two points. *First*, as things now stand, how they will be able to find food and raiment for a hundred thousand useless mouths and backs. And *secondly*, there being a round million of creatures in human figure throughout this kingdom, whose whole subsistence put into a common stock would leave them in debt two millions of pounds sterling—adding those who are beggars by profession, to the bulk of farmers, cottagers, and labourers, with their wives and children, who are beggars in effect; I desire those politicians, who dislike my overture, and may perhaps be so bold to attempt an answer, that they will first ask the parents of these mortals, whether they would not at this day think it a great happiness to have been sold for food at a year old, in the manner I prescribe, and thereby have avoided such a perpetual scene of misfortunes as they have since gone through, by the oppression of landlords, the impossibility of paying rent without money or trade, the want of common sustenance, with neither house nor clothes to cover them from the inclemencies of the weather, and the most inevitable prospect of entailing the like, or greater miseries, upon their breed for ever.

I profess in the sincerity of my heart, that I have not the least personal interest in endeavouring to promote this necessary work, having no other motive than the publick good of my country, by advancing our trade, providing for infants, relieving the poor, and giving some pleasure to the rich. I have no children by which I can propose to get a single penny; the youngest being nine years old and my wife past child-bearing.

VOCABULARY

alms: money or food to relieve the poor 1
sustenance: nourishment and other support 1
prodigious: extraordinary amount 2
dam: mother 4
raiment: clothing 4
fricasee: stew 9
ragout: stew 9
repine: express discontent 14
shambles: slaughterhouse 16
discoursing: talking about 17
encumbrance: burden 19
inducement: motivation 26
emulation: imitation 26
propagation: reproduction 27
yearling: 1-year-old 27
expedients: temporary means to an end 29
parsimony: thriftiness 29
factions: sects 29

effectual: effective 32
overture: advance 32
inclemencies: severity, lack of mercy 32

AUDIENCE AND PURPOSE

1. At what point did you become aware that the essay is ironic?
2. What is Swift's purpose besides exposing the problems of poverty in Ireland?
3. What methods does he use to shock the reader? Give examples.

CONTENT

1. How does the conclusion reinforce the irony of the essay?
2. How does the narrator see himself? Give examples. How does the reader see him? Give examples.
3. What is the narrator's attitude toward the rich and the English? What is the real underlying attitude of the author, and how do you know?

STYLE AND STRUCTURE

1. How does word choice contribute to the effect of this essay?
2. Why does the narrator provide such a long introduction to his proposal?
3. Is there any reason for the order of the advantages given in the proposal?
4. Give some examples of specific details and concrete images, and explain why Swift includes them.

George Orwell

George Orwell (1903–50), born Eric Arthur Blair, was an English novelist and essayist. His most famous novels are *Nineteen Eighty-Four* (1949) and *Animal Farm* (1945), both brilliant satires that attacked totalitarianism. His essays are well-known and exemplary of the form. They are collected in the four-volume *Collected Essays, Journalism, and Letters of George Orwell*, published in 1968. The following famous essay was written in 1950.

POLITICS AND THE ENGLISH LANGUAGE

Most people who bother with the matter at all would admit that the English language is in a bad way, but it is generally assumed that we cannot by conscious action do anything about it. Our civilization is decadent and our language—so the argument runs—must inevitably share in the general collapse. It follows that any struggle against the abuse of language is a sentimental archaism, like preferring candles to electric light or hansom cabs to airplanes. Underneath this lies the half-conscious belief that language is a natural growth and not an instrument which we shape for our own purposes.

Now, it is clear that the decline of a language must ultimately have political and economic causes: it is not due simply to the bad influence of this or that individual writer. But an effect can become a cause, reinforcing the original cause and producing the same effect in an intensified form, and so on indefinitely. A man may take to drink because he feels himself to be a failure, and then fail all the more completely because he drinks. It is rather the same thing that is happening to the English language: It becomes ugly and inaccurate because our thoughts are foolish, but the slovenliness of our language makes it easier for us to have foolish thoughts. The point is that the process is reversible. Modern English, especially written English, is full of bad habits which spread by imitation and which can be avoided if one is willing to take the necessary trouble. If one gets rid of these habits one can think more clearly, and to think clearly is a necessary first step toward political regeneration: so that the fight against bad English is not frivolous and is not the exclusive concern of professional writers. I will come back to this presently, and I hope that by that time the meaning of what I have said here will have become clearer. Meanwhile, here are five specimens of the English language as it is now habitually written.

These five passages have not been picked out because they are especially bad—I could have quoted far worse if I had chosen—but because they illustrate various of the mental vices from which we now suffer. They are a little below the average, but are fairly representative samples. I number them so that I can refer back to them when necessary:

1. I am not, indeed, sure whether it is not true to say that the Milton who once seemed not unlike a seventeenth-century Shelley had not become, out of an experience ever more bitter in each year, more alien [*sic*] to the founder of that Jesuit sect which nothing could induce him to tolerate.

   —Professor Harold Laski, essay in *Freedom of Expression*

2. Above all, we cannot play ducks and drakes with a native battery of idioms which prescribes such egregious collocations of vocables as the Basic *put up with* for *tolerate* or *put at a loss* for *bewilder*.

   —Professor Lancelot Hogben, *Interglossa*

3. On the one side we have the free personality: by definition it is not neurotic, for it has neither conflict nor dream. Its desires, such as they are, are transparent, for they are just what institutional approval keeps in the forefront of consciousness; another institutional pattern would alter their number and intensity; there is little in them that is natural, irreducible, or culturally dangerous. But *on the other side*, the social bond itself is nothing but the mutual reflection of these self-secure integrities. Recall the definition of love. Is not this the very picture of a small academic? Where is there a place in this hall of mirrors for either personality or fraternity?

   —Essay on psychology in *Politics* (New York)

4. All the "best people" from the gentlemen's clubs, and all the frantic fascist captains, united in common hatred of Socialism and bestial horror of the rising tide of the mass revolutionary movement, have turned to acts of provocation, to foul incendiarism, to medieval legends of poisoned wells, to legalize their own destruction of proletarian organizations, and rouse the agitated petty-bourgeoisie to chauvinistic fervor on behalf of the fight against the revolutionary way out of the crisis.

   —Communist pamphlet

5. If the new spirit *is* to be infused into this old country, there is one thorny and contentious reform which must be tackled, and that is the humanization and galvanization of the B.B.C. Timidity here will bespeak canker and atrophy of the soul. The heart of Britain may be sound and of strong beat, for instance, but the British lion's roar at present is like that of Bottom in Shakespeare's *Midsummer Night's Dream*—as gentle as any sucking dove. A virile new Britain cannot continue indefinitely to be traduced in the eyes or rather ears, of the world by the effete languors of Langham Place, brazenly masquerading as "standard English." When the Voice of Britain is heard at nine o'clock, better far and infinitely less ludicrous to hear aitches honestly dropped than the present priggish, inflated, inhibited, school-ma'amish arch braying of blameless bashful mewing maidens!

—Letter in *Tribune*

Each of these passages has faults of its own, but, quite apart from avoidable ugliness, two qualities are common to all of them. The first is staleness in imagery; the other is lack of precision. The writer either has a meaning and cannot express it, or he inadvertently says something else, or he is almost indifferent as to whether his words mean anything or not. This mixture of vagueness and sheer incompetence is the most marked characteristic of modern English prose, and especially of any kind of political writing. As soon as certain topics are raised, the concrete melts into the abstract and no one seems able to think in turns of speech that are not hackneyed: prose consists less and less of *words* chosen for the sake of their meaning, and more and more of *phrases* tacked together like the sections of a prefabricated henhouse. I list below, with notes and examples, various of the tricks by means of which the work of prose-construction is habitually dodged:

5 *Dying metaphors.* A newly invented metaphor assists thought by evoking a visual image, while on the other hand a metaphor which is technically "dead" (e.g., *iron resolution*) has in effect reverted to being an ordinary word and can generally be used without loss of vividness. But in between these two classes there is a huge dump of worn-out metaphors which have lost all evocative power and are merely used because they save people the trouble of inventing phrases for themselves. Examples are: *Ring the changes on, take up the cudgels for, toe the line, ride rough-shod over, stand shoulder to shoulder with, play into the*

hands of, no axe to grind, grist to the mill, fishing in troubled waters, rift within the lute, on the order of the day, Achilles' heel, swan song, hotbed. Many of these are used without knowledge of their meaning (what is a "rift," for instance?), and incompatible metaphors are frequently mixed, a sure sign that the writer is not interested in what he is saying. Some metaphors now current have been twisted out of their original meaning without those who use them even being aware of the fact. For example, *toe to line* is sometimes written *toe the line*. Another example is *the hammer and the anvil*, now always used with the implication that the anvil gets the worst of it. In real life it is always the anvil that breaks the hammer, never the other way about: a writer who stopped to think what he was saying would be aware of this, and would avoid perverting the original phrase.

Operators or *verbal false limbs*. These save the trouble of picking out appropriate verbs and nouns, and at the same time pad each sentence with extra syllables which give it an appearance of symmetry. Characteristic phrases are *render inoperative, militate against, make contact with, be subjected to, give rise to, give grounds for, have the effect of, play a leading part (role) in, make itself felt, take effect, exhibit a tendency to, serve the purpose of, etc., etc.* The keynote is the elimination of simple verbs. Instead of being a single word, such as *break, stop, spoil, mend, kill*, a verb becomes a *phrase*, made up of a noun or adjective tacked on to some general-purpose verb such as *prove, serve, form, play, render*. In addition, the passive voice is wherever possible used in preference to the active, and noun constructions are used instead of gerunds (*by examination of* instead of *by examining*). The range of verbs is further cut down by means of the *-ize* and *de-* formations, and the banal statements are given an appearance of profundity by means of the *not un-* formation. Simple conjunctions and prepositions are replaced by such phrases as *with respect to, having regard to, the fact that, by dint of, in view of, in the interests of, on the hypothesis that;* and the ends of sentences are saved from anticlimax by such resounding commonplaces as *greatly to be desired, cannot be left out of account, a development to be expected in the near future, deserving of serious consideration, brought to a satisjying conclusion,* and so on and so forth.

Pretentious diction. Words like *phenomenon, element, individual* (as noun), *objective, categorical, effective, virtual, basic, primary, promote, constitute, exhibit, exploit, utilize, eliminate, liquidate*, are used to dress up simple statements and give an air of scientific impartiality to biased judgments. Adjectives like *epoch-making, epic, historic, unforgettable, triumphant, age-old, inevitable, inexorable, veritable*, are used to dignify the sordid processes of international politics, while writing that aims at glorifying war usually takes on an archaic color, its characteristic words being: *realm, throne, chariot, mailed fist, trident, sword, shield, buckler, banner, jackboot, clarion.* Foreign words and expressions such as *cul de sac, ancien régime, deus ex machina, mutatis mutandis, status quo, gleichschaltung, weltanschauung*, are used to give an air of culture and elegance. Except for the useful abbreviations *i.e., e.g.*, and *etc.*, there is no real need for any of the hundreds of foreign phrases now current in English. Bad writers, and especially scientific, political, and sociological writers, are nearly always haunted by the notion that Latin or Greek words are grander than Saxon ones, and unnecessary words like *expedite, ameliorate, predict, extraneous, deracinated, clandestine, subaqueous*, and hundreds of others constantly gain ground from their Anglo–Saxon opposite numbers.[1] The jargon peculiar to Marxist writing (*hyena, hangman, cannibal, petty bourgeois, these gentry, lackey, flunkey, mad dog, White Guard*, etc.) consists largely of words and phrases translated from Russian, German, or French; but the normal way of coining a new word is to use a Latin or Greek root with the appropriate affix and, where necessary, the size formation. It is often easier to make up words of this kind (*deregionalize, impermissible, extramarital, nonfragmentary* and so forth) than to think up the English words that will cover one's meaning. The result, in general, is an increase in slovenliness and vagueness.

Meaningless words. In certain kinds of writing, particularly in art criticism and literary criticism, it is normal to come across long passages which are almost completely lacking in meaning.[2] Words like *romantic, plastic, values, human, dead, sentimental, natural, vitality*, as used in art criticism, are strictly meaningless, in the sense that they not only do not point to any discoverable object, but are hardly ever expected to do so by the reader. When one critic writes, "The outstanding feature of Mr. X's work is its

1 An interesting illustration of this is the way in which the English flower names which were in use till very recently are being ousted by Greek ones, *snapdragon* becoming *antirrhinum*, *forget-me-not* becoming *myosotis*, etc. It is hard to see any practical reason for this change of fashion: it is probably due to an instinctive turning away from the more homely word and a vague feeling that the Greek word is scientific.

2 Example: "Comfort's catholicity of perception and image, strangely Whitmanesque in range, almost the opposite in aesthetic compulsion, continues to evoke that trembling atmospheric accumulative hinting at a cruel, an inexorably serene timelessness.... Wrey Gardiner scores by aiming at simple bull's-eyes with precision. Only they are not so simple, and through this contented sadness runs more than the surface bittersweet of resignation." (*Poetry Quarterly.*)

living quality," while another writes, "The immediately striking thing about Mr. X's work is its peculiar deadness," the reader accepts this as a simple difference of opinion. If words like *black* and *white* were involved, instead of the jargon words *dead* and *living*, he would see at once that language was being used in an improper way. Many political words are similarly abused. The word *Fascism* has now no meaning except in so far as it signifies "something not desirable." The words *democracy, socialism, freedom, patriotic, realistic, justice*, have each of them several different meanings which cannot be reconciled with one another. In the case of a word like *democracy*, not only is there no agreed definition, but the attempt to make one is resisted from all sides. It is almost universally felt that when we call a country democratic we are praising it: consequently the defenders of every kind of régime claim that it is a democracy, and fear that they might have to stop using the word if it were tied down to any one meaning. Words of this kind are often used in a consciously dishonest way. That is, the person who uses them has his own private definition, but allows his hearer to think he means something quite different. Statements like *Marshal Pétain was a true patriot, The Soviet press is the freest in the world, The Catholic Church is opposed to persecution*, are almost always made with intent to deceive. Other words used in variable meanings, in most cases more or less dishonestly, are: *class, totalitarian, science, progressive, reactionary, bourgeois, equality*.

Now that I have made this catalogue of swindles and perversions, let me give another example of the kind of writing that they lead to. This time it must of its nature be an imaginary one. I am going to translate a passage of good English into modern English of the worst sort. Here is a well-known verse from *Ecclesiastes*:

> I returned and saw under the sun, that the race is not to the swift, nor the battle to the strong, neither yet bread to the wise, nor yet riches to men of understanding, nor yet favour to men of skill; but time and chance happeneth to them all.

Here it is in modern English:

> Objective consideration of contemporary phenomena compels the conclusion that success or failure in competitive activities exhibits no tendency to be commensurate with innate capacity, but that a considerable element of the unpredictable must invariably be taken into account.

10 This is a parody, but not a very gross one. Exhibit (3), above, for instance, contains several patches of the same kind of English. It will be seen that I have not made a full translation. The beginning and ending of the sentence follow the original meaning fairly closely, but in the middle the concrete illustrations—race, battle, bread—dissolve into the vague phrase "success or failure in competitive activities." This had to be so, because no modern writer of the kind I am discussing—no one capable of using phrases like "objective consideration of contemporary phenomena"—would ever tabulate his thoughts in that precise and detailed way. The whole tendency of modern prose is away from concreteness. Now analyze these two sentences a little more closely. The first contains forty-nine words but only sixty syllables, and all its words are those of everyday life. The second contains thirty-eight words of ninety syllables: eighteen of its words are from Latin roots, and one from Greek. The first sentence contains six vivid images, and only one phrase ("time and chance") that could be called vague. The second contains not a single fresh, arresting phrase, and in spite of its ninety syllables it gives only a shortened version of the meaning contained in the first. Yet without a doubt it is the second kind of sentence that is gaining ground in modern English. I do not want to exaggerate. This kind of writing is not yet universal, and outcrops of simplicity will occur here and there in the worst-written page. Still, if you or I were told to write a few lines on the uncertainty of human fortunes, we should probably come much nearer to my imaginary sentence than to the one from *Ecclesiastes*.

As I have tried to show, modern writing at its worst does not consist of picking out words for the sake of their meaning and inventing images in order to make the meaning clearer. It consists in gumming together long strips of words which have already been set in order by someone else, and making the results presentable by sheer humbug. The attraction of this way of writing is that it is easy. It is easier—even quicker, once you have the habit—to say *In my opinion it is not an unjustifiable assumption that* than to say *I think*. If you use ready-made phrases, you not only don't have to hunt about for words; you also don't have to bother with the rhythms of your sentences, since these phrases are generally so arranged as to be more or less euphonious. When you are composing in a hurry—when you are dictating to a stenographer, for instance, or making a public speech—it is natural to fall into a pretentious, Latinized style. Tags like *a consideration which we should do well to bear in mind* or *a conclusion to which all of us would readily assent* will save many a sentence from coming down with a bump. By using stale metaphors, similes, and idioms, you save much mental effort, at the cost of leaving your meaning vague, not only for your reader but for yourself. This is the significance of mixed metaphors. The sole aim of a metaphor is to call up a visual image. When these images clash—as in *The Fascist octopus has sung its swan song, the jackboot is thrown into the melting pot*—it can be taken as certain that the writer is not seeing a mental image of the objects he is naming; in other words he is not really thinking. Look again at the examples I gave at the beginning of this essay. Professor Laski (1) uses five negatives in fifty-three words. One of these is superfluous, making nonsense of the whole passage, and in addition there is the slip—alien for akin—making further nonsense, and several avoidable pieces of clumsiness which increase the general vagueness. Professor Hogben (2) plays duck and drakes with a battery which is able to write prescriptions, and, while disapproving of the everyday phrase *put up with*, is unwilling to look *egregious* up in the dictionary and see what it means; (3), if one takes an uncharitable attitude towards it, is simply meaningless: probably one could work out its intended meaning by reading the whole of the article in which it occurs. In (4), the writer knows more or less what he wants to say, but an accumulation of stale phrases chokes him like tea leaves blocking a sink. In (5), words and meaning have almost parted company. People who write in this manner usually have a general emotional meaning—they dislike one thing and want to express solidarity with another—but they are not interested in the detail of what they are saying. A scrupulous writer, in every sentence that he writes, will ask himself at least four questions, thus: What am I trying to say? What words will express it? What image or idiom will make it clearer? Is this image fresh enough to have an effect? And he will probably ask himself two more: Could I put it more shortly? Have I said anything that is avoidably ugly? But you are not obliged to go to all this trouble. You can shirk it by simply throwing your mind open and letting the ready-made phrases come crowding in. They will construct your sentences for you—even think your thoughts for you, to a certain extent—and at need they will perform the important service of partially concealing your meaning even from yourself. It is at this point that the special connection between politics and the debasement of language becomes clear.

In our time it is broadly true that political writing is bad writing. Where it is not true, it will generally be found that the writer is some kind of rebel, expressing his private opinions and not a "party line." Orthodoxy, of whatever color, seems to demand a lifeless, imitative style. The political dialects to be found in pamphlets, leading articles, manifestoes, White Papers and the speeches of undersecretaries do, of course, vary from party to party, but they are all alike in that one almost never finds in them a fresh, vivid, homemade turn of speech. When one watches some tired hack on the platform mechanically repeating the familiar phrases—*bestial atrocities, iron heel, bloodstained tyranny, free peoples of the world, stand shoulder to shoulder*—one often has a curious feeling that one is not watching a live human being but some kind of dummy: a feeling which suddenly becomes stronger at moments when the light catches the speaker's spectacles and turns them into blank discs which seem to have no eyes behind them. And this is not altogether fanciful. A speaker who uses that kind of phraseology has gone some distance toward turning himself into a machine. The appropriate noises are coming out of his larynx, but his brain is not involved as it would be if he were choosing his words for himself. If the speech he is making is one that he is accustomed to make over and over again, he may be almost unconscious of what he is saying, as one is when one utters the responses in church. And this reduced state of consciousness, if not indispensable, is at any rate favorable to political conformity.

In our time, political speech and writing are largely the defense of the indefensible. Things like the continuance of British rule in India, the Russian purges and deportations, the dropping of the atom bombs on Japan, can indeed be defended, but only by arguments which are too brutal for most people to face, and which do not square with the professed aims of political parties. Thus political language has to consist largely of euphemism, question-begging and sheer cloudy vagueness. Defenseless villages are bombarded from the air, the inhabitants driven out into the countryside, the cattle machine-gunned, the huts set on fire with incendiary bullets: this is called *pacification*. Millions of peasants are robbed of their farms and sent trudging along the roads with no more than they can carry: this is called *transfer of population* or *rectification of frontiers*. People are imprisoned for years without trial, or shot in the back of the neck or sent to die of scurvy in Arctic lumber camps: this is called *elimination of unreliable elements*. Such phraseology is needed if one wants to name things without calling up mental pictures of them. Consider for instance some comfortable English professor defending Russian totalitarianism. He cannot say outright, "I believe in killing off your opponents when you can get good results by doing so." Probably, therefore, he will say something like this: "While freely conceding that the Soviet régime exhibits certain features which the humanitarian may be inclined to deplore, we must, I think, agree that a certain curtailment of the right to political opposition is an unavoidable concomitant of transitional periods, and that the rigors which the Russian people have been called upon to undergo have been amply justified in the sphere of concrete achievement."

The inflated style is itself a kind of euphemism. A mass of Latin words fall upon the facts like soft snow, blurring the outlines and covering up all the details. The great enemy of clear language is insincerity. When there is a gap between one's real and one's declared aims, one turns as it were instinctively to long words and exhausted idioms, like a cuttlefish squirting out ink. In our age there is no such thing as "keeping out of politics." All issues are political issues, and politics itself is a mass of lies, evasions, folly, hatred, and schizophrenia. When the general atmosphere is bad, language must suffer. I should expect to find — this is a guess which I have not sufficient knowledge to verify — that the German, Russian and Italian languages have all deteriorated in the last ten or fifteen years, as a result of dictatorship.

15 But if thought corrupts language, language can also corrupt thought. A bad usage can spread by tradition and imitation, even among people who should and do know better. The debased language that I have been discussing is in some ways very convenient. Phrases like *a not unjustifiable assumption, leaves much to be desired, would serve no good purpose, a consideration which we should do well to bear in mind*, are a continuous temptation, a packet of aspirins at one's elbow. Look back through this essay, and for certain you will find that I have again and again committed the very faults I am protesting against. By this morning's post I have received a pamphlet dealing with conditions in Germany. The author tells me that he "felt impelled" to write it. I open it at random, and here is almost the first sentence that I see: "[The Allies] have an opportunity not only of achieving a radical transformation of Germany's social and political structure in such a way as to avoid a nationalistic reaction in Germany itself, but at the same time of laying the foundations of a co-operative and unified Europe." You see, he "feels impelled" to write — feels, presumably, that he has something new to say — and yet his words, like cavalry horses answering the bugle, group themselves automatically into the familiar dreary pattern. This invasion of one's mind by ready-made phrases (*lay the foundations, achieve a radical transformation*) can only be prevented if

one is constantly on guard against them, and every such phrase anaesthetizes a portion of one's brain.

I said earlier that the decadence of our language is probably curable. Those who deny this would argue, if they produced an argument at all, that language merely reflects existing social conditions, and that we cannot influence its development by any direct tinkering with words and constructions. So far as the general tone or spirit of a language goes, this may be true, but it is not true in detail. Silly words and expressions have often disappeared, not through any evolutionary process but owing to the conscious action of a minority. Two recent examples were *explore every avenue* and *leave no stone unturned*, which were killed by the jeers of a few journalists. There is a long list of flyblown metaphors which could similarly be got rid of if enough people would interest themselves in the job; and it should also be possible to laugh the *not un-* formation out of existence,[3] to reduce the amount of Latin and Greek in the average sentence, to drive out foreign phrases and strayed scientific words, and, in general, to make pretentiousness unfashionable. But all these are minor points. The defense of the English language implies more than this, and perhaps it is best to start by saying what it does *not* imply.

To begin with it has nothing to do with archaism, with the salvaging of obsolete words and turns of speech, or with the setting up of a "standard English" which must never be departed from. On the contrary, it is especially concerned with the scrapping of every word or idiom which has outworn its usefulness. It has nothing to do with correct grammar and syntax, which are of no importance so long as one makes one's meaning clear, or with the avoidance of Americanisms, or with having what is called a "good prose style." On the other hand it is not concerned with fake simplicity and the attempt to make written English colloquial. Nor does it even imply in every case preferring the Saxon word to the Latin one, though it does imply using the fewest and shortest words that will cover one's meaning. What is above all needed is to let the meaning choose the word, and not the other way about. In prose, the worst thing one can do with words is to surrender to them. When you think of a concrete object, you think wordlessly, and then, if you want to describe the thing you have been visualizing you probably hunt about till you find the exact words that seem to fit it. When you think of some-

3 One can cure oneself of the *not un-* formation by memorizing this sentence: *A not unblack dog was chasing a not unsmall rabbit across a not ungreen field.*

thing abstract you are more inclined to use words from the start, and unless you make a conscious effort to prevent it, the existing dialect will come rushing in and do the job for you, at the expense of blurring or even changing your meaning. Probably it is better to put off using words as long as possible and get one's meaning as clear as one can through pictures or sensations. Afterward one can choose—not simply *accept*—the phrases that will best cover the meaning, and then switch round and decide what impression one's words are likely to make on another person. This last effort of the mind cuts out all stale or mixed images, all prefabricated phrases, needless repetitions, and humbug and vagueness generally. But one can often be in doubt about the effect of a word or a phrase, and one needs rules that one can rely on when instinct fails. I think the following rules will cover most cases:

(i) Never use a metaphor, simile, or other figure of speech which you are used to seeing in print.
(ii) Never use a long word where a short one will do.
(iii) If it is possible to cut a word out, always cut it out.
(iv) Never use the passive where you can use the active.
(v) Never use a foreign phrase, a scientific word, or a jargon word if you can think of an everyday English equivalent.
(vi) Break any of these rules sooner than say anything outright barbarous.

These rules sound elementary, and so they are, but they demand a deep change of attitude in anyone who has grown used to writing in the style now fashionable. One could keep all of them and still write bad English, but one could not write the kind of stuff that I quoted in those five specimens at the beginning of this article.

I have not here been considering the literary use of language, but merely language as an instrument for expressing and not for concealing or preventing thought. Stuart Chase and others have come near to claiming that all abstract words are meaningless, and have used this as a pretext for advocating a kind of political quietism. Since you don't know what Fascism is, how can you struggle against Fascism? One need not swallow such absurdities as this, but one ought to recognize that the present political chaos is connected with the decay of language, and that one can probably bring about some improvement by starting at the verbal end. If you simplify your English, you are freed from the worst follies of orthodoxy. You cannot speak any of the necessary dialects, and when you make a stupid remark its stupidity will be obvious, even to yourself. Political language—and with variations this is true of all political parties, from Conservatives to Anarchists—is designed to make lies sound truthful and murder respectable, and to give an appearance of solidity to pure wind. One cannot change this all in a moment, but one can at least change one's own habits, and from time to time one can even, if one jeers loudly enough, send some worn-out and useless phrase —some *jackboot, Achilles' heel, hotbed, melting pot, acid test, veritable inferno*, or other lump of verbal refuse—into the dustbin where it belongs.

VOCABULARY

decadent: marked by decay or decline 1
archaism: something no longer in use 1
hansom cab: a covered carriage with the driver's seat elevated behind 1
egregious: obviously bad 3
collocations: arrangements of words 3
vocables: words composed of sounds or letters without regard to meaning 3
galvanization: electrification, stimulation 3
atrophy: weaken from disuse 3
virile: manly 3
effete: weak, effeminate 3
languors: sluggishness 3
brazenly: brashly 3
evocative: capable of summoning up, re-creating 5
symmetry: beauty of form arising from balance 6
keynote: setting the tone 6
banal: dull, ordinary 6
categorical: absolute 7
inexorable: relentless, inflexible 7
expedite: bring to a hasty conclusion 7
ameliorate: improve 7
extraneous: additional 7
deracinated: uprooted 7
clandestine: secret 7
subaqueous: under water 7
totalitarian: controlled by a central government 8
reactionary: ultraconservative 8
bourgeois: middle class 8
commensurate: measured, weighted 9

parody: an imitation meant to ridicule 10
humbug: nonsense 11
euphonious: pleasing to hear 11
superfluous: unnecessary 11
scrupulous: honest 11
orthodoxy: standard practice 12
euphemism: word or phrase that disguises something ugly 13
cuttlefish: mollusk with a calcified internal shell 14
colloquial: spoken 17
quietism: passive attitude toward worldly affairs 18

AUDIENCE AND PURPOSE

1. What is Orwell's thesis statement?
2. Why does Orwell want to stress the link between language and politics?
3. It is interesting that Orwell takes it upon himself quite literally to teach the reader how to use English properly. How is this teaching made acceptable and not condescending?

CONTENT

1. Is Orwell right when he claims "if you or I were to write a few lines on the uncertainty of human fortunes" we would produce something closer to his parody than to the simplicity of the Bible? Comment on the effectiveness of his parody.
2. Look at some of Orwell's examples of egregious language. How are they examples of lack of thought?
3. Orwell argues that the English language suffers from decadence. What does he argue contributes to that decadence?

STYLE AND STRUCTURE

1. Why does Orwell start with bad examples of English?
2. How does Orwell try to demonstrate the relation between politics and bad language throughout?
3. What metaphors does Orwell himself use? Are these phrases, to use his terminology, living or dying?

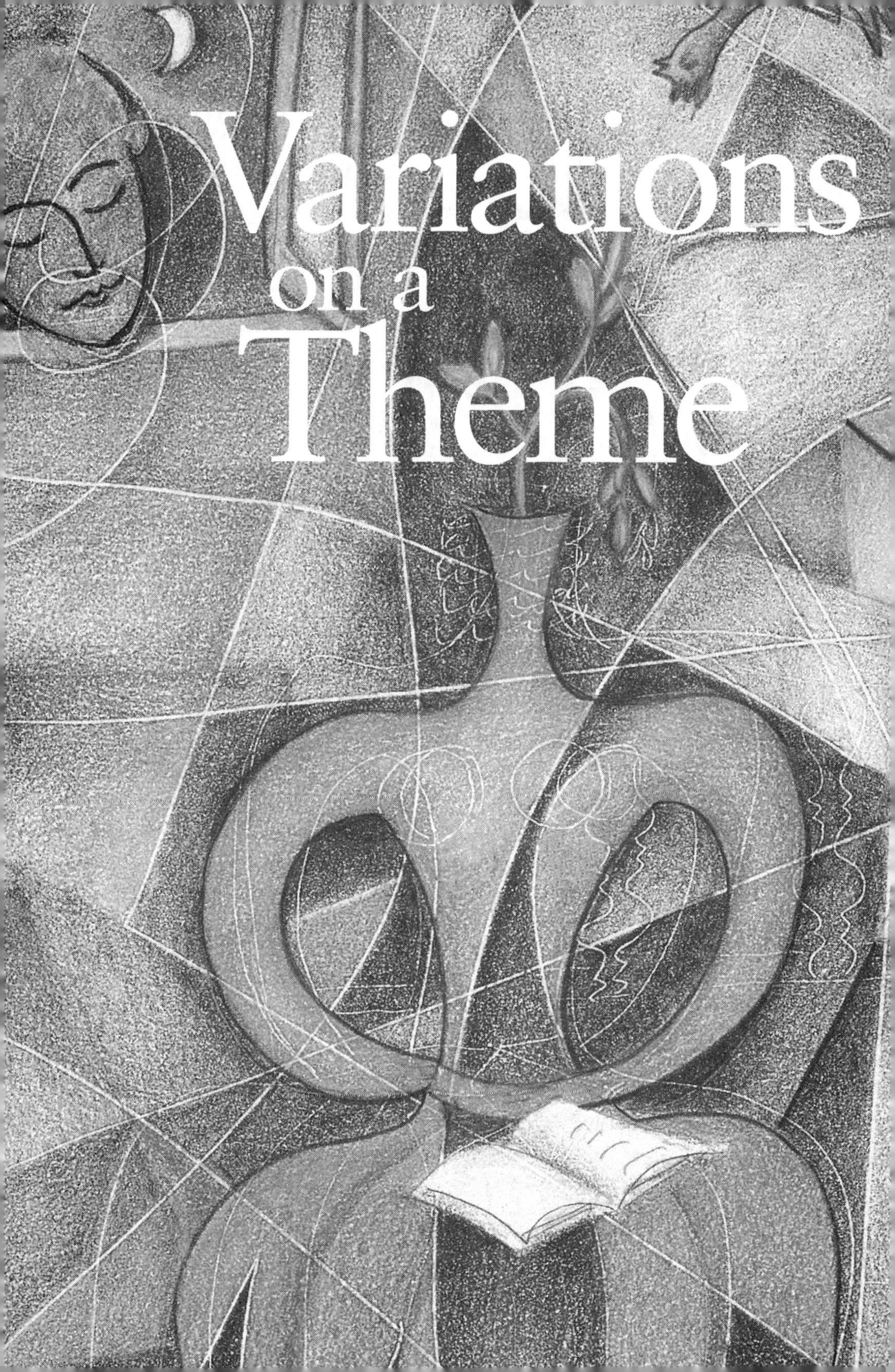
Variations
on a
Theme

VARIATIONS ON A THEME: EXPLORING MULTICULTURALISM

Comparing Arguments on Multiculturalism

The essays contained in this section are organized according to similarity of theme. They explore multiculturalism and its effect on individual identity. From a number of perspectives, authors discuss the challenges and consequences of seeing themselves defined by mainstream culture and struggle to define who they are as members of a distinctive group.

As raw materials that you can use to write response pieces, these essays can help you formulate your thoughts on a larger issue and scrutinize how various authors approach the same subject matter. Your interest here is how the material is developed, where the controversial issues are, and what you can do that will help you come to grips with the issues in your own writing. Because the concerns of these essays are topical, they can help you think about how you can develop critical reading skills to find problematic areas in the arguments with which you are presented. This kind of critical reading is the core of any research essay, which demands that you make sense of a number of conflicting points in the material you uncover in your search. While one reading of an essay might first be primarily for information, your second reading of it needs to consider the ways the author's argument presents controversial material. Looking at how an author makes his or her case can help you figure out where an argument is vulnerable or where you could use some of its strengths to support your own position on the subject.

The fundamentals of writing a research essay are here, in other words, without the necessity for you to do the research. The grouped essays represent a variety of conflicting opinions and perspectives, and your job as a reader is to come to your own conclusions, educated and enlightened by what you have read and what you can bring to the subject from your own background and understanding of the subject under discussion. Use these authors' words and opinions in different ways: use them as authorities who reinforce your point of view; use them as punching bags when you think they need to be taken to task for their naiveté or bias; use them as sources of information that can lead you further or as launching points for your own view of the subject matter.

Whether you accept or reject an author's point of view, such critical reading will help you approach any text with more questions, with more of a sense of the issues to be explored, and with less intimidation. Comparing authors' arguments on a related subject is a good way to prepare yourself to enter the conversation with them and write something back in response. Most essay writing, after all, whether in newspapers, scholarly articles, or books, focuses on how to resolve problems in order to arrive at the truth. Your task as an essay writer is to participate in that continuing conversation using all the knowledge, information, and experience that you can bring to the task.

Neil Bissoondath

Neil Bissoondath (b. 1955) was born in Trinidad and raised as a Hindu before moving to Canada. He is well known for his critiques of multiculturalism and is the host of the documentary series *Vision World. Selling Illusions* (1994), the work from which this excerpt was taken, won the Gordon Montador Award. Bissoondath's latest novel is *The Worlds Within Her* (1998).

MARGINALIZATION

One never really gets used to the conversation. It will typically go something like this:

"What nationality are you?"

"Canadian."

"No, I mean, what nationality are you *really*?"

There is probably not a person who has emigrated to Canada from a hot, moist country who has not been asked: "Why in the world did you come here, to this cold and beachless land, from *such a beautiful place*"? It is a question simplistic in the asking; it assumes so much. But it is also a question breath-taking in the response; it ignores so much.

Your first thought, as you take a deep breath, is: What does this person, fantasizing about perpetual sunstroke, want to hear? A cry of desperation? *Yes! Yes! God, why have I done this to myself?*

Your second thought is: Don't you read the newspapers? Don't you know what's happening in the world?

And your third thought, in growing desperation, is: Where do I begin?

No obvious point of departure offers itself because you know that your reasons for leaving "such a beautiful place" are so complex that your questioner would require a whirlwind tour of history, politics and economics all mixed together with a healthy dose of reality. So you simply plunge ahead, hastily tossing out words—depending on where you come from—like "political corruption," "torture," "violence," "murder," "oppression," and you watch your questioner's eyes glaze over, his gaze grow distant, his face tighten into a barely restrained scepticism. He has seen tourist posters, he has watched "Travel, Travel" on television, he subscribes to *National Geographic*. And you know that your words are competing hopelessly in his head with stylized visions of sun, sea and sand, that your version of reality cannot hope to vanquish the Tropics à la Club Med.

10 Should you manage to complete your answer—and more often than not the reception proves too disheartening halfway through—you frequently run into the stunningly unanswerable: "Yes, but we have all that in Canada, too...."

You nod, despite the obscenity of the remark which, in its ignorance, in its heartlessness, devalues so much Third World pain, so much Third World struggle; for to reject this assertion is to lose all hope of convincing your questioner that, in coming here, you have immeasurably improved your lot—and it is suddenly vital that you do so. You need to narrow that gap; you need to prove that your decision to move here was neither whimsical nor erroneous. Yes, you agree, there is political corruption in Canada, and violence and murder—isn't there everywhere?—and the native peoples may have something to say about oppression and torture of a kind, but.... You offer the merest of acknowledgements, for, in the end, the conversation is really about the weather.

So you talk about growing up in the hot, moist country. You talk about the heat and the humidity and the sensation of physical oppression. You tell of sitting and reading and, with no greater physical exertion, of sweating like a pig. You tell of laboured breathing, of your energy drained and the soporific effect of the air itself. You dramatize: A hurricane hit the island once...

But winter! comes the response. All that snow, all that slush, the bite of the wind on your nose, ears, teeth: the endless inhumanity of it all!

You reveal your perversity: You enjoy winter. No, you don't ski, you haven't quite managed to get the hang of skating, you don't even enjoy watching hockey. But you need less sleep during the winter months, your concentration improves, your productivity goes up, your sense of well-being is sweetened.

15 But you can't go outside in shorts and a T-shirt the way you can in "your" country...

There's no point in explaining that Canada is now your country—you have been distanced from the beginning, seen merely as some exoticism on two legs—so you remark that to go outside in "my" country is often to enter a sunlight strong enough to crisp your skin, a heat so powerful it causes you to shiver even as it sucks your strength out through your pores. So, if you can afford it, you prefer to stay indoors, shut off from the sweltering world in a room defined by shadows and the hum of an air-conditioner.

But isn't winter equally imprisoning? Who wants to go out into a world that resembles a freezer gone wild?

The point, though, is that with the proper clothing you can, whereas the portable air-conditioner has not yet been invented.

But for your questioner, caressing images of coconut trees swaying in the breeze, all of this is beside the point. He has been to the Bahamas or Jamaica or Cuba; he has experienced life in the islands, life lived on the sand.

And this is the crux of the problem. Experiencing the tropics only as a two-week visitor, passport and return air-ticket safely tucked away in a pocket, he can afford to speculate on the leavened delights of life in tropical zones. But you grew up there, you consider the experience from a rather different point of view. So the simplistic question brings two completely opposed visions hurtling towards one another. Yet you pursue the answer because the question itself is mildly insulting; it assumes your philosophy of life and your urge to accomplishment are sufficiently shallow that you would choose your country of residence based on mere meteorology.

So, despite the beauty left behind, you look fondly on the blowing snow, the frigid wind and the treacherous ice of February. You smile to yourself, you smile at your questioner, for you know that all this, even with its challenge, is symbolic of a greater freedom than you have ever known.

Your questioner smiles back and, after a moment of silence, asks what food people eat in "your" country.

Pizza, you say. Big Macs, Kentucky Fried Chicken ...

To be simply Canadian, untinged by the exoticism of elsewhere, seems insufficient, even unacceptable, to many other Canadians. The fact clearly stems, in part, from the simple human attraction to the exotic. But it seems to me that it also has much to do with a wider issue: the uncertainty we feel as a people.

We reveal this uncertainty in a variety of ways, including our newly minted concern for traditions, but particularly through that quintessential (and possibly eternal) Canadian question: Who are we? The usual answer—"Well, we're not like the Americans ..."—is insufficient: a self-perception cast in the negative can never satisfy (although it can obsess: in John Robert Colombo's *The Dictionary of Canadian Quotations*, "Canada" requires fewer than nine columns while "Canada & the United States" fills more than seventeen).

Nor might we be pleased by the impression offered of Canada by Naipaul's Nazruddin: "I felt the place was a hoax. They thought they were part of the West, but really they had become like the rest of us who had run to them for safety. They were like people far away, living on other people's land and off other people's brains, and that was all they thought they should do. That was why they were so bored and dull."

American novelist Alison Lurie's take is more personal: "[H]e wasn't hateful, or cruel, or cold-hearted, or neurotic. But he seemed to be ... I don't know ... a Canadian."

There are many visions of us, many answers to that question of who we are, some complimentary, some critical. And so, ourselves lacking a full and vigorous response ("A Canadian," the English essayist J.B. Priestley once remarked, "is lost when he asks himself what a Canadian is") we search for distinctiveness —exoticism—wherever we can find it. And we find it most readily in our compatriots most recently arrived.

For people I think of as "professional ethnics"—they who enjoy the role of the exotic and who depend on their exoticism for a sense of self—this is not an unpleasant state of affairs. But for those who would rather be accepted for their individuality, who resent being distinguished only by their differences, it can prove a matter of some irritation, even discomfort. The game of exoticism can cut two ways: it can prevent an individual from being ordinary, and it can prevent that same individual from being accepted.

Trudi Hanley, a twenty-one-year-old black woman who works in a field—modelling—where exoticism can reasonably be expected to be an advantage, once spoke to a reporter of the excuses used by those reluctant to hire her: "My nose was too big. I was too black. I was too different. We have enough ethnics. I heard them all."

But the finest example of this exclusion remains the sprinter Ben Johnson. Within a shattering twenty-four-hour period in Seoul, Korea, Mr. Johnson was transformed in media reports from being the Canadian who had won Olympic gold through effort to the Jamaican immigrant who had lost it through use of drugs. The only thing swifter than Mr. Johnson's drug-enhanced achievement was his public demotion from "one of us" to "one of them." The exotic multicultural concept of the everlasting immigrant has come to function as an institutional system for the marginalization of the individual: Ben Johnson was, in other words, a Canadian when convenient, an immigrant when not. Had he, success or failure, been accepted as being simply Canadian and not "Jamaican-Canadian," it would have been difficult for anyone to distance him in this way.

Thus the weight of the multicultural hyphen, the pressure of the link to exoticism, can become onerous—and instead of its being an anchoring definition, it can easily become a handy form of estrangement. Dr. John Polanyi, born elsewhere, is the *Canadian* Nobel-prize-winning chemist. Michael Ondaatje, born elsewhere, is the *Canadian* Booker-prize-winning novelist. Valery Fabrikant, born elsewhere, is the *Russian émigré* murderer.

This hyphen, even when it is there in spirit only, is a curious beast. It appears to mean so much and is yet so often indicative of so little.

Ali Sharrif, a Somali immigrant who freelances for *NOW* magazine in Toronto, began wondering why the city's black community had failed to come to the aid of Somalis in conflict with long-time residents of six apartment buildings in Toronto. He telephoned a man identified only as a "well-known Toronto black activist" and was told, "You see, it's hard to place the Somalis. They really are not black in the true sense of the word." He explained that the black community in North America saw Somalis and other people from the Horn of Africa as Muslims and Arabs first, Africans second. Somalis, who to those without the distinguishing eye bear a strong resemblance to Ethiopians, are Muslims but not Arabs, Africans but not black, and in Metro Toronto they find acceptance and support difficult to obtain. Sharrif ends his article on a note that is part plaintive, part angry: "Most of the Somalis I know, casual acquaintances and friends, really want to be part of the black community. But their fate might be that they are considered black, but not black enough to be really black."

Too much of this, not enough of that: it is a problem. There are people of African descent, born in the Caribbean, immigrants to Canada, who describe themselves as African-Canadians, a phrase now deemed more acceptable than "coloured" or even "black." Yet I cannot help wondering how, say, former South African president F.W. de Klerk would be described should events force him to flee his country for a Canadian haven: would he too be an African-Canadian? And what about, say, Muammar al-Qaddafi? Libya too is in Africa. I am uncertain, then, as to the precise meaning of phrases such as African-Canadian or Italian-Canadian or Greek-Canadian, particularly when applied to people whose experience of these foreign lands is most likely historical, touristic or anecdotal: what conclusions are to be drawn from them? Their principal effect, I would suggest, is not to define the word "Canadian" but to mark a distance from it, the hyphen that links them a sign of an acceptable marginalization.

If the questions of degree of race and ethnicity, and of that troublesome hyphen, unsettle me, it is because they strike close to home—as they strike close to home for the growing number of Canadians whose personal relationships entail a commingling of ethnicities. It is a realm that must be entered with care, for the very language we use is a minefield of offence.

One of my favourite *New Yorker* fillers—those little nuggets of linguistic curios with which the magazine rounds out its articles—concerned a U.S. newspaper that reported on the restructuring program instituted by a faltering company. Not only would the plan save jobs in the long run, the newspaper reported, but it was expected eventually to put the company's books back in the African-American.

Back in the *what*?

The newspaper subsequently ran a correction explaining that it had meant to say that the company's finances would be back in the—uhh—black. It blamed overzealousness on the part of a copy-editor.

40 The trend to more specific ethnic self-identification is a complex one. What is one to make, for instance, of Sir Peter Ustinov, he of the Russian surname, the British manner (Jacques Parizeau with a sense of humour and no chip on the shoulder) and a family history that ties together influences from Russia, Italy, France, Germany, Switzerland and, by virtue of a great-great-grandmother, Ethiopia (which may qualify him as a person of colour)?

A similar deconstruction would make of me an Indian-West-Indian (or, more accurately, an Indian-Trinidadian-West-Indian) by birth and an Indian-Trinidadian-West-Indian-Canadian by choice. My companion's ethnicity is less complex. She would be a Franco-Québécoise-Canadian (barring possible confirmation of a family legend that tells of an infusion of native blood somewhere in the distant past).

But what then of our daughter?

With her mixture of heritages, should she one day be asked to define her ethnicity, she would be obliged to take a deep breath before replying that she is "a Franco-Québécoise-First Nations-Indian-Trinidadian-West-Indian-Canadian." Or something of the sort. (I am assuming here that the actual order of the ethnicities is not subject to political considerations, but I may be wrong.) I do shudder, though, for the children she may one day have should she choose to have a family with someone of different but equally complex composition.

There is an interest here, it seems to me, in a certain simplicity, a simplicity that my daughter might find in moving away from an ethnic concept of self-definition (without abandoning the knowledge of it) towards a self-definition based on her homeland. But, as I found out after the publication of an article I wrote on the subject, even the word "homeland" is problematic.

I had written in the article of the many young men, born and bred in Canada of parents from Croatia, who had returned to that unhappy land to take up arms in its defence. I was puzzled by their actions, concerned about the implications for Canada, saddened by the thought of young men eager to go off to war. The following week, a Montreal writer and editor named François Hébert penned a reply to my piece in which he defended the right of these young men to go to the aid of, as he put it, their homeland. I had not questioned their right, but what struck me in the reply was the defining of Croatia as the "homeland" of these young men.

My understanding of the word would have defined Croatia as the homeland of these young men's parents or grandparents, while their homeland would be Canada, the land of their birth and upbringing. I felt that to view their *ancestral* land as their homeland was to wilfully distance them, to make them marginal to the Canadian context. It was to define the belonging of others through the prism of one's own personal and political needs, in a way not very different from the historical view of that young woman on the phone-in show in Washington.*

To consider the ancestral land as the true homeland is to risk engaging a dizzying absurdity, for it would mean that my homeland is India, a place I have never visited and have little wish to. It would mean that Lucien Bouchard's would be neither Quebec nor Canada but France; Brian Mulroney's would be Ireland, David Suzuki's Japan, Nino Ricci's Italy and so on. Only aboriginals, then, could claim Canada as their homeland—unless it is true that they happen to have migrated here thousands of years ago from another continent, in which case they're out of luck. And what is one to make of the homelands of people like Pierre-Marc Johnson, Claude Ryan, Jeanne Blackburn and others complicated by history?

And what of my daughter's homeland? Does she have two, India and France? How much time must go by, then, how many cultural changes are required, before one's homeland is no longer that of one's ancestors? Is there a moment when one stops being, in the eyes of others, an alien, an exile, an immigrant?

It seems to me vital that, as unfashionable or as outdated as it may seem to some in their rush both to claim and to impose

* Editor's note: Neil Bissoondath refers to material in the source text that is not included in this reprinted excerpt.

narrow ethnicity and tribal exoticism, that my daughter should grow up to think of her homeland as simply Canada and of herself as simply Canadian. In this way, there will be no other "homeland" to which others can wilfully consign—and therefore distance—her, alienating her from the mainstream and thereby withholding her rightful place in the land of her birth.

There is also a strong element of marginalization in the Sikh-turban issue. The controversy of turbans in Legion halls and in the RCMP is in itself an indication of the failure of multiculturalism programs to go beyond superficiality in explaining us to each other. To view the turban as just another kind of hat, with no significance beyond sheltering the head, is to say that a cross worn on a chain is of no significance beyond a decoration for the neck: it is to reveal a deep ignorance of the ways and beliefs of others. To ban either in any context is to revel in that ignorance and to alienate the wearer by rejecting an intimate and fundamental part of his or her self.

The marginalization to which we so easily subject one another comes frequently in times of economic hardship. The stresses of unemployment—the difficulty of the present and the unimaginable idea of a future—create a need for scapegoats: we need something or someone to blame. We can rail against politicians, taxes, corporations—but these are all distant, untouchable.

No one is more easily blamed for the lack of opportunity than the obvious "foreigner" cleaning tables in the local doughnut shop or serving behind the counter at McDonald's. Maybe he has brown skin, maybe he speaks with an accent: clearly he is out of place here, filling a paid position that should by rights have gone to a "real" Canadian. All differences, always so close to the surface, are seized upon, turned into objects of ridicule and resentment, the psychology of exoticism once more cutting both ways.

Encouraging people to view each other as simply Canadian, discouraging the use of the marginalizing hyphen, would not solve such problems—humans, in times of fear and anger, have a unique ability for seeking out bull's-eyes in each other—but it might help deflect some of the resentment, so that in expressing our pain we do not also alienate our fellow citizens. Differences between people are already obvious enough without their being emphasized through multiculturalism policy and its growing cult of racial and ethnic identity.

VOCABULARY

soporific: sleep-inducing 12
leavened: lightened 20
quintessential: most typical or representative 25
onerous: burdensome 32
curios: things considered rare, novel, or bizarre 37
deflect: turn aside 53

AUDIENCE AND PURPOSE

1. Whom do you think Bissoondath identifies as his audience for this essay?
2. What problems does Bissoondath find in the concept of the Canadian identity?
3. What is Bissoondath's point about immigrant identity in Canada? Where does he make his point?

CONTENT

1. What are the author's objections to the exotic roles usually ascribed to those who immigrate to Canada?
2. What point does Bissoondath make about Ben Johnson's rise and fall as an athlete in Canada?
3. What problem does the author find in the "multicultural hyphen," as he calls it?
4. Why does Bissoondath use the example of his daughter to demonstrate the absurdity of our existing notions of identity? Why is the concept of the "ancestral homeland" unsatisfactory?

STYLE AND STRUCTURE

1. Why does Bissoondath begin with such a long anecdotal introduction?
2. Why does he use the pronoun "you" to write this introduction?
3. Why is the introduction written in the present tense?
4. In the conclusion, Bissoondath explains his notion of marginalization. How does this argument tie in with the point he makes in his introduction?

David Suzuki

David Suzuki (b. 1936) is a geneticist, writer, and journalist. His CBC TV show, *The Nature of Things*, has been broadcast for many years. He has published many books, including *Metamorphosis: Stages in a Life* (1987), from which this excerpt is taken, as well as ten books for children. Suzuki holds a PhD in Zoology from the University of Chicago, and is currently working in the Sustainable Development Research Institute (SDRI) at the University of British Columbia.

ANCESTORS — THE GENETIC SOURCE

My genes can be traced in a direct line to Japan. I am a pure-blooded member of the Japanese race. And whenever I go there, I am always astonished to see the power of that biological connection. In subways in Tokyo, I catch familiar glimpses of the eyes, hairline or smile of my Japanese relatives. Yet when those same people open their mouths to communicate, the vast cultural gulf that separates them from me becomes obvious: English is my language, Shakespeare is my literature, British history is what I learned and Beethoven is my music.

For those who believe that in people, just as in animals, genes are the primary determinant of behaviour, a look at second- and third-generation immigrants to Canada gives powerful evidence to the contrary. The overriding influence is environmental. We make a great mistake by associating the inheritance of physical characteristics with far more complex traits of human personality and behaviour.

Each time I visit Japan, I am reminded of how Canadian I am and how little the racial connection matters. I first visited Japan in 1968 to attend the International Congress of Genetics in Tokyo. For the first time in my life, I was surrounded by people who all looked like me. While sitting in a train and looking at the reflections in the window, I found that it was hard to pick out my own image in the crowd. I had grown up in a Caucasian society in which I was a minority member. My whole sense of self had developed with that perspective of looking different. All my life I had wanted large eyes and brown hair so I could be like everyone else. Yet on that train, where I did fit in, I didn't like it.

On this first visit to Japan I had asked my grandparents to contact relatives and let them know I was coming. I was the first in the Suzuki clan in Canada to visit them. The closest relative on my father's side was my grandmother's younger brother, and we arranged to meet in a seaside resort near his home. He came to my hotel room with two of his daughters. None of them spoke any English, while my Japanese was so primitive as to be useless. In typical Japanese fashion, they showered me with gifts, the most important being a package of what looked like wood carved in the shape of bananas! I had no idea what it was. (Later I learned the package contained dried tuna fish from which slivers are shaved off to flavour soup. This is considered a highly prized gift.) We sat in stiff silence and embarrassment, each of us struggling to dredge up a common word or two to break the quiet. It was excruciating! My great uncle later wrote my grandmother to tell her how painful it had been to sit with her grandson and yet be unable to communicate a word.

5 To people in Japan, all non-Japanese—black, white or yellow—are *gaijin* or foreigners. While *gaijin* is not derogatory, I find that its use is harsh because I sense doors clanging shut on me when I'm called one. The Japanese do have a hell of a time with me because I look like them and can say in perfect Japanese, "I'm a foreigner and I can't speak Japanese." Their reactions are usually complete incomprehension followed by a sputtering, "What do you mean? You're speaking Japanese." And finally a pejorative, "Oh, a *gaijin*!"

Once when my wife, Tara, who is English, and I went to Japan we asked a man at the travel bureau at the airport to book a *ryokan*—a traditional Japanese inn—for us in Tokyo. He found one and booked it for "*Suzuki-san*" and off we went. When we arrived at the inn and I entered the foyer, the owner was confused by my terrible Japanese. When Tara entered, the shock was obvious in his face. Because of my name, they had expected a "real" Japanese. Instead, I was a *gaijin* and the owner told us he wouldn't take us. I was furious and we stomped off to a phone booth where I called the agent at the airport. He was astonished and came all the way into town to plead our case with the innkeeper. But the innkeeper stood firm and denied us a room. Apparently he had accepted *gaijin* in the past with terrible consequences.

As an example of the problem, Japanese always take their shoes off when entering a *ryokan* because the straw mats (*tatami*) are quickly frayed. To a Japanese, clomping into a room with shoes on would be comparable to someone entering our homes and spitting on the floor. Similarly, the *ofuro*, or traditional tub, has hot clean water that all bathers use. So one must first enter the bathroom, wash carefully and rinse off *before* entering the tub. Time in the *ofuro* is for relaxing and soaking. Again, Westerners who lather up in the tub are committing a terrible desecration.

To many Canadians today, the word "Jap" seems like a natural abbreviation for Japanese. Certainly for newspaper headlines it would seem to make sense. So people are often shocked to see me bristle when they have used the word Jap innocently. To Japanese-Canadians, Jap or Nip (from "*Nippon*") were epithets used generously during the pre-war and war years. They conjure up all of the hatred and bigotry of those times. While a person using the term today may be unaware of its past use, every Japanese-Canadian remembers.

The thin thread of Japanese culture that does link me to Japan was spun out of the poverty and desperation of my ancestors. My grandparents came to a Canadian province openly hostile to their strange appearance and different ways. There were severe restrictions on how much and where they could buy property. Their children, who were born and raised in Canada, couldn't vote until 1948 and encountered many barriers to professional training and property ownership. Asians, regardless of birthplace, were third-class citizens. That is the reality of the Japanese-Canadian experience and the historical cultural legacy that came down to the third and fourth generations—to me and my children.

10 The first Japanese immigrants came to Canada to make their fortunes so they could return to Japan as people of wealth. The vast majority was uneducated and impoverished. But in the century spanning my grandparents' births and the present, Japan has leapt from an agrarian society to a technological and economic giant.

Now, the Japanese I meet in Japan or as recent immigrants to Canada come with far different cultural roots. Present-day Japanese are highly educated, upper-middle class and proud of their heritage. In Canada they encounter respect, envy and curiosity in sharp contrast to the hostility and bigotry met by my grandparents.

Japanese immigrants to North America have names that signify the number of generations in the new land (or just as significantly, that count the generational distance *away* from Japan). My grandparents are *Issei*, meaning the first generation in Canada. Most *Issei* never learned more than a rudimentary knowledge of English. *Nisei*, like my parents, are the second generation here and the first native-born group. While growing up they first spoke Japanese in the home and then learned English from playmates and teachers. Before the Second World War, many *Issei* sent their children to be educated in Japan. When they returned to Canada, they were called *Kika-nisei* (or *Kibei* in the United States). Most have remained bilingual, but many of the younger *Nisei* now speak Japanese with difficulty because English is their native tongue. My sisters and I are *Sansei* (third generation); our children are *Yonsei*. These generations, and especially *Yonsei*, are growing up in homes where English is the only spoken language, so they are far more likely to speak school-taught French as their second language than Japanese.

Most *Sansei*, like me, do not speak Japanese. To us, the *Issei* are mysteries. They came from a cultural tradition that is a hundred years old. Unlike people in present-day Japan, the *Issei* clung tightly to the culture they remembered and froze that culture into a static museum piece like a relic of the past. Not being able to speak each other's language, *Issei* and *Sansei* were cut off from each other. My parents dutifully visited my grandparents and we children would be trotted out to be lectured at or displayed. These visits were excruciating, because we children didn't understand the old culture, and didn't have the slightest interest — we were Canadians.

My father's mother died in 1978 at the age of ninety-one. She was the last of the *Issei* in our family. The final months of her life, after a left-hemisphere stroke, were spent in that terrible twilight — crippled, still aware, but unable to communicate. She lived the terminal months of her life, comprehending but mute, in a ward with Caucasian strangers. For over thirty years I had listened to her psychologically blackmailing my father by warning him of her imminent death. Yet in the end, she hung on long after there was reason to. When she died, I was astonished at my own reaction, a great sense of sadness and regret at the cleavage of my last link with the source of my genes. I had never been able to ask what made her and others of her generation come to Canada, what they felt when they arrived, what their hopes and dreams had been, and whether it was worth it. And I wanted to thank her, to show her that I was grateful that, through them, I was born a Canadian.

VOCABULARY

pejorative: disparaging, negative 5
desecration: violation of the sacred 7
epithets: disparaging or abusive word 8
cleavage: split 14

AUDIENCE AND PURPOSE

1. Although this is a personal essay, Suzuki uses it to make a general point. Explain how the title relates to that point.

2. This is an expository essay and not a persuasive one. How does Suzuki nevertheless make it clear that genetic inheritance is only part of the story?
3. Whom does Suzuki assume his audience to be?

CONTENT

1. What examples does Suzuki use to demonstrate that he is a *gaijin* in Japan?
2. Why do the Japanese find the nickname "Jap" or "Nip" so degrading?
3. What is the point of Suzuki's discussion of the number of generations he is away from his Japanese heritage?
4. How has the Canadian perception of the Japanese changed in recent decades?

STYLE AND STRUCTURE

1. How does Suzuki create for the reader his sense of himself as an outsider, both in Canada and in Japan?
2. Why is genetic inheritance an appropriate topic for Suzuki? What hint do you get of that connection?
3. Why does Suzuki end with the story of his grandmother's death?

Sun-Kyung Yi

Sun-Kyung Yi (b. 1967) is a journalist and a producer living in Toronto. Her television documentary *Scenes from a Corner Score,* about a Korean immigrant family, was broadcast on CBC TV. *Hide & Seek: An Underground Trilogy* (1997) is a story of three illegal immigrants trying to survive in a hostile country. *Thai Girls* (1998) is a look at the lives of two women who came to Canada and became prostitutes. The article reprinted below is from *The Globe and Mail.*

AN IMMIGRANT'S SPLIT PERSONALITY

I am Korean-Canadian. But the hyphen often snaps in two obliging me to choose to act as either a Korean or a Canadian, depending on where I am and who I'm with. After 16 years of living in Canada, I discovered that it's very difficult to be both at any given time or place.

When I was younger, toying with the idea of entertaining two separate identities was a real treat, like a secret game for which no one knew the rules but me.

I was known as Angela to the outside world, and as Sun-Kyung at home. I ate bologna sandwiches in the school lunch room and rice and kimchee for dinner. I chatted about teen idols and giggled with my girlfriends during my classes, and ambitiously practiced piano and studied in the evenings, planning to become a doctor when I grew up. I waved hellos and goodbyes to my teachers, but bowed to my parents' friends visiting our home.

I could also look straight in the eyes of my teachers and friends and talk frankly with them instead of staring at my feet with my mouth shut when Koreans talked to me.

5 Going outside the home meant I was able to relax from the constraints of my cultural conditioning, until I walked back in the door and had to return to being an obedient and submissive daughter.

The game soon ended when I realized that it had become a way of life, that I couldn't change the rules without disappointing my parents and questioning all the cultural implications and consequences that came with being a hyphenated Canadian.

Many have tried to convince me that I am a Canadian, like all other immigrants in the country, but those same people also ask me which country I came from with great curiosity, following with questions about the type of food I ate and the language I spoke. It's difficult to feel a sense of belonging and acceptance when you are regarded as "one of them." "Those Koreans, they work hard.... You must be fantastic at math and science." (No.) "Do your parents own a corner store?" (No.)

Koreans and Canadians just can't seem to merge into "us" and "we."

Some people advised me that I should just take the best of both worlds and disregard the rest. That's ideal, but unrealistic when my old culture demands a complete conformity with very little room to manoeuvre for new and different ideas.

10 After a lifetime of practice, I thought I could change faces and become Korean on demand with grace and perfection. But working with a small Korean company in Toronto proved me wrong. I quickly became estranged from my own people.

My parents were ecstatic at the thought of their daughter finally finding her roots and having a working opportunity to speak my native tongue and absorb the culture. For me, it was the most painful and frustrating 2 $^{1}/_{2}$ months of my life.

When the president of the company boasted that he "operated little Korea," he meant it literally. A Canadianized Korean was not tolerated. I looked like a Korean, therefore I had to talk, act, and think like one, too. Being accepted meant a total surrender to ancient codes of behaviour rooted in Confucian thought, while leaving the "Canadian" part of me out in the parking lot with my '86 Buick.

In the first few days at work, I was bombarded with inquiries about my marital status. When I told them I was single, they spent the following days trying to match me up with available bachelors in the company and the community.

I was expected to accept my inferior position as a woman and had to behave accordingly. It was not a place to practice my feminist views, or be an individual without being condemned. Little Korea is a place for men (who filled all the senior positions) and women don't dare to speak up or disagree with their male counterparts.

15 The president (all employees bow to him and call him Mr. President) asked me to act more like a lady and smile. I was openly scorned by a senior employee because I spoke more fluent English than Korean. The cook in the kitchen shook her head in disbelief upon discovering that my cooking skills were limited to boiling a package of instant noodles. "You want a good husband, learn to cook," she advised me.

In less than a week I became an outsider because I refused to conform and blindly nod my head in agreement to what my elders (which happened to be everybody else in the company) said.

A month later, I was demoted because "members of the workplace and the Korean community" had complained that I just wasn't "Korean enough," and I had "too much power for a single woman." My father suggested that "when in Rome do as the Romans." But that's exactly what I was doing. I am in Canada so I was freely acting like a Canadian, and it cost me my job.

My father also said, "It doesn't matter how Canadian you think you are, just look in the mirror and it'll tell you who you *really* are." But what he didn't realize is that an immigrant has to embrace the new culture to enjoy and benefit from what it has to offer. Of course, I will always be Korean by virtue of my appearance and early conditioning, but I am also happily Canadian and want to take full advantage of all that such citizenship confers.

But for now I remain slightly distant from both cultures, accepted fully by neither. The hyphenated Canadian personifies the ideal of multiculturalism, but unless the host culture and the immigrant cultures can find ways to merge their distinct identities, sharing the best of both, this cultural schizophrenia will continue.

AUDIENCE AND PURPOSE

1. What point does Yi make about being a "hyphenated Canadian"?
2. In what way is the hyphenated term "Korean-Canadian" an apt one to describe Yi's existence in Canada?
3. What in Yi's experience demonstrates the need to merge two identities? Why is such merging difficult to achieve?

CONTENT

1. Find examples of the cultural differences between Koreans and Canadians in Yi's essay.
2. How, according to Yi, do some Canadians view Korean immigrants? What stereotypes come into play?
3. Why did Yi's boss in "little Korea" reject Canadianized Koreans like Yi?
4 Why does the split personality approach that Yi masters as a child not work when she becomes an adult?

STYLE AND STRUCTURE

1. How does Yi use detail to conjure up her childhood experiences for the reader?

2. The experience of working in "little Korea" that ends the piece emphasizes the problems that Yi encounters as a woman. Discuss her examples.
3. At first the notion of two identities seems innocent, but by the end, the author calls it "cultural schizophrenia." How does the notion of the split personality become more intolerable as the essay progresses?

Drew Hayden Taylor

Drew Hayden Taylor (b. 1962) was born on the Curve Lake Reserve in Ontario. He is a writer, director, and journalist in theatre, on radio, on television, and in the press. His best-known work is one-act plays, among them *Toronto at Dreamer's Rock* (1990) and *Education Is Our Right* (1990). He has also written a full-length play entitled *The Bootlegger Blues* (1991). Taylor is known for his humour and for his use of elements of traditional Native storytelling.

PRETTY LIKE A WHITE BOY: THE ADVENTURES OF A BLUE EYED OJIBWAY

In this big, huge world, with all its billions and billions of people, it's safe to say that everybody will eventually come across personalities and individuals that will touch them in some peculiar yet poignant way. Individuals that in some way represent and help define who you are. I'm no different, mine was Kermit the Frog. Not just because Natives have a long tradition of savouring Frogs' legs, but because of his music. If you all may remember, Kermit is quite famous for his rendition of "It's Not Easy Being Green." I can relate. If I could sing, my song would be "It's Not Easy Having Blue Eyes in a Brown Eyed Village."

Yes, I'm afraid it's true. The author happens to be a card-carrying Indian. Once you get past the aforementioned eyes, the fair skin, light brown hair, and noticeable lack of cheekbones, there lies the heart and spirit of an Ojibway storyteller. Honest Injun, or as the more politically correct term may be, honest aboriginal.

You see, I'm the product of a white father I never knew, and an Ojibway woman who evidently couldn't run fast enough. As a kid I knew I looked a bit different. But, then again, all kids are paranoid when it comes to their peers. I had a fairly happy childhood, frolicking through the bullrushes. But there were certain things that, even then, made me notice my unusual appearance. Whenever we played cowboys and Indians, guess who had to be the bad guy, the cowboy.

It wasn't until I left the Reserve for the big bad city, that I became more aware of the role people expected me to play, and the fact that physically I didn't fit in. Everybody seemed to have this preconceived idea of how every Indian looked and acted. One guy, on my first day of college, asked me what kind of horse I preferred. I didn't have the heart to tell him "hobby."

5 I've often tried to be philosophical about the whole thing. I have both white and red blood in me, I guess that makes me pink. I am a "Pink" man. Try to imagine this, I'm walking around on any typical Reserve in Canada, my head held high, proudly announcing to everyone "I am a Pink Man." It's a good thing I ran track in school.

My pinkness is constantly being pointed out to me over and over and over again. "You don't look Indian?" "You're not Indian, are you?" "Really?!?" I got questions like that from both white and Native people, for a while I debated having my Status card tattooed on my forehead.

And like most insecure people and specially a blue eyed Native writer, I went through a particularly severe identity crisis at one point. In fact, I admit it, one depressing spring evening, I dyed my hair black. Pitch black.

The reason for such a dramatic act, you may ask? Show Business. You see, for the last eight years or so, I've worked in various capacities in the performing arts, and as a result I'd always get calls to be an extra or even try out for an important role in some Native oriented movie. This anonymous voice would phone, having been given my number, and ask if I would be interested in trying out for a movie. Being a naturally ambitious, curious, and greedy young man, I would always readily agree, stardom flashing in my eyes and hunger pains from my wallet.

A few days later I would show up for the audition, and that was always an experience. What kind of experience you may ask? Picture this, the picture calls for the casting of seventeenth-century Mohawk warriors living in a traditional longhouse. The casting director calls the name "Drew Hayden Taylor" and I enter.

10 The casting director, the producer, and the film's director look up from the table and see my face, blue eyes flashing in anticipation. I once was described as a slightly chubby beachboy. But even beachboys have tans. Anyway, there would be a quick flush of confusion, a recheck of the papers, and a hesitant "Mr. Taylor?" Then they would ask if I was at the right audition. It was always the same. By the way, I never got any of the parts I tried for, except for a few anonymous crowd shots. Politics tells me it's because of the way I look, reality tells me it's probably because I can't act. I'm not sure which is better.

It's not just film people either. Recently I've become quite involved in Theatre, Native theatre to be exact. And one cold October day I was happily attending the Toronto leg of a province-wide tour of my first play, *Toronto at Dreamer's Rock*. The place was sold out, the audience very receptive and the performance was wonderful. Ironically one of the actors was also half white.

The director later told me he had been talking with the actor's father, an older Non-Native type chap. Evidently he had asked a few questions about me, and how I did my research. This made the director curious and he asked about his interest. He replied "He's got an amazing grasp of the Native situation for a white person."

Not all these incidents are work related either. One time a friend and I were coming out of a rather upscale bar (we were out YUPPIE watching) and managed to catch a cab. We thanked the cab driver for being so comfortably close on such a cold night, he shrugged and nonchalantly talked about knowing what bars to drive around. "If you're not careful, all you'll get is drunk Indians." I hiccuped.

Another time this cab driver droned on and on about the government. He started out by criticizing Mulroney, and eventually to his handling of the Oka crisis. This perked up my ears, until he said "If it were me, I'd have tear-gassed the place by the second day. No more problem." He got a dime tip. A few incidents like this and I'm convinced I'd make a great undercover agent for one of the Native political organizations.

15 But then again, even Native people have been known to look at me with a fair amount of suspicion. Many years ago when I was a young man, I was working on a documentary on Native culture up in the wilds of Northern Ontario. We were at an isolated cabin filming a trapper woman and her kids. This one particular nine-year-old girl seemed to take a shine to me. She followed me around for two days both annoying me and endearing herself to me. But she absolutely refused to believe that I was Indian. The whole film crew tried to tell her but to no avail. She was certain I was white.

Then one day as I was loading up the car with film equipment, she asked me if I wanted some tea. Being in a hurry I declined the tea. She immediately smiled with victory crying out "See, you're not Indian, all Indians drink tea!"

Frustrated and a little hurt I whipped out my Status card and thrust it at her. Now there I was, standing in a Northern Ontario winter, showing my Status card to a nine-year-old non-status Indian girl who had no idea what one was. Looking back, this may not have been one of my brighter moves.

But I must admit, it was a Native woman that boiled everything down in one simple sentence. You may know that woman, Marianne Jones from "The Beachcombers" television series. We were working on a film together out west and we got to gossiping. Eventually we got around to talking about our respective villages. Hers on the Queen Charlotte Islands, or Haida Gwaii as the Haida call them, and mine in central Ontario.

Eventually childhood on the Reserve was being discussed and I made a comment about the way I look. She studied me for a moment, smiled, and said "Do you know what the old women in my village would call you?" Hesitant but curious, I shook my head. "They'd say you were pretty like a white boy." To this day I'm still not sure if I like that.

20 Now some may argue that I am simply a Métis with a Status card. I disagree, I failed French in grade 11. And the Métis as everyone knows have their own separate and honourable culture, particularly in western Canada. And of course I am well aware that I am not the only person with my physical characteristics.

I remember once looking at a video tape of a drum group, shot on a Reserve up near Manitoulin Island. I noticed one of the drummers seemed quite fairhaired, almost blond. I mentioned this to my girlfriend of the time and she shrugged saying "Well, that's to be expected. The highway runs right through the Reserve."

Perhaps I'm being too critical. There's a lot to be said for both cultures. For example, on the left hand, you have the Native respect for Elders. They understand the concept of wisdom and insight coming with age.

On the white hand, there's Italian food. I mean I really love my mother and family but seriously, does anything really beat good Veal Scallopini? Most of my aboriginal friends share my fondness for this particular brand of food. Wasn't there a warrior at Oka named Lasagna? I found it ironic, though curiously logical, that Columbus was Italian. A connection I wonder?

Also Native people have this wonderful respect and love for the land. They believe they are part of it, a mere chain in the cycle of existence. Now, as many of you know, this conflicts with the accepted Judeo-Christian i.e. western view of land management. I even believe somewhere in the first chapters of the Bible it says something about God giving man dominion over Nature. Check it out, Genesis 4:?, "Thou shalt clear cut." So I grew up understanding that everything around me is important and alive. My Native heritage gave me that.

25 And again, on the white hand, there's breast implants. Darn clever them white people. That's something Indians would never have invented, seriously. We're not ambitious enough. We just take what the Creator decides to give us, but no, not the

white man. Just imagine it, some serious looking white man, and let's face it people, we know it was a man who invented them, don't we? So just imagine some serious looking white doctor sitting around in his laboratory muttering to himself, "Big tits, big tits, hmm, how do I make big tits?" If it was an Indian, it would be "Big tits, big tits, white women sure got big tits" and leave it at that.

So where does that leave me on the big philosophical scoreboard, what exactly are my choices again; Indians — respect for elders, love of the land. White people — food and big tits. In order to live in both cultures I guess I'd have to find an Indian woman with big tits who lives with her grandmother in a cabin out in the woods and can make Fettuccini Alfredo on a wood stove.

Now let me make this clear, I'm not writing this for sympathy, or out of anger, or even some need for self-glorification. I am just setting the facts straight. For as you read this, a new Nation is born. This is a declaration of independence, my declaration of independence.

I've spent too many years explaining who and what I am repeatedly, so as of this moment, I officially secede from both races. I plan to start my own separate nation. Because I am half Ojibway, and half Caucasian, we will be called the Occasions. And I of course, since I'm founding the new nation, will be a Special Occasion.

AUDIENCE AND PURPOSE

1. This essay is personal, but it does have an implicit point. Explain what Taylor's point is.
2. Why does Taylor use humour to make his point?
3. In some ways this could be called an essay of self-definition. How does Taylor accomplish this purpose?

CONTENT

1. How does the author feel about belonging neither to the white community nor to the Native community?
2. How does Taylor deal with the stereotypes associated with Native people?
3. What is the role of show business in maintaining stereotypes of Native people?
4. What is the legacy of Native culture for Taylor?

STYLE AND STRUCTURE

1. How does Taylor use stereotypes as the basis for some of his humour?
2. How does Taylor poke fun at the pretensions of white people?
3. Why is the declaration of independence in the conclusion both humorous and poignant?

Eva Hoffman

Eva Hoffman (b. 1945) was born in Poland, and her family immigrated to Canada when she was 14. She completed a PhD in English at Harvard University and now works as an editor for *The New York Times*. Hoffman has written an autobiography, *Lost in Translation* (1989), and *Exit into History: A Journey through the New Eastern Europe* (1993).

LOST IN TRANSLATION

Every day I learn new words, new expressions. I pick them up from school exercises, from conversations, from the books I take out of Vancouver's well-lit, cheerful public library. There are some turns of phrase to which I develop strange allergies. "You're welcome," for example, strikes me as a gaucherie, and I can hardly bring myself to it—I suppose because it implies that there's something to be thanked for, which in Polish would be impolite. The very places where the language is at its most conventional, where it should be most taken for granted, are the places where I feel the prick of artifice.

Then there are words to which I take an equally irrational liking, for their sound, or just because I'm pleased to have deduced their meaning. Mainly they're words I learn from books, like "enigmatic" or "insolent"—words that have only a literary value, that exist only as signs on the page.

But mostly, the problem is that the signifier has become severed from the signified. The words I learn now don't stand for things in the same unquestioned way they did in my native tongue. "River" in Polish was a vital sound, energized with the essence of riverhood, of my rivers, of my being immersed in rivers. "River" in English is cold—a word without an aura. It has no accumulated associations for me, and it does not give off the radiating haze of connotation. It does not evoke.

The process, alas, works in reverse as well. When I see a river now, it is not shaped, assimilated by the word that accommodates it to the psyche—a word that makes a body of water a river rather than an uncontained element. The river before me remains a thing, absolutely other, absolutely unbending to the grasp of my mind.

5 When my friend Penny tells me that she's envious, or happy, or disappointed, I try laboriously to translate not from English to Polish but from the word back to its source, to the feeling from which it springs. Already, in that moment of strain, spontaneity

of response is lost. And anyway, the translation doesn't work. I don't know how Penny feels when she talks about envy. The word hangs in a Platonic stratosphere, a vague prototype of all envy so large, so all-encompassing that it might crush me—as might disappointment or happiness.

I am becoming a living avatar of structuralist wisdom; I cannot help knowing that words are just themselves. But it's a terrible knowledge, without any of the consolations that wisdom usually brings. It does not mean that I'm free to play with words at my wont; anyway, words in their naked state are surely among the least satisfactory play objects. No, this radical disjoining between word and thing is a desiccating alchemy, draining the world not only of significance but of its colors, striations, nuances—its very existence. It is the loss of a living connection.

The worst losses come at night. As I lie down in a strange bed in a strange house—my mother is a sort of housekeeper here, to the aging Jewish man who has taken us in return for her services—I wait for that spontaneous flow of inner language which used to be my nighttime talk with myself, my way of informing the ego where the id had been. Nothing comes. Polish, in a short time, has atrophied, shriveled from sheer uselessness. Its words don't apply to my new experiences; they're not coeval with any of the objects, or faces, or the very air I breathe in the daytime. In English, words have not penetrated to those layers of my psyche from which a private conversation could proceed. This interval before sleep used to be the time when my mind became both receptive and alert, when images and words rose up to consciousness, reiterating what had happened during the day, adding the day's experiences to those already stored there, spinning out the thread of my personal story.

Now, this picture-and-word show is gone; the thread has been snapped. I have no interior language, and without it, interior images—those images through which we assimilate the external world, through which we take it in, love it, make it our own—become blurred too. My mother and I met a Canadian family who live down the block today. They were working in their garden and engaged us in a conversation of the "Nice weather we're having, isn't it?" variety, which culminated in their inviting us into their house. They sat stiffly on their couch, smiled in the long pauses between the conversation, and seemed at a loss for what to ask. Now my mind gropes for some description of them, but nothing fits. They're a different species from anyone I've met in Poland, and Polish words slip off them without sticking. English words don't hook on to anything. I try, deliberately, to come up with a few. Are these people pleasant or dull? Kindly or silly? The words float in an uncertain space. They come up from a part of my brain in which labels may be manufactured but which has no connection to my instincts, quick reactions, knowledge. Even the simplest adjectives sow confusion in my mind; English kindliness has a whole system of morality behind it, a system that makes "kindness" an entirely positive virtue. Polish kindness has the tiniest element of irony. Besides, I'm beginning to feel the tug of prohibition, in English, against uncharitable words. In Polish, you can call someone an idiot without particularly harsh feelings and with the zest of a strong judgment. Yes, in Polish these people might tend toward "silly" and "dull"—but I force myself toward "kindly" and "pleasant." The cultural unconscious is beginning to exercise its subliminal influence.

The verbal blur covers these people's faces, their gestures with a sort of fog. I can't translate them into my mind's eye. The small event, instead of being added to the mosaic of consciousness and memory, falls through some black hole, and I fall with it. What has happened to me in this new world? I don't know. I don't see what I've seen, don't comprehend what's in front of me. I'm not filled with language anymore, and I have only a memory of fullness to anguish me with the knowledge that, in this dark and empty state, I don't really exist.

10 For my birthday, Penny gives me a diary, complete with a little lock and key to keep what I write from the eyes of all intruders. It is that little lock—the visible symbol of the privacy in which the diary is meant to exist—that creates my dilemma. If I am indeed to write something entirely for myself, in what language do I write? Several times, I open the diary and close it again. I can't decide. Writing in Polish at this point would be a little like resorting to Latin or ancient Greek—an eccentric thing to do in a diary, in which you're supposed to set down your most immediate experiences and unpremeditated thoughts in the most unmediated language. Polish is becoming a dead language, the language of the untranslatable past. But writing for nobody's eyes in English? That's like doing a school exercise, or performing in front of yourself, a slightly perverse act of self-voyeurism.

Because I have to choose something, I finally choose English. If I'm to write about the present, I have to write in the language of the present, even if it's not the language of the self. As a result, the diary becomes surely one of the more impersonal exercises of that sort produced by an adolescent girl. These are no sentimental effusions of rejected love, eruptions of familial anger, or consoling broodings about death. English is not the language of such emotions. Instead, I set down my reflections on the ugliness of wrestling; on the elegance of Mozart, and on how Dostoyevsky puts me in mind of El Greco. I write down Thoughts. I Write.

There is a certain pathos to this naïve snobbery, for the diary is an earnest attempt to create a part of my persona that I imagine I would have grown into in Polish. In the solitude of this most private act, I write, in my public language, in order to update what might have been my other self. The diary is about me and not about me at all. But on one level, it allows me to make the first jump. I learn English through writing, and, in turn, writing gives me a written self. Refracted through the double distance of English and writing, this self—my English self—becomes oddly objective; more than anything, it perceives. It exists more easily in the abstract sphere of thoughts and observations than in the world. For a while, this impersonal self, this cultural negative capability, becomes the truest thing about me. When I write, I have a real existence that is proper to the activity of writing—an existence that takes place midway between me and the sphere of artifice, art, pure language. This language is beginning to invent another me. However, I discover something odd. It seems that when I write (or, for that matter, think) in English, I am unable to use the word "I." I do not go as far as the schizophrenic "she"—but I am driven, as by a compulsion, to the double, the Siamese-twin "you."

My voice is doing funny things. It does not seem to emerge from the same parts of my body as before. It comes out from somewhere in my throat, tight, thin, and mat—a voice without the modulations, dips, and rises that it had before, when it went from my stomach all the way through my head. There is, of course, the constraint and the self-consciousness of an accent that I hear but cannot control. Some of my high school peers accuse me of putting it on in order to appear more "interesting." In fact, I'd do anything to get rid of it, and when I'm alone, I practice sounds for which my speech organs have no intuitions, such as "th" (I do this by putting my tongue between my teeth) and "a," which is longer and more open in Polish (by shaping my mouth into a sort of arrested grin). It is simple words like "cat" or "tap" that give me the most trouble, because they have no context of other syllables, and so people often misunderstand them. Whenever I can, I do awkward little swerves to avoid them, or pause and try to say them very clearly. Still, when people — like salesladies — hear me speak without being prepared to listen carefully, they often don't understand me the first time around. "Girls' shoes," I say, and the "girls' " comes out as a sort of scramble. "Girls' shoes," I repeat, willing the syllable to form itself properly, and the saleslady usually smiles nicely, and sends my mother and me to the right part of the store. I say "Thank you" with a sweet smile, feeling as if I'm both claiming an unfair special privilege and being unfairly patronized.

It's as important to me to speak well as to play a piece of music without mistakes. Hearing English distorted grates on me like chalk screeching on a blackboard, like all things botched and badly done, like all forms of gracelessness. The odd thing is that I know what is correct, fluent, good, long before I can execute it. The English spoken by our Polish acquaintances strikes me as jagged and thick, and I know that I shouldn't imitate it. I'm turned off by the intonations I hear on the TV sitcoms — by the expectation of laughter, like a dog's tail wagging in supplication, built into the actors' pauses, and by the curtailed, cutoff rhythms. I like the way Penny speaks, with an easy flow and a pleasure in giving words a fleshly fullness; I like what I hear in some movies; and once the Old Vic comes to Vancouver to perform *Macbeth*, and though I can hardly understand the particular words, I am riveted by the tones of sureness and command that mold the actors' speech into such majestic periods.

15 Sociolinguists might say that I receive these language messages as class signals, that I associate the sounds of correctness with the social status of the speaker. In part, this is undoubtedly true. The class-linked notion that I transfer wholesale from Poland is that belonging to a "better" class of people is absolutely dependent on speaking a "better" language. And in my situation especially, I know that language will be a crucial instrument, that I can overcome the stigma of my marginality, the weight of presumption against me, only if the reassuringly right sounds come out of my mouth.

Yes, speech is a class signifier. But I think that in hearing these varieties of speech around me, I'm sensitized to something else as well — something that is a matter of aesthetics, and even of psychological health. Apparently, skilled chefs can tell whether a dish from some foreign cuisine is well cooked even if they have never tasted it and don't know the genre of cooking it belongs to. There seem to be some deep-structure qualities — consistency proportions of ingredients, smoothness of blending — that indicate culinary achievement to these educated eaters' taste buds. So each language has its own distinctive music, and even if one doesn't know its separate components, one can pretty quickly recognize the propriety of the patterns in which the components are put together, their harmonies and discords. Perhaps the crucial element that strikes the ear in listening to living speech is the degree of the speaker's self-assurance and control.

As I listen to people speaking that foreign tongue, English, I can hear when they stumble or repeat the same phrases too many times, when their sentences trail off aimlessly—or, on the contrary, when their phrases have vigor and roundness, when they have the space and the breath to give a flourish at the end of a sentence, or make just the right pause before coming to a dramatic point. I can tell, in other words, the degree of their ease or disease, the extent of authority that shapes the rhythms of their speech. That authority—in whatever dialect, in whatever variant of the mainstream language—seems to me to be something we all desire. It's not that we all want to speak the King's English, but whether we speak Appalachian or Harlem English, or Cockney, or Jamaican Creole, we want to be at home in our tongue. We want to be able to give voice accurately and fully to ourselves and our sense of the world. John Fowles, in one of his stories in *The Ebony Tower* has a young man cruelly violate an elderly writer and his manuscripts because the legacy of language has not been passed on to the youthful vandal properly. This seems to me an entirely credible premise. Linguistic dispossession is a sufficient motive for violence, for it is close to the dispossession of one's self. Blind rage, helpless rage is rage that has no words—rage that overwhelms one with darkness. And if one is perpetually without words, if one exists in the entropy of inarticulateness, that condition itself is bound to be an enraging frustration. In my New York apartment, I listen almost nightly to fights that erupt like brushfire on the street below—and in their escalating fury of repetitious phrases ("Don't do this to me, man, you fucking bastard, I'll fucking kill you"), I hear not the pleasures of macho toughness but an infuriated beating against wordlessness, against the incapacity to make oneself understood, seen. Anger can be borne—it can even be satisfying—if it can gather into words and explode in a storm, or a rapier-sharp attack. But without this means of ventilation, it only turns back inward, building and swirling like a head of steam—building to an impotent, murderous rage. If all therapy is speaking therapy—a talking cure—then perhaps all neurosis is a speech dis-ease.

VOCABULARY

gaucherie: awkwardness 1
artifice: device or trick 1
signifier/signified: the word/the thing to which it refers 3
aura: atmosphere 3
avatar: embodiment 6
structuralist: one who studies words as abstract entities 6
wont: habit 6
desiccating: drying up 6
alchemy: pseudoscience that sought to turn base metals into gold 6
striations: streaks 6
nuances: subtle details 6
atrophied: wasted 7
coeval: contemporary, of the same age 7
prohibition: ban 8
subliminal: unconscious 8
effusions: outpourings 11
negative capability: self-effacement 12
mat: unpolished, dull 13
curtailed: cut short 14
aesthetics: the study of beauty 16
dispossession: loss of home or security 17
entropy: steady disintegration 17

AUDIENCE AND PURPOSE

1. Why does Hoffman use the perspective of a young woman who has not mastered English, even though she is looking back in time?
2. What is the main point of the essay? How does it relate to the title?
3. Why does the author feel that she does not exist in this new language?

CONTENT

1. Why does Hoffman feel that translation is inadequate?
2. What are some of the cultural assumptions that a person's use of language reveals? How does Hoffman feel judged in her use of her new language?
3. Why is the choice of language in the diary a particularly baffling problem? Why do you suppose "I" is a difficult word for Hoffman to write though "you" is acceptable?
4. Why does Hoffman think speech is a "class signifier"?

STYLE AND STRUCTURE

1. In some ways Hoffman's command of language now belies her account of dispossession. How does her struggle to achieve fluency in language illustrate its psychological importance?
2. The author compares use of language with both music and food. How are these things related, in Hoffman's view?
3. In her conclusion, Hoffman speculates that all neurosis is "speech dis-ease." How has she shown this "dis-ease" in her account of childhood losses of language?

Rohinton Mistry

Rohintin Mistry (b. 1952) was born in Bombay, India, and immigrated to Canada in 1975. In 1985, he was awarded the Canadian Fiction Contributor's Prize. In 1987, *Tales from Firozsha Baag* was published, from which this excerpt is taken. His novel *Such a Long Journey* won the Governor General's Award in 1991. Since that time Mistry has published another novel, *A Fine Balance* (1995). His stories are strongly autobiographical and often reflect life in Bombay.

LEND ME YOUR LIGHT

> ... your lights are all lit—then where do you go with your lamp? My house is all dark and lonesome,—lend me your light.
>
> *Rabindranath Tagore*
> *Gitanjali*

We both left Bombay the same year. Jamshed first, for New York, then I, for Toronto. As immigrants in North America, sharing this common experience should have salvaged something from our acquaintanceship. It went back such a long way, to our school days at St Xavier's.

To sustain an acquaintance does not take very much. A friendship, that's another thing. Strange, then, that it has ended so completely, that he has erased himself out of our lives, mine and Percy's; now I cannot imagine him even as a mere bit player who fills out the action or swells a procession.

Jamshed was my brother's friend. The three of us went to the same school. Jamshed and my brother, Percy, both four years older than I, were in the same class, and spent their time together. They had to part company during lunch, though, because Jamshed did not eat where Percy and I did, in the school's drill-hall-cum-lunchroom.

The tiffin carriers would stagger into the school compound with their long, narrow rickety crates on their heads, each with fifty tiffin boxes, delivering lunches from homes in all corners of the city. When the boxes were unpacked, the drillhall would be filled with a smell that is hard to forget, thick as swill, while the aromas of four hundred steaming lunches started to mingle. The smell must have soaked into the very walls and ceiling, there to age and rancify. No matter what the hour of the day, that hot and dank grotto of a drillhall smelled stale and sickly, the way a vomit-splashed room does even after it is cleaned up.

Jamshed did not eat in this crammed and cavernous interior. Not for him the air redolent of nauseous odours. His food arrived precisely at one o'clock in the chauffeur-driven, air-conditioned family car, and was eaten in the leather-upholstered luxury of the back seat, amidst his collection of hyphenated lavishness.

In the snug dining-room where chauffeur doubled as waiter, Jamshed lunched through his school-days, safe from the vicissitudes of climate. The monsoon might drench the tiffin carriers to the bone and turn cold the boxes of four hundred waiting schoolboys, but it could not touch Jamshed or his lunch. The tiffin carriers might arrive glistening and stinking of sweat in the hot season, with scorching hot tiffin boxes, hotter than they'd left the kitchens of Bombay, but Jamshed's lunch remained unaffected.

During the years of high school, my brother, Percy, began spending many weekend afternoons at his friend's house at Malabar Hill. Formerly, these were the afternoons when we used to join Pesi *paadmaroo* and the others for our most riotous times in the compound, the afternoons that the adults of Firozsha Baag would await with dread, not knowing what new terrors Pesi had devised to unleash upon the innocent and the unsuspecting.

But Percy dropped all this for Jamshed's company. And when he returned from his visits, Mummy would commence the questioning: What did he eat? Was Jamshed's mother home? What did the two do all afternoon? Did they go out anywhere? And so on.

Percy did not confide in me very much in those days. Our lives intersected during the lunch routine only, which counted for very little. For a short while we had played cricket together with the boys of Firozsha Baag. Then he lost interest in that too. He refused to come when Daddy would take the whole gang to the Marine Dri *maidaan* on Sunday morning. And soon, like all younger brothers, I was seen mainly as a nuisance.

But my curiosity about Percy and Jamshed was satisfied by Mummy's interrogations. I knew that the afternoons were usually spent making model airplanes and listening to music. The airplanes were simple gliders in the early years; the records, mostly Mantovani and from Broadway shows. Later came more complex models with gasoline engines and remote control, and classical music from Bach and Poulenc.

The model-airplane kits were gifts from Jamshed's itinerant aunties and uncles, purchased during business trips to England or the U.S. Everyone except my brother and I seemed to have uncles and aunties smitten by wanderlust, and Jamshed's supply line from the western world guaranteed for him a steady diet of foreign clothes, shoes, and records.

One Saturday, Percy reported during question period that Jamshed had received the original soundtrack of *My Fair Lady*. This was sensational news. The LP was not available in Bombay, and a few privately imported or "smuggled" copies, brought in by people like Jamshed's relatives, were selling in the black market for two hundred rupees. I had seen the records displayed side by side with foreign perfumes, chocolates, and cheeses at the pavement stalls of smugglers along Flora Fountain.

Sometimes, these stalls were smashed up during police raids. I liked to imagine that one day a raid would occur as I was passing, and in the mêlée and chaos of the clash, *My Fair Lady* would fly through the air and land at my feet, unnoticed by anyone. Of course, there wasn't much I could have done with it following the miracle, because our old gramophone played only 78 rpms.

After strenuous negotiations in which Mummy, Percy, and I exhausted ourselves, Percy agreed to ask his friend if I could listen to the album. Arrangements were made. And the following Saturday we set off for Jamshed's house. From Firozsha Baag, the direction of Malabar Hill was opposite to the one we took to go to school every morning, and I was not familiar with the roads the bus travelled. The building had a marble lobby, and the lift zoomed us up smoothly to the tenth floor before I had time to draw breath. I was about to tell Percy that we needed one like this in Firozsha Baag, but the door opened. Jamshed welcomed us graciously, then wasted no time in putting the record on the turntable. After all, that was what I had come for.

15 The afternoon dragged by after the sound-track was finished. Bored, I watched them work on an airplane. The box said it was a Sopwith Camel. The name was familiar from the Biggles books Percy used to bring home. I picked up the lid and read dully that the aircraft had been designed by the British industrialist and aeronautical engineer, Thomas Octave Murdoch Sopwith, born 1888, and had been used during the First World War. Then followed a list of parts.

Later, we had lunch, and they talked. I was merely the kid brother, and nobody expected me to do much else but listen. They talked of school and the school library, of all the books that the library badly needed; and of the *ghatis* who were flooding the school of late.

In the particular version of reality we inherited, *ghatis* were always flooding places, they never just went there. *Ghatis* were flooding the banks, desecrating the sanctity of institutions, and taking up all the coveted jobs. *Ghatis* were even flooding the colleges and universities, a thing unheard of. Wherever you turned, the bloody *ghatis* were flooding the place.

With much shame I remember this word *ghati*. A suppurating sore of a word, oozing the stench of bigotry. It consigned a whole race to the mute roles of coolies and menials, forever unredeemable.

During one of our rare vacations to Matheran, as a child, I watched with detachment while a straining coolie loaded the family's baggage on his person. The big metal trunk was placed flat on his head, with the leather suitcase over it. The enormous hold-all was slung on his left arm, which he raised to steady the load on his head, and the remaining suitcase went in the right hand. It was all accomplished with much the same approach and consideration used in loading a cart or barrow—the main thing was balance, to avoid tipping over. This skeletal man then tottered off towards the train that would transport us to the little hill station. There, similar skeletal beings would be waiting with rickshaws. Automobiles were prohibited in Matheran, to preserve the pastoral purity of the place and the livelihood of the rickshawallas.

Many years later I found myself at the same hill station, a member of my college hikers' club, labouring up its slopes with a knapsack. Automobiles were still not permitted in Matheran, and every time a rickshaw sped by in a flurry of legs and wheels, we'd yell at the occupant ensconced within: "Capitalist pig! You bastard! Stop riding on your brother's back!" The bewildered passenger would lean forward for a moment, not quite understanding, then fall back into the cushioned comfort of the rickshaw.

But this type of smug socialism did not come till much later. First we had to reckon with school, school uniforms, brown paper covers for textbooks and exercise books, and the mad morning rush for the school bus. I remember how Percy used to rage and shout at our scrawny *ghaton* if the pathetic creature ever got in his way as she swept and mopped the floors. Mummy would proudly observe, "He has a temper just like Grandpa's." She would also discreetly admonish Percy, since this was in the days when it was becoming quite difficult to find a new *ghaton*, especially if the first one quit due to abuse from the scion of the family and established her reasons for quitting among her colleagues.

I was never sure why some people called them *ghatons* and others, *gungas*. I suppose the latter was intended to placate—the collective conferment of the name of India's sacred river balanced the occasions of harshness and ill-treatment. But the good old days, when you could scream at a *ghaton* and could kick her and hurl her down the steps, and expect her to show up for work next morning, had definitely passed.

After high school, Percy and Jamshed went to different colleges. If they met at all, it would be at concerts of the Bombay Chamber Orchestra. Along with a college friend, Navjeet, and some others, my brother organized a charitable agency that collected and distributed funds to destitute farmers in a small Maharashtrian village. The idea was to get as many of these wretched souls as possible out of the clutches of the village money-lenders.

Jamshed showed a very superficial interest in what little he knew about Percy's activities. Each time they met, he would start with how he was trying his best to get out of the country. "Absolutely no future in this stupid place," he said. "Bloody corruption everywhere. And you can't buy any of the things you want, don't even get to see a decent English movie. First chance I get, I'm going abroad. Preferably the U.S."

After a while, Percy stopped talking about his small village, and they only discussed the concert program or the soloist's performance that evening. Then their meetings at concerts ceased altogether because Percy now spent very little time in Bombay.

Jamshed did manage to leave. One day, he came to say good-bye. But Percy was away working in the small village: his charitable agency had taken on the task full time. Jamshed spoke to those of us who were home, and we all agreed that he was doing the right thing. There just weren't any prospects in this country; nothing could stop its downhill race towards despair and ruin.

My parents announced that I, too, was trying to emigrate, but to Canada, not the U.S. "We will miss him if he gets to go," they told Jamshed, "but for the sake of his own future, he must. There is a lot of opportunity in Toronto. We've seen advertisements in newspapers from England, where Canadian Immigration is encouraging people to go to Canada. Of course, they won't advertise in a country like India — who would want these bloody *ghatis* to come charging into their fine land? — but the office in New Delhi is holding interviews and selecting highly qualified applicants." In the clichés of our speech was reflected the cliché which the idea of emigration had turned into for so many. According to my parents, I would have no difficulty being approved, what with my education, and my westernized background, and my fluency in the English language.

And they were right. A few months later things were ready for my departure to Toronto.

VOCABULARY

tiffin: British term for a midday meal 4
swill: edible refuse used as food for swine 4
rancify: become rancid or stale 4
vicissitudes: hardships 6
itinerant: travelling 11
suppurating: oozing 18
coolies: low-paid unskilled workers, often from the East 18
menials: those who perform lowly tasks 18
ensconced: sheltered, settled 20
admonish: scold 21
scion: descendant, child 21

AUDIENCE AND PURPOSE

1. Why do you think Mistry chose the title for this essay?
2. How does the early account of lunch make the reader aware of class differences that the child himself does not comment on?
3. How does the mention of the *ghatis* fit into the author's account of life in India?

CONTENT

1. How does Mistry give us a sense of the social classes that could be distinguished in Bombay?
2. How does Mistry contrast himself and Jamshed (who both left Bombay in the same year)? How does Mistry show contrasting approaches to the problems of achieving one's goal in life?
3. How is the idea of immigration to Canada from India a cliché, in Mistry's estimation?

STYLE AND STRUCTURE

1. How does the accumulation of detail add authenticity to this autobiographical account?
2. Why does Mistry quote his parents' clichéd and biased speech at the end of the essay?
3. How does Mistry's essay use subtle details to reveal the powerful role of Westernized things in the life of Bombay?

Jan Wong

Jan Wong (b. 1952) is the Canadian-born Chinese author of *Red China Blues* (1997), from which this excerpt is taken, and a reporter and columnist for *The Globe and Mail.* She went to China in 1972 at the height of the Cultural Revolution. Her book is a memoir of the twelve years she spent living and working in mainland China.

JAN WONG WANTS TO SEE CANADIANS DE-HYPHENATE THEMSELVES

In 1880, a teenager from south China joined a team of coolies blasting tunnels through the Rocky Mountains. When the Canadian Pacific Railway was completed several years later, the American contractor reneged on his pledge to provide passage home.

Chang Hooie had a choice: spend his savings on a ticket home, or stay and work some more. He stayed, and I'm grateful.

Yesterday, on the final Canada Day of the century, I thought about Grandfather Chong and what it means to be a Canadian. And I don't mean a hyphenated Canadian.

Growing up in Montreal in the 1960s, I once called myself a Chinese-Canadian, perhaps because my classmates always asked where I was born.

5 Montreal, I'd reply.

Where were you *really* born? they'd persist.

The Montreal General, I'd say.

My Canadian-born parents encouraged a Chinese identity, giving me Chinese language and dance lessons. But I was a fake, hopeless at math and chemistry, a disaster at piano competitions.

Still, something stuck. At university, I majored in Asian studies. I even went to China. Oddly, the more Chinese I learned and the more history and culture I absorbed, the less Chinese I felt.

10 One day, an epiphany: I am Canadian.

I no longer hyphenate myself, for the same reason Peter Gzowski doesn't call himself a Polish-Canadian, or Elvis Stojko call himself a ... What is he anyway? (After much research, I found out he's a Hungarian-Slovenian-Canadian.)

To be sure, I'm often reminded of my otherness. But when someone praises my grasp of English, I always remember to return the compliment. In my local park, the other parents shun me, but the Filipina-Canadian and Jamaican-Canadian nannies always greet me.

Notice I hyphenate them. I think hyphenating is natural for the first generation, who are still rooted in the old country. It's optional for the second.

But by the third generation, we're definitely Canadian. When new immigrants cut in at Chinatown cash registers, I bark at them to get in line. It will only be a generation or two, I console myself, before their offspring become unassuming donut-eaters.

15 In a Toronto library, I once scanned the microfilm of the 1901 national census. When I finally spotted Grandfather Chong's name, I was so excited I dropped my quarters for the photocopier. Under race, it described him as "Y" for yellow, under religion, "a Confucian," under trade, "a laundryman." It also showed that he became a Canadian citizen in 1899, exactly 100 years ago.

I know the CPR paid Grandfather Chong half what it paid white workers. I know that my other three grandparents paid the head tax. I know that they couldn't vote until after the Second World War.

For my Aunt Ming, the first Chinese-Canadian woman to become an anesthetist, July 1 is "Chinese Humiliation Day." That's the day Ottawa passed the Chinese Immigration Act, a racial ban that stretched from 1923 to 1947.

To me, that's history. I remember only to ensure it doesn't happen to anyone else. Nor do I expect a head-tax refund. That was my grandparents' money, not mine. I'm just glad they came.

Canada's most precious contribution to the 20th century is that we look forward, not backward, and that we all want to live together. Unlike those in Somalia or Ireland or Kosovo, we needn't worry that our neighbour will kill us because of what our ancestors did to theirs 400 years ago.

20 Here, we eat our differences. Where else can you have Ethiopian one night, Armenian the next, Cambodian the third?

I'm not denying my ethnicity. I'm affirming it. I'm just one more piece of the mosaic.

Besides, China doesn't need one more person claiming to be Chinese. It already has 1.3 billion. Canada has only 30 million, and we're in grave danger of losing 6 million of them. We need every single one we can get.

VOCABULARY

coolies: low-paid unskilled workers, often from the East 1
epiphany: moment of realization, awakening 10

AUDIENCE AND PURPOSE

1. Why does Jan Wong argue that she is Canadian rather than Chinese-Canadian?
2. Why does she consider the last Canada Day of the century to be an appropriate moment to consider her identity?
3. In what sense does Wong consider identity partly a historical fact?

CONTENT

1. Why does Wong consider the hyphen a generational matter?
2. What stereotypes of the Chinese does Wong mention?
3. How is the Canadian mosaic related to Wong's sense of her ethnic identity?
4. Why does Wong include so much history?

STYLE AND STRUCTURE

1. How does Wong's use of language make the essay personal?
2. Why does Wong begin with a reference to a man whom she only later identifies as her grandfather?
3. Why does Wong end with a reference to Canada's own cultural identity crisis?

Jamaica Kincaid

Jamaica Kincaid was born in 1949 in Antigua. She left the island at the age of 17 and now lives in Vermont. Her status as an exile is the subject of much of her writing. Kincaid examines critically both the narrowness of life in her native Antigua and in materialistic and often ignorant North America.

A SMALL PLACE

If you go to Antigua as a tourist, this is what you will see. If you come by aeroplane, you will land at the V.C. Bird International Airport. Vere Cornwall (V.C.) Bird is the Prime Minister of Antigua. You may be the sort of tourist who would wonder why a Prime Minister would want an airport named after him — why not a school, why not a hospital, why not some great public monument? You are a tourist and you have not yet seen a school in Antigua, you have not yet seen the hospital in Antigua, you have not yet seen a public monument in Antigua. As your plane descends to land, you might say, What a beautiful island Antigua is — more beautiful than any of the other islands you have seen, and they were very beautiful, in their way, but they were much too green, much too lush with vegetation, which indicated to you, the tourist, that they got quite a bit of rainfall, and rain is the very thing that you, just now, do not want, for you are thinking of the hard and cold and dark and long days you spent working in North America (or, worse, Europe), earning some money so that you could stay in this place (Antigua) where the sun always shines and where the climate is deliciously hot and dry for the four to ten days you are going to be staying there; and since you are on your holiday, since you are a tourist, the thought of what it might be like for someone who had to live day in, day out in a place that suffers constantly from drought, and so has to watch carefully every drop of fresh water used (while at the same time surrounded by a sea and an ocean — the Caribbean Sea on one side, the Atlantic Ocean on the other), must never cross your mind.

You disembark from your plane. You go through customs. Since you are a tourist, a North American or European — to be frank, white — and not an Antiguan black returning to Antigua from Europe or North America with cardboard boxes of much needed cheap clothes and food for relatives, you move through customs swiftly, you move through customs with ease. Your bags are not searched. You emerge from customs into the hot, clean air: immediately you feel cleansed, immediately you feel blessed (which is to say special); you feel free. You see a man, a taxi driver; you ask him to take you to your destination; he quotes you a price. You immediately think that the price is in the local currency, for you are a tourist and you are familiar with these things (rates of exchange) and you feel even more free, for things seem so cheap, but then your driver ends by saying, "In U.S. currency." You may say, "Hmmmm, do you have a formal sheet that lists official prices and destinations?" Your driver obeys the law and shows you the sheet, and he apologises for the incredible mistake he has made in quoting you a price off the top of his head which is so vastly different (favouring him) from the one listed. You are driven to your hotel by this taxi driver in his taxi, a brand-new Japanese-made vehicle. The road on which you are travelling is a very bad road, very much in need of repair. You are feeling wonderful, so you say, "Oh, what a marvellous change these bad roads are from the splendid highways I am used to in North America." (Or, worse, Europe.) Your driver is reckless; he is a dangerous man who drives in the middle of the road when he thinks no other cars are coming in the opposite direction, passes other cars on blind curves that run uphill, drives at sixty miles an hour on narrow, curving roads when the road sign, a rusting, beat-up thing left over from colonial days, says 40 MPH. This might frighten you (you are on your holiday; you are a tourist); this might excite you (you are on your holiday; you are a tourist), though if you are from New York and take taxis you are used to this style of driving: most of the taxi drivers in New York are from places in the world like this. You are looking out the window (because you want to get your money's worth); you notice that all the cars you see are brand-new, or almost brand-new, and that they are all Japanese-made. There are no American cars in Antigua — no new ones, at any rate; none that were manufactured in the last ten years. You continue to look at the cars and you say to yourself, Why, they look brand-new, but they have an awful sound, like an old car — a very old, dilapidated car. How to account for that? Well, possibly it's because they use leaded gasoline in these brand-new cars whose engines were built to use non-leaded gasoline, but you musn't ask the person driving the car if this is so, because he or she has never heard of unleaded gasoline. You look closely at the car; you see that it's a model of a Japanese car that you might hesitate to buy; it's a model that's very expensive; it's a model that's quite impractical for a person who has to work as hard as you do and who watches every penny you earn so that you can afford this holiday you are on.

How do they afford such a car? And do they live in a luxurious house to match such a car? Well, no. You will be surprised, then, to see that most likely the person driving this brand-new car filled with the wrong gas lives in a house that, in comparison, is far beneath the status of the car; and if you were to ask why you would be told that the banks are encouraged by the government to make loans available for cars, but loans for houses not so easily available; and if you ask again why, you will be told that the two main car dealerships in Antigua are owned in part or outright by ministers in government. Oh, but you are on holiday and the sight of these brand-new cars driven by people who may or may not have really passed their driving test (there was once a scandal about driving licences for sale) would not really stir up these thoughts in you. You pass a building sitting in a sea of dust and you think, It's some latrines for people just passing by, but when you look again you see the building has written on it PIGOTT'S SCHOOL. You pass the hospital, the Holberton Hospital, and how wrong you are not to think about this, for though you are a tourist on your holiday, what if your heart should miss a few beats? What if a blood vessel in your neck should break? What if one of those people driving those brand-new cars filled with the wrong gas fails to pass safely while going uphill on a curve and you are in the car going in the opposite direction? Will you be comforted to know that the hospital is staffed with doctors that no actual Antiguan trusts; that Antiguans always say about the doctors, "I don't want them near me"; that Antiguans refer to them not as doctors but as "the three men" (there are three of them); that when the Minister of Health himself doesn't feel well he takes the first plane to New York to see a real doctor; that if any one of the ministers in government needs medical care he flies to New York to get it?

It's a good thing that you brought your own books with you, for you couldn't just go to the library and borrow some. Antigua used to have a splendid library, but in The Earthquake (everyone talks about it that way—The Earthquake; we Antiguans, for I am one, have a great sense of things, and the more meaningful the thing, the more meaningless we make it) the library building was damaged. This was in 1974, and soon after that a sign was placed on the front of the building saying, THIS BUILDING WAS DAMAGED IN THE EARTHQUAKE OF 1974. REPAIRS ARE PENDING. The sign hangs there, and hangs there more than a decade later, with its unfulfilled promise of repair, and you might see this as a sort of quaintness on the part of these islanders, these people descended from slaves—what a strange, unusual perception of time they have. REPAIRS ARE PENDING, and here it is many years later, but perhaps in a world that is twelve miles long and nine miles wide (the size of Antigua) twelve years and twelve minutes and twelve days are all the same. The library is one of those splendid old buildings from colonial times, and the sign telling of the repairs is a splendid old sign from colonial times. Not very long after The Earthquake Antigua got its independence from Britain, making Antigua a state in its own right, and Antiguans are so proud of this that each year, to mark the day, they go to church and thank God, a British God, for this. But you should not think of the confusion that must lie in all that and you must not think of the damaged library. You have brought your own books with you, and among them is one of those new books about economic history, one of those books explaining how the West (meaning Europe and North America after its conquest and settlement by Europeans) got rich: the West got rich not from the free (free—in this case meaning got-for-nothing) and then undervalued labour, for generations, of the people like me you see walking around you in Antigua but from the ingenuity of small shopkeepers in Sheffield and Yorkshire and Lancashire, or wherever; and what a great part the invention of the wristwatch played in it, for there was nothing noble-minded men could not do when they discovered they could slap time on their wrists just like that (isn't that the last straw; for not only did we have to suffer the unspeakableness of slavery, but the satisfaction to be had from "We made you bastards rich" is taken away, too), and so you needn't let that slightly funny feeling you have from time to time about exploitation, oppression, domination develop into full-fledged unease, discomfort; you could ruin your holiday. They are not responsible for what you have; you owe them nothing; in fact, you did them a big favour, and you can provide one hundred examples. For here you are now, passing by Government House. And here you are now, passing by the Prime Minister's Office and the Parliament Building, and overlooking these, with a splendid view of St. John's Harbour, the American Embassy. If it were not for you, they would not have Government House, and Prime Minister's Office, and Parliament Building and embassy of powerful country. Now you are passing a mansion, an extraordinary house painted the colour of old cow dung, with more aerials and antennas attached to it than you will see even at the American Embassy. The people who live in this house are a merchant family who came to Antigua from the Middle East less than twenty years ago. When this family first came to Antigua, they sold dry goods door to door from suitcases they carried on their backs. Now they own a lot of Antigua; they regularly lend money to the government, they build enormous (for Antigua), ugly (for Antigua), concrete buildings in Antigua's capital, St. John's, which the government then rents for huge sums of money; a member of their family is the Antiguan Ambassador to Syria; Antiguans hate them. Not far from this mansion is another mansion, the home of a drug smuggler. Everybody knows he's a drug smuggler, and if just as you were driving by he stepped out of his door your driver might point him out to you as the notorious person that he is, for this drug smuggler is so rich people say he buys cars in tens — ten of this one, ten of that one — and that he bought a house (another mansion) near Five Islands, contents included, with cash he carried in a suitcase: three hundred and fifty thousand American dollars, and, to the surprise of the seller of the house, lots of American dollars were left over. Overlooking the drug smuggler's mansion is yet another mansion, and leading up to it is the best paved road in all of Antigua — even better than the road that was paved for the Queen's visit in 1985 (when the Queen came, all the roads that she would travel on were paved anew, so that the Queen might have been left with the impression that riding in a car in Antigua was a pleasant experience). In this mansion lives a woman sophisticated people in Antigua call Evita. She is a notorious woman. She's young and beautiful and the girlfriend of somebody very high up in the government. Evita is notorious because her relationship with this high government official has made her the owner of boutiques and property and given her a say in cabinet meetings, and all sorts of other privileges such a relationship would bring a beautiful young woman.

Oh, but by now you are tired of all this looking, and you want to reach your destination — your hotel, your room. You long to refresh yourself; you long to eat some nice lobster, some nice local food. You take a bath, you brush your teeth. You get dressed again; as you get dressed, you look out the window. That water — have you ever seen anything like it? Far out, to the horizon, the colour of the water is navy-blue; nearer, the water is the colour of the North American sky. From there to the shore, the water is pale, silvery, clear, so clear that you can see its pinkish-white sand bottom. Oh, what beauty! Oh, what beauty! You have never seen anything like this. You are so excited. You breathe shallow. You breathe deep. You see a beautiful boy skimming the water, godlike, on a Windsurfer. You see an incredibly unattractive, fat, pastrylike-fleshed woman enjoying a walk on the beautiful sand, with a man, an incredibly unattractive, fat, pastrylike-fleshed man; you see the pleasure they're taking in their surroundings. Still standing, looking out the window, you see yourself lying on the beach, enjoying the amazing sun (a sun so powerful and yet so beautiful, the way it is always overhead as if on permanent guard, ready to stamp out any cloud that dares to darken and so empty rain on you and ruin your holiday; a sun that is your personal friend). You see yourself taking a walk on that beach, you see yourself meeting new people (only they are new in a very limited way, for they are people just like you). You see yourself eating some delicious, locally grown food. You see yourself, you see yourself... You must not wonder what exactly happened to the contents of your lavatory when you flushed it. You must not wonder where your bathwater went when you pulled out the stopper. You must not wonder what happened when you brushed your teeth. Oh, it might all end up in the water you are thinking of taking a swim in; the contents of your lavatory might, just might, graze gently against your ankle as you wade carefree in the water, for you see, in Antigua, there is no proper sewage-disposal system. But the Caribbean Sea is very big and the Atlantic Ocean is even bigger; it would amaze even you to know the number of black slaves this ocean has swallowed up. When you sit down to eat your delicious meal, it's better that you don't know that most of what you are eating came off a plane from Miami. And before it got on a plane in Miami, who knows where it came from? A good guess is that it came from a place like Antigua first, where it was grown dirt-cheap, went to Miami, and came back. There is a world of something in this, but I can't go into it right now.

5 The thing you have always suspected about yourself the minute you become a tourist is true: A tourist is an ugly human being. You are not an ugly person all the time; you are not an ugly person ordinarily; you are not an ugly person day to day. From day to day, you are a nice person. From day to day, all the people who are supposed to love you on the whole do. From day to day, as you walk down a busy street in the large and modern and prosperous city in which you work and live, dismayed, puzzled (a cliché, but only a cliché can explain you) at how alone you feel in this crowd, how awful it is to go unnoticed, how awful it is to go unloved, even as you are surrounded by more people than you could possibly get to know in a lifetime that lasted for millennia, and then out of the corner of your eye you see someone looking at you and absolute pleasure is written all over that person's face, and then you realise that you are not as revolting a presence as you think you are (for that look just told you so).

And so, ordinarily, you are a nice person, an attractive person, a person capable of drawing to yourself the affection of other people (people just like you), a person at home in your own skin (sort of; I mean, in a way; I mean, your dismay and puzzlement are natural to you, because people like you just seem to be like that, and so many of the things people like you find admirable about yourselves—the things you think about, the things you think really define you—seem rooted in these feelings): a person at home in your own house (and all its nice house things), with its nice back yard (and its nice back-yard things), at home on your street, your church, in community activities, your job, at home with your family, your relatives, your friends—you are a whole person. But one day, when you are sitting somewhere, alone in that crowd, and that awful feeling of displacedness comes over you, and really, as an ordinary person you are not well equipped to look too far inward and set yourself aright, because being ordinary is already so taxing, and being ordinary takes all you have out of you, and though the words "I must get away" do not actually pass across your lips, you make a leap from being that nice blob just sitting like a boob in your amniotic sac of the modern experience to being a person visiting heaps of death and ruin and feeling alive and inspired at the sight of it; to being a person lying on some faraway beach, your stilled body stinking and glistening in the sand, looking like something first forgotten, then remembered, then not important enough to go back for; to being a person marvelling at the harmony (ordinarily, what you would say is the backwardness) and the union these other people (and they are other people) have with nature. And you look at the things they can do with a piece of ordinary cloth, the things they fashion out of cheap, vulgarly colored (to you) twine, the way they squat down over a hole they have made in the ground, the hole itself is something to marvel at, and since you are being an ugly person this ugly but joyful thought will swell inside you: their ancestors were not clever in the way yours were and not ruthless in the way yours were, for then would it not be you who would be in harmony with nature and backwards in that charming way? An ugly thing, that is what you are when you become a tourist, an ugly, empty thing, a stupid thing, a piece of rubbish pausing here and there to gaze at this and taste that, and it will never occur to you that the people who inhabit the place in which you have just paused cannot stand you, that behind their closed doors they laugh at your strangeness (you do not look the way they look); the physical sight of you does not please them; you have bad manners (it is their custom to eat their food with their hands; you try eating their way, you look silly; you try eating the way you always eat, you look silly); they do not like the way you speak (you have an accent); they collapse helpless from laughter, mimicking the way they imagine you must look as you carry out some everyday bodily function. They do not like you. *They do not like me!* That thought never actually occurs to you. Still, you feel a little uneasy. Still, you feel a little foolish. Still, you feel a little out of place. But the banality of your own life is very real to you; it drove you to this extreme, spending your days and your nights in the company of people who despise you, people you do not like really, people you would not want to have as your actual neighbour. And so you must devote yourself to puzzling out how much of what you are told is really, really true (Is ground-up bottle glass in peanut sauce really a delicacy around here, or will it do just what you think ground-up bottle glass will do? Is this rare, multicoloured, snout-mouthed fish really an aphrodisiac, or will it cause you to fall asleep permanently?). Oh, the hard work all of this is, and is it any wonder, then, that on your return home you feel the need of a long rest, so that you can recover from your life as a tourist?

That the native does not like the tourist is not hard to explain. For every native of every place is a potential tourist, and every tourist is a native of somewhere. Every native everywhere lives a life of overwhelming and crushing banality and boredom and desperation and depression, and every deed, good and bad, is an attempt to forget this. Every native would like to find a way out, every native would like a rest, every native would like a tour. But some natives—most natives in the world—cannot go anywhere. They are too poor. They are too poor to go anywhere. They are too poor to escape the reality of their lives; and they are too poor to live properly in the place where they live, which is the very place you, the tourist, want to go—so when the natives see you, the tourist, they envy you, they envy your ability to leave your own banality and boredom, they envy your ability to turn their own banality and boredom into a source of pleasure for yourself.

VOCABULARY

latrines: bathrooms 2
cliché: expression that has become meaningless from repetition 5
banality: ordinary dullness 5
aphrodisiac: drug that increases one's sexual desire 5

AUDIENCE AND PURPOSE

1. Why does Kincaid use the pronoun "you" throughout the essay?
2. How does the bitterness grow as the essay develops? Give examples.
3. Why does Kincaid write about the ugly tourist to readers who are likely themselves tourists?

CONTENT

1. What do you find out about the cars on the island?
2. What do you find out about the hospital on Antigua?
3. How does Kincaid contrast the appearance of the sea with its function?
4. Kincaid insists through repetition on how ugly the tourist is. Why?

STYLE AND STRUCTURE

1. Why does Kincaid write such long sentences?
2. What is the effect of parentheses throughout the essay?
3. Why does Kincaid trace the history of Antigua through the tourist's eyes from arrival at the airport to discoveries made on the journey?
4. Why is there so much repetition of the word "poor" in the conclusion?

Richard Rodriguez

Richard Rodriguez (b. 1944) has written for major American magazines and journals, and he appears on *The News Hour with Jim Lehrer* on PBS. He has written two books, one an autobiography, *Hunger of Memory: The Education of Richard Rodriguez* (1981). His second book, *Days of Obligation* (1992), was a finalist for the Pulitzer Prize.

ARIA

Supporters of bilingual education today imply that students like me miss a great deal by not being taught in their family's language. What they seem not to recognize is that, as a socially disadvantaged child, I considered Spanish to be a private language. What I needed to learn in school was that I had the right—and the obligation—to speak the public language of *los gringos*. The odd truth is that my first-grade classmates could have become bilingual, in the conventional sense of that word, more easily than I. Had they been taught (as upper-middle-class children are often taught early) a second language like Spanish or French, they could have regarded it simply as that: another public language. In my case such bilingualism could not have been so quickly achieved. What I did not believe was that I could speak a single public language.

Without question, it would have pleased me to hear my teachers address me in Spanish when I entered the classroom. I would have felt much less afraid. I would have trusted them and responded with ease. But I would have delayed—for how long postponed?—having to learn the language of public society. I would have evaded—and for how long could I have afforded to delay?—learning the great lesson of school, that I had a public identity.

Fortunately, my teachers were unsentimental about their responsibility. What they understood was that I needed to speak a public language. So their voices would search me out, asking me questions. Each time I'd hear them, I'd look up in surprise to see a nun's face frowning at me. I'd mumble, not really meaning to answer. The nun would persist, "Richard, stand up. Don't look at the floor. Speak up. Speak to the entire class, not just to me!" But I couldn't believe that the English language was mine to use. (In part, I did not want to believe it.) I continued to mumble. I resisted the teacher's demands. (Did I somehow suspect that once I learned public language my pleasing family life would be changed?) Silent, waiting for the bell to sound, I remained dazed, diffident, afraid.

Because I wrongly imagined that English was intrinsically a public language and Spanish an intrinsically private one, I easily noted the difference between classroom language and the language of home. At school, words were directed to a general audience of listeners. ("Boys and girls.") Words were meaningfully ordered. And the point was not self-expression but to make oneself understood by many others. The teacher quizzed: "Boys and girls, why do we use that word in this sentence? Could we think of a better word to use there? Would the sentence change its meaning if the words were differently arranged? And wasn't there a better way of saying much the same thing?" (I couldn't say. I wouldn't try to say.)

5 Three months. Five. Half a year passed. Unsmiling, ever watchful, my teachers began to connect my behavior with the difficult progress my older sister and brother were making. Until one Saturday morning three nuns arrived at the house to talk to our parents. Stiffly, they sat on the blue living room sofa. From the doorway of another room, spying the visitors, I noted the incongruity—the clash of two worlds, the faces and voices of school intruding upon the familiar setting of home. I overheard one voice gently wondering, "Do your children speak only Spanish at home, Mrs. Rodriguez?" While another voice added, "That Richard especially seems so timid and shy."

That Rich-heard!

With great tact the visitors continued, "Is it possible for you and your husband to encourage your children to practice their English when they are home?" Of course, my parents complied. What would they not do for their children's well-being? And how could they have questioned the Church's authority which those women represented? In an instant, they agreed to give up the language (the sounds) that had revealed and accentuated our family's closeness. The moment after the visitors left, the change was observed. "*Ahora*, speak to us *en inglés*," my father and mother united to tell us.

At first, it seemed a kind of game. After dinner each night, the family gathered to practice "our" English. (It was still then *inglés*, a language foreign to us, so we felt drawn as strangers to it.) Laughing, we would try to define words we could not pronounce. We played with strange English sounds, often overanglicizing our pronunciations. And we filled the smiling gaps of our sentences with familiar Spanish sounds. But that was cheating, somebody shouted. Everyone laughed. In school, meanwhile, like my brother and sister, I was required to attend a daily tutoring session. I needed a full year of special attention. I also needed my teachers to keep my attention from straying in class by calling out, *Rich-heard*—their English voices slowly prying loose my ties to my other name, its three notes, *Ri-car-do*. Most of all I needed to hear my mother and father speak to me in a moment of seriousness in broken—suddenly heartbreaking—English. The scene was inevitable: One Saturday morning I entered the kitchen where my parents were talking in Spanish. I did not realize that they were talking in Spanish however until, at the moment they saw me, I heard their voices change to speak English. Those *gringo* sounds they uttered startled me. Pushed me away. In that moment of trivial misunderstanding and profound insight, I felt my throat twisted by unsounded grief. I turned quickly and left the room. But I had no place to escape to with Spanish. (The spell was broken.) My brother and sisters were speaking English in another part of the house.

Again and again in the days following, increasingly angry, I was obliged to hear my mother and father: "Speak to us *en inglés*." (*Speak*.) Only then did I determine to learn classroom English. Weeks after, it happened: One day in school I raised my hand to volunteer an answer. I spoke out in a loud voice. And I did not think it remarkable when the entire class understood. That day, I moved very far from the disadvantaged child I had been only days earlier. The belief, that calming assurance that I belonged in public, had at last taken hold.

10 Shortly after, I stopped hearing the high and loud sounds of *los gringos*. A more and more confident speaker of English, I didn't trouble to listen to *how* strangers sounded, speaking to me. And there simply were too many English-speaking people in my day for me to hear American accents anymore. Conversations quickened. Listening to persons who sounded eccentrically pitched voices, I usually noted their sounds for an initial few seconds before I concentrated on *what* they were saying. Conversations became content-full. Transparent. Hearing someone's *tone* of voice—angry or questioning or sarcastic or happy or sad—I didn't distinguish it from the words it expressed. Sound and word were thus tightly wedded. At the end of a day, I was often bemused, always relieved, to realize how "silent," though crowded with words, my day in public had been. (This public silence measured and quickened the change in my life.)

At last, seven years old, I came to believe what had been technically true since my birth: I was an American citizen.

But the special feeling of closeness at home was diminished by then. Gone was the desperate, urgent, intense feeling of being at home; rare was the experience of feeling myself individualized by family intimates. We remained a loving family, but one greatly changed. No longer so close; no longer bound tight by the pleasing and troubling knowledge of our public separateness. Neither my older brother nor sister rushed home after school anymore. Nor did I. When I arrived home there would often be neighborhood kids in the house. Or the house would be empty of sounds.

Following the dramatic Americanization of their children, even my parents grew more publicly confident. Especially my mother. She learned the names of all the people on our block. And she decided we needed to have a telephone installed in the house. My father continued to use the word *gringo*. But it was no longer charged with the old bitterness or distrust. (Stripped of any emotional content, the word simply became a name for those Americans not of Hispanic descent.) Hearing him, sometimes, I wasn't sure if he was pronouncing the Spanish word *gringo* or saying gringo in English.

Matching the silence I started hearing in public was a new quiet at home. The family's quiet was partly due to the fact that, as we children learned more and more English, we shared fewer and fewer words with our parents. Sentences needed to be spoken slowly when a child addressed his mother or father. (Often the parent wouldn't understand.) The child would need to repeat himself. (Still the parent misunderstood.) The young voice, frustrated, would end up saying, "Never mind"—the subject was closed. Dinners would be noisy with the clinking of knives and forks against dishes. My mother would smile softly between her remarks; my father at the other end of the table would chew and chew at his food, while he stared over the heads of his children.

15 My *mother!* My *father!* After English became my primary language, I no longer knew what words to use in addressing my parents. The old Spanish words (those tender accents of sound) I had used earlier—*mamá* and *papá*—I couldn't use anymore. They would have been too painful reminders of how much had changed in my life. On the other hand, the words I heard neighborhood kids call their parents seemed equally unsatisfactory. *Mother* and *Father*; *Ma, Papa, Pa, Dad, Pop* (how I hated the all American sound of that last word especially)—all these terms I felt were unsuitable, not really terms of address for *my* parents. As a result, I never used them at home. Whenever I'd speak to my parents, I would try to get their attention with eye contact alone.

In public conversations, I'd refer to "my parents" or "my mother and father."

My mother and father, for their part, responded differently, as their children spoke to them less. She grew restless, seemed troubled and anxious at the scarcity of words exchanged in the house. It was she who would question me about my day when I came home from school. She smiled at small talk. She pried at the edges of my sentences to get me to say something more. (What?) She'd join conversations she overheard, but her intrusions often stopped her children's talking. By contrast, my father seemed reconciled to the new quiet. Though his English improved somewhat, he retired into silence. At dinner he spoke very little. One night his children and even his wife helplessly giggled at his garbled English pronunciation of the Catholic Grace before Meals. Thereafter he made his wife recite the prayer at the start of each meal, even on formal occasions, when there were guests in the house. Hers became the public voice of the family. On official business, it was she, not my father, one would usually hear on the phone or in stores, talking to strangers. His children grew so accustomed to his silence that, years later, they would speak routinely of his shyness. (My mother would often try to explain: Both his parents died when he was eight. He was raised by an uncle who treated him like little more than a menial servant. He was never encouraged to speak. He grew up alone. A man of few words.) But my father was not shy, I realized, when I'd watch him speaking Spanish with relatives. Using Spanish, he was quickly effusive. Especially when talking with other men, his voice would spark, flicker, flare alive with sounds. In Spanish, he expressed ideas and feelings he rarely revealed in English. With firm Spanish sounds, he conveyed confidence and authority English would never allow him.

The silence at home, however, was finally more than a literal silence. Fewer words passed between parent and child, but more profound was the silence that resulted from my inattention to sounds. At about the time I no longer bothered to listen with care to the sounds of English in public, I grew careless about listening to the sounds family members made when they spoke. Most of the time I heard someone speaking at home and didn't distinguish his sounds from the words people uttered in public. I didn't even pay much attention to my parents' accented and ungrammatical speech. At least not at home. Only when I was with them in public would I grow alert to their accents. Though, even then, their sounds caused me less and less concern. For I was increasingly confident of my own public identity.

I would have been happier about my public success had I not sometimes recalled what it had been like earlier, when my family had conveyed its intimacy through a set of conveniently private sounds. Sometimes in public, hearing a stranger, I'd hark back to my past. A Mexican farmworker approached me downtown to ask directions to somewhere, "*¿Hijito . . . ?*" he said. And his voice summoned deep longing. Another time, standing beside my mother in the visiting room of a Carmelite convent, before the dense screen which rendered the nuns shadowy figures, I heard several Spanish-speaking nuns—their busy, singsong overlapping voices—assure us that yes, yes, we were remembered, all our family was remembered in their prayers. (Their voices echoed faraway family sounds.) Another day, a dark-faced old woman—her hand light on my shoulder—steadied herself against me as she boarded a bus. She murmured something I couldn't quite comprehend. Her Spanish voice came near, like the face of a never-before-seen relative in the instant before I was kissed. Her voice, like so many of the Spanish voices I'd hear in public, recalled the golden age of my youth. Hearing Spanish then, I continued to be a careful, if sad, listener to sounds. Hearing a Spanish-speaking family walking behind me, I turned to look. I smiled for an instant, before my glance found the Hispanic-looking faces of strangers in the crowd going by.

Today I hear bilingual educators say that children lose a degree of "individuality" by becoming assimilated into public society. (Bilingual schooling was popularized in the seventies, that decade when middle-class ethnics began to resist the process of assimilation—the American melting pot.) But the bilingualists simplistically scorn the value and necessity of assimilation. They do not seem to realize that there are *two* ways a person is individualized. So they do not realize that while one suffers a diminished sense of *private* individuality by becoming assimilated into public society, such assimilation makes possible the achievement of *public* individuality.

20 The bilingualists insist that a student should be reminded of his differences from others in mass society, his heritage. But they equate mere separateness with individuality. The fact is that only in private—with intimates—is separateness from the crowd a prerequisite for individuality. (An intimate draws me apart, tells me that I am unique, unlike all others.) In public, by contrast, full individuality is achieved, paradoxically, by those who are able to consider themselves members of the crowd. Thus it happened for me: Only when I was able to think of myself as an American, no

longer an alien in *gringo* society, could I seek the rights and opportunities necessary for full public individuality. The social and political advantages I enjoy as a man result from the day that I came to believe that my name, indeed, is *Rich-heard Road-ree-guess*. It is true that my public society today is often impersonal. (My public society is usually mass society.) Yet despite the anonymity of the crowd and despite the fact that the individuality I achieve in public is often tenuous — because it depends on my being one in a crowd — I celebrate the day I acquired my new name. Those middle-class ethnics who scorn assimilation seem to me filled with decadent self-pity, obsessed by the burden of public life. Dangerously, they romanticize public separateness and they trivialize the dilemma of the socially disadvantaged.

My awkward childhood does not prove the necessity of bilingual education. My story discloses instead an essential myth of childhood — inevitable pain. If I rehearse here the changes in my private life after my Americanization, it is finally to emphasize the public gain. The loss implies the gain: The house I returned to each afternoon was quiet. Intimate sounds no longer rushed to the door to greet me. There were other noises inside. The telephone rang. Neighborhood kids ran past the door of the bedroom where I was reading my schoolbooks — covered with shopping-bag paper. Once I learned public language, it would never again be easy for me to hear intimate family voices. More and more of my day was spent hearing words. But that may only be a way of saying that the day I raised my hand in class and spoke loudly to an entire roomful of faces, my childhood started to end.

VOCABULARY

diffident: lacking confidence 3
intrinsically: inherently 4
menial: lowly 16
effusive: talkative 16
tenuous: unsteady 20

AUDIENCE AND PURPOSE

1. Why does Rodriguez use the title "Aria" for his essay?
2. What does Rodriguez argue is the problem with bilingual education?
3. What point does Rodriguez make about his childhood experiences in the last paragraph?

CONTENT

1. What did Rodriguez gain and lose in being assimilated into an English-speaking environment?
2. How did Rodriguez's relation to his parents change?
3. How did Rodriguez's parents themselves change?

STYLE AND STRUCTURE

1. Lewis Thomas in his essay "Seven Wonders" (also in this anthology) makes the point that childhood is meant for learning language. How is this point exemplified in Rodriguez's essay?
2. What details does Rodriguez use to touch the reader?
3. How does Rodriguez insist on the uniqueness of his individual experience?
4. Why does Rodriguez end with his sense of the inevitable loss of childhood?

Ward Churchill

Ward Churchill (b. 1947) is co-director of the American Indian Movement of Colorado and vice chairperson of the American Anti-Defamation Council. He is an associate professor of American Indian Studies and Communications at the University of Colorado/Boulder, where he also serves as associate director of the Center for Studies of Ethnicity and Race in America. His works include *Indians Are Us* (1994), *Fantasies of the Master Race* (1992), and *Struggle for the Land* (1992).

CRIMES AGAINST HUMANITY

During the past couple of seasons, there has been an increasing wave of controversy regarding the names of professional sports teams like the Atlanta "Braves," Cleveland "Indians," Washington "Redskins," and Kansas City "Chiefs." The issue extends to the names of college teams like Florida State University "Seminoles," University of Illinois "Fighting Illini," and so on, right on down to high school outfits like the Lamar (Colorado) "Savages." Also involved have been team adoption of "mascots," replete with feathers, buckskins, beads, spears, and "warpaint" (some fans have opted to adorn themselves in the same fashion), and nifty little "pep" gestures like the "Indian Chant" and "Tomahawk Chop."

A substantial number of American Indians have protested that use of native names, images and symbols as sports team mascots and the like is, by definition, a virulently racist practice. Given the historical relationship between Indians and non-Indians during what has been called the "Conquest of America," American Indian Movement leader (and American Indian Anti-Defamation Council founder) Russell Means has compared the practice to contemporary Germans naming their soccer teams the "Jews," "Hebrews," and "Yids," while adorning their uniforms with grotesque caricatures of Jewish faces taken from the Nazis' anti-Semitic propaganda of the 1930s. Numerous demonstrations have occurred in conjunction with games—most notably during the November 15, 1992 match-up between the Chiefs and Redskins in Kansas City—by angry Indians and their supporters.

In response, a number of players—especially African Americans and other minority athletes—have been trotted out by professional team owners like Ted Turner, as well as university and public school officials, to announce that they mean not to insult but to honor native people. They have been joined by the television networks and most major newspapers, all of which have editorialized that Indian discomfort with the situation is "no big deal," insisting that the whole thing is just "good, clean fun." The country needs more such fun, they've argued, and "a few disgruntled Native Americans" have no right to undermine the nation's enjoyment of its leisure time by complaining. This is especially the case, some have argued, "in hard times like these." It has even been contended that Indian outrage at being systematically degraded—rather than the degradation itself—creates "a serious barrier to the sort of intergroup communication so necessary to a multicultural society such as ours."

Okay, let's communicate. We are frankly dubious that those advancing such positions really believe their own rhetoric, but, just for the sake of argument, let's accept the premise that they are sincere. If what they say is true, then isn't it time we spread such "inoffensiveness" and "good cheer" around among *all* groups so that *everybody* can participate *equally* in fostering the round of national laughs they laugh for? Sure it is—the country can't have too much fun or "intergroup involvement"—so the more, the merrier. Simple consistency demands that anyone who thinks the Tomahawk Chop is a swell pastime must be just as hearty in their endorsement of the following ideas—by the logic used to defend the defamation of American Indians—should help us all really start yukking it up.

5 First, as a counterpart to the Redskins, we need an NFL team called "Niggers" to honor Afro-Americans. Half-time festivities for fans might include a simulated stewing of the opposing coach in a large pot while players and cheerleaders dance around it, garbed in leopard skins and wearing fake bones in their noses. This concept obviously goes along with the kind of gaiety attending the Chop, but also with the actions of the Kansas City Chiefs, whose team members—prominently including black team members—lately appeared on a poster looking "fierce" and "savage" by way of wearing Indian regalia. Just a bit of harmless "morale boosting," says the Chiefs' front office. You bet.

So that the newly-formed Niggers sports club won't end up too out of sync while expressing the "spirit" and "identity" of Afro-Americans in the above fashion, a baseball franchise—let's call this one the "Sambos"—should be formed. How about a basketball team called the "Spearchuckers"? A hockey team called the "Jungle Bunnies"? Maybe the "essence" of these teams could be depicted by images of tiny black faces adorned with huge pairs of lips. The players could appear on TV every week or so gnawing on chicken legs and spitting watermelon seeds at one another. Catchy, eh? Well, there's "nothing to be upset about," according to those who love wearing "war bonnets" to the Super Bowl or having "Chief Illiniwik" dance around the sports arenas of Urbana, Illinois.

And why stop there? There are plenty of other groups to include. "Hispanics"? They can be "represented" by the Galveston "Greasers" and San Diego "Spics," at least until the Wisconsin "Wetbacks" and Baltimore "Beaners" get off the ground. Asian Americans? How about the "Slopes," "Dinks," "Gooks," and "Zipperheads"? Owners of the latter teams might get their logo ideas from editorial page cartoons printed in the nation's newspapers during World War II: slant-eyes, buck teeth, big glasses, but nothing racially insulting or derogatory, according to the editors and artists involved at the time. Indeed, this Second World War-vintage stuff can be seen as just another barrel of laughs, at least by what current editors say are their "local standards" concerning American Indians.

Let's see. Who's been left out? Teams like the Kansas City "Kikes," Hanover "Honkies," San Leandro "Shylocks," Daytona "Dagos," and Pittsburgh "Polacks" will fill a certain social void among white folk. Have a religious belief? Let's all go for the gusto and gear up the Milwaukee "Mackerel Snappers" and Hollywood "Holy Rollers." The Fighting Irish of Notre Dame can be rechristened the "Drunken Irish" or "Papist Pigs." Issues of gender and sexual preferences can be addressed through creation of teams like the St. Louis "Sluts," Boston "Bimbos," Detroit "Dykes," and the Fresno "Fags." How about the Gainesville "Gimps" and Richmond "Retards," so the physically and mentally impaired won't be excluded from our fun and games?

Now, don't go getting "overly sensitive" out there. None of this is demeaning or insulting, at least not when it's being done to Indians. Just ask the folks who are doing it, or their apologists like Andy Rooney in the national media. They'll tell you —as in fact they *have* been telling you—that there's been no harm done, regardless of what their victims think, feel, or say. The situation is exactly the same as when those with precisely the same mentality used to insist that Step 'n' Fetchit was okay, or Rochester on the Jack Benny Show, or Amos and Andy, Charlie Chan, the Frito Bandito, or any of the other cutesy symbols making up the lexicon of American racism. Have we communicated yet?

10 Let's get just a little bit real here. The notion of "fun" embodied in rituals like the Tomahawk Chop must be understood for what it is. There's not a single non-Indian example used above which can be considered socially acceptable in even the most marginal sense. The reasons are obvious enough. So why is it different where American Indians are concerned? One can only conclude that, in contrast to the other groups at issue, Indians are (falsely) perceived as being too few, and therefore too weak, to defend themselves effectively against racist and otherwise offensive behavior.

Fortunately, there are some glimmers of hope. A few teams and their fans have gotten the message and have responded appropriately. Stanford University, which opted to drop the name "Indians" from Stanford, has experienced no resulting drop-off in attendance. Meanwhile, the local newspaper in Portland, Oregon recently decided its long-standing editorial policy prohibiting use of racial epithets should include derogatory team names. The Redskins, for instance, are now referred to as "the Washington team," and will continue to be described in this way until the franchise adopts an inoffensive moniker (newspaper sales in Portland have suffered no decline as a result).

Such examples are to be applauded and encouraged. They stand as figurative beacons in the night, proving beyond all doubt that it is quite possible to indulge in the pleasure of athletics without accepting blatant racism into the bargain.

NUREMBERG PRECEDENTS

On October 16, 1946, a man named Julius Streicher mounted the steps of a gallows. Moments later he was dead, the sentence of an international tribunal composed of representatives of the United States, France, Great Britain, and the Soviet Union having been imposed. Streicher's body was then cremated, and—so horrendous were his crimes thought to have been—his ashes dumped into an unspecified German river so that "no one should ever know a particular place to go for reasons of mourning his memory."

Julius Streicher had been convicted at Nuremberg, Germany of what were termed "Crimes Against Humanity." The lead prosecutor in his case—Justice Robert Jackson of the United States Supreme Court—had not argued that the defendant killed anyone, nor that he had personally committed any especially violent act. Nor was it contended that Streicher had held any particularly important position in the German government during the period in which the so-called Third Reich had exterminated some 6,000,000 Jews, as well as several million Gypsies, Poles, Slavs, homosexuals, and other untermenschen (subhumans).

The sole offense for which the accused was ordered put to death was in having served as publisher/editor of a Bavarian tabloid entitled *Der Sturmer* during the early-to-mid 1930s, years before the Nazi genocide actually began. In this capacity, he had penned a long series of virulently anti-Semitic editorials and "news" stories, usually accompanied by cartoons and other images graphically depicting Jews in extraordinarily derogatory fashion. This, the prosecution asserted, had done much to "dehumanize" the targets of his distortion in the mind of the German public. In turn, such dehumanization had made it possible—or at least easier—for average Germans to later indulge in the outright liquidation of Jewish "vermin." The tribunal agreed, holding that Streicher was therefore complicit in genocide and deserving of death by hanging.

During his remarks to the Nuremberg tribunal, Justice Jackson observed that, in implementing its sentences, the participating powers were morally and legally binding themselves to adhere forever after to the same standards of conduct that were being applied to Streicher and the other Nazi leaders. In the alternative, he said, the victorious allies would have committed "pure murder" at Nuremberg—no different in substance from that carried out by those they presumed to judge—rather than establishing the "permanent benchmark for justice" which was intended.

Yet in the United States of Robert Jackson, the indigenous American Indian population had already been reduced, in a process which is ongoing to this day, from perhaps 12.5 million in the year 1500 to fewer than 250,000 by the beginning of the 20th century. This was accomplished, according to official sources, "largely through the cruelty of [Euro-American] settlers," and an informal but clear governmental policy which had made it an articulated goal to "exterminate these red vermin," or at least whole segments of them.

Bounties had been placed on the scalps of Indians—any Indians—in places as diverse as Georgia, Kentucky, Texas, the Dakotas, Oregon, and California, and had been maintained until resident Indian populations were decimated or disappeared altogether. Entire peoples such as the Cherokee had been reduced to half their size through a policy of forced removal from their homelands east of the Mississippi River to what were then considered less preferable areas in the West.

Others, such as the Navajo, suffered the same fate while under military guard for years on end. The United States Army had also perpetrated a long series of wholesale massacres of Indians at places like Horseshoe Bend, Bear River, Sand Creek, the Washita River, the Marias River, Camp Robinson, and Wounded Knee.

Through it all, hundreds of popular novels—each competing with the next to make the Indians appear more grotesque, menacing, and inhuman—were sold in the tens of millions of copies in the U.S. Plainly, the Euro-American public was being conditioned to see Indians in such a way as to allow their eradication to continue. And continue it did until the Manifest Destiny of the U.S.—a direct precursor to what Hitler would subsequently call Lebensraumpolitik (the politics of living space)—was consummated.

By 1900, the national project of "clearing" Native Americans from their land and replacing them with "superior" Anglo-American settlers was complete: the indigenous population had been reduced by as much as 98 percent while approximately 97.5 percent of their original territory had "passed" to the invaders. The survivors had been concentrated, out of sight and mind of the public, on scattered "reservations," all of them under the self-assigned "plenary" (full) power of the federal government. There was, of course, no Nuremberg-style tribunal passing judgment on those who had fostered such circumstances in North America. No U.S. official or private citizen was ever imprisoned—never mind hanged—for implementing or propagandizing what had been done. Nor had the process of genocide afflicting Indians been completed. Instead, it merely changed form.

Between the 1880s and the 1980s, nearly half of all Native American children were coercively transferred from their own families, communities, and cultures to those of the conquering society. This was done through compulsory attendance at remote boarding schools, often hundreds of miles from their homes, where native children were kept for years on end while being systematically "deculturated" (indoctrinated to think and act in the manner of the Euro-Americans rather than Indians). It was also accomplished through a pervasive foster home and adoption program—including "blind" adoptions, where children would be permanently denied information as to who they were/are and where they'd come from—placing native youths in non-Indian homes.

The express purpose of all this was to facilitate a U.S. governmental policy to bring about the "assimilation" (dissolution) of indigenous societies. In other words, Indian cultures as such were to be caused to disappear. Such policy objectives are directly contrary to the United Nations 1948 Convention on Punishment and Prevention of the Crime of Genocide, an element of international law arising from the Nuremberg proceedings. The forced "transfer of the children" of a targeted "racial, ethnical, or religious group" is explicitly prohibited as a genocidal activity under the Convention's second article.

Article II of the Genocide Convention also expressly prohibits involuntary sterilization as a means of "preventing births among" a targeted population. Yet, in 1975, it was conceded by the U.S. government that its Indian Health Service (IHS) then a subpart of the Bureau of Indian Affairs (BIA), was even then conducting a secret program of involuntary sterilization that had affected approximately 40 percent of all Indian women. The program was allegedly discontinued and the IHS was transferred to the Public Health Service, but no one was punished. In 1990, it came out that the IHS was inoculating Inuit children in Alaska with Hepatitis-B vaccine. The vaccine had already been banned by the World Health Organization as having a demonstrated correlation with the HIV-Syndrome which is itself correlated to AIDS. As this is written, a "field test" of Hepatitis-A vaccine, also HIV-correlated, is being conducted on Indian reservations in the northern plains region.

The Genocide Convention makes it a "crime against humanity" to create conditions leading to the destruction of an identifiable human group, as such. Yet the BIA has utilized the government's plenary prerogatives to negotiate mineral leases "on behalf of" Indian peoples, paying a fraction of standard royalty rates. The result has been "super profits" for a number of preferred U.S. corporations. Meanwhile, Indians, whose reservations ironically turned out to be in some of the most mineral-rich areas of North America, which makes us, the nominally wealthiest segment of the continent's population, live in dire poverty.

By the government's own data in the mid-1980s, Indians received the lowest annual and lifetime per capita incomes of any aggregate population group in the United States. Concomitantly, we suffer the highest rate of infant mortality, death by exposure and malnutrition, disease, and the like. Under such circumstances, alcoholism and other escapist forms of substance abuse are endemic in the Indian community, a situation which leads both to a general physical debilitation of the population and a catastrophic accident rate. Teen suicide among Indians is several times the national average.

The average life expectancy of a reservation-based Native American man is barely 45 years; women can expect to live less than three years longer.

Such itemizations could be continued at great length, including matters like the radioactive contamination of large portions of contemporary Indian Country, the forced relocation of traditional Navajos, and so on. But the point should be made. Genocide, as defined in international law, is a continuing fact of day-to-day life (and death) for North American's native peoples. Yet there has been—and is—only the barest flicker of public concern about, or even consciousness of, this reality. Absent any serious expression of public outrage, no one is punished and the process continues.

A salient reason for public acquiescence before the ongoing holocaust in Native North America has been a continuation of the popular legacy, often through more effective media. Since 1925, Hollywood has released more than 2,000 films, many of them rerun frequently on television, portraying Indians as strange, perverted, ridiculous, and often dangerous things of the past. Moreover, we are habitually presented to mass audiences one-dimensionally, devoid of recognizable human motivations and emotions; Indians thus serve as props, little more. We have thus been thoroughly and systematically dehumanized.

Nor is this the extent of it. Everywhere, we are used as logos, as mascots, as jokes: "Big-Chief" writing tablets, "Red Man" chewing tobacco, "Winnebago" campers, "Navajo" and "Cherokee" and "Pontiac" and "Cadillac" pickups and automobiles. There are the Cleveland "Indians," the Kansas City "Chiefs," the Atlanta "Braves" and the Washington "Redskins" professional sports teams—not to mention those in thousands of colleges, high schools, and elementary schools across the country—each with their own degrading caricatures and parodies of Indians and/or things Indian. Pop fiction continues in the same vein, including an unending stream of New Age manuals purporting to expose the inner works of indigenous spirituality in everything from pseudo-philosophical to do-it-yourself styles. Blond yuppies from Beverly Hills amble about the country claiming to be reincarnated 17th century Cheyenne Ushamans ready to perform previously secret ceremonies.

In effect, a concerted, sustained, and in some ways accelerating effort has gone into making Indians unreal. It is thus of obvious importance that the American public begin to think about the implications of such things the next time they witness a gaggle of face-painted and war-bonneted buffoons doing the "Tomahawk Chop" at a baseball or football game. It is necessary that they think about the implications of the grade-school teacher adorning their child in turkey feathers to commemorate Thanksgiving. Think about the significance of John Wayne or Charleton Heston killing a dozen "savages" with a single bullet the next time a western comes on TV. Think about why Land-o-Lakes finds it appropriate to market its butter with the stereotyped image of an "Indian princess" on the wrapper. Think about what it means when non-Indian academics profess—as they often do—to "know more about Indians than Indians do themselves." Think about the significance of charlatans like Carlos Castaneda and Jamake Highwater and Mary Summer Rain and Lynn Andrews churning out "Indian" bestsellers, one after the other, while Indians typically can't get into print.

Think about the real situation of American Indians. Think about Julius Streicher. Remember Justice Jackson's admonition. Understand that the treatment of Indians in American popular culture is not "cute" or "amusing" or just "good, clean fun."

Know that it causes real pain and real suffering to real people. Know that it threatens our very survival. And know that this is just as much a crime against humanity as anything the Nazis ever did. It is likely that the indigenous people of the United States will never demand that those guilty of such criminal activity be punished for their deeds. But the least we have the right to expect—indeed, to demand—is that such practices finally be brought to a halt.

VOCABULARY

virulently: poisonously 2
regalia: insignia or decorations of any rank or position 5
epithet: disparaging name that characterizes a person or thing 11
derogatory: insulting, negative 11
moniker: name 11
indigenous: native 17
decimated: destroyed 18
plenary: complete; for attendance by all members 21
prerogatives: rights 25
aggregate: group 26
concomitantly: at the same time 26
endemic: constantly present 26
salient: apparent 29
acquiescence: consent 29

AUDIENCE AND PURPOSE

1. Why does Churchill give this essay the title "Crimes Against Humanity"?
2. How does Churchill show the importance of language and of the media in the depiction of racial stereotypes?
3. How does Churchill use hypothetical examples to reduce to absurdity the notion that using Aboriginal names and stereotypes about Aboriginals is just "good, clean fun"?

CONTENT

1. What comparisons does Churchill draw between the case of Julius Streicher and the media today?
2. In what ways does Churchill argue that Aboriginals of North America have been victims of attempted genocide similar to the holocaust?
3. Churchill cites the Genocide Convention to show how Aboriginal peoples have been targeted. Explain.

STYLE AND STRUCTURE

1. How does Churchill get the reader involved in his examples?
2. Churchill begins with something that may seem trivial and ends by returning to it, this time charged with meaning. How does his essay itself show the power of words?
3. Examine how Churchill uses repetition to make his conclusion powerful. What, finally, does Churchill want to do about the problem?

CREDITS

Atwood, Margaret "God Is in the Details: The Shakers Knew When to Stop" appeared in *The New York Times Magazine*, April 18, 1999. Reprinted by permission of *The New York Times*. "Approximate Homes" from *Writing Home, A PEN Canada Anthology*, edited by Constance Rooke. McClelland & Stewart, Inc. *The Canadian Publishers*. Copyright © 1997. Reproduced by permission of the author.

Baker, Russell "Francs and Beans" from *So This is Depravity* by Russell Baker © 1985. Used with permission of NTC/Contemporary Publishing Group, Inc.

Bissoondath, Neil "Marginalization" from *Selling Illusions: The Cult of Multiculturalism in Canada* by Neil Bissoondath. Copyright © 1994 by Neil Bissoondath. Reprinted by permission of Penguin Books Canada Limited.

Byatt, A.S. "Narrate or Die: Why Scheherazade Keeps on Talking" appeared in *The New York Times Magazine*, April 18, 1999. Copyright 1998 by Antonia Byatt. Reprinted by permission of Sterling Lord Literistic, Inc.

Churchill, Ward "Crimes Against Humanity" appeared in *Z Magazine*, March 1993. Reprinted by permission of the author.

Davies, Robertson "Stratford Forty Years Ago" from *Happy Alchemy: Writings on the Theatre and Other Lively Arts* by Robertson Davies. Copyright © 1997 by Pendragon Ink. Reprinted by permission of Penguin Books Canada Limited.

Diamond, Jared "Invention Is the Mother of Necessity" appeared in *The New York Times Magazine*, April 18, 1999. Copyright © 1999 by the New York Times Co. Reprinted by permission.

Dobbs, Kildare "The Schools" from *Smiles and Chukkers and Other Vanities* by Kildare Dobbs. Copyright © 1994 by Kildare Dobbs. By permission of Little, Brown and Company, Inc.

Doidge, Norman "Do Children 'Get' Irony? Duhhhh!" first appeared in *The National Post*, June 2, 1999. Reprinted by permission of the author.

Eco, Umberto "How the Bean Saved Civilization" appeared in *The New York Times Magazine*, April 18, 1999. Reprinted by permission of the author.

Flowers, Betty S. "Madman, Architect, Carpenter, Judge: Roles and the Writing Process" from Proceedings of the Conference of College Teachers of English of Texas 44, September 1979. Reprinted by permission of the author.

Ginzburg, Natalia "He and I" translated by Dick Davis from *The Art of the Personal Essay: An Anthology from the Classical Era to the Present*, edited by Phillip Lopate. Reprinted by permission of Dick Davis.

Grady, Wayne "The Metric System (Sort of)" originally appeared in *Saturday Night*, March 1999. Reprinted by permission of the author.

Gzowski, Peter "And the Best Damn Stew-Maker Too" from *Selected Columns from Canadian Living* by Peter Gzowski. Used by permission, McClelland & Stewart, Inc. *The Canadian Publishers.*

Hoffman, Eva "Lost in Translation" from *Lost in Translation* by Eva Hoffman. Copyright © 1989 by Eva Hoffman. Used by permission of Dutton, a Division of Penguin Putnam Inc.

Hurtig, Mel "Never Heard of Them ... They Must Be Canadian" from *At Twilight in the Country* © 1996 by Mel Hurtig. Reprinted by permission of Stoddart Publishing Co. Ltd.

Iyer, Pico "In Praise of the Humble Comma" appeared in *Time*, June 13, 1983. Copyright © 1983 Time, Inc. Reprinted by permission. "Lonely Places" from *Falling Off the Map: Some Lonely Places of the World* by Pico Iyer. Copyright © 1993 by Pico Iyer. Reprinted by permission of Alfred A. Knopf, a Division of Random House, Inc.

Kahn, Jennifer "I Don't Want to Go Forth and Multiply" first appeared in Salon.com, at http://www.Salon.com. An on-line version remains in the Salon archives. Reprinted with permission.

Katz, Sidney " 'Tis the Season to Be Kissing" first appeared in *The Globe and Mail* as " 'Tis the Season for Kissing," February 14, 1982. Reprinted by permission of the author.

Kincaid, Jamaica "A Small Place" excerpted from *A Small Place* by Jamaica Kincaid. Copyright © 1988 by Jamaica Kincaid. Reprinted by permission of Farrar, Straus and Giroux, LLC.

Kurzweil, Ray "When Machines Think" appeared in *Maclean's*, March 1, 1999. Reprinted by permission of Ray Kurzweil.

MacLennan, Hugh "If You Drop a Stone ..." from *The Other Side of Hugh MacLennan, Selected Essays Old and New*, edited by Elspeth Cameron. Macmillan of Canada, © 1978. Reprinted by permission of McGill University, the Hugh MacLennan Estate.

McQueen, Ann Marie "My Fling with Men's Mags" appeared in *The Globe and Mail*, June 28, 1999. Reprinted by permission of the author.

Manguel, Alberto "Point of Order" appeared in *The New York Times Magazine*, April 18, 1999. Reprinted by permission of the author.

Masson, Jeffrey Moussaieff and Susan McCarthy "Shame, Blushing, and Hidden Secrets" from *When Elephants Weep: The Emotional Lives of Animals* by Jeffrey Moussaieff Masson and Susan McCarthy, Delta Trade Paperbacks, © 1995 by Jeffrey Masson and Susan McCarthy. Used by permission of Delacorte Press, a Division of Random House, Inc.

Mistry, Rohinton "Lend Me Your Light" from *Tales from the Firozsha Baag* by Rohinton Mistry. Used by permission, McClelland & Stewart, Inc. *The Canadian Publishers.*

Mitford, Jessica "The Story of Service" from *The American Way of Death Revisited* by Jessica Mitford. Copyright © 1998 by the Estate of Jessica

Mitford. Reprinted by permission of Alfred A. Knopf, a Division of Random House, Inc.

Nilsen, Alleen Pace "Sexism in English: A 1990s Update" from *Language Awareness Essays for College Writers*, edited by Paul Eschholz. St. Martin's Press, 1996. Reprinted by permission of the author.

Oates, Joyce Carol "When Tristram Met Isolde" appeared in *The New York Times Magazine*, April 18, 1999. Copyright © 1999 Joyce Carol Oates. Distributed by The New York Times Special Features/Syndication Sales.

Orwell, George "Politics and the English Language" from *Shooting an Elephant and Other Essays* by George Orwell. Copyright © George Orwell 1946. Reprinted by permission of Bill Hamilton as the Literary Executor of the Estate of the Late Sonia Brownell Orwell and Seeker & Warburg Ltd.

Postman, Neil "The Ideology of Machines: Computer Technology" from *Technopoly: The Surrender of Culture to Technology*, © 1992, Vintage Books.

Rheingold, Howard "Look Who's Talking" originally appeared in *Wired*, January 1999. Reprinted by permission of the author.

Ritter, Erika "Guilt" from *Urban Scrawl: The World as Seen through the Bemused Eyes of Erika Ritter*, Macmillan of Canada. Copyright © 1984 Erika Ritter. With permission of the author.

Roberts, Paul "How to Say Nothing in 500 Words" from *Understanding English* by Paul Roberts. Copyright 1958 by Paul Roberts. Reprinted by permission of Addison-Wesley Educational Publishers, Inc.

Rodriguez, Richard "Aria" from *Hunger of Memory* by Richard Rodriguez. Copyright © 1982 by Richard Rodriguez. Reprinted by permission of David R. Godine, Publisher, Inc.

Rushdie, Salman "American Culture Is Not the Enemy" originally appeared in *The Globe and Mail*, March 8, 1999. Copyright © 1999 by Salman Rushdie. Reprinted by permission of The Wylie Agency.

Suzuki, David "Lessons Taught by Nature" from *Earth Time* by David Suzuki. Copyright © 1998 by David Suzuki. Reprinted by permission of Stoddart Publishing Co. Ltd. "Ancestors — The Genetic Source" from *Metamorphosis: Stages in a Life* by David Suzuki. Copyright © 1987 by David Suzuki. Reprinted by permission of Stoddart Publishing Co. Ltd.

Swerdlow, Joel L. "The Power of Writing" appeared in *National Geographic*, August 1999. Joel Swerdlow/NGS Image Collection. Reprinted by permission of National Geographic Society.

Tannen, Deborah "Listening to Men, Then and Now" appeared in *The New York Times Magazine*, May 16, 1999. Copyright © Deborah Tannen. Reprinted by permission.

Taylor, Drew Hayden "Pretty Like a White Boy: The Adventures of a Blue Eyed Ojibway" from *An Anthology of Canadian Native Literature in English*, edited by Daniel D. Moses and Terry Goldie. Oxford University Press, 1992. Reprinted by permission of the author.

Thomas, Dylan "Memories of Christmas" from *Quite Early One Morning* by Dylan Thomas. Reprinted by permission of David Higham Associates.

Thomas, Lewis "Seven Wonders" from *Late Night Thoughts on Listening to Mahler's Ninth* by Lewis Thomas. Copyright © 1983 by Lewis Thomas. Used by permission of Viking Penguin, a Division of Penguin Putnam, Inc.

Tierney, John "Our Oldest Computer, Upgraded" appeared in *The New York Times Magazine*, September 28, 1997. Copyright © 1997 by The New York Times Co. Reprinted by permission.

White, E.B. "Once More to the Lake" from *One Man's Meat*, text copyright © 1941 by E.B. White. Reprinted by permission of Tilbury House, Publishers, Gardiner, Maine.

Wong, Jan "Jan Wong Wants to See Canadians De-Hyphenate Themselves" appeared in *The Globe and Mail*, July 2, 1999. Reprinted by permission of *The Globe and Mail.*

Yi, Sun-Kyung "An Immigrant's Split Personality." Reprinted by permission of the author.

INDEX OF AUTHORS